Dr Richard Race, Roeham

Philosophy, Methodology and E

7

Philosophy, Methodology and Educational Research

Edited by

David Bridges and Richard Smith

Blackwell
Publishing

First published as Volume 40, Nos 2 & 4 of *the Journal of Philosophy of Education*. 'The Contested Nature of Empirical Educational Research (and Why Philosophy of Education Offers Little Help)' by D.C. Phillips was published in Volume 39, No 4.

BLACKWELL PUBLISHING
350 Main Street, Malden, MA 02148-5020, USA
9600 Garsington Road, Oxford OX4 2DQ, UK
550 Swanston Street, Carlton, Victoria 3053, Australia

First published 2007 by Blackwell Publishing Ltd

Library of Congress Cataloging-in-Publication Data has been applied for

Philosophy, methodology, and educational research / edited by David Bridges and Richard Smith.
          p. cm.
  "First published as volume 40, nos 2 & 4 of the Journal of philosophy of education"—T.p. verso.
  Includes bibliographical references and index.
  ISBN 978-1-4051-4513-8 (pbk.: alk. paper) 1. Education—Research—Methodology. 2. Education—Philosophy. I. Bridges, David, 1941- II. Smith, Richard (Richard D.) III. Journal of philosophy of education.

  LB1028.P47 2007
  370.1—dc22

A catalogue record for this title is available from the British Library.

Set in Advent 3B2
by Macmillan India Ltd.
Printed and bound in the UK
by TJ International, Padstow, Cornwall

For further information on
Blackwell Publishing, visit our website:
www.blackwellpublishing.com

Contents

Notes on Contributors   vii

Preface   xi

1. Philosophy, Methodology and Educational Research:
   Introduction   1
   David Bridges and Richard Smith

2. The Myth of 'Scientific Method' in Contemporary Educational Research   11
   Darrell Patrick Rowbottom and Sarah Jane Aiston

3. As if by Machinery: The Levelling of Educational Research   31
   Richard Smith

4. 'A Demented Form of the Familiar': Postmodernism and
   Educational Research   43
   Maggie MacLure

5. The Disciplines and Discipline of Educational Research   61
   David Bridges

6. Consistency, Understanding and Truth in Educational
   Research   75
   Andrew Davis

7. No Harm Done: The Implications for Educational Research
   of the Rejection of Truth   89
   Stefan Ramaekers

8. The Quantitative-Qualitative Distinction and the Null
   Hypothesis Significance Testing Procedure   107
   Nimal Ratnesar and Jim Mackenzie

9. A View from Somewhere: Explaining the Paradigms of
   Educational Research   117
   Hanan A. Alexander

10. Philosophy, Methodology and Action Research   133
    Wilfred Carr

11. Educational Research as a Form of Democratic Rationality   149
    John Elliott

12. Philosophical Research and Educational Action Research 167
Marianna Papastephanou

13. Why Generalisability is not Generalisable 185
Lynn Fendler

14. On Generalising from Single Case Studies: Epistemological
Reflections 199
Colin W. Evers and Echo H. Wu

15. Epistemological Issues in Phenomenological Research:
How Authoritative are People's Accounts of their own
Perceptions? 215
Bas Levering

16. Reasons and Causes in Educational Research: Overcoming
Dichotomies and Other Conceptual Confusions 227
Paul Smeyers

17. Philosophy's Contribution to Social Science Research on
Education 251
Martyn Hammersley

18. US Graduate Study in Education Research: From Methodology
to Potential Totalization 265
Lynda Stone

19. Shovelling Smoke? The Experience of Being a Philosopher
on an Educational Research Training Programme 283
Judith Suissa

20. Induction into Educational Research Networks: The Striated
and the Smooth 299
Naomi Hodgson and Paul Standish

21. The Contested Nature of Empirical Educational Research
(and Why Philosophy of Education Offers Little Help) 311
D.C. Phillips

22. On the Limits of Empirical Educational Research, Beyond
the Fantasy: A Rejoinder to D.C. Phillips 333
Paul Smeyers

Index 351

Notes on Contributors

Sarah Jane Aiston is a lecturer in the Centre for Learning, Teaching and Research in Higher Education at Durham University, UK. Her research concerns the history of women in education and students' conceptions of research. Her recent publications include 'A Woman's Place: Male Representations of University Women in the Student Press of the University of Liverpool 1944–1979' in *Women's History Review* and 'A Maternal Identity? The Family Lives of British Women Graduates pre and post 1945' in *History of Education*.

Hanan A. Alexander chairs the Department of Education at the University of Haifa, Israel, where he teaches philosophy of education and coordinates with colleagues an integrated introduction to educational research. He is also Head of the University's Centre for Jewish Education, a Senior Research Fellow of the Van Leer Jerusalem Institute, a Senior Fellow of the Institute for Philosophy, Politics and Religion of Jerusalem's Shalem Center and a Visiting Fellow of St Edmund's College, Cambridge. His book *Reclaiming Goodness: Education and the Spiritual Quest* (University of Notre Dame Press, 2001) is winner of a 2001–2 National Jewish Book Award in the US.

David Bridges is Professorial Fellow at the University of East Anglia and Chair of the Von Hügel Institute at St Edmund's College, Cambridge, UK where he is also a Fellow. He chairs the Philosophy of Education Society of Great Britain and is a Council member of both the British and the European Educational Research Associations. He has substantial experience in ethnographically grounded applied research and has written extensively in recent years on issues in the philosophy of educational research. His publications include *The Ethics of Educational Research* (Blackwell 2002) edited with Mike McNamee and *'Fiction Written under Oath'? Essays in philosophy and educational research* (Kluwer, 2003).

Wilfred Carr is Professor of the Philosophy of Education at the University of Sheffield, UK, where until recently he was Head of the School of Education and Dean of the Faculty of Social Sciences. He is an Honorary Vice-President of the Philosophy of Education Society of Great Britain and a member of its Executive Committee. His books include: *Becoming Critical* (co-authored with Stephen Kemmis) and *For Education*, both of which have been translated into Spanish and Chinese. He edited The *RoutledgeFalmer Reader in Philosophy of Education* and is Executive Editor of the Journal *Pedagogy, Culture and Society*.

Andrew Davis is a Research Fellow in the School of Education, University of Durham, UK. He trained as an analytical philosopher, before gaining substantial experience as a primary teacher and then university lecturer in philosophy of education and mathematics education. His research interests include applying analytical philosophy, especially philosophy of mind, to educational policy issues such as assessment. His recent publications focus on the social character of learning. In 2006 he co-authored the third edition of the best-selling *Mathematical Knowledge for Primary Teachers* and in 2007 he produced a second edition of his IMPACT book on educational assessment for the Philosophy of Education Society of Great Britain.

John Elliott is Emeritus Professor of Education in the Centre for Applied Research in Education, which he directed from 1996–99, at the University of East Anglia, UK. He is well-known internationally for his role in developing the theory and practice of action research in the contexts of curriculum and teacher development. He was an Advisory Professor to the Hong Kong Institute of Education (2001–2006) and is currently a consultant to the Hong Kong Government on the strategic development of its curriculum reforms. His recent publications include *'Reflecting Where the Action Is': The Selected Works of John Elliott* in the Routledge World Library of Educationalists (2007).

Colin W. Evers is a Professor of Education at the University of Hong Kong, People's Republic of China. He studied mathematics, philosophy and education before taking his Ph.D in philosophy of education at the University of Sydney. His teaching and research interests are in educational theory, research methodology and administrative theory. He has co-edited and co-authored six books on educational administration, including *Knowing Educational Administration*, *Exploring Educational Administration* and *Doing Educational Administration* (written with Gabriele Lakomski) and many papers in his areas of research interest.

Lynn Fendler is an Assistant Professor of Teacher Education at Michigan State University, USA, where she teaches philosophy of education, research paradigms and curriculum theory in the master's and doctoral programs. She also supervises teacher preparation for the secondary education program in World Languages. Lynn's research areas include postmodern and critical theories of education, historiography, rhetoric, and continental philosophy. Lynn was a founding member of the Foucault and Education Special Interest Group of the American Educational Research Association (AERA), and recipient of the 2004 Lilly Teaching Endowment Fellowship and the 2007 University Teacher-Scholar award.

Martyn Hammersley is Professor of Educational and Social Research at the Open University, UK. His early research was in the sociology of education. Much of his more recent work has been concerned with the methodological issues surrounding social and educational enquiry. His most recent books are: *Taking Sides in Social Research* (Routledge, 2000); *Educational Research, Policymaking and Practice* (Paul Chapman, 2002); and *Media Bias in Reporting Social Research? The case of reviewing ethnic inequalities in education* (Routledge, 2006). He is currently working on the issue of research ethics.

Naomi Hodgson is a doctoral student at the Institute of Education, University of London, UK, supervised by Professor Paul Standish. Her research focuses on ideas of citizenship in Europe and their contemporary relationship to education. Her Master's dissertation, completed at the University of Sheffield in 2006, was entitled *Educational research, Foucault, and the study of citizenship*. Her Master's and doctoral study are funded by the Economic and Social Research Council (ESRC). Naomi has written, with Paul Standish, a contribution entitled *Network, Critique, Conversation: Towards a Rethinking of Educational Research Methods Training* to a book emanating from the Leuven Research Community on networks and technologies in educational research (Springer, forthcoming).

Bas Levering is an Associate Professor of Philosophy of Education at Utrecht University and a professor of Pedagogy at Fontys Professional University in Tilburg, both in The Netherlands. His main methodological work is on the relationship between phenomenology and ordinary language analysis. Among his numerous articles and books is (with Max van Manen) *Childhood's Secrets. Intimacy, Privacy and the Self Reconsidered* (New York 1996), now available in seven languages. Currently he is involved in international research on dual wage-earners and the division of pedagogical tasks between parents and professional childcare. Levering is European Editor of the *International Journal of Qualitative Methods*.

Jim Mackenzie has a background in philosophical logic. He teaches philosophy of education at the University of Sydney, Australia, and has published both on the formal logic of dialogue, for example 'Four dialogue systems', *Studia Logica* 49 (1990), and on a variety of topics related to education, including 'The new professor of theology' *Journal of Philosophy of Education* 28 (1994), and 'The idea of literacy', *Journal of Philosophy of Education* 34 (2000).

Maggie MacLure is Professor of Education in the Education and Social Research Institute at Manchester Metropolitan University, UK. Her research interests include qualitative methodology, especially discourse analysis, deconstruction and poststructuralist approaches. She is the author of *Discourse in Educational and Social Research* (Open University Press).

Marianna Papastephanou has studied and researched in Cardiff, Wales and Berlin and taught at Cardiff University. She is currently teaching at the Department of Education, University of Cyprus, as an Assistant Professor in Philosophy of Education. She is the editor of *K.O. Apel: From A Transcendental- Semiotic Point of View* (Manchester: Manchester University Press, 1998) and author of numerous articles on the Frankfurt School, political philosophy, postmodernism, and education from a continental-philosophical point of view.

D.C. Phillips, an Australian by birth, is Professor Emeritus of Education, and by courtesy of Philosophy, at Stanford University, USA. A member of the US National Academy of Education and a Fellow of the International Academy of Education, and a past-president of the Philosophy of Education Society, he is the author or co-author or editor of twelve books and over a hundred book and encyclopaedia chapters and journal articles. Two recent books are *Postpositivism and Educational Research* (with Nicholas Burbules), and *The Expanded Social Scientist's Bestiary* (both Rowman and Littlefield 2000). Several of his recent papers critique the use of randomized experiments as the 'gold standard' of rigour in educational research.

Stefan Ramaekers is a philosopher of education in the Department of Education at the Faculty of Psychology and Educational Sciences, K.U. Leuven, Belgium. His interests and activities focus on scepticism and its implications in the human condition, Wittgenstein, Nietzsche and Cavell. He has written recently about scepticism in educational theory and research in the *Journal of Philosophy of Education, Educational Theory* and in edited collections.

Nimal Ratnesar is currently a graduate student at the University of Sydney, Australia. His interests include the methodological issues that arise within the educational (and social) research discourse context as well as the broader matter of how we make meaningful sense of things at all. He has taught and tutored mathematics, physics and statistics.

Darrell Patrick Rowbottom is a postdoctoral research associate in philosophy of science at the Universities of Edinburgh and Bristol, UK, on a project concerning the interface between physics and biology. His forthcoming papers include 'Beyond Empiricism and Rationalism: Stance Epistemology' in *Synthese*, 'Intersubjective Corroboration' in *Studies in History and Philosophy of Science* and 'The Insufficiency of the Dutch Book Argument' in *Studia Logica.*

Paul Smeyers is Full Professor, K.U. Leuven, Belgium, President of the International Network of Philosophers of Education, and chairs the Research Community, Philosophy and History of the Discipline of Education: Evaluation and Evolution of the Criteria for Educational Research. With Blake, Smith and Standish he co-authored *Thinking Again* (1998), *Education in an Age of Nihilism* (2000), *The Therapy of Education* (2006) and co-edited *The Blackwell Guide to the Philosophy of Education*

(2003). With Depaepe he co-edited *Beyond Empiricism. On Criteria for Educational Research* (2003), *Educational Research: why 'what works' doesn't work* (2006) and *Educational Research/Networks and Technologies* (2007).

Richard Smith is Professor of Education and Director of the Combined Degrees in Arts and Social Sciences at the University of Durham, UK. He is Editor of the new journal *Ethics and Education*, and Associate Editor of the *Journal of Philosophy of Education*. His most recent book is (with Paul Smeyers and Paul Standish) *The Therapy of Education* (Palgrave Macmillan, 2006). His principal research interests are in the philosophy of education and the philosophy of social science.

Paul Standish is Professor of Philosophy of Education at the University of London Institute of Education. His teaching combines analytical and continental philosophical approaches in the study of questions concerning the nature of teaching and learning, citizenship and democracy, technology, and higher education. His recent books, in various collaborations with Nigel Blake, Paul Smeyers and Richard Smith, include *Thinking Again: Education after Postmodernism* (Bergin & Garvey, 1998), *Education in an Age of Nihilism* (RoutledgeFalmer, 2000), *The Blackwell Guide to Philosophy of Education* (Blackwell, 2003) and *The Therapy of Education* (Palgrave Macmillan, 2006). He is Editor of the *Journal of Philosophy of Education*.

Lynda Stone is Professor, Philosophy of Education at the University of North Carolina at Chapel Hill, USA. With degrees from the Universities of California, Berkeley and Stanford, she has had a career of over forty years in education teaching and research. Her scholarly interests focus on social and feminist theory, philosophy of history, and philosophy of education including philosophy of educational research. Recent papers compare and contrast Kuhn and Foucault for research and consider character education from a Foucauldian perspective. Recent publications appear in *Journal of Philosophy of Education*, *Studies in Philosophy and Education*, *Educational Philosophy and Theory*, and *Journal of Thought*.

Judith Suissa is Lecturer in Philosophy of Education at the Institute of Education, University of London, UK. Her research interests include radical and libertarian education, theories of human nature, and philosophical perspectives on childhood and the parent-child relationship. Her book, *Anarchism and Education: A Philosophical Perspective* was published by Routledge in 2006.

Echo H. Wu is currently a Ph.D student in the Curry School of Education at the University of Virginia, USA and a research assistant at the National Research Center on the Gifted and Talented (NRC/GT). She earned an MEd from the University of New South Wales in Sydney, and an MPhil specializing in gifted education at The University of Hong Kong. Her research interests include parenting the gifted and talented, concepts of giftedness and talented performance, cultural issues related to gifted education, instructional strategies and social-emotional issues of children with special needs, counselling the gifted and talented, and qualitative research methodology.

Preface

Complaints about the quality of educational research arise perennially, and these come from a number of quarters. There are those who would emphasise only 'what works'—without so much as a flicker of discomfort over the vagueness of this phrase or any inclination to question what it is that would constitute working well. There are those who imagine that educational research can take medical research as its model, the randomised control trial being its optimum methodological form—without any apparent awareness of the range of non-empirical enquiry that has in fact informed educational policy and practice. And there are those within educational research whose identity is so staked in paradigm wars and their aftermath that they become ideologically insulated from the questions that teachers, policy-makers and researchers need to ask. These are among the factors that contribute to the crisis of confidence from which educational research so often suffers. This is a crisis that is manifested in the self-consciousness about methodology that characterises many publications in the field—especially publications about the nature of educational research—and that runs through so much research methods training. Indeed the latter sometimes involves an odd mix of banal catalogues of method with abstract and largely bogus categorisations of theoretical stances (interpretivist, objectivist, subjectivist, feminist, epistemological, ontological . . .).

In this context the publication of *Philosophy, Methodology and Educational Research* is especially to be welcomed. The carefully argued essays collected here bring clarity where there has been confusion and demonstrate ways of enquiry and sources of insight whose practical salience is too often suppressed or overlooked. The volume brings together papers previously published in two issues of the *Journal of Philosophy of Education* with some further essays and a revised introduction. It is a sequel to *The Ethics of Educational Research*, which attracted widespread interest in the broader international educational research community. On that occasion we had reason to thank Mike McNamee and David Bridges for their judgement and imagination in creating a lively and stimulating collection. In the preparation of the present volume—the purpose and content of which are detailed in the introduction that follows—David Bridges has collaborated with Richard Smith to produce a carefully orchestrated examination of philosophical questions central to educational research and social science methodology. The contributors demonstrate a level of critical engagement with these questions that is rarely found, and they suggest ways beyond the points of impasse and the ideological self-consciousness to which educational research too readily succumbs. *Philosophy, Methodology and Educational Research* addresses topics of pressing importance for anyone involved in educational research or in social science more generally, and we have every confidence that the volume will have impact and enduring influence.

Paul Standish
Series Editor

1
Philosophy, Methodology and Educational Research: Introduction

DAVID BRIDGES AND RICHARD SMITH

This book is addressed both to philosophers of education and to the many colleagues in the wider educational research community whose interests lead them into questions about the nature of different forms of educational enquiry, their methodological foundations, their claims to illuminate our experience and their relationship to policy and practice. This is intriguing territory in which philosophers of education can engage fruitfully with colleagues from other traditions, and we hope that the chapters included here will encourage such engagement.

Philosophy, we would argue, has a unique and indispensable contribution to make to educational as well as other forms of social science research. Philosophical considerations must, of course, inform the ethical and social principles which underpin such research—and some of these considerations were explored in an earlier volume in this series (McNamee and Bridges 2002). They also inform our understanding of the very nature of what it is we are engaged with in educational research (brains or minds? experienced phenomena or objects in a real world?), the different kinds of claims we make to know or understand these and the methods we employ to enquire into them. This is, more particularly, the territory of this volume.

As Wilfred Carr observed in a paper to a BERA/EERA conference in September 1995: 'Research ... always conveys a commitment to philosophical beliefs even if this is unintended and even though it remains implicit and unacknowledged ... [Researchers] cannot evade the responsibility for critically examining and justifying the philosophical ideas that their enquiries incorporate. It follows that philosophical reflection and argumentation are central features of the methods and procedures of educational research' (Carr, 1995, p. 1).

Educational researchers are constantly confronted by the need to make sense of how educational theory, policy and practice are to be investigated and understood, not least in order to justify their own work. What kinds of enquiry provide what kinds of understanding of education? How can such enquiry inform practical decisions, whether in the context of general policy-making or in more particular settings? What kinds of inferences can we draw from what kind of evidence? What sorts of assumptions can we make about the stuff of educational experience and the way it is constructed or reconstructed in thought and language? (Is learning, for example, best understood by observing electrical activity in the brain, through the instruments of behavioural observation or by eliciting reflective or phenomenological accounts of people's states of mind?) What part does the subjectivity of the enquirer play in this enquiry and construction? How are power and knowledge connected and implicated in educational processes, not least those of educational research itself?

Philosophy contributes to all of these questions and thus provides some of the essential *underpinning of research* in the social sciences—the 'underlabourer' view of philosophy referred to below (p. 231); but it may itself actually *constitute such research*. This latter claim, that research in the social sciences is necessarily and ineliminably philosophical, was most fully set out in Peter Winch's seminal *The Idea of a Social Science and its Relation to Philosophy* (1958) (again, see below, p. 230 ff.). The chapters in this volume illustrate both kinds of contribution.

One thing that philosophy supplies is a history of rehearsal of the central arguments that arise here, the depth of which is such as to expose the embeddedness of any one point of view in more far-reaching sets of assumptions. It can offer forms of analysis and argument which enable us better to understand what might be at stake in any particular view-point and to come to a view for which there is a discernible, appropriate warrant, albeit one which is always exposed to critique. The nature and force of such arguments are themselves, of course, philosophical questions, just as the nature and force of evidence in science or history, of reasoning in mathematics or of commentary in literary criticism raise philosophical questions. In the context of educational research, the contributors to this volume offer analysis and reasoned argument while at the same time they question over-simplified notions of what counts as analysis and reason.

Neither the importance of the contribution which philosophy makes to broadly empirical enquiry nor that of philosophical research in education itself can be taken for granted. In this volume our contributors share with many colleagues in the wider research community a concern over the tendency to see educational research as essentially, or even solely, a matter of discovering 'what works'—a tendency whose reductivism and anti-intellectualism is all too apparent, for example, in the 'What Works Clearinghouse' in the United States (see http://www.whatworks.ed.gov/) and even in the rather more liberal regime of the E-PPI (Evidence for Policy and Practice Information and Coordinating Centre) 'systematic research reviews' in the UK. A recent philosophical discussion of these developments in Smeyers and Depaepe (2006) provides some of the background to contributions to be found here.

What may seem the wholly reasonable expectation that reforms and initiatives should be based on evidence rather than hunch or ideology often has an alarming way of sliding into the dogma that the only research that really counts is the kind that, on the analogy of medical research, is based on randomised control trials. On the basis of just which randomised control trials, we might ask, has this been shown to be anything other than dogma? We are offered what is at its core a philosophical position about the kind of evidence that can inform human action which is itself, however, philosophically indefensible. It is also an extremely damaging position in the sense that it consigns to oblivion philosophy, history, much sociology and, in fact, anything that is explicitly theoretical, as well as more specific forms of enquiry that identify themselves, for example, as life history research, illuminative case studies, deconstructive approaches and discourse analysis. In so doing it eliminates from the examination of educational policy many of the sources which can claim to provide some of the most nuanced, sensitive, contextually informed, critical and meaningful insights into this particular sphere of human experience and behaviour. Philosophers of education have common cause with those working in these other traditions in resisting the intellectual impoverishment of educational enquiry but also a shared obligation, perhaps, to examine critically and to explain the nature of the contribution which they can make to such enquiry.

This volume has, then, a number of interconnected themes, and the chapters may be read in different ways to contribute to their discussion. These include:

- examination of the idea of educational research as 'scientific' and challenges to this conception—an examination most closely related to the 'what works' debate (Aiston/Rowbottom, Smith and MacLure);
- analysis of the different forms of enquiry which might be thought to constitute educational research and their claims on our belief (Bridges, Davis, and Ramaekers);
- consideration of the (over-crudely drawn) qualitative/quantitative divide in educational research (Ratnesar/MacKenzie and Alexander);
- discussion of action research as a resolution of the (equally crudely drawn) divide between educational theory and practice (Carr, Elliott and Papastephanou);
- examination of specific issues in the logic of educational research—notably the question of the generalisability of research findings (Fendler and Evers/Wu);
- analysis of the contribution of philosophy itself to educational enquiry (Alexander, Hammersley, Levering and Smeyers);
- examination of issues raised in initiating newcomers to the educational—including the philosophical—research community (Suissa, Stone and Hodgson/Standish);
- a call for philosophers of education to engage with the detail of empirical research (Phillips)—and a response (Smeyers)

A number of contributions address more than one of these interconnected themes, but we here introduce the chapters in this order.

THE IDEA OF EDUCATIONAL RESEARCH AS 'SCIENTIFIC' AND CHALLENGES TO THIS CONCEPTION (AISTON/ROWBOTTOM, SMITH AND MACLURE)

The Latin word *scientia*, from which our word 'science' comes, originally meant nothing more than 'systematic knowledge of the true causes of particular things' (Smith, 1997, p. 16), as opposed to the revealed knowledge that came from religion. It did not mean what we have came to designate in the 20th century as the 'natural sciences' (ibid.). It was in the 16th and 17th centuries, in what is usually called the Era of Scientific Revolutions, that 'science' began to acquire its modern connotations of empiricism and experimentalism. Thus conceived, 'science' began to seem, because of its remarkable discoveries and inventions, the most respectable kind of systematic knowledge, which is why the social sciences came to be so called and why, riding on the prestige of experimental science, some people talk of management science, political science and even the science of literary criticism. We are talking here specifically of the British and Anglophone tradition. Things are otherwise elsewhere. The German language, for example, does not speak of the social sciences but of the *Geisteswissenschaften*, sometimes translated as the 'humanities' or the 'humanistic study of culture' (literally it means the ways of knowing the human mind or spirit, *Geist*), and distinguishes the *Geisteswissenschaften* from the *Naturwissenschaften* or ways of knowing the natural world. In France, the phrase *les sciences de l'éducation* applies to all systematic and disciplined forms of enquiry and not just to those that are closest to the physical sciences. Continental Europe is more hospitable to theory than the Anglophone countries. It is a sobering thought that the influence of the scientific paradigm may be largely an accident of history and of the English language.

Behind the 'what works' dogma there seem to lurk not only the idea that 'science' supplies the model to which all claims to knowledge should aspire, but fantasies and misconceptions concerning science itself. Sarah Aiston and Darrell Rowbottom, in this volume, examine these misconceptions, and analyse the false contrasts often drawn between 'scientific' and 'non-scientific' approaches. They see here the origins of the idea that educational research is centrally a matter of employing particular methods, an idea they find prevalent in standard research methods textbooks.

It was Francis Bacon who in the early 17th century provided theoretical underpinning for the new paradigm of knowledge, and in this collection Richard Smith traces back to Bacon and his legacy the modern ambition to formulate 'research methods' for the social sciences that can be applied regardless of the acumen of the researcher employing them. Smith argues that that this ambition is still with us and that it deprives educational research of the wider range of ideas and theories that should inform it. On the other hand, too much emphasis is placed on one distinguishing feature of the social sciences, the fact that we are ourselves the objects of our study, risks leading to a kind of solipsism, equally uninformed by ideas from the wider world of theory and literature.

MacLure elaborates on the theme that, far from being obliged to discover 'what works' in the classroom, educational research can be conceived in other terms than the instrumental. The idea that research should be useful is a particular perspective, typical of the age in which we live, to which there are alternatives. It does not reflect some eternal verity. One task for educational research, she argues, is to resist the demand for practical solutions to practical problems, the demand for closure and oversimplification. Enquiry into education can make the over-familiar seem properly strange; it can be playful and thus help us to resist the dreary, limited and limiting solemnities of educational policy, practice and research.

THE DIFFERENT FORMS OF ENQUIRY WHICH MIGHT CONSTITUTE EDUCATIONAL RESEARCH AND THEIR CLAIMS ON OUR BELIEF (BRIDGES, DAVIS AND RAMAEKERS)

The variety of forms which educational research can take is the theme of David Bridges' chapter. This traces the fragmentation and expansion of the intellectual traditions from which educational research has drawn from what were at one stage regarded as the 'foundation disciplines' of psychology, sociology, history and philosophy and considers the claim that educational research does not merely require multi- or inter-disciplinary approaches but is now in a 'post-disciplinary' era. He argues that discipline in the sense of adherence to some shared understanding of and commitment to rules of enquiry, albeit in diverse forms, is what makes a 'community of arguers' possible.

Andrew Davis argues that an obsession with scientific notions of objectivity, truth and consistency can blind us to the fact that science is not the only activity in our world. The arts give us other notions of objectivity altogether. Consistency in assessing the arts, he shows, is compatible with defensible accounts of truth and objectivity, and this suggests ways in which consistency should be understood in many forms of educational research.

To some MacLure's 'demented form of the familiar' may seem to conjure the bug-bear of postmodernism, an alarming state of affairs leading to nihilism or an 'anything goes' philosophy. Stefan Ramaekers shows, however, that such fears are ungrounded. Postmodern or poststructural currents in educational thought may shift the emphasis away from the search for 'truth', but they do so by focusing on a different set of issues and questions, particularly ones where what education means to the individual moves back to the centre of the picture.

THE QUALITATIVE/QUANTITATIVE DIVIDE IN EDUCATIONAL RESEARCH (RATNESAR/MACKENZIE AND ALEXANDER)

Nimal Ratnesar and Jim Mackenzie accuse educational researchers of a tendency to ignorance of other kinds of research, and of making an over-simple division into the quantitative and the qualitative. Misunderstanding of the null hypothesis significance testing procedure is just one symptom of mechanical and thoughtless use of statistics. Here too are to be found the view that 'science progresses through accumulating publicly verifiable empirical facts and through mechanical procedures and experiments which anybody can repeat at will' and the characteristics of 'a kind of positivism that disavows the intuitions and judgements of the researcher'. Research worthy of the name requires intellectual commitment, judgement, imagination and many other qualities. The house of knowledge, as Ratnesar and Mackenzie memorably note, has many mansions.

Alexander challenges what he argues is the sterile tendency to polarise educational research between the constructivist extreme at one end and positivistic science at the other and he locates educational research firmly in the *Geisteswissenschaften*, placing at its heart the business of understanding education as an intentional activity, replete with the purposes and meanings with which people invest it. He emphasises the importance of ideals and values: 'educational research worthy of the name must be conducted within the context of explicit and adequately defended visions of the good'. A view of the higher ideals that govern human activities (which some at least would see as an essentially philosophical project) is, on this argument, necessary to making sense of quantitative as well as qualitative research.

ACTION RESEARCH AS A RESOLUTION OF THE DIVIDE BETWEEN EDUCATIONAL THEORY AND PRACTICE (CARR, ELLIOTT AND PAPASTEPHANOU)

The critique of narrow and technicist forms of scientificity in educational research is extended in a group of contributions which turn instead towards action research as a form of research practice which brings theory and practice together. Wilfred Carr argues that the recovery of the Aristotelian tradition of 'practical philosophy', with the notion of *phronesis* or practical judgement at its heart, gives us crucial insight into the kind of business that education uniquely is. It is the predecessor of the action research that is widely regarded, across a range of professions, as a mode of reflection on and improvement of practice distinguished by an epistemological basis other than the scientific paradigm.

John Elliott too believes that 'research on education', to use his phrase, is impoverished by assimilation to the model of the physical sciences. By contrast he distinguishes 'educational research' as a 'form of disciplined conversation' carried on by those on the inside of education as a practice and governed by a conception of rationality that is both different from the scientific kind and more democratic in its nature.

Marianna Papastephanou is, perhaps, rather less impressed by the claims of action research to incorporate philosophical thought. She finds it frequently lacking in imagination and critical power. In particular, she claims, it is often naive about the relationship between theory and practice and about questions of power, and it risks reinforcing the political and professional *status quo*. She concludes that educational action research needs to draw on deeper and rich theoretical resources if it is to realise its potential.

THE GENERALISABILITY OF RESEARCH FINDINGS (FENDLER, EVERS AND WU)

A key issue in a number of research traditions is the issue of the extent to which general beliefs can be legitimately drawn from specific and sometimes very limited research evidence. We do not attempt to address this question comprehensively, but two contributions offer interesting insights into it. Lynn Fendler approaches the question of generalisability employing a Foucauldian approach and thus illustrates the useful of this approach in showing us where ideas that we now take for granted come from. The idea of generalisability itself, Fendler shows, does not represent an eternal and unquestionable verity. It is the product of historical factors that characterise the period we have come to think of as modernity, including the increasing popularity of measurement as a technology for governing society, and including too the strange shift in which 'statistics' changed its meaning from knowledge of statecraft to the application of mathematical formulae to the understanding of human society. Thus generalisability is a local and contingent phenomenon and so, rather wonderfully, it is not itself universally generalisable.

Colin Evers and Echo Wu tackle what they acknowledge to be the 'complex and difficult matter' of generalising from a single case. They manage nevertheless to indicate a number of grounds for concluding that such generalisation cannot be ruled out as methodologically unsound in the way it would tend to be in the physical sciences. For example, particular cases may have sophisticated structures, governed for instance by culture, language and practices, and these can be the basis for the judgement that one particular case is similar to another.

THE CONTRIBUTION OF PHILOSOPHY ITSELF TO EDUCATIONAL ENQUIRY (LEVERING, SMEYERS AND HAMMERSLEY)

Philosophy does not have to be thought of as a preliminary, perhaps ground-clearing, exercise that comes before 'real' or proper research, for example, in the Lockean tradition that makes the philosopher an under-labourer to the scientist. Philosophy makes claim to being research itself rather than a preliminary to it in the school of thought known as phenomenology, central to which is the exploration of what presents itself to us in conscious experience. For much educational research subjectivity is conceived as a problem, and the goal is objectivity understood as the absence of subjectivity. However, as Bas Levering explains, from a phenomenological point of view subjectivity is not so much a problem as an inevitable starting-point. It is not that people's accounts of their own experiences and perceptions are indubitable, since clearly they are not: it is rather that ways need to be found to distinguish convincing interpretations from unconvincing ones, and this is what phenomenological research undertakes.

Perhaps the most forthright claim that social science is essentially philosophical in nature is associated with Peter Winch and his (1958) book, *The Idea of a Social Science and its Relation to Philosophy*. For Winch there is no easy distinction between how the world is and how we conceptualise the world. Philosophy deals with 'what it makes sense to say', and in Winch's famous words, 'any worthwhile study of society must be philosophical in character'. Taking a strongly but not uncritically Winchean stance, Paul Smeyers shows how and in what sense human behaviour is often helpfully to be understood in terms of reasons rather than causes.

A corollary of this is that, as an investigation of the social world, educational research must take a more pluralistic form than common theorisations of research methodology tend to allow. Hammersley criticises both research methodology that ignores philosophical considerations and those who appear to believe that philosophy itself, conceived in one way or another, constitutes the methodology of most significance to social science research in education. Philosophy is necessary to clarify values and principles, especially, but it cannot, he argues, itself provide a framework to structure ideals of knowledge, truth and objectivity.

INITIATING NEWCOMERS TO THE EDUCATIONAL— INCLUDING THE PHILOSOPHICAL—RESEARCH COMMUNITY (STONE, SUISSA, HODGSON AND STANDISH)

The authors of the last group of chapters are concerned particularly with research training and the induction of postgraduate students into educational research via conferences and publication. Such initiation provides something of a touchstone for understanding what the practice of philosophy entails in a research environment in which it has a function either as an underpinning to other research methodologies or as a form of enquiry in its own right. Lynda Stone argues that graduate research training values method as technology for its own sake, and thus involves a kind of technologisation. Her focus is on the US context, but her analysis is widely applicable.

Judith Suissa offers a reflective and personal account of her experience of designing and teaching a philosophy module as part of a research training programme for students studying for research degrees in education. She suggests that such graduate students may benefit more from the opportunity to work together studying different writers, theories and traditions than from the kind of methodological courses that Lynda Stone describes.

Finally, Naomi Hodgson and Paul Standish explore ways in which a narrow and self-referential, but to all appearances eminently reasonable, discourse of research method has been created in such a way that an orthodoxy has been constructed, with a consequent neutralisation and domestication of critique. Drawing on the distinction made by Deleuze and Guattari between the 'striated' and the 'smooth', and questioning the operation of the networks into which new researchers are initiated, they argue for an 'orientation towards becoming': this requires of educational research an 'engagement with the philosophical questions inherent in education ... and dialogue with the knowledge of the social sciences in order to challenge [educational research's] sense of its purpose, of its history, and of its relationship to that which it seeks to study and improve'.

It is this engagement that all the contributors to both of this volume regard as essential and central to any worthwhile research into education.

A CALL FOR ENGAGEMENT BY PHILOSOPHERS OF EDUCATION WITH THE DETAIL OF EMPIRICAL RESEARCH (PHILLIPS)— AND A RESPONSE (SMEYERS)

To some extent this book has made a claim on behalf of philosophy for the attention of other sections of the research community and in particular those whose work is empirically based. It has illustrated and sometimes argued for the contribution of philosophy to the understanding and advance of debates about issues of research methodology and also to areas of substantive educational enquiry to which it can contribute in its own right.

Dennis Phillips' contribution goes some way to turn the tables on the philosophical community and is an explicit attempt 'to goad philosophers of education into paying more detailed attention to empirical educational research' and to resist the abstract generalities which are, he argues, characteristic of too much philosophical writing in this field. Unless philosophers pay close attention to the detail of empirical research and the ways in which it is constructed, argues Phillips, they cannot expect the wider research community to take their critique to heart. Not only this, but such attention would force philosophers to think more deeply about real problems rather than about 'problems that emanate from our "idealised" but uninformed models of what happens in research and about how research decisions are made'.

Paul Smeyers responds to Dennis Phillips not so much with immediate dissent but by taking his advice—and applying it to a consideration of first a qualitative study of the professional development of primary school teachers and then a quantitative study of class size. Paul Smeyers uses this examination to identify some of the problems which Phillips' position might entail. He argues that it is not so much whether we need to study empirical educational research which is the issue, but rather the nature of the research that is genuinely helpful for an understanding of the field of education.

Thus empirical researchers are enjoined to engage in the philosophical issues which are integral to any educational research undertaking—and philosophers are enjoined to give more careful attention to the work with which empirical researchers are primarily occupied. We hope that this book will contribute to a fruitful dialogue between these two communities.

REFERENCES

Carr, W. (1995) Philosophy and Educational Research: Paper presented to roundtable session of BERA/EERA Conference, Bath, UK.

McNamee, M. and Bridges, D. (eds) (2002) *The Ethics of Educational Research* (Oxford, Blackwell).

Smeyers, P. and Depaepe, M. (eds) (2006) *Educational Research: Why 'What Works' Doesn't Work* (Dordrecht, Springer).

Smith, R. (1997) *The Norton History of the Human Sciences* (New York, W.W. Norton).

Winch, P. (1958) *The Idea of a Social Science and its Relation to Philosophy* (London, Routledge).

2
The Myth of 'Scientific Method' in Contemporary Educational Research

DARRELL PATRICK ROWBOTTOM AND SARAH JANE AISTON

As a rule, I begin my lectures on Scientific Method by telling my students that scientific method does not exist and I ought to know, having been, for a time at least, the one and only professor of this non-existent subject within the British Commonwealth ... my subject does not exist because subject matters in general do not exist. There are no subject matters; no branches of learning—or, rather, of inquiry: there are only problems, and the urge to solve them.
(Popper, 1983, Preface, 'On the Non-Existence of Scientific Method')

Rationality, then, consists primarily in eliminating errors and learning from them. This process is not peculiar to empirical science, nor is empirical science furthered by empirical testing alone ...
(O'Hear, 1980, p. 111)

I INTRODUCTION

Educational research has been plagued by dubious bifurcations, the most significant of which is between 'positivism', according to which social sciences ought to be modelled on the natural sciences, and 'interpretivism', which rejects this view.[1] However, the association of 'positivism' with modern science is misguided since, as Carr and Kemmis point out (1986, p. 71), one need only carry out a historical analysis of the nature of progress in science to see that positivist notions 'lay down ideals for the conduct of research that are ... unrealistic and irrelevant'. As they go on to note (1986, p. 120), the philosophy of science 'generates an image of science very different from the orthodox positivist account', yet this rather outdated account continues to dominate educational research. As we shall argue, such an account is not only unrealistic and irrelevant, but also divisive and detrimental to social science.

There are a number of educational researchers who acknowledge that such a misconception of science is problematic, and emphasise, in particular, the narrow perception of science that it involves. For example, Lather (2004, p. 760), in discussing the No Child Left Behind Act and the legislation of scientific method in educational research in the U.S., objects to 'how the narrowly defined sense of science-based evidence in this effort at the federal level works to discipline educational research'. Similarly, Davis and Sumara (2005) discuss 'complexity science' in an attempt to widen the conception of science. However, both Lather and Davis *et al.* argue from what might be described as an interpretative/critical position, which serves to perpetuate the polarisation between 'science' and 'non-science' on the basis of method.[2] So while we wholeheartedly support the notion of widening the conception of science, we suggest that we should widen it even further, by rejecting the idea of a scientific method, and recognise that good inquiry—rather than 'doing science'—is what really matters. Surely it is a much more powerful argument, in objecting to the aforementioned US legislation, for instance, to look to the history and philosophy of science, and what scientists *actually* do, in order to point out the misconception of science that is operating.

This chapter is sympathetic to Pring (2000) and Phillips (2005). The former discusses the 'false dualism' that has arisen between the quantitative and qualitative tradition, commenting that (2000, p. 57): 'the polarization between two paradigms, which is so typical of so much theoretical writing on educational research, bears little relation to the complexity of research practice'. He further notes that (2000, p. 87) 'in failing to do a proper philosophical job, educational researchers have drawn too sharp a contrast'. The latter claims the educational research community is beset by a 'confusion of tongues', and suggests (2005, p. 7) that 'those who dismiss scientific educational research as being misguided ... have failed to consider there may be other fruitful ways to characterise this scientific paradigm'. He concludes that :

> ... attempts to delineate 'the central method of science'—the attempt to give a simple 'gold standard' account of the 'nature of science'—must always be quite arbitrary; perhaps it was recognition of all of this that led Percy Bridgman, a Nobel Laureate in Physics, to remark that 'the scientist has no other method than doing his damnedest' (2005, p. 19).

We endeavour to advance this view by considering a concrete example of how science and scientists are misrepresented. Specifically, we examine one of the most widely known contemporary textbooks on educational research—*Research Methods in Education* by Cohen, Manion, and Morrison—which is currently in its fifth edition. We take this to be important since the contents of such books have real consequences, e.g. in shaping young researchers' conceptions of, and thereby approaches to, educational research.[3]

It is important to note that Cohen *et al.* (2003) draw heavily on the work of others, in advancing their view of research, and are therefore something of an incidental target.[4] They are simply representative of a wider problem, although they are surely blameworthy in so far as they do not seem to have grasped—or even, perhaps, properly read—all of the material that they refer to. (As we shall see, they murder the philosophy of Popper.) In the present climate of mechanical regurgitation, textbooks contain references to quotations lifted from other textbooks—see, for instance, the indirect quotation of Mouly, in Wellington (2000, p. 12). The system is closed, stale, and self-referential.

II ESTABLISHING THE PROBLEM

In this section, we examine some of the misconceptions which are apparent in the early discussions of Cohen *et al.* (2003, p. ch.1), and then endeavour to diagnose the underlying problem and its source.

First, we tackle what might be called their view of science from *without*: of the differences between laypeople and scientists. They imply that scientists do not posit causal relations in the same fashion as laypeople—and/or ought not to—because they do not, like everyone else, proceed by trial and error. But we reject both the view that scientists are especially empowered to discover causal relations, and that they do not make causal posits without 'rigorous experimentation'.

Second, we address their view of science from *within*: of what scientists must assume, either explicitly or implicitly. In reference to ontology and epistemology, we demonstrate that a positivistic approach does not necessarily map onto a realist one, and indeed that an anti-positivistic approach does not necessarily map onto a nominalist one, as they mistakenly claim. Furthermore, we show that they misunderstand what nominalism is, and actually *assume it* in presenting their view of a 'concept' as a necessary tool of science. This renders their account internally inconsistent, because if one did have to be a nominalist in order to be a scientist—which is, incidentally, false—then this would show that there could not be 'an objectivist' and 'a subjectivist' approach *within* science, in the fashion that they contend. We continue by suggesting that there seem to be some deeper ontological assumptions, about perception and learning, which underlie their misconceptions.

Third, and finally, we endeavour to bring together our discussion of these misconceptions of scientists and science—both from *without*, and from *within*—by showing that they assume there to be a special method in natural science, because they also believe there is an ultimate authority upon which knowledge-claims can rest. It is this, we contend, which leads to the false dichotomy that has become enshrined in educational research, and the inauthentic polarisation of social scientists into two radically separate camps.

A(i)   Misconceptions from Without: 'Laypeople' versus 'Scientists'

Cohen *et al.* (2003, p. 4) present a narrative that over-emphasises the differences between 'laypeople' and 'scientists', in which the former are portrayed as implausibly dim-witted characters for whom: 'The chance occurrence of two events in close proximity is sufficient reason to predicate a causal link between them'. However, if one recognises that two events occur 'in close proximity' *by chance*, one is hardly going to think that one has caused the other! (This reading might seem unfair. But notice that a 'reason' must, presumably, take propositional form.) Moreover, even if 'mere' replaces 'chance', their claim seems to be based on the ageing presupposition that we can never *perceptually* distinguish a causal conjunction of events from a coincidental one; as Hume (1748, p. 144) put it: 'All events seem entirely loose and separate. One follows another; but we can never observe any tye between them'. Yet plausibly, our experience of causally related kinds of events is neither entirely uniform, nor fully coherent. We blink our eyes, hold our bodies in different postures, find ourselves in different locations, suffer lapses of concentration, and so on, and so forth. (Similarly, there is an extremely tricky question about how we *individuate* events.) It is rather a wonder that we posit any causal connections at all, if we cannot notice them. Further, if Cohen *et al.* are correct, it is a wonder that 'laypeople' do not associate their personal existences, construed as the set of events involving them, as necessary for the continuation of other events in the wider world.

Of scientists, by contrast, they write that (Cohen *et al.* 2003, p. 4) 'only as a result of rigorous experimentation will they postulate a relationship between two phenomena'. But if this is so, then we cannot account for the diverse theoretical activities of those whom we intuitively want to label 'scientists', both past and present. We all agree, presumably, that Einstein was a scientist, and think that his special and general theories of relativity are scientific. Yet as Zahar (1989, pp. 88–90) convincingly argues, Einstein postulated relationships between phenomena on the basis of heuristic principles, since he believed that: 'Science should present us with a coherent, unified, harmonious, simple and organically compact picture of the world'. On this matter, a quotation directly from Einstein is appropriate:

> It is my conviction that we are able, through pure mathematical construction, to find those concepts and the law-like connections between them which yield the key to the understanding of natural phenomena ... The really creative principle is in mathematics. In a certain sense I therefore consider it to be true—as was the dream of the Ancients—that pure thought is capable of grasping reality (1934, p. 116).

Whether or not it is true that pure thought can grasp (certain aspects of) reality, Einstein certainly made free causal posits, albeit ones that were susceptible to *future* testing, in advancing his relativistic theories. We see no obvious reason for thinking that he was wrong on either score. Pure mathematics seems to be the paradigm of *a priori* inquiry, and it surely involves research. Yet according to Cohen *et al.* (2003) 'research' must base 'its operations on the inductive-deductive model' and be 'empirical'.

A(ii)   Misconceptions from Within: 'Subjectivism' versus 'Objectivism'

The following figure, which is similar to the one that Cohen *et al.* (2003) reproduce from Burrell and Morgan (1979), will set the scene for what follows:

A Scheme for Analysing Assumptions about the Nature of Social Science				
The Subjectivist Approach to Social Science				The Objectivist Approach to Social Science
Nominalism	←	Ontology	→	Realism
Anti-positivism	←	Epistemology	→	Positivism
Voluntarism	←	Human Nature	→	Determinism
Idiographic	←	Methodology	→	Nomothetic

Figure 1

It is our contention that this is a thoroughly misguided polarisation: that one need not adopt either of these approaches, but can mix and match individual components of each, and even adopt a quietist stance on some. In order to advance it, we will focus on the relationship between ontology and epistemology, since it strikes us that the issue of 'Human Nature' is precisely an ontological one, and that the question of 'Methodology' is to be answered, if it can be answered, by appeal to both ontological and epistemological concerns. We should add that although we *do* accept there are important relations between one's metaphysical and epistemological views, we believe that these are both entirely different to, and far more complicated than, those suggested by Figure 1. In fact, we think that such oversimplification is dangerous, and does grave injustice to the subtleties of human thought.

We will start at the top of Figure 1, with 'what is known in philosophy as the nominalist-realist debate' according to Cohen *et al.* (2003, p. 6). On the one hand, we are told, the nominalist 'holds that objects of thought are merely words and that there is no independently accessible thing constituting the meaning of a word'. On the other, apparently, the realist believes that 'objects have an independent existence and are not dependent for it on the knower'. *Prima facie*, this seems simple enough.

When we consider the foregoing explanation of 'nominalism' a little more carefully, however, it appears incoherent. If objects of thought were *merely* words, then what could words be? How, that is to say, could the so-called 'nominalist' have grasped that there are words, above and beyond objects of thought? What Cohen *et al.* seem to be describing is someone who is very confused: almost as confused, perhaps, as they are. Any claim about 'objects of thought' being 'merely words' would have to be purely verbal—and hence, rather uninteresting.

Cohen *et al.* would have done well to have consulted the entry for 'nominalism' in the Oxford English Dictionary (1994): '*Philos.* The doctrine that universals or abstract concepts are mere names without any corresponding reality'. Nominalists need not deny the existence of any given concrete particular, or indeed their non-verbal, non-conceptual, access to it. They need not, that is, deny that they are directly acquainted with things that are red, square, and so forth. What they will deny, *qua* nominalists, is that this means there are such separate entities as 'redness', and 'squareness'. They can think that Big Ben exists quite independently of them, their language, their thoughts, etc. It therefore emerges, rather remarkably, that they can be 'realists' according to Cohen *et al.*

What's more, Cohen *et al.* (2003, pp. 13–14) unwittingly assume a nominalist stance, a few pages later, in discussing 'The Tools of Science': '*Concepts* express generalizations from particulars ... scientific concepts ... do not exist independently of us: they are indeed our inventions enabling us to acquire some understanding at least of the apparent chaos of nature'. Thus they preclude the possibility, according to Fig. 1, of any scientist adopting an 'objectivist' approach.[5]

This elementary error might have been avoided by reading the work of such metaphysicians as Lowe (2002, chaps.19–20), who goes to considerable lengths not only to explain the difference between nominalism and realism, but also the underlying categorial distinctions between particular and universal, and abstract and concrete.[6] And the following introductory passage in Loux, 1998, makes their misunderstanding crystal clear:

> Although almost everyone will concede that some of our ways of classifying objects reflect our interests, goals, and values, few will deny that many of our ways of sorting things are fixed by the objects themselves. It is not as if we just arbitrarily choose to call some things triangular, others circular, and still others square ... Likewise, it is not a mere consequence of human thought or language that there are elephants, oak trees, and paramecia. They come that way, and our language and thought reflect these antecedently given facts about them.

> There are, then, objective similarities among things. Prior to our classifying them in the ways we do, the familiar objects of the everyday world agree in their characteristics, features, or attributes. This is not a claim born of any metaphysical theory. It is, on the contrary, a prephilosophical truism, but one that has given rise to significant philosophical theorizing ... [I]s there a very general type or form of fact such that, given any case of attribute agreement, that case obtains because and only because some fact of the relevant very general type or form obtains? (Loux, 1998, p. 21)

So one striking consequence of the view of 'concepts' blithely assumed by Cohen *et al.* is that we cannot discover natural kinds—e.g. recognize them, and assign them names in order to rigidly designate them—such as dogs, gold, and electrons. Rather, according to their view, such classifications would seem to be socially, or even personally, constructed. Again, it seems as if they are somehow assuming that concrete particulars are accessible, in a manner that abstracta are not. To hark back to the earlier discussion of Hume, this would seem to be because they adopt, without explanation or justification, a contentious—and dated—view of our perception being rooted in 'sense data'. As Morris Raphael Cohen put it, inveighing against the sensationalist and physicalist trends of the time:

> That all knowledge begins with the perception of the individual and then goes on by abstraction to the universal is a widespread dogma ... We are impressed with a stranger's beauty, agreeableness, or reliability before we can specify his features or traits. It is therefore quite in harmony with fact to urge that the perception of universals is as primary as the perception of particulars. The process of reflection is necessary to make the universal clear and distinct, but as the discriminating element in observation it aids us to recognize the individual ... A student will make little progress in geometry if his attention is solicited by the special features of his particular diagram rather than by the universal relations which the diagram imperfectly embodies ... without some perception of the abstract or universal traits which the new shares with the old, we cannot recognize or discover new truths (Cohen, 1931, pp. 124–125).

Underlying a lot of what Cohen *et al.* (2003) say is the notion of representation: words represent ideas, but not presumably things, theories represent facts, whatever those are, and our thought represents the world, whatever that is. But notice that if we are really stuck in such a game of representation, we cannot directly refer to the world, or things, such as ourselves, in it. In such a game 'thought represents the world' loses its intuitive sense, and would be more clearly expressed as 'thought represents the-world-as-thought'. We may then go on to legitimately question whether we have a pure notion of representation, or only understand 'representation-as-thought'. In the end, our sentence will become 'thought-as-thought-represents-as-thought-the-world-as-thought'. Not much is left. Similarly, we might reflect on whether 'concept' is a concept, not to mention whether 'sense data' is a concept on to which 'concepts' are supposed to be imposed. All this is summed up very clearly by Bonjour:

> While it is clear enough that concepts are at least roughly the philosophical descendants of the *ideas* invoked by earlier philosophers like Locke, and also that talk of concepts (or ideas or notions) often seems virtually unavoidable in philosophical discourse, none of that helps in any very immediate way to clarify exactly what such talk is about. Perhaps the clearest point of agreement is that the possession of the concept of an X by a person is to be identified with that person's having a certain cluster of intellectual abilities: the ability to think of X's, to classify things as X's, and, in some cases at least, to recognize X's in appropriate circumstances. But none of this makes it very clear how a concept can be itself an object of knowledge in a way that makes knowledge of concepts an alternative to knowledge of the world (1998, pp. 150–151).

B   A Diagnosis of the Problem

The difficulties we have seen above are characteristic of the opacity of Cohen *et al.* Looking again to Burrell and Morgan (1979), for example, they claim that one might view knowledge as 'hard, objective and tangible', which makes it sound, to us, rather like a table. We guess this means that truth must be understood to be absolute, and perhaps as 'correspondence to fact', in the fashion defended by Alston (1996). But how, we ask, does one's belief in this entail that one must adopt 'an observer role, together with an allegiance to the methods of natural science'? We fail to see how anyone could think so, without importing some serious metaphysical baggage. We fail, in particular, to see why one need even believe in 'the methods of natural science'. Further, it seems to us that one does not even have to believe either that there *is* such a thing as knowledge, or that 'knowledge' denotes one particular sort of thing, in order to be a scientist, social or otherwise. That is, in either a descriptive or a normative sense.

What one does have to believe, presumably, is that there is some sort of aim to one's activity. But even then it is unclear whether one need believe that it has a purpose *in itself*, above and beyond its purpose *for oneself*: 'the aim of chess is to give checkmate' is, on the face of it, a category mistake. And more importantly, individual scientists have differed considerably on their views about 'the aims of science', yet nevertheless made very worthy contributions. For Niels Bohr, 'There is no quantum world. There is only abstract quantum physical description. It is wrong to think that the task of physics is to find out how nature *is*. Physics concerns what we can *say* about nature' (Squires, 1994, pp. 117–118). Yet on his reasons for challenging the Copenhagen view of quantum mechanics, of which Bohr was a key architect, Bohm (1987, p. 33) says: 'What I felt to be especially unsatisfactory was the fact that the quantum theory had no place in it for an adequate notion of an independent actuality . . . the theory could not go beyond the phenomena or appearances'. It is even plausible that such differences in personal opinion are beneficial for science itself: they motivate the exploration of different avenues.

So to sum up, we have found so far that: (a) Cohen *et al.* accord special authority to scientists; (b) such authority is supposed to be due, in part if not in whole, to a particular set of (implicit or explicit) assumptions required for the practice of science; (c) the assumptions which Cohen *et al.* believe are required are not, in fact, required; and (d) this mistake seems to arise because Cohen *et al.* are motivated by unarticulated assumptions about how it is that we interact with the external—with respect to perception, in particular. We are now going to endeavour to show that (a) and (d) are closely associated with another view that we have already touched upon above, and also think is false, namely that there is a (natural) scientific method.

Now to return to the view of knowledge as 'hard, objective, and tangible', we think it is telling that Cohen *et al.* (2003, pp. 6–8) describe it as 'positivist', although they subsequently admit that they are not precisely sure what 'positivism' means, above and beyond the 'residual meaning . . . always present . . . from an acceptance of natural science as the paradigm of human knowledge'. For it would follow that one could only be a 'positivist', in their sense, provided that there were *really* something special about natural science which one could appeal to, in order to properly demarcate it from other forms of inquiry. The two obvious options are social structure, and method. We rule out the first, since in so far as it is contingent—inquirers in different disciplines could ape the current structure in natural science—it is hardly interesting. Therefore, if there is no method to natural science, or science in general, then there cannot be any grounds for 'positivism'. But there cannot be any grounds for 'anti-positivism', in the sense of Cohen *et al.* (2003), either. This is because no inquirer can seriously object to 'the ways of the natural scientist' (2003, p. 6), if there are no such (necessary) ways above and beyond those of *any* decent inquirer. All that one could be objecting to, it would seem, is a mere fiction.

Philosophers of science cannot be readily identified as members of warring camps, and their positions cannot be readily individuated on the basis of the categories that Cohen *et al.* employ. It therefore seems to follow, provided that such philosophers have sustainable positions on the nature of science (and/or inquiry), that scientists themselves need not be forced to adopt one of the curiously extreme positions which Cohen *et al.* indicate. It is worth bearing this in mind when we look at the work of Popper and Bartley, below.

III POPPER AND BARTLEY TO THE RESCUE: SCIENCE WITHOUT METHOD

As we have seen, one of the central assumptions underlying the approach of Cohen *et al.* (2003), which is representative of an unfortunate trend in educational research, is that there *is* a scientific method (or a natural scientific method). Yet given that they cite Popper (1959), it is somewhat of a surprise that they do not question this; that is, until one notices that they associate his work with the following claim of any given theory (Cohen *et al.*, 2003, p. 12): 'If repeated attempts to disconfirm its various hypotheses fail, then greater confidence can be placed in its validity'. This is wrong on two counts. First, Popper (1959, p. 267) writes: '[I]t is not so much the number of corroborating instances which determines the degree of corroboration as *the severity of the various tests* to which the hypothesis in question can be, and has been, subjected'. Second, Popper (1959, pp. 278–280) writes: 'Science is not a system of certain, or well-established, statements; nor is it a system which steadily advances towards a state of finality. Our science is not knowledge (epistēmē): it can never claim to have attained truth, or even a substitute for it, such as probability . . .'. And just in case this is not clear enough, Popper (1959, pp. 415–419) adds:

> As to degree of corroboration, it is nothing but a measure of the degree to which a hypothesis *h* has been tested, and of the degree to which it has stood up to tests. It must not be interpreted, therefore, as a degree of the rationality of our belief in the *truth* of *h* . . . Rather, it is a measure of the rationality of *accepting*, tentatively, a problematic guess, knowing that it

is a guess—but one that has undergone searching examinations ... '*accept*' but only in the sense that we select it as worthy to be subjected to further criticism, and to the severest tests we can design.

Taken in isolation, the recognition that Cohen *et al.* (2003) have misunderstood Popper is, of course, rather uninteresting. But it is precisely by coming to grips with his rejection of the notion of induction—including the so-called '*combined inductive-deductive* approach', which Cohen *et al.* (2003) posit—that one can come to free oneself from the obsession with appeals to authorities—to what might be referred to as 'comprehensive rationalism', as we shall shortly see—and thereby from the misguided notion that science has a special method. That is, above and beyond 'the one method of all *rational discussion*, and therefore of the natural sciences as well as of philosophy ... stating one's problem clearly and examining its various proposed solutions *critically*' (Popper, 1959, p. 16).

If this is unclear, let us explain the point as follows: as we have shown, Cohen *et al.* (2003) suggest there is a special route to knowledge, via access to the particular in our 'sense-data'. So they suggest, if you like, a 'solid foundation' for knowledge, upon which theories can be constructed: can be proven, or 'probabilified', variously. Their clearest statement of this view, which they take to be a prerequisite for any scientist, is the following:

> [C]ertain kinds of reliable knowledge can only originate in experience ... Empirical here means that which is verifiable by observation; and evidence, yielding proof or strong confirmation, in probability terms, of a theory or hypothesis in a research setting (Cohen *et al.*, 2003, p. 10).

Illustrative of this is their earlier contention that (Cohen *et al.*, 2003, pp. 4–5) 'deductive reasoning is based on the syllogism', and suggestion that 'deduction' has 'weaknesses'. Yet as Popper explains:

> We no longer look upon a deductive system as one that establishes the truth of its theorems by deducting them from 'axioms' whose truth is quite certain (or self-evident, or beyond doubt); rather, we consider a deductive system as *one that allows us to argue its various assumptions rationally and critically*, by systematically working out their consequences. Deduction is not used merely for the purposes of *proving* conclusions; rather, it is used as an instrument of rational criticism ... By looking upon inductive probability as a measure of the reasonableness of our beliefs or the reliability of our knowledge, the devotee of probable induction makes it clear that he still clings, like Bacon, to a weakened ideal of *epistēmē*. He conceives his evidential statements *e* as playing a part analogous to that of the self-evident axioms supposed to 'prove' our theorems. And he conceives his hypothesis *h* as playing a part analogous to that of theorems whose truth is made certain by deduction from the axioms; only, that induction being weaker than deduction, we now get merely an *Ersatz* certainty: probability comes in as the substitute, or surrogate, of certainty ... (Popper, 1983, pp. 221–222).

So as we shall show, the ultimate problem with the approach of Cohen *et al.*—their belief in some 'special method', due to a particular way in which we build upon a putative 'solid foundation'—is that belief in any ultimate authority would seem to be an act of faith. Similarly, such a 'special method' could not, on pain of vitiating circularity, be used to derive its own support: that there are 'sense data', that we have direct access to—or, say, 'knowledge by acquaintance' with—a class of physical entities, or whatever other poison it is that one prefers. In the words of Popper:

> Two attitudes or tendencies that are at times found together foster a belief in induction. One is the wish for a super-human authority—the authority of science, far above human whims, and exemplified in the 'exact' science of mathematics, and in the natural sciences, so far as they are based, firmly and squarely upon fact: verified, confirmed fact. The other is the wish to see in science not the work of an inspiration or revelation of the human spirit, but a more or less mechanical compilation which in principle might be performed by machines. (For what else are we but machines?) At bottom, the two tendencies may be one: the tendency to debunk man ... (Popper, 1983, p. 258).

Is it unfair for us to suggest that this is the case for Cohen *et al.* (2003), as our chosen proponents of 'the myth of scientific method' in educational research? We think not, since they ally themselves with the following sentiment of Barratt (1971): 'The decision for empiricism as an act of scientific faith signifies that the best way to acquire reliable knowledge is the way of evidence obtained by direct experience'. This ought really to be rather shocking. If empiricism—and hence, the employment of Cohen *et al.*' s alleged 'scientific method'—is based on *faith*, then we ought to be absolutely free to adopt a different kind of faith, and completely ignore the products, advocates, and practitioners, of science. For 'creation science', astrology, or the reading of tea leaves, would be on precisely the same final footing. Enter what Bartley dubs the *tu quoque* move:

> In sum, the belief that rationality is ultimately limited, by providing an excuse for irrational commitment, enables a Protestant, or any other irrationalist, to make an irrational commitment without losing intellectual integrity. But at the same time, anyone who makes use of this excuse may not, in integrity, *criticize* the holder of a different commitment. One gains the right to be irrational at the expense of losing the right to criticize. One gains immunity from criticism for one's own commitment by making any criticism of commitments impossible ... Moreover if everyone *has* to be a subjectivist, there is a sort of consolation: nobody can look in from the outside. Everyone is alone, inside his own mirror cage, staring at his own face (Bartley, 1962, pp. 103–104).

Here, Bartley has in mind the 'comprehensive rationalist', a title which Popper (1966, pp. 249–254) awarded to the individual who does not 'accept anything that cannot be defended by means of argument or experience', and thereby holds to a principle such that 'any assumption which cannot be supported either by argument or by experience is to be discarded'. But the problem with such a principle is that since it cannot by itself be defended by argument or experience, it would seem to rule itself out. In fact, it is for similar reasons that the foremost advocate of contemporary empiricism, namely Van Fraassen (2002, p. 41), has recently denied the claim that: 'For each philosophical position X there exists a statement X+ such that to have (or take) position X is to believe (or decide to believe) that X+'.[7] Straightforwardly, why take the *theory* (T) that our observations have a reliable character—or are some sort of 'route to knowledge'—any more seriously than a given theory (T') that some observations are being used to test? *Why?* Let us return to Bartley:

> The most common conception of rationalist identity, comprehensive rationalism, combines two requirements. (1) A rationalist accepts any position that can be justified or established by appeal to the rational criteria or authorities; and (2) he accepts *only* those positions that can be so justified ... In the stereotyped way in which it is usually told, the history of modern philosophy focuses attention on a number of basically subordinate questions that arise only if comprehensive rationalism is assumed to be possible. Among these, the most important has probably been: What is the nature of the rational authority or criterion to which a rationalist appeals to justify all his opinions? The various theories of knowledge are functions of the answers philosophers have given to this question. These answers fall into two main categories:

> (1) According to the intellectualists (or Rationalists—with a capital 'R'), the rational authority lies in the intellect (or Reason). A rationalist justifies his beliefs by appealing to intellectual intuition.

> (2) According to the empiricists, the rational authority lies in sense experience. An empiricist justifies his beliefs by appealing to sense observation.

> The history of these answers is one of failure (Bartley, 1962, pp. 109–110).

Now according to Bartley, what is required for a truly critical rationalism—a 'comprehensively critical rationalism' (1962), or 'pancritical rationalism' (1984)—is to avoid appeals to authority, and to banish dogmatism, while simultaneously making no concessions to irrationalism or fideism. His solution is to invoke the blindingly simple idea of assessment of the current state of the ongoing debate, and preference on the basis of that assessment. That is, in so far as there is to be 'faith' in anything, this would be 'faith' in ourselves: but that can hardly be any sort of 'faith', since we do not have any option on this level. The core idea is that we can 'step outside' of theories, with respect to any irrational attachment we may have to them. Bartley writes:

The test statements are intended to be hypothetical, and criticisable and revisable, just like everything else in the system; there is no justification, no proof, no fixed point anywhere. There is nothing 'basic' about basic statements. And hence no possibility of dogmatism with respect to them. If such basic statements happen to be incompatible with a theory, then the theory is false *relative to them*; and they are false *relative to the theory*. There is no question of theory proving reports wrong, or reports proving theory wrong. *Both* could be wrong: neither is 'basic' ... [O]ne steps outside the positionality of the theory to comment on the state of examination of the theory, treating the theory as an object, not as one's point of view, and oneself coming from beyond the theory ... (Bartley, 1984, pp. 215–216).

Our only objection to this is that Bartley does not go quite far enough. A theory can be *'false' relative to some basic propositions* (expressed by statements, or sentence types, no doubt), but this 'falsity' is in its own turn *relative to a particular system of logic*. (We say propositions, because there is the additional issue of falsity with respect to hermeneutic appraisal of sentence types within a language.[8] And indeed, matters become even more complicated when translation functions between languages are required—say when the basic statements are in one language, and the theory is in another.) Still further, even at this level—of recognising an inconsistency between a class of basic statements and a theory, given a system of logic—*we are still fallible*. For if there were to be any suggestion that we were not, then some sort of 'ground' to inquiry would be advocated here, after all. What we need, instead, is a frank admission that we can change the logic, change the basic statements we hypothesise as being acceptable, change the theory, change the language in which we work, change our interpretation of the basic statements or theory, or throw a whole system out as entirely unworkable. But we take this to be precisely the strength of a critical approach. It has no boundaries, yet no infinite regress is on the cards: its potential is unlimited. As Popper put it:

[N]on-demonstrability of any kind never worries the critical rationalist. For his critical arguments—just like the theories which he is criticising in terms of them—are conjectural ... It is only the demand for proof or justification that generates an infinite regress, and creates a need for an ultimate *term* of the discussion (Popper, 1983, pp. 28–29).

So what is so desirable about pancritical rationalist approach is that its practitioner's issuances cannot be readily dismissed as products of a particular form of faith, or 'irrational' commitment.[9] Its scope is such that its possessor might nevertheless come to reject rationalism—understood as the theory (or *explicit policy*) that one ought to adopt her approach—and perhaps also come, thereby, to adopt a different attitude. Further, she will still enjoy serious advantages:

If the rationalist were in fact *committed* to rationalism, he would be entitled to treat such people as they treat him: he could regard them as members of a different *ecclesia*, or ultimately committed religiously community, whom—since real argument was impossible—he could best hope to convert through nonrational persuasion. But since the rationalist ... need be committed neither to his rationalism nor to any other of his beliefs, he need not repudiate people with whom he fundamentally disagrees. In principle, he can act toward them in a remarkable way (Bartley, 1984, pp. 161–162).

The ethical desirability of such an approach is, we hope, clear. But it should also be noticed that there is plausibly an *epistemic* advantage for the rationalist. Bartley (1984, p. 163) sums this up elegantly: '[I]f we treat our opponents in a discussion *not as they treat us, but as we would have them treat us*, it is we who profit ... We may learn from the criticisms of our opponents even when their own practice prevents them from learning from us'.

In closing this section, it is worth adding that a rejection of the notion of scientific method is *descriptively* supported by an examination of actual practice in modern physics—that is, in one of the 'natural sciences' which is supposed to involve particular 'methodological ways' (Cohen *et al.*, 2003, p. 6). This, for Cushing, answers the question of whether scientific methodology is 'interestingly' atemporal as follows:

'[N]o', once the caveat implied by 'interestingly' has been clarified. By the term 'interesting' I refer here to constraints, on scientific practice and reasoning, that would go beyond normal, commonsense demands placed on everyday argument (such as the usual rules of deductive reasoning, say, or some acknowledgement of the importance of facts) ... there are no invariant (ahistorical, atemporal) characteristics of science that distinguish it from nonscience. [D]istinguishing characteristics of scientific practice and reasoning ... are not universal across all of science for all time unless we make vague, elastic claims that can be fit to almost anything (Cushing, 1990, §1).

IV   THE ALTERNATIVE VIEW OF INQUIRY: MODES OF CRITICISM

In attacking the widespread dogma that there is, or ought to be, a 'scientific method'—above and beyond the method of inquiry, we re-emphasise—it is tempting to be almost entirely destructive, in the manner of Feyerabend (1975). But the view we advocate is amenable to a constructive alternative to the standard view of 'method', as we shall now endeavour to illustrate, albeit in a brief and tentative manner. As our starting point, we again look to Bartley:

We have at least four means for eliminating error by criticizing our conjectures and speculations. These checks are listed in descending order according to their importance and to the rigor with which they may be applied:

(1) The check of *logic*: Is the theory in question consistent?

(2) The check of *sense observation*: Is the theory *empirically* refutable by some sense observation? And if it is, do we know of any refutation of it?

(3) The check of *scientific theory*: Is the theory, whether or not in conflict with sense observation, in conflict with any scientific hypotheses?

(4) The check of the *problem*: What problem is the theory intended to solve? Does it do so successfully? (Bartley, 1962, p. 158).

This is some sort of start. But first, we do not agree that any one of these tests is more 'important' than any other; for a theory is either true or false, and any means by which it can be excluded, if false, is surely as 'important' as any other. Second, we are not really sure about the third check, since it implies that 'scientific hypotheses' are more valuable than others held in the light of critical discussion. Why not make mention of metaphysical or mathematical theories, in this regard? Why not just lose the word 'scientific' altogether, since it has such unfortunate authoritarian baggage? It is due precisely to these concerns that Bartley (1984, p. 204) later states: 'Where such theories are brought into clash with scientific theories, and thus are criticizable in terms of these scientific theories, one must not assume too readily, however, that the observation-irrefutable but theory-refutable statement is wrong and the observation-refutable scientific hypothesis is right'. This is what one would expect from the architect of pancritical rationalism. Indeed we might also expect, and be glad to find from his personal correspondence, that he believed 'there is a "check of metaphysics", as well as a check on metaphysics'.[10] This being the case, we might well want to change (3) to a check on the *external consistency* of a given theory. Call this (3*).

This model of modes of criticism might be further improved by invoking the distinction between *immanent* and *transcendent* criticism. Indeed, checks (1) and (4) might be thought of precisely as *immanent* (when we have opted to hold the system of logic constant), whereas checks (2) and (3*) are *transcendent*. And we might ask, further, whether there could be other forms of immanent or transcendent criticism. Here are a few suggestions, and we draw on Kuhn's (1977, p. 321) notion of 'theoretical virtues' in order to make some of them:

(5) The check of simplicity. Does the theory constitute the simplest available way to solve the problem it is designed to solve?

(6) The check of fruitfulness. Has the theory proven fruitful, in conjunction with other theories, in suggesting new approaches, disclosing unexpected observations, or serving as an auxiliary to allow their testing by observation?

(7) The check of conceivability (or intuition). Does the theory have any consequences which do not, in the current status of the debate, seem conceivable (and/or intuitable)?

(8) The check of possibility. Is the theory possibly true, in a *non-epistemic* sense?

We now make a few remarks about these suggestions, although more—say about scope, or accuracy—could be made. With respect to (5), which can be understood immanently and transcendently, simplicity is, at the very least, a *pragmatic* virtue. But might simplicity not also be an epistemic, in so far as truth-conducive, virtue, even if only in *ceteris paribus* cases of comparison? The critical rationalist can remain neutral, but entertain the possibility. (There is nothing 'inductive' about such a suggestion).

As to (6), which is a transcendent check, it is sometimes the case that a particular theory seems to be responsible for great progress, and hence there is a sense in which it is natural to want to stick with it for longer, *ceteris paribus*. So this check is somewhat Lakatosian: it is effectively a check on whether the theory constitutes, or is a part of, a progressive research programme.[11] Is it merely pragmatic, though? The answer seems to lie in the affirmative, since it is clear that any false theory can nonetheless be useful in a limited class of applications. Yet it is equally clear that as long as its employment leads to great successes, it is not unreasonable to continue to employ it, *even if there are some serious suspicions about its falsity*. It should be added that there is no tension with respect to the truth-goal, here. For example, we might be interested in the truth of the theory (T') that 'Use of theory T is still driving technology ahead'. And we might want to invite those with counter-theories to start employing those, if we suspect T to be false on the basis of other checks, in order to see whether those can be equally as fruitful, or even more so.

(7) and (8) might be linked, somewhat, if there is a link between conceivability and possibility. Such a suggestion is not against the spirit of pancritical rationalism—since it does not involve the advocacy of radical intellectualism (*qua* the positing of 'firm foundations' for knowledge)—as Popper himself makes clear in writing:

> My opinion is that we can readily admit that we possess something which may be described as 'intellectual intuition'; or more precisely, that certain of our intellectual experiences may be thus described. Everybody who 'understands' an idea, or a point of view, or an arithmetical method, for instance, multiplication, in the sense that he has 'got the feel of it', might be said to understand that thing intuitively; and there are countless intellectual experiences of that kind. But I would insist, on the other hand, that these experiences, important as they may be for our scientific endeavours, can never serve to establish the truth of any idea or theory, however strongly somebody may feel intuitively, that it must be true, or it is 'self-evident' ... Such intuitions cannot even serve as an argument, although they may encourage us to look for arguments (Popper, 1966, p. 18).

Prima facie, the final comment might seem damning. But 'sense impressions' cannot serve as arguments either, *even if there are such things*, from the perspective of the pancritical rationalist. On the contrary, it might be suggested that arguments *emerge* out of intuition, sensory experience, or even a subtle interplay of the two. But if our focus is to be on arguments, then let them be assessed on their own merits, no matter what their source. In short, if there is to be a check (2), then why not a check (7)? Or more plausibly, a check (8) in so far as what can be intuited *serves to reveal or enable* arguments for what is possible? Analogously, it may be said that 'sense-impressions' could only *play a part* in allowing observation *statements* to be made; that is, only *play a part* in allowing a check (2). It might be added that (1) is plausibly only a special case of check (8), in so far as it is a check on strict and narrow logical possibility.

In closing this section, we ought to add that pancritical rationalists are free to discuss precisely what does, or should, count as successful criticism! Further, they are free to critically examine one another's values, the wisdom of being (or striving to be) a pancritical rationalist, and so on, and so forth. So this means that the approach we advocate may even be compatible with the reticulated view of scientific rationality, plus a 'top-up' of the requirement of a critical attitude, according to which:

> There is no single 'right' goal for inquiry because it is evidently legitimate to engage in inquiry for a wide variety of reasons and with a wide variety of purposes .... To say as much is not, however, to take the bite out of the demand for rationality ... But beyond demanding that our cognitive goals must reflect our best beliefs about what is and is not possible, that our methods must stand in an appropriate relation to our goals, and that our implicit and explicit values must be synchronized, there is little more that the theory of rationality can demand (Laudan, 1984, pp. 63–64).

This is not to deny that truth, say, is important.[12] It is just to say that it need not be correct to say that all inquiry must be aimed at the truth (in a correspondence sense), rather than other pragmatically valuable goals, such as the empirical adequacy explained by Van Fraassen (1980).

V   A FAREWELL TO DOGMATISM

The problem we have identified is neither simply a *product* of textbooks on educational research, nor is its impact limited to that domain. Its significance is far wider, as indicated by the restrictive views of 'proper scientific method' with respect to determining what counts as 'good evidence' on which to base policy.[13] The point is just that what works in one context need not do so in another, and that this goes for successful experimental practice as much it does for theory-construction and theory-choice. (Needless to say, what counts as 'working' can also change.) To be a good inquirer, it is not only necessary to be willing to carefully consider the truth of those propositions pertinent to the problem one is investigating. Rather, one must also consider how best to tackle the problem, and even whether it *is* a genuine problem. And just as a rake is not well suited to sweeping a path, a random field trial is unsuitable for discovering the (actual, rather than apparent) motion of the planets. It follows that methodological flexibility, rather than rigid adherence to externally imposed standards, is necessary to allow inquiry to flourish. To a certain extent, scientists can, and must, police themselves: to enforce obedience to 'the methods' is just to impede progress, by preventing the exploration of new avenues.

By adopting a radically new approach to educational research, we can liberate ourselves from the dungeon of dogmatism. On the conceptual level, we need to recognize that it is the difference between good and bad inquiry with which we should be concerned, with respect to the question of overarching method, and that inquiry is multi-faceted. On the practical level, we should be concerned with the genuine 'fitness for purpose' of different *local* methods, in specific contexts, irrespective of whether they have been associated with 'positivists', 'interpretivists', lions, witches, or wardrobes.[13] But by this, we do not mean that we should just 'pull the correct tool' from the 'scientific tool-box': we should be willing to design and craft our very own tools, when appropriate.

We end as we began, by leaving the final word to Popper:

> [I]t is all guesswork, *doxa* rather than *epistēmē* ... Science has no authority. It is not the magical product of the given, the data, the observations. It is not a gospel of truth. It is you and I who make science, as well as we can. It is you and I who are responsible for it (1983, p. 259).

NOTES

1. Different terminology is used to refer to this distinction. For example, Merton (1998) refers to positivism/postpositivism and interpretative/constructivist paradigms, whilst Pring (2000) makes reference to the scientific and constructivist paradigms. We acknowledge that a third paradigm, the 'emancipatory' or 'critical' paradigm, is often referred to.
2. For example, Lather (2004) draws on 'Foucauldian', feminist and postcolonial readings in providing a 'critical'—in the sense of the critical paradigm—approach to US legislation. Similarly, Davis and Sumara (2005) make reference to the work of Rorty, Irigary and Derrida.
3. For a discussion of students' conceptions of educational research, see Aiston and Meyer, 2006.
4. Another suitable textbook would be Ary *et al.* (1990), although the problem is not limited just to textbooks on *educational* research: it is a problem within social sciences generally. See for example, Burns, 2001; Bryman, 2001.
5. Since we will be focusing on his philosophy, it is worth noting the view of Popper (1983, p. 262, fn. 2), who is presumably supposed to fit, but fails to fit, one of the 'objectivist' or 'subjectivist' moulds: '[N]ominalism ... asserts that meaningful words *are* nothing but names of things (or of memory images of things) and ... thereby gives an essentialist answer to an (implied) essentialist question—and a wrong answer to boot'.
6. See also Lowe (1995), where the distinction between semantic and metaphysical understandings of 'abstract' is covered in greater detail, and a metaphysical view of abstracta, according to which they are entities without spatiotemporal properties, is defended.
7. For a more refined discussion, see Teller, 2004; Van Fraassen, 2004; and Rowbottom, 2005.
8. On this, see Rowbottom, 2006, §2.
9. Notice, however, an important distinction between being convinced, and being committed:

We can assume or be *convinced* of the truth of something without being *committed* to its truth ... [A] pancritical rationalist, like other people, holds countless unexamined presuppositions and assumptions, many of which may be false. His rationality consists in his willingness to submit these to critical consideration when he discovers them or when they are pointed out to him (Bartley, 1984, p. 121).

10. We refer to an unpublished letter addressed to Rafe Champion, dated May 3 1986, from which we quote with the permission of the Estate of William Warren Bartley.
11. See Lakatos, 1970.
12. But for a critique of Laudan's 'reticulated view', and an argument in favour of a 'hierarchical view', see Worrall, 1988.
13. See Phillips, 2005, for instance, on how the US Congress restricted 'research funds in education to *scientifically rigorous research, as defined narrowly by the use of randomized experimental or field trial designs* (the so-called RFT, the "gold standard" methodology) ...'.
14. We recognise that there are those who already adopt such a local approach, but think that this is typically on the basis of a failure to consider the conceptual level. We actually *motivate* their position.

REFERENCES

Aiston, S. J. and Meyer, J. H. F. (2006) Improving Research as Learning Outcomes: responses to variations in students' conceptions of educational research, in: C. Rust (ed.) *Improving Student Learning Through Assessment* (Oxford, Oxford Center for Staff and Learning Development).
Alston, W. P. (1996) *A Realist Conception of Truth* (Ithaca, NY, Cornell University Press).
Ary, D., Jacobs, L. C. and Razavieh, A. (1990) *Introduction to Research in Education* (London, Holt, Rinehard, and Winston).
Barratt, P. E. H. (1971) *Bases of Psychological Methods* (Queensland, John Wiley and Sons).
Bartley, W. W. (1962) *The Retreat to Commitment*, 1st edn (New York, Alfred A. Knopf).
Bartley, W. W. (1984) *The Retreat to Commitment*, 2nd edn (La Salle, IL, Open Court).
Bohm, D. (1987) Hidden Variables and the Implicate Order, in: Hiley and Peat (eds) (1987).
Bonjour, L. (1998) *In Defense of Pure Reason* (Cambridge, Cambridge University Press).
Brampton, K. C. (1964) Nominalism and the Law of Parsimony, *The Modern Schoolman*, 41, pp. 273–281.
Bryman, A. (2001) *Social Research Methods* (Oxford, Oxford University Press).
Burns, R. B. (2001) *Introduction to Research Methods* (London, Sage).
Burrell, G. and Morgan, G. (1979) *Sociological Paradigms and Organisational Analysis* (London, Heinemann Educational Books).
Carr, W. and Kemmis, S. (1986) *Becoming Critical: Education, knowledge and action research* (London, Falmer Press).
Cohen, L., Manion, L. and Morrison, K. (2003) *Research Methods in Education* (London, Routledge Falmer).
Cushing, J. T. (1990) Is Scientific Methodology Interestingly Atemporal?, *British Journal of the Philosophy of Science*, 41, pp. 177–194.
Davis, B. and Sumara, D. J. (2005) Challenging Images of Knowing: Complexity science and educational research, *International Journal of Qualitative Studies in Education*, 18, pp. 305–321.
Einstein, A. (1934) *Mein Weltbild* (Frankfurt am Main, Ullstein).
Feyerabend, P. K. ([1975] 1993) *Against Method* (London, Verso).
Hiley, B. J. and Peat, F. D. (eds) (1987) *Quantum Implications: Essays in honour of David Bohm* (London, Routledge).
Hume, D. ([1748] 1999) *An Enquiry Concerning Human Understanding*, T. L. Beauchamp, ed. (Oxford, Oxford University Press).
Kuhn, T. (1977) *The Essential Tension: Selected studies in scientific tradition and change* (Chicago, IL, University of Chicago Press).
Lakatos, I. (1970) Methodology of Scientific Research Programmes, in: Lakatos and Musgrave (eds), pp. 91–196.

Lakatos, I. and Musgrave, A. (eds) (1970) *Criticism and the Growth of Knowledge* (Cambridge, Cambridge University Press).

Laudan, L. (1984) *Science and Values: The aims of science and their role in scientific debate* (Berkeley, CA, University of California Press).

Lather, P. (2004) Scientific Research in Education: A critical perspective, *British Educational Research Journal*, 30, pp. 759–772.

Loux, M. J. (1998) *Metaphysics: A contemporary introduction* (London, Routledge).

Lowe, E. J. (1995) The Metaphysics of Abstract Objects, *The Journal of Philosophy*, 92.10, pp. 509–524.

Lowe, E. J. (2002) *A Survey of Metaphysics* (Oxford, Oxford University Press).

Merton, D. (1998) *Research Methods in Education and Psychology* (London, Sage).

O'Hear, A. (1980) *Karl Popper* (London, Routledge and Kegan Paul).

Phillips, D. C. (2005) A Guide for the Perplexed: Scientific educational research, methodology and the gold versus platinum standards, presented at EARLI: Integrating Multiple Perspectives on Effective Learning Environments, University of Cyprus, 23–27th August 2005.

Popper, K. R. (1959) *The Logic of Scientific Discovery* (London, Routledge).

Popper, K. R. (1966) *The Open Society and Its Enemies, Volume II: Hegel and Marx*, 5th edn (London, Routledge).

Popper, K. R. (1983) *Realism and the Aim of Science* (London, Routledge).

Pring, R. (2000) *Philosophy of Educational Research* (London, Continuum).

Rowbottom, D. P. (2005) The Empirical Stance vs. The Critical Attitude, *South African Journal of Philosophy*, 24.3, pp. 200–223.

Rowbottom, D. P. (2006) On the Significance of 'World 3' for the Depersonalisation of Inquiry and the Democratisation of Education, *Learning for Democracy*, 2.2, (Forthcoming).

Squires, E. (1994) *The Mystery of the Quantum World* (Bristol, Institute of Physics).

Teller, P. (2004) What is a Stance?, *Philosophical Studies*, 121, pp. 159–170.

Van Fraassen, B. C. (1980) *The Scientific Image* (Oxford, Oxford University Press).

Van Fraassen, B. C. (2002) *The Empirical Stance* (New Haven, CT, Yale University Press).

Van Fraassen, B. C. (2004) Replies to Discussion on *The Empirical Stance*, *Philosophical Studies*, 121, pp. 171–192.

Wellington, J. (2000) *Educational Research: Contemporary issues and practical approaches* (London, Continuum).

Worrall, J. (1988) The Value of a Fixed Methodology, *British Journal of the Philosophy of Science*, 39, pp. 263–275.

Zahar, E. (1989) *Einstein's Revolution: A Study in Heuristic* (La Salle, IL, Open Court).

3
As if by Machinery: The Levelling of Educational Research

RICHARD SMITH

I

In his Preface to the *Novum Organum*, Francis Bacon writes that in what follows he will be setting out a new method for establishing 'progressive stages of certainty': essentially a method for reaching scientific knowledge. He aims to sweep away the authority of Aristotle, whose texts were scrutinised in the Middle Ages for answers that could and should be read in the book of nature. For Bacon the evidence of the senses is important, but, crucially, 'the mental operation which follows the act of sense' needs to be fundamentally reconceived. There is only one way for things to be put on a sound footing,

> Namely, that the entire work of the understanding be commenced afresh, and the mind itself be from the very outset not left to take its own course, but guided at every step, and the business be done as if by machinery.[1]

Bacon draws a comparison: we would make no progress in construction and engineering if we worked with our bare hands, 'without help or force of instruments'. Imagine, he writes, working on the quarrying and erection of a 'vast obelisk' without any mechanical devices to help us. Suppose we simply sent for more workers, or presently made a selection of the stronger and sent home the rest; or that we asked our workers to present themselves 'with hands, arms, and sinews well anointed and medicated according to the rules of art'. We would be thought foolish if we went about matters like this. But this is how people typically proceed in their intellectual endeavours, joining 'mad effort and useless combination of forces'.

> When they hope great things either from the number and co-operation or from the excellency and acuteness of individual wits; yea, and when they endeavour by Logic (which may be considered as a kind of athletic art) to strengthen the sinews of the understanding; that they are but applying

the naked intellect all the time; whereas in every great work to be done by the hand of man it is manifestly impossible, without instruments and machinery, either for the strength of each to be exerted or the strength of all to be united.

Later in the *Novum Organum* Bacon spells out the thoroughly egalitarian implications of his ideas. The course he proposes for the 'discovery of sciences' does not require any great intellectual qualities of the researcher. Indeed, if the researcher has such qualities they must be restrained: 'The understanding must not therefore be supplied with wings, but rather hung with weights, to keep it from leaping and flying' (I. CIV). That Bacon's approach requires no talent is, he thinks, precisely one of its merits. It 'leaves but little to the acuteness and strength of wits, but places all wits and understandings nearly on a level' (I. LXI[2]). Geometry supplies an analogy: it takes skill to draw a circle or straight line freehand, and not everyone has such skill. Virtually anyone, however, can execute the task with the aid of rule or compass (ibid.). The essential thing, therefore, is to possess a method: not the mere groping in the dark that is naïve empiricism, but the 'true method of experience' that 'first lights the candle, and then by means of the candle shows the way' (I. LXXXII). 'A method rightly ordered leads by an unbroken route through the woods of experience to the open ground of axioms' (ibid.). Towards the end of the first book of the *Novum Organum* (I. CXXII) Bacon re-emphasises that almost anyone can use the new method he advocates:

> For my way of discovering sciences goes far to level men's wits, and leaves but little to individual excellence;[3] because it performs everything by the surest rules and demonstrations.

This claim has not been well received by editors and historians of ideas. Robertson (1905) notes that the similar passage from *Novum Organum* I. LXI (quoted above) 'is one of the passages of Bacon on which Macaulay is justly severe', and he quotes one Professor Fowler to the effect that 'Bacon's promise never has been and never can be fulfilled' (p. 270). It is usual to note that Bacon's method of eliminative induction simply cannot do the job required of it. Gjertsen (1992) for instance points out that it presupposes that the list of hypotheses or evidence that we are presented with is complete; it would for example lend support to the conclusion that, on the basis of the forms of heat and energy then known, the earth could not possibly have sustained life forms for more than ten or fifteen millions years. The verdict of time is that Bacon's legacy is not any kind of method but rather a climate of opinion in which empirical science is held to trump all other kinds of knowledge—not an entirely fair verdict in the light of Bacon's own strictures on unreflective empiricism (cf. I. LXIV) and his well-known warnings about the four kinds of Idols that I allude to briefly at the end of the chapter. Appleyard (1992, p. 51) sums up the widespread verdict: 'he remains a hero of the scientist who aspired primarily to virtues of forthrightness, realism and practicality. The Baconian gets on with the job'.

It was specifically in inspiring the quest for method that Bacon was so influential. Descartes's famous *Discourse*, for example, published seventeen years after the appearance of *Novum Organum*, has as its full title *Discourse on the Method of Rightly Conducting the Reason and Seeking for Truth in the Sciences*. Descartes had written *Regulae* or *Rules for the Direction of the Mind* around ten years earlier (though it was not published until 1701): here he states flatly in Rule 4 that 'We need a method if we are to investigate the truth of things'. The search for reliable scientific method continues with (among other cases) David Hume's eight rules 'by which to judge of cause and effects' (*A Treatise of Human Nature*, Book I, part 3, section 15) and John Stuart Mill's four 'experimental methods' (*System of Logic*, Book 3, ch. 8). Hume is worth quoting here at some length since he is so perceptive of the limitations of setting out the rules of any such method. After enumerating his eight rules he writes:

> Here is all the LOGIC I think proper to employ in my reasoning; and perhaps even this was not very necessary, but might have been supply'd by the natural principles of our understanding. Our scholastic head-pieces and logicians shew no such superiority above the mere vulgar in their reason and ability, as to give us any inclination to imitate them in delivering a long system of rules and precepts to direct our judgement, in philosophy. All the rules of this nature are very easy in their invention, but extremely difficult in their application; and even experimental philosophy, which seems the most natural and simple of any, requires the utmost stretch of human judgement (ibid.).

This puts the matter very aptly. Whatever rules of method are stipulated, their application will still require judgement. There cannot be further rules for their application; or if there are, there cannot be an endless series of such rules. Sooner or later, and probably sooner rather than later, judgement must be applied. And judgement is not a faculty that can be readily 'levelled', in Bacon's terms. The qualities that make up judgement—flexibility, attentiveness, suitable experience and so on—are found more in some people than in others. They are found for instance in those who have a rich acquaintance with the subject-matter in hand, and in those prepared to attune themselves to the subject-matter rather than to treat it as one more field for the operation of pre-established skills and techniques.

The thoroughly egalitarian implications of the Baconian search for method and for what Gaukroger (2001, p. 3) calls a 'nonelitist' form of science were well understood in the eighteenth and early nineteenth centuries. Denis Diderot for instance paid homage to Bacon in his 'Introduction' to the *Encyclopédie*, and de Maistre was inclined to hold him responsible for the French Revolution. These implications are perhaps less obvious today; but the notion that there exist research methods that can be acquired relatively straightforwardly by almost any aspiring researcher, irrespective of his or her general intellectual sophistication, quality of judgement and understanding of the subject being researched, is nevertheless prevalent, and can perhaps be seen essentially as a continuation of the Baconian tradition. Any number of textbooks offer their readers knowledge of research techniques: chapters on ethnomethodology, participant observation, interviewing, discourse analysis, grounded theory, and a plethora of 'isms'. Courses on research methods leave students under the impression that they can write a dissertation on 'whether the National Curriculum is improving children's reading skills'; they are upset when it is suggested that hard thinking needs to be done about just what counts as reading, and whether or not it consists of skills. 'If it doesn't', said one, 'then it's difficult to see how the question could be researched': a revealing insight into the way in which the nature of research is here being conceived.

The problem here is not confined to educational research but is found in the social sciences more widely. Andrew Sayer (1994, p. 2) for example writes: 'It is quite extraordinary to compare the attention given in social science courses to "methods" in the narrow sense of statistical techniques, interviewing and survey methods and the like, with the blithe disregard of questions of how we conceptualise, theorise and abstract. ("Never mind the concepts, look at the techniques" might be the slogan)'.

John Law (2004) complains that 'method in social science . . . is enacted in a set of nineteenth- or even seventeenth-century Euro-American blinkers' (p. 143), the problem being in his view the 'hegemonic and dominatory pretensions of certain versions or *accounts* of method' (p. 4) and the normativities that the textbooks on research methods legislate (ibid.). Method becomes automatic 'mechanical replacement' (p. 11).

The point here is of course not that ethnomethodology, participant observation and the rest are without value: of course they have their uses, and many classic pieces of educational research have employed them to good effect. The problem is precisely one of 'replacement', as Law puts it above: where they stand in for the cultivation of judgement and insight, and for acquaintance with the broader background of ideas and theory; where emphasis on the acquisition of such techniques even distracts from such cultivation and acquaintance and diminishes the time available for them. Richard Pring makes a similar point when he complains that 'much educational research espouses controversial philosophical positions without any recognition of the philosophical problems which they raise and which often have been well rehearsed by philosophers from Plato onwards' (Pring, 2000, pp. 5–6). Pring gives examples such as facile talk of knowledge as a social construct or truth as a personal one.

Here are two examples from my own recent experience. The first is the often-made claim that all knowledge—or all *true* knowledge, perhaps—arises in the context of problems to be solved. The implications of this argument, if it could be sustained, would be considerable: it could be used to support curriculum reform in the direction of discovery learning or something very like it. It would be a valuable weapon in the battle that its proponents like to think of themselves as waging against didacticism or the assumption that teaching consists of pouring facts into receptive heads. Now to those who have taken issue with this particular line of thought it seems promiscuous to call *all* learning a matter of solving problems. There are cases where it is such a matter, as when your car refuses to start and in consequence you learn the function of the spark plugs and the use of certain kinds of aerosol spray. There are other cases, however. which are very different. If you move into the house next door to me and I tell you that the window-cleaner comes on alternate Tuesdays you have clearly learned something you did not know before. But the solving of a problem hardly arises, since the possibility of window-cleaners might not have crossed your mind: you certainly were not wondering when the window-cleaners call. Those committed to the idea that all true learning is problem solving however, tend to be ready to insist that the new information only makes sense and thus constitutes learning if the new home-owner is eager to keep their new property clean and attractive and thus is faced with the problem of how to do so. Now this seems to be an excellent example of what Antony Flew (1971, p. 267) has called the 'since it is trivially true it must be importantly true manoeuvre', familiar to any philosopher who has had to deal with the claim that there is no such thing as truly unselfish action since whatever we do we must in some sense have wanted to do it. So too there is a trivial sense in which perhaps all learning can be called problem solving, which is not the same and more substantial sense as when you peer beneath the bonnet of your unresponsive car and wish you had learned more about the workings of the internal combustion engine.

The second example is of a proposal to study the 'cognitive facility'[4] of university entrants, comparing first-year students at a new and at a relatively traditional university. Here 'cognitive facility' was conceived as the extent to which students understood what was expected of them in the new learning environment, possessed the ability to make sense of course requirements, to seek clarification where necessary and so on. The proposal was unimpeachable in the ways in which it sought to measure and compare such 'facility' (for example between students attending different kinds of universities, and between students from different kinds of schools). But it seemed extraordinary, in the broader context in which in many western nations we no longer seem clear about the purposes of universities, to locate the problem in young people as the extent to which they do or do not possess particular skills. What is at stake here should be reasonably clear to anyone who has wondered if stress-management courses for employees rightly locate the problem to which they are meant to be an answer. Alarm-bells should ring in the head of anyone who has made any acquaintance with Plato's strictures against such sophists as Gorgias for peddling mere *empeiriai*, context-free techniques or 'knacks'.[5]

It is difficult to write in this way without seeming to commit a particular offence, consideration of which will take us into the second half of this chapter. My argument may appear to imply that it is not good enough to be a humble, jobbing researcher: the honest seeker after educational truth has it seems to be something of a philosopher, to be on nodding terms with key points in the intellectual history of the west, and to be familiar with dead, white, male thinkers such as Plato and Kant. Thus it may seem to smell unacceptably of elitism, or to require educational researchers to submit to the condescension of their educational betters. To this perhaps the only suitable reply is to observe that the Baconian legacy of seeking to 'level men's wits' certainly tends to abolish intellectual hierarchies and differences, except of course those that separate people who have acquired methods and techniques from those who have not. But the legacy has not yet been shown to be a sound one.

II

We have not yet however delineated the full extent of the problem here. For in the field of education there are those whose democratic ambitions, so to speak, extend still further. They would have every teacher be a researcher: a researcher of her own classroom and her own practice in it. Now to the extent that research involves command of methods and techniques, it is perhaps implausible that any and every teacher, busy with the demands of the classroom and every latest government directive, can find time to acquire such methods: ethnomethodology, participant observation, interviewing, discourse analysis and the rest. But of course this is not what is intended. The process by which and the sense in which the universal teacher comes to be identified as a researcher is a subtle one and worth investigating in detail.

In their 1987 book *Reflective Teaching in the Primary School* Andrew Pollard and Sarah Tann begin: 'The main aim of this book is to support student teachers and teachers who wish to reflect upon their teaching in a systematic fashion' (p. xi). By pp. 4 ff the form of reflection is commonly identified as *enquiry*, an identification made explicit in places, such as p. 26, which contains the heading 'Issues to be considered when planning classroom enquiry'. There is a revealing passage on p. 10, where the authors turn to Donald Schon for support for their particular notion of reflection (or enquiry). The classroom, they say, does not lend itself to rigorous analysis (that is, research as traditionally conceived on the scientific model) but can draw on 'a type of knowledge-in-action, that is, knowledge that is inherent in professional action ... Schon also argues that it is possible to recognise reflection-in-action, in which adjustments to action are made in the light of experience'. Here they quote from Schon:

> When someone reflects-in-action, he becomes a *researcher* in the practice context (ibid., my emphasis).

The reflective teacher has become a researcher in the space of a dozen pages.

In a sense to make this move is to make the positive claim that there is a kind of research rather different from that of the professional researcher: 'action-research', which Pollard and Tann describe as encouraging teachers 'to assume the role of researcher in their own classrooms as part of their professional, reflective stance' (p. 25). I do not mean to dismiss action-research: it has expanded the horizons and enhanced the understanding of generations of teachers and others (see John Elliott's chapter). Of course there is a literature critical of it, for instance on the grounds that it is often guilty of a narrow instrumentalism. But this is not the kind of line I wish to take, not least because (again) the full extent of the problem here has not yet emerged. A short detour is required.

One of the most fundamental differences between research in the physical or 'hard' sciences and research in the social sciences is that the latter is reflective, as it is often put. That is to say, because the social sciences deal with humankind the researcher's object of study necessarily includes himself or herself. The chemist researching the properties of a compound is not required to empathise with it, to consider how easily such compounds get stereotyped, or to reflect 'There but for the grace of God go I'. The researcher investigating the effect of social class on educational achievement, on the other hand, is finding out something about herself— as one who comes from a particular social class and has attained a certain level of educational achievement—as well as about other people. To make such a discovery is in itself to change as a person, since to acquire self-knowledge, to whatever extent, is to be altered from the relatively unaware previous self. The effect of such change is to transform the relationship between the researcher and the researched, in an iterative and in principle endless process.

This feature of social science is of course well known and familiar in the literature. Hume noted that 'we ourselves are not only the beings, that reason, but also one of the objects, concerning which we reason' (*A Treatise of Human Nature*, 1969, Introduction, p. 43). Roger Smith (1997) writes in similar vein:

> The core problem is simple enough: how, objectively, can we observe ourselves? By the process of observation, do we not make ourselves into something different? This is the problem of the human capacity for reflection; it is the nature of being human to reflect and through reflection to alter human experience and action. The subject does not stay still (p. 15).

This kind of thinking has been valuable in moving social science away from the paradigm of the physical sciences. It has brought a liberation, in particular from the fantasy that there are appropriate 'research methods' conceived as wholly objective techniques for operating on human beings as if they were one more kind of inert subject matter. There is however a cost to be paid for these advantages. In much educational research literature, particularly that influenced by the 'reflective teacher' and action-research paradigms, the proper insistence that the researcher's object of study necessarily *includes* himself or herself seems to have become the expectation that the researcher (the teacher-as-researcher, or reflective teacher-as-enquirer) should *focus* or himself or herself.

A particularly egregious example of this is Jean McNiff's (1993) *Teaching as Learning: An Action Research Approach.* Central to her conception of research is 'an understanding of the self by the self' (p. 19). She explicitly rejects what she thinks of as the dominant view of educational research: this is research undertaken by researchers who are situated outside the classroom and who then impose their so-called knowledge on teachers. These and other 'experts', a group that seems to contain most academics, are of no more than 'entertainment value' (p. 14). All such external and objectified knowledge is to be swept away in favour of 'self-reflective research', which not only provides a proper base for learning, but *is* learning' (p. 20). It is not surprising, in view of this conception of research, that she declares that her book 'is part of the developing story of my life' (p. 1) and includes her own poetry as if its apparently indubitable authenticity guaranteed its epistemological status. (See Newby, 1994, for an acute review of the book.)

It is tempting to dismiss McNiff's writing as an extreme case, perhaps the high-water mark of action-research in its most in-bred form. Recent interest in postmodernism, however, has given this 'inward turn', this focusing on the self, a new and distinctive twist. Brown and Jones write in *Action Research and Postmodernism* (2001, p. 5):

> The book explores the notion of the 'teacher as researcher' seen as the framing of relevant aspects of practice in reflective writing which enables a move from mere description to an understanding of the intricacies of such descriptions. The book also addresses the ways in which social norms and structures work at coercing these descriptions. Such an approach, however, has the potential to lead not to the unlocking of complexity but to the elucidation of rigid preconceptions which serve only to confirm injustices of the 'found' world. Hitherto, action research has assumed a reality which can be uncovered and then altered in some way or improved upon for emancipatory purposes. This however begs key questions about where our ideas of what counts as 'improvement' come from. How can the researcher both 'observe' reality as well as being part of it and thus be implicated in its continual creation and recreation? These issues are much more complex than action research has acknowledged so far. We need to move beyond the notion of the 'reflective practitioner' to encompass poststructuralism which attends more to the way in which we construct reality.

It is not easy to see quite what this manifesto amounts to. The suggestion seems to be that the action researcher, instead of imagining she is reflecting on some kind of given reality, instead reflects on the multi-layered textuality that is often mistaken for reality (perhaps because there is nothing outside of text, as Derrida is taken to have demonstrated or at least *written*) and creates further layers herself. Some confirmation that this is what is intended seems to be offered on p. 8:

> Our premise is that the practitioner researching in their classroom brings about perceived changes both through acting in the classroom itself and in

producing writing commenting on this classroom practice. That is to say, written descriptions of classroom practice, undertaken by the practitioner, effectively change the reality attended to by that practitioner.

Accordingly much of the text of the book consists of the authors' reflections not simply on their lives and educational practice, but on the written form those reflections take ('As the closures went ahead I chose to apply for teacher of Home Economics ... I wish to examine ways in which personal identity may be constructed. From my reading of Lacan ... (p. 81)). Far from simply reflecting on self, these action researchers reflect on reflections on the self. Stronach and MacLure, in *Educational Research Undone: The Postmodern Embrace*, take matters a stage still further, examining the ways in which teachers become these action researchers who reflect thus. They write of the stories that action researchers tell about themselves:

> These stories both appeal to the notion of a core self, whose inclinations towards action research were inscribed in the past, and produce that core self in the telling. The core or essential self is both cause and effect of the narrative. People become action researchers by having always been, in some protean sense, action researchers (p. 126).

Having seen off the unpleasant dualities that might be lurking here (past/ present, self/story), Stronach and MacLure are attracted to the idea that the action researcher might best be thought of at the hyphen, 'between those boundaries that are inevitably implicated in narratives of becoming an action researcher' (p. 129).

Brown and Jones cheerfully acknowledge the introspective quality of their own text: 'Philosophy and self-narrative are not the same thing ... it is, however, this sort of intention that is held in the narrative product of practitioner-oriented research' (p. 183). And what, we might ask them, is the ultimate purpose of this 'research'?

> We have sought to reconceptualise the task of the practitioner-researcher. ... We have nudged away from Habermasian-style victory narratives in which research is targeted at creating a better world ... (p. 68).

But why indulge in such prolonged introspection, if emancipation is a chimaera and the creation of a better world nothing but modernist illusion?

III

I have in this chapter given an account of how theory and its abstractions—which meant, for Francis Bacon, the works of the ancient writers and of Aristotle in particular—have tended to be rejected in favour of the democracy of skills and techniques. And I have argued that two tendencies then come into play: the discovery that any techniques worth having are by no means simple to acquire and deploy, and the dawning realisation that, as a species of social science, educational research can scarcely omit some degree of self-reflection on the part of the researcher herself. Scepticism about science, or about scientism, and so about distinct research techniques or methods, works to feed this interest in the self. Finally, with the assistance of a few ideas from the more modish parts of what is taken to be postmodernism, the self (or, of course, multiple selves) and the textuality of self or selves naturally come to take centre stage.

The chapter has been in part an exercise in genealogy of the Nietzschean or Foucauldian kind, in that when we understand how our current ways of thinking about research have specific historical origins and trajectories over time it is easier to see them as contingent and temporary, rather than as universal and inevitable, and to imagine alternatives to them. One way to make progress in imagining alternatives is to ask: what does this tendency for educational research to divide into two camps or strands, the mechanical and the solipsistic, work to marginalise or exclude? What ways of thinking, acting and writing does it make less possible to engage in or be open to?

Both strands, I suggest, are inimical to the creative imagination that has the courage to take wings and fly beyond what is already known (contrast Bacon, *Novum Organum* I. CIV, quoted above), that is prepared to speculate, to theorise, even to entertain utopian visions. (Bacon himself, as the author of the utopian *New Atlantis*, was such a visionary even while he was prescribing a more pedestrian route for everyone else.) The mechanical strand cannot admit what it sees as flights of fancy, ungrounded in objective procedures. Here is the familiar polarisation of the scientific—or the would-be scientific—and the romantic. The solipsistic strand, despite its apparently romantic focus on self, is too little interested in others' viewpoints and perspectives, and not always very interested in quite what they are viewpoints and perspectives *on*. The egalitarian leanings of both strands, forays into postmodernism notwithstanding, make them suspicious of ideas that do not come from their own tribes and trades.

A second exclusion is the idea of judgement and of subjectivity. The Baconian reaction against Aristotle had the unfortunate consequence that in its exaltation of what we now call scientific reason on the one hand and technical or instrumental reason on the other it consigned to obscurity for several centuries Aristotle's subtle account in the *Nicomachean Ethics* of what he calls *phronesis*, practical reason or practical judgement: an obscurity from which *phronesis*, and its significance for education especially, have only recently begun to emerge.[6] *Phronesis*, to simplify a complex picture, is characterised by sensitivity to situated particulars and concrete cases, and by flexibility; it is a property of people of a certain character, who have relevant experience and know how to use it wisely. There are no algorithms or rules for its operation. To the question 'what is the right way of looking at this situation?' the only answer often seems to be 'the way that the *phronimos*, the person of good practical judgement, looks at it'. This can be put somewhat paradoxically by noting that objectivity requires a proper subjectivity. To apprehend the world aright involves being appropriately open and receptive. *Phronesis* thus looks to the mechanistically-minded too close to an objectionable subjectivity, while the solipsist is too immersed in her own reflections to be interested in a *theory* of subjectivity and judgement, particularly a complex one formulated by a philosopher entirely innocent of the world of the modern classroom.

In summarising what he calls 'the general criticism' or verdict on Bacon, Hans-Georg Gadamer (1975, pp. 312–313) writes that 'his methodological suggestions are disappointing. They are too vague and have produced little ... His real achievement is, rather, that that he undertakes a comprehensive examination of the prejudices that hold the human mind captive and lead it away from the true knowledge of things, thus carrying out a methodical self-purification of the mind that is more a discipline than a method'.

Bacon identifies four kinds of prejudices, or fixations, which he calls 'idols'. The 'Idols of the Tribe' are the common tendencies of humankind in general, such as the tendency to exaggerate or distort. The 'Idols of the Cave' are the idiosyncrasies of individuals, arising for instance from temperament, education, habit and environment. 'Men become attached to certain particular sciences and speculations ... because they have bestowed the greatest pains upon them and become most habituated to them' (*Novum Organum* I. LIV: the physicist sees physics everywhere, we might say). The 'Idols of the Theatre' are due to false learning. Systems and philosophies harden into dogmas, for instance where the scientist over-generalises on the basis of only a few experiments. Bacon gives as an example William Gilbert, whose experiments with the lodestone led him to believe that magnetism was a universally present, though hidden, force (I. LIV). What Bacon calls 'the Empirical school of philosophy' gives birth to dogmas particularly 'deformed and monstrous' (I. LXIV). He writes (ibid.):

> With regard to philosophies of this kind there is one caution not to be omitted; for I foresee that if ever men are roused by my admonitions to betake themselves seriously to experiment and bid farewell to sophistical doctrines, then indeed through the premature hurry of the understanding to leap or fly to universals and principles of things, great danger may be apprehended from philosophies of this kind, against which evil we ought even now to prepare.

In other words Bacon's own ambition to formulate precise rules for the 'work of the understanding' carried the seeds of its own distortion. This is an evil against which we did not sufficiently prepare; and in narrow conceptions of 'research methods', especially in education, it has even now come to pass.

NOTES

1. All translations are by Ellis and Spedding, in Robertson, 1905.
2. *Nostra vero inveniendi scientias ea est ratio, ut non multum ingeniorum acumini et robori relinquatur; sed quae ingenia et intellectus fere exaequet.*

3. *Nostra enim via inveniendi scientias exaequat fere ingenia, et non multum excellentiae eorum relinquit.*
4. 'Cognitive facility' was not the term used in the proposal. I have changed it in the interests of anonymity.
5. This is not of course to imply wholesale acceptance of those strictures.
6. Especially in the writings of Hans-Georg Gadamer, e.g. *Truth and Method*, 1975. For its implications for the social sciences, as the social sciences are generally understood in English-speaking countries, see Flyvbjerg, 2001; for a rich and detailed treatment that is attentive to the implications for education, see Dunne, 1993. See also Smith (forthcoming).

REFERENCES

Appleyard, B. (1993) *Understanding the Present: Science and the Soul of Modern Man* (London, Pan).

Brown, T. and Jones, L. (2001) *Action Research and Postmodernism* (Buckingham, Open University Press).

Carr, W. (2004) Philosophy and Education, *Journal of Philosophy of Education*, 38.1, pp. 55–73.

Dunne, J. (1993) Back to the Rough Ground: 'Phronesis' and 'Techne' in Modern Philosophy and in Aristotle (Notre Dame, IN, University of Notre Dame Press).

Flew, A. (1971) *An Introduction to Western Philosophy* (London, Thames & Hudson).

Flyvbjerg, B. (2001) *Making Social Science Matter: Why Social Inquiry Fails and How it Can Succeed Again*, trans. S. Sampson (Cambridge, Cambridge University Press).

Gadamer, H. G. (1975) *Truth and Method* [*Wahrheit und Methode*, 1960], trans. G. Barden and J. Cumming (London, Sheed & Ward).

Gaukroger, S. (2001) *Francis Bacon and the Transformation of Early-Modern Philosophy* (Cambridge, Cambridge University Press).

Gjertsen, D. (1992) *Science and Philosophy: Past and Present* (London, Penguin).

Hume, D. (1969) *A Treatise of Human Nature* (London, Penguin).

Law, J. (2004) *After Method* (London, Routledge).

McNiff, J. (1993) *Teaching as Learning: An Action Learning Approach* (London, Routledge).

Newby, M. (1994) Living Theory or Living Contradiction?, *Journal of Philosophy of Education*, 28.1, pp. 119–126.

Pollard, A. and Tann, S. (1987) *Reflective Teaching in the Primary School* (London, Cassell).

Pring, R. (2000) *Philosophy of Educational Research* (London, Continuum).

Robertson, J. (1905) *The Philosophical Works of Francis Bacon* (London, Routledge).

Sayer, A. (1994) *Method in Social Science* (London, Routledge).

Smith, R. (1997) *The Norton History of the Human Sciences* (New York, W.W. Norton).

Smith, R. (forthcoming) Technical Difficulties: The Workings of Practical Judgement, in: M. Depaepe and P. Smeyers (eds) *The Relevance of Educational Research: why 'what works' doesn't work* (Dordrecht, Springer).

Stronach, I. and MacLure, M. (1997) *Educational Research Undone: The Postmodern Embrace* (Milton Keynes, Open University Press).

4
'A Demented Form of the Familiar': Postmodernism and Educational Research

MAGGIE MACLURE

An antagonism results when the presence of the 'Other' disrupts a discourse so thoroughly as to prevent it from being itself.

(Jones, 1994. p. 212)

A contemporary is not always someone who lives at the same time, nor someone who speaks of overtly 'current' questions. But it is someone in whom we recognize a voice or gesture which reaches us from a hitherto unknown but immediately familiar place, something which we discover we have been waiting for, or rather which has been waiting for us, something which was there, imminent.

(Nancy, 1996. p. 108)

INTRODUCTION

I was originally invited to write this chapter under the title of 'The Compatibility of Postmodernisms with the Project of Educational Research'. But compatibility is too cosy. I prefer to think in terms of a productive *in*compatibility of postmodernism and educational research, and indeed of postmodernism and philosophy. What interests me about postmodernism is its capacity for unsettling the customary arrangements of the disciplines or domains that it tangles with.

Postmodernism, in my preferred reading at any rate, is eccentric—off-centre, de-centred. As a result of its eccentricity, postmodernism is sometimes able to pose questions and mobilise issues that are hidden or taken for granted.[1] This, I think, is postmodernism's dubious gift to educational research, and in particular to methodology: to unsettle the still core of habit and order in the uncertain hope of shaking things up, asking new questions, estranging the familiar. It is not really a matter, therefore, of a relationship between two self-standing entities that may or may not be compatible. I am persuaded rather by accounts of postmodernism as emanating from the 'inside' of whatever is its (supposedly) modernist antagonist—literary theory, educational research, philosophy, anthropology, sociology and so on.[2] In these accounts, postmodernism emerges from a discipline's internal, irreconcilable contradiction: from whatever it is that a discipline or system of thought tries to (has to) suppress in order to go on 'being itself', as Jones puts it in the opening quotation above.

Why dwell on the mischief of postmodernism though, rather than continue for as long as possible to ignore or condemn it (a defensive posture that has been maintained more staunchly in education than many other fields of inquiry)? Why not carry on professing the Enlightenment values that education and educational research supposedly still embody—faith in progress, rationality, access to truth and the agency of the centred self? It seems to me that the antagonism of postmodernism is called for, as well as called forth, by contemporary conditions. Policy discourses in the UK betray an intense fear of uncertainty and contradiction, and seem ever more intent on the suppression of dissent, diversity, complexity and unpredictability. Curriculum, assessment and inspection programmes, with their emphasis on uniformity of delivery and outcomes, attempt to repress the gaps and discontinuities out of which teaching, learning and research issue. Research is disciplined by audit and a retreat to simplistic notions of science (cf. Strathern, 2000a; Lather, 2005; MacLure, 2005). What such policies attempt to suppress is education's 'Other'—the pain, conflict, failure, chance, irrationality, desire, judgement, frailty, frivolity and singularity that are also, unavoidably, implicated in the rationalist projects of teaching, learning and research.

But education's Other also returns, I have suggested, as *postmodernism*. The remainder of this chapter considers what methodology under the auspices of postmodernism might involve. It asks how method might resist, rather than collude with, the rage for closure that animates contemporary policy. Qualitative method, despite its aspirations to openness, nuance and multiple perspectives, and its repudiation of the patriarchal assurance of positivism, still inclines towards closure. It is for instance often nostalgic for reconciliation of difference between researchers and their 'subjects', seeking to close the gap between their incommensurable realities, or their unequal power. Yet also wanting other, contradictory closures—of generalisation, abstraction and mastery, the prerogative to arbitrate amongst competing realities, to have the last word. It looks for bedrock truths in 'grounded' theorising; or convivial truths in narrative approaches, or experiential truths in action research. It still wants access to the real: the real person behind the frailties of performance, the real world behind the fabrications of writing, even though at other times, in other moments, it knows there is no direct access to these. It is still pretty much in thrall to the closures of innocent knowing, clear vision and settled accounts (cf. Lather, 1996; MacLure, 2003).

For the most part, qualitative research is still conducted, then, as an Enlightenment practice: seeking to dispel illusion and illuminate the dark places of ignorance with the light of reason. In one sense, this is unavoidable: none of us can fully escape the 'closure of metaphysics' (Spivak, 1976, xx). We can't give up our longing for what Taussig (1993) calls the 'true real'. Nor should we, since that is the real that works for us. But with Taussig, I want to argue that method could work more provocatively, and politically, if it addressed the strange and fascinating ways in which that true real is produced and haunted by 'representational gimmicks', replicas, mimetic machines and magic (1993, xvii). This chapter tries to conjure a method that could productively engage its own representational gimmickry and mimicry, and attend to the irrational, the sensual, the forgotten, the perverse and the marginal aspects of education that are repressed by policy, custom and the grim pursuit of progress, but that return as ghosts to haunt it. In keeping with a postmodern disrespect for boundaries, the argument wanders through surrealism and the baroque, and takes its examples from illusionistic paintings and outmoded popular entertainments such as the magic lantern, the peep show and that favourite replicant of the Enlightenment, the clockwork automaton.

'PREPOSTEROUS' POSTMODERNISM

I'm not really sure that I want to call that method by the name of 'postmodernism'. I have avoided using the word in my own writing over the last few years, partly because of its unavoidable tendency to deflect engagement and provoke instead a routine recitation of accusations—self-indulgence, arrogance, vanity, relativism, frivolity, etc.—and an endless round of territorial and definitional disputes. (Who's in and who's out? What's the difference between postmodernism and poststructuralism? Does deconstruction 'belong'?)[3] Principally though, I have avoided postmodernism because I have become more and more interested in its *untimeliness*. Although it seems to be a phenomenon of the second half of the twentieth century, it may be that what is called postmodernism is the contemporary outbreak of a repressed Otherness that has haunted all closure-seeking systems or philosophies, at least since the late 16th/early 17th centuries (conventionally tagged as the beginning of 'modernity').[4] As the 'Other' that disrupts discourse from within—its 'spectral double' to use Butler's term (2004, p. 233)—postmodernism seems to have affinities with the philosophy and art of the baroque, with the literary Gothic of the 19th century and with surrealism. Perhaps, then, postmodernism is just one manifestation of the spectre that has stalked modernity as its *impensé*: the trace of its ineffable, uncanny, dark Other.[5]

   This chapter traces some possible entanglements of postmodernism with surrealism and the baroque, and teases out some implications for methodology.[6] I am not the first to notice such entanglements (see for example Caws, 1997). Below are some of the traits that they seem to share. Although they are presented here as a list, they are baroquely entwined.

   Defamiliarisation—the estrangement of the familiar.
   The attempt to 'represent the unrepresentable' (Jay, 1993, p. 48).
   The nausea, exhilaration or melancholy that the necessary failure of this project inaugurates.
   Loss of mastery of self and of other.

Embrace of the nonrational.

Theatricality—life, art and philosophy as performance, productive of doubles, mirrors, copies, fakes, simulacra and apparitions.

Resistance to generalisation, abstraction or totalisation.

Attention to fragments, details and marginalia.

Epistemic excess—i.e. overflowing of boundaries and structures.

Confusion of opposites such as reality and representation, light and dark, life and death, surface and depth.

Fragmentary or distorting representational strategies—montage, assemblage, blurring of boundaries between word and image, oscillations of scale and focus.

I do not mean to suggest that postmodernism, surrealism and the baroque are all 'the same': e.g., versions or expressions of an underlying or overarching principle—a move that would lock them all back into the enclosures of Enlightenment logic. Nor (for the same reason) am I suggesting a 'tradition' or filiation from past to present, baroque to postmodernism. The untimely relation between past and present is precisely at issue here. Bal's (baroque) notion of 'preposterous history' appeals, as a play on the temporal confounding of 'pre' and 'post' that understands the past 'as it is enfolded into the present that constructs it' (1999, p. 21). This is an enfolding that also embraces the analyst or researcher, who changes the past through her interventions, and is in turn changed by them. Perhaps one way of reading the preposterous relation between postmodernism, surrealism and the baroque would be as a Derridean chain of 'undecidables'—words that perform the undoing of the binary distinctions on which Enlightenment thought hangs (e.g., Derrida, 1983). Or perhaps these words are the intermittent sounding of that 'voice or gesture' that introduces the contemporary, of which Nancy (1996) writes in the quotation that prefixes this chapter.

In its entanglements with the surreal and the baroque, this chapter lines itself up with anti-Enlightenment forms of theorising that embrace the 'disappointment' of certainty (cf. Stronach and MacLure, 1997, pp. 4–5). Researchers and writers who practice disappointment invoke a shifting lexicon of 'trouble' words—failure, disconcertion, bafflement, bother, 'stuck places', entanglement, ruin, haunting, melancholy, not to mention trouble itself[7]—to worry away at the 'Other' of Enlightenment. They interest themselves in the realities and subjectivities that are occluded by Western culture's triumphal stories of progress, reason and order. Disappointment might sound like a rather passive state. This chapter focuses, however, on the more animated aspect of anti-Enlightenment figuration—the fascination, fear, frisson, surprise, vertigo or wonder that might be released by the disappointment of certainty and the embrace of the smoke-and-mirrors machinery of representation and writing.

SURREALIST ENCOUNTERS

There is a half-submerged story of intellectual and cultural work over the last century that tells of its haunting by surrealism. Surrealism has irrupted, or seeped, into art, literature, anthropology, sociology and

Marxism, challenging prevailing definitions of their 'proper' business and bringing to each its eccentric energy. Clifford (1981) traces the inter-connections of ethnography and surrealism in 1930s France, when boundaries—between science and aesthetics, reality and imagination, fieldwork and exploration, collecting and documenting, political inter-vention and artistic expression, literary and academic writing—seem to have been less strictly patrolled than they are these days. Surrealists and ethnographers shared an interest in the realities that were repressed by the taxonomic orders of Western rationality, and looked to 'primitive' cultures and to the unconscious as sources of disruptive energy.[8] 'Ethnographic surrealism', as defined by Clifford, values 'fragments, curious collections and unexpected juxtapositions', putting these to work to 'provoke manifestations of extraordinary realities drawn from the domain of the erotic, the exotic, and the unconscious' (1981, p. 118).

Surrealism has never completely disappeared from the cultural and political landscape, though it has been dismissed many times as frivolous and outmoded. The surrealist opposition to Enlightenment rationality, and to the global aggressions of Left and Right that it rationalised, has proved enduringly powerful, for instance, for anti-colonial art and politics. Artists and authors have used surrealist representational strategies to trace subaltern identities and release some usable energy from the toxic mixture of Western/Northern domination and local cultures (e.g., Spiteri and LaCoss, 2003). The ambivalent and disturbing energies of surrealism have also been of use to feminist art and activism (cf. Chadwick, 1998; Caws, 1997). Despite its abject status within whatever is the cultural status quo of the time, or precisely because of that abjection, surrealism is always being disinterred or strangely encountered one more time.

MIRRORS AND MAGIC LANTERNS: BENJAMIN'S *PHANTASMAGORIA*

Walter Benjamin's work, which has been widely reclaimed for postmodernism, is also intricately folded both into surrealism (Cohen, 1993) and into the baroque (Buci-Glucksmann, 1994).[9] In his attempt to develop a post-Enlightenment Marxism, disengaged from the metaphors of progress that had failed to free the masses, Benjamin strove for moments of 'profane illumination' in the discarded commodities, frivolous pursuits and mundane events of everyday life in industrial society. Like the surrealists, Benjamin was interested in the revolutionary potential of the *familiar* as a site of potential disruption and estrangement, where something might momentarily jolt people out of the frenetic paralysis of modernity. The familiar could not be looked straight in the face; could not be appropriated, subjected to reason, or brought within totalising schemes. It had to be viewed awry, through 'a dialectical optic that perceives the everyday as impenetrable, the impenetrable as everyday' (Benjamin, 1979, p. 237). For Benjamin, the familiar was a strange place, occupying 'all those incomplete territories overflowing classical rationality (childhood, female culture, the world of the defeated, the experiences of history)' (Buci-Glucksmann, 1994, p. 45).

Benjamin chose to dwell, therefore, at the point of dialectical impasse, where the dualities of Enlightenment thought (reality/illusion, reason/ unreason, subject/object, familiar/strange) come to a standstill. He saw modernity as a *phantasmagoria*—a magic lantern show of ghosts and illusions (Benjamin, 2002). The phantasmagoria, with its artificial illumination, theatricality, deception and seductive appeal to the masses, also represented a post-Enlightenment critical apparatus that no longer believed in the possibility of escape from the entanglements of ideology (see Cohen, 1993). The observer of the phantasmagoria is both participant and dupe, caught up in the pleasurable frisson of its machinations even while knowing them to be fraudulent.

Benjamin detected phantasmagorias in the Parisian arcades, the World Exhibitions, and popular entertainments of the 19th century such as optical toys and panoramas—all sites where the products of technology and the fruits of imperialism were assembled to entertain and seduce the populace with false promises of abundance and mastery over nature. Other examples of the phantasmagorical included photography, wax museums, fashion and transgressive urban characters such as the prostitute, the lesbian and the androgyne—whom Benjamin, after Baudelaire, understood both as debased products of modernity (the commodity made flesh, the unhomely woman) and as figures of '*heroic protest against this modernity*' (Buci-Glucksmann, 1994, p. 104, original emphasis). The phantasmagoria does not merely stand, therefore, for the narcoleptic delusions of capital. This would confine it to the Enlightenment horizon that Benjamin hoped to transgress. It is, rather, an ambiguous figuration of delusion and fascination, life and death, which simultaneously emerges from modernity and undermines the rationality of the centred subject. The Gothic artifice of the phantasmagoria blocks the gambits of distancing, elevation, rank ordering and self-certainty that are characteristic of Enlightenment method.

Benjamin was also a practitioner of non-academic, non-transparent, poetic forms of writing of the kind that have become familiar within postmodern texts. Cohen describes his phantasmagorical strategy as one of inciting 'all manner of irrational states: fascination, enchantment, melancholy, frustration, distraction' (1993, p. 252). She places Benjamin within a submerged tradition of 'Gothic' Marxism which aims to understand 'how the irrational pervades existing society and dreams of using it to effect social change' (1993, pp. 1–2). Buci-Glucksmann (1994, p. 45) calls it a 'torn Marxism', reading Benjamin as a practitioner of 'baroque reason'—a reason born out of, and into, catastrophe, driven by a 'logic of dislocation'. Writing, living and dying 'under the sign of failure' (Cohen, 2004, p. 200) and the looming shadow of Fascism, Benjamin was perhaps the pre-eminent methodologist of disappointment.

BAROQUE ENTANGLEMENTS

The art and philosophy of the baroque (dated roughly, and retrospectively, from the end of the 16th century) currently provide one of the most fertile sources of reclaimed transgressive energy. From art theory (Bal, 1999), to actor network theory (Law, 2003; Kwa, 2002) to continental philosophy (Deleuze, 1992, Buci-Glucksmann, 1999; Badie, nd), to surrealism (Caws, 1997), the baroque provides exemplars of an entangled, confounded vision that resists the god's eye perspective and the false clarity of scientism. Baroque figures and metaphors—the ruin, the labyrinth, the library, the (distorting) mirror and (above all perhaps) the fold—speak to contemporary imaginaries of the postmodern (cf. Turner, 1994), as does the appetite for spectacle, the melancholic 'intertwining of death and desire' (Jay, 1993, pp. 47–8), and the blurring of distinctions between subject and object, surface and depth, reality and representation. The 'voice or gesture' of the baroque is thus 'contemporary' again, to requote Nancy (1996). It is recognisable in the refusal of clarity, mastery and the single point of view, the radical uncertainty about scale, boundaries and coherence, and the acceptance of the obligation to get entangled in the details and decorations, rather than rise above them. These are all recognisable injunctions, or descriptions, for research under the sign of postmodernism.

METHODOLOGY UNDER THE AUSPICES OF POSTMODERNISM
Fracturing the Familiar

What, then, are the implications of the foregoing for methodology? I want firstly to suggest that educational research might try to generate some of the *defamiliarising* energy sought by Benjamin and the surrealists—not in order to be able to 'look back' at the familiar and see it more clearly, but rather to split it open: to see what might burst out of the 'dehiscent gap' (Buci-Glucksmann, 1994, p. 49). Our ways of seeing education are so deeply ingrained with discursive familiarity and 'mythic immediacy' (Buck-Morss, 1991, x) that we are more-or-less insulated from surprise and wonder.[10] What is needed is the kind of transgressive jolt that comes from encountering a 'demented form of the familiar' (Fer, 1993, p. 176)[11]; or suddenly glimpsing the demented in the all-too familiar. The political ends of such research would have more in common with Breton's 'flea-market vision of social change' (Cohen, 1993, p. 110) than with more ambitious narratives of emancipation or revolution—a matter of sifting through the everyday texts of education for the 'fascinating' or 'perverse' details that force us to think again, and more slowly, about what is taken for granted. It might, like Benjamin, devote itself to seeking out 'counterimages that rubbed against the grain of the semantics of progress' (Buck-Morss, 1991, p. 92). It might encourage new ways of 'reading' and 'writing' the social, based on anti-taxonomic, analogical, juxtapositional strategies such as collage or montage. Its architecture might more closely resemble a cabinet of curiosities, or a labyrinth, than the hierarchies of a 'table' or paradigm.

An Analytics of Entanglement

A postmodern method would resist building hierarchies, frameworks, abstractions or other methodological crows' nests from which to look down from a distance on the details or the 'data'—i.e., the 'feckless particulars' (Krauss, 1993, p. 103) of educational scenes. It might adopt instead a baroque sensibility that looks for ways of working with, and deeply within, the intricate entanglements of global and local, representation and reality, sensual and intellectual, particular and general, and so on. An example can be found in Law (2003) who unfolds a baroque attitude to the 'global' that challenges common assumptions about its size and scale. Against the idea that the global is big and all-encompassing—a kind of biggest box or largest frame for locating the local—Law looks for a global that is small, 'broken, poorly formed and comes in patches' (p. 5 of 15). Adopting the principle of monadology from Leibniz/Deleuze, Law assumes that phenomena are already present in the smallest particulars of practices and institutions. He provides an example in an analysis of British aircraft development in the 1950s, starting from a technical formula for calculating the best (i.e., least lethal, most efficient) wing design. In a quintessentially baroque movement, Law peers 'into' the formula, intensifying the 'magnification' of his view and opening up its folds and layers, until he comes upon 'the Russians'—not 'out there in the global environment' of the Cold War, but in 'sets of assumptions traded in conversation or memos between young men working on the same corridor' (p. 7 of 15).

Instead of ascending to ever-higher levels of abstraction or explanatory power (or purer states of authenticity), a baroque analytic preserves, and indeed intensifies, the complexity of the specific. It enacts a 'logic of ramification' (Bal, 1999, p. 24) that proliferates meanings and new connections, rather than converging on generalities or coalescing within boundaries. It does not aspire to clarity, never achieves full coherence, and is 'tolerant of the implicit' (Law, 2003, p. 9 of 15). It is 'wavering' in its scale and focus (Bal, 1999, p. 24). Entities are not, therefore, intrinsically big or small, containing or contained: the size, significance and dimensions of the object under study depend on how the folds of the fabric of the world are disposed at the place where we start ravelling and unravelling some of its threads. What size, for instance, is 'the classroom'? From some vantage points it is small and surrounded, buffeted or embraced by bigger stuff such as policy, society, history; or pushed into a tiny corner of insignificance by the more pressing claims of lives lived more vividly 'elsewhere'. From others it's an expansive terrain, pock-marked by unevenly distributed fragments of 'policy' or 'society', torn by competing theories, with hidden depths and varying topologies of fear, desire, dedication, exile, silences, play, censure, effort, power, missed chances, pools of conversation, sparks of interest, blame, thwarted or fulfilled ambitions, feats of memory.

The Recalcitrance of the Object

A postmodern method would respect the recalcitrance of the object of study—not only its complexity but also its capacity for resisting social explanation and for unsettling the composure of researchers. The recalcitrance of objects is commended by Latour (2000), who argues for a social science that renders its objects able to 'strike back' (p. 107).

Objects, says Latour, should be allowed to manifest their intransigent thingness or 'objectity' in the face of the rule- or pattern-seeking propensities of conventional social science (p. 116). Such a refocusing on the object would represent a shift of attention in qualitative methodology, which has been preoccupied with questions of subjectivity (cf. Lather, 2005). It would also represent a 'return' to a baroque attitude, which likewise takes the object as the focus of its curiosity. However, a baroque engagement with objects ultimately unsettles clear distinctions between subject and object: its oscillations of scale and its 'microscopic' intensity lead to loss of mastery, both of the object and the subject. 'Subjectivity and the object become co-dependent, folded into one another', writes Bal (1999, p. 28), 'and this puts the subject at risk'. The paradoxes and aporias of the baroque point of view, and the perplexing effects on the viewer, have interested contemporary cultural critics and philosophers: Velasquez's *Las Meninas*, for instance, has been an object of fascination for Foucault (1970) and many others.

This 'shared entanglement' (Bal, 1999, p. 30) of subject and object is unmistakable in *trompe l'oeil* painting and sculpture—a form of art, or perhaps anti-art, favoured by baroque artists and again by the surrealists. The *trompe l'oeil* 'fools the eye' by imitating its object so faithfully that the onlooker is momentarily gripped by an inability to tell the difference between representation and reality, original and copy. The little frisson of vertigo sparked by the *trompe l'oeil* marks a moment of ontological panic. Unable to deploy the usual strategies for mastering the visual field and penetrating 'through' the picture to the meaning, object or reality that lies beyond, the viewer is momentarily trapped in an uncanny space where the usual distance between subject and object has suddenly collapsed. As many commentators have noted, the picture seems to 'look back' at the viewer, and its uncanny effects have frequently been associated with death, haunting, hallucination or magic (Badie, nd; Bryson, 1990, Baudrillard, 1998; MacLure, 2003).[12] The *trompe l'oeil*, according to Badie, opens a 'breach' in baroque space that interferes/misplays (*déjoue*) not only with the laws of representation, but with those of objectivity and of meaning itself (nd, p. 6 of 12)). The *trompe l'oeil* is, in short, an irruption of Otherness into the scene of representation and mastery. It is a 'demented form of the familiar'. It is 'intractable' (ibid.). It is recalcitrant.

There are *trompe l'oeil* moments in research—fleeting instances where the object of the inquiry (who may, of course, also be a subject) is able to become recalcitrant: to deflect the research gaze and resist being made an example of. Here is one such moment, from the start of a life history interview with a teacher, which took place many years ago now.

trompe l'oeil interview fragment

Teacher: Right—question one.

M. MacLure: (disconcerted) Question one—oh yes—I haven't got a check-list fortunately.

T: Jolly good.

MM: Perhaps the best way is to go backwards—right? How did you get here?

T: By car.

Like a *trompe l'oeil* painting of the back of a painting, or of a cupboard whose half-open, painted door opens only onto the depthless surface of its painted interior, the illusion of interpretive depth suddenly evaporates.[13] The interviewee performs a kind of impersonation of an interviewee that confounds the queasy camaraderie of the interview genre, exposing instead its creaky discursive stage machinery for conjuring truth and insight. The performance destabilises my self-assurance and calls attention to the necessary illusion involved in attempting access to 'inner' things such as a person's thoughts or his authentic self.

Little irruptions of the ridiculous into the precarious order of the research encounter happen quite often but they seldom surface in research reports or research method texts, being edited out or written off as false starts, trivia or failures of technique. And the experience of estrangement that they provoke is generally fleeting: as with the *trompe l'oeil* painting, it 'exhausts itself in its effects' (Badie, nd). Such moments are easily forgotten, though as the example above indicates, they may return to haunt you. A postmodern method might try to resist the forgetting of these moments, when research is prevented from 'being itself' by the apparition of the Other, to allude to the quotation that opens this chapter. It would look for ways of reminding itself of the delirious nature of the distance between self and other on which interpretive penetration or analytic mastery depend.

The Debt to Frivolity

Recalcitrance has also been noted, and commended, as a self-protective stance by postcolonial subjects and other marginalised persons, for whom visibility and availability to the administrative gaze often means oppression and loss of agency (e.g., Bhabha, 1994). The deadly seriousness of subaltern recalcitrance often has a *frivolous* aspect, mixing mimicry with mockery to unsettle the composure of the masterful gaze—as indeed does the example from the life history interview above. There is frivolity too in the trickster and joker figures who inhabit the myths, stories and dreams studied by anthropologists and literary theorists, and who have returned in the guise of the ambivalent agency of the poststructuralist subject (cf. Haraway, 1992; Johnston, 1987). There is frivolity in the camp aesthetics of queer theory; in the 'excremental literature' of writers in postcolonial Africa who wallow in the abject discourse of filth for subversive purposes (Esty, 1999); in the surrealist-inflected work of South American artists such as Nadin Ospina, whose pre-Columbian Mickey Mouse mocks the erasures of globalisation and colonisation, and the pretensions of the Western/Northern art establishment.[14]

Frivolity resists appropriation or incorporation (cf. Derrida, 1980). Too frothy, and simultaneously too mundane, it 'resists elevation to generality' (Smith, 1995, p. 27). Frivolity introduces Otherness into the binary distinctions that are used to settle methodological and philosophical questions—researcher/researched, observer/observed, subjective/objective and so on (MacLure, forthcoming).[15] I want to suggest that researchers and educators should not be too assiduous in their suppression of the frivolous in the (supposed) interests of the serious. Children after all seem to live and learn without concerning themselves too much with the distinction, at least until formal education tells them otherwise.

Anyway, the distinction between the serious and the frivolous has never been all that clear-cut. To take one example, the makers of the clockwork automata that diverted the princes and the public in 18th Century Europe often represented their creations as experiments at the frontiers of anatomy or physics, and several were also associated with technological innovations in industrial processes. Vaucanson, whose flute player was presented as a model of the respiratory system, was also an inventor of weaving looms (Sayous, nd). The automata built by Jacquet-Droz wrote messages and played musical instruments, their tunes or sentences pre-selected by a rudimentary form of programming that was also the principle underlying the pattern-setting machinery of the emerging textile industry (Sayous, nd). Von Kempelen, who invented the most famous automaton of all, the chess-playing 'Turk', is reported as also having invented a steam lift, a drainage pump for mines, a 'talking machine', a system of writing for the blind and hydraulic systems for fountains (Standage, 2004). As with the phantasmagoria, distinctions between serious and frivolous pursuits, science and entertainment, are blurred in the figure of the automaton.

It is worth looking a little closer at the adventures of Von Kemplen's 'Turk', who toured the capitals of Europe between 1770 and the early 1900s and also visited the US and Cuba, taking on human opponents and usually beating them (Shaffer, 1997; Standage, 2004).[16] The Turk seems to have insinuated himself, not only into the story of Enlightenment science and the industrial revolution, but also into the cultural text of the past two and a half centuries. He is reputed to have spurred Edmund Cartwright to develop the power loom, and to have inspired the very young Charles Babbage to think productively about the calculating machines that prefigured computers. Edgar Allan Poe wrote a newspaper article and, later, a short story, solving the mystery of his operation. Among other luminaries that the Turk is reputed to have encountered are Napoleon, Catherine the Great, Frederick the Great and Benjamin Franklin. These disseminations of the Turk were not halted when it became known that the automaton was a fake—its arms were operated by a person crouched inside its cabinet (variously imagined in contemporary accounts to be a hunchback, a child or an amputee). The Turk's deceptions brought him new admirers including the magician Robert-Houdin and the circus entrepreneur P.T. Barnum. He also makes an appearance in Walter Benjamin's writing, not as an object of admiration, but as a figure for the critique of historical materialism—the 'puppet' that always gets to win the philosophical argument by illegitimately smuggling in the 'hunchback' of theology (1968, p. 253). In his more recent manifestations the Turk is written into the history of artificial intelligence (e.g. Schaffer, 2004).

Right 'inside' the big stories of the Enlightenment, the industrial revolution and the information revolution sits the frivolous figure of the automaton, therefore, folded into the narratives of science, technology, entertainment, philosophy, medicine and magic, and interfering with the distinctions among them. Perhaps the strange fascination of the Turk, the proliferation of stories about him (many of which are probably untrue), and his reappearances across the decades testify to a continuing need for wonders and cyborgs, and a lingering dissatisfaction with the fortified boundaries that are still supposed to keep nature and technology, science and art, human and non-human apart.[17]

The entanglements of frivolity and science are no less apparent today, especially perhaps in the field of virtual technologies. Huhtamo (2002) argues that the antecedents of the 'virtual museums' of cyberspace, and perhaps even of the World Wide Web itself can be traced, not to just to the serious pursuits of Big Science or Art (of the capital 'A' variety), but also to the entertainment technologies and public spectacles of the 19th and early 20th centuries, and the domestic and frivolous pleasures that these offered to a highly participative audience. For instance, the non-linear architecture of the Web, offering multiple routes and intimate pleasures, activated by the desires and inclinations of the individual viewer, can be traced, he argues, to such things as the world fairs and exhibitions, Disneyland, penny arcades, peep show, magic lanterns and optical toys (the mutoscope, phenakistoscope, stereoscope, etc.). These are the kinds of pleasures and devices that also interested the surrealists and Walter Benjamin. So here we are, back at the profane illumination of the peep show and the smoke and mirrors of the magic lantern. A postmodern method would resist the forgetting of the debt to frivolity. It would assume an ethical stance of recalcitrance towards the po-faced, risk-averse literalism that permeates education.[18]

The Peep Show

A postmodern method would also recognise, as did the surrealists, the inescapable absurdity of the postures adopted by the viewing subject, and the strange insights to be gained by contemplating objects under conditions of intimacy, distortion or difficulty. In addition to their fascination with optical toys and fairground technologies, the surrealists secreted their objects and art works in suitcases, boxes and cabinets, sometimes in the form of doubles or miniatures. They required viewers to glimpse their work through peep-holes or by pressing levers (e.g., Huhtamo, 2002). This interest in occluded vision and a seductive address to the viewer was part of a wider interest in the delimitation of the visible and the invisible, in the erotics of the look, and in what could be 'seen' by not looking at things directly. By interfering with the remote and indifferent mastery of the gaze, the surrealists pursued and glimpsed shadowy things, and attempted to catch the viewer's complicity in the act of looking. This is also a baroque vision that Caws (1997, p. 4), explicitly associating it with surrealism, describes as 'fascination with what is complex, multiple, clouded and changeable'. Optical instruments, which have always wavered on the boundary between science and entertainment, were objects of special fascination during the baroque. Stafford (2001, p. 6) describes the effect on the subject of such 'devices of wonder' as *intensification*—a kind of exhilaration of the senses that sets perception, cognition and imagination in motion. Learning, fascination, enchantment and seduction are caught up in each other, and in a complex relation to the object. 'Capturing devices' such as prisms, mirrors, microscopes, perspective boxes and magic lanterns 'focused, abstracted, diminished or multiplied objects', according to Stafford (ibid.). In the spirit of the baroque, they 'concentrated, conjoined and metamorphosed the universe's unruly singularities' (pp. 6–7).

Perhaps a postmodern method could consider alternative visual apparatuses such as the peep show or the magic lantern (phantasmagoria) as new imaginaries for the relation to the object. Or at least contemplate its point of view as delimited by the aperture of the peep-hole rather than the proscenium arch or other more expansive openings onto the scene of research. The peep show brings the viewer into an intimate relation with the object, one into which desire, wonder and Otherness are folded, and out of which something might issue that would never be seen by shining a bright light upon the object in the empty space of reason and looking at it as hard as possible. But the peepshow also calls attention to the compromised, voyeuristic nature of the researcher gaze and the unavoidable absurdity of the research posture. To view the delights of the peep show you have to bend down, present your backside to public view, put yourself at risk. You may start out standing, as Bob Dylan wrote, 'but you will wind up peeking through [a] keyhole down upon your knees'.[19] What would such a method look like?

CONCLUSION

These times are not as dark as the ones that enfolded Benjamin and the surrealists, but they are dark enough. Clifford's description of the phantasmagorical 'normality' that mobilised surrealism/ethnography between the wars seems all too evident again now.

> The sort of normality or common sense that can amass empires in fits of absent-mindedness or wander routinely into world wars is seen as a contested reality to be subverted, parodied and transgressed (Clifford, 1981, pp. 117–8).

Or as Lyotard asserted, 'We have paid a high enough price for the nostalgia for the one and the whole' (1984, pp. 81–82).

It was a chance encounter with an exhibition of illusionistic paintings of the 17th century (which I did not at that time know as baroque) that led me to stumble across surrealism, so the notion of the lucky find and of 'objective chance' haunt this chapter too. The notion of *déjouer,* discussed by Krauss (1993) seems apt. *Déjouer* means to foil or baffle, but also to 'mis-play'—that is, to undermine the game from within. Postmodernism might be read as one such mis-playful project.

NOTES

1. See Derrida (1990) on the necessity of eccentricity.
2. See Butler (2004, chapter 11) for an account of philosophy's antagonism to its own 'Other'.
3. An alternative refusal of the term 'postmodernism' might be grounded in an appeal to contemporary conditions as a time of 'post-methodology', as Lather (2005) suggests. However this would be to retain a certain temporality that this chapter attempts to disrupt.
4. See Turner (1993) for a discussion of postmodernism's relation to modernity.
5. I am 'quoting' here from Foster's (1993) description of surrealism as the *impensé* of modernism.
6. For lack of space, this chapter does not pursue possible *gothic* entanglements. See Castricano (2001) and Cohen (2004) for a gothic reading of, respectively, Derrida and Benjamin.
7. Under the umbrella of 'post-Enlightenment' theorising I would include deconstruction, poststructuralism, postmodernism, queer theory and other not-so-emphatically-named orientations. Users of trouble-words include: *disconcertion*—Taussig (1993); *bafflement*—Krauss (1993); *failure*—Visweswaran (1994), Cohen, 2004; *entanglement*—Bal (1999); *ruin*—St Pierre and Willow (2000); *trouble*—Butler (1990); *melancholy*—Buci-Glucksmann (1994); *haunting*—Derrida (1994), amongst many other writers. Critiques of 'clarity' as a methodological or policy goal are also practices of disappointment: cf. Scheurich, 2000; Lather, 1996; St. Pierre, 2000; MacLure, 2003, chapter 6.
8. Another such encounter between surrealism and anthropology took place in the UK around the same time, with the establishment of Mass Observation: cf. MacClancy, 1995.
9. The 'Walter Benjamin' conjured in these pages is, of course, only one of many Benjamins. This account might easily be accused, by writers who know much more than I about their subject, of 'finding' just the sort of post-humanist exemplar that it set out to look for. It is heavily indebted to Margaret Cohen (1993) and Christine Buci-Glucksmann (1994) for their differently brilliant books on Benjamin.
10. Buck-Morss was writing of Benjamin's aim of fracturing 'the mythic immediacy of the present' (1991, x).
11. This was how Ray and Dora Maar described Meret Oppenheim's famous fur-lined cup and saucer (reported in Fer, 1993, p. 176).
12. The implications of *trompe l'oeil* for methodology in educational research are pursued in more detail in MacLure, 2003, chapter 9).
13. Examples by the 17th century artist Gijsbrechts, together with a range of other baroque and surrealist *trompe l'oeil* works, can be viewed online: see Zamora (nd).
14. The work of Chris Ofili provides another well-known instance of 'excremental' art (follow links from 'Collections' at the Tate Museum Online: http://www.tate.org.uk/). Ospina's work can be seen at http://www.nadinospina.com/menu.htm (accessed January 2006).
15. Frivolity is, of course, one of the crimes of which postmodernism has repeatedly been accused.
16. The Turk has gone through several incarnations since his death in a fire in 1854, including a recent reconstruction: see photograph and description at: http://www.grg.org/Turk.htm (accessed September 2005).
17. Louise Morley pointed out, after a seminar presentation of this chapter at the University of Sussex, that the Turk has long been invoked, pejoratively, as the figure of the 'Other' in contexts of European cultural anxiety about boundaries. She called attention to one such manifestation that was occurring at the time of the seminar (October, 2005): the panic about the spread of 'bird flu', in which Turkey was repeatedly identified in the media as the locus of the immediate threat to Europe.

18. I have in mind here the effects of the extreme regulation of educational practices brought about by the spread of the 'audit culture' (cf. Power, 1999; Strathern, 2000). The pursuit of accountability, 'transparency', effectiveness, 'quality' and ever-rising standards has, in the view of critics, produced a highly managed, risk-averse educational milieu, which is intolerant of diversity, suspicious of professional expertise and fearful of uncertainty. In such a milieu, diversions—from the prescriptions of policy, the surveillance of 'quality assurance' procedures, or the goal-oriented strictures of the daily lesson plan—are not encouraged. Curricula and pedagogy are pre-specified in detail and assessed in depth; training is 'delivered' according to scripts; reports are written according to recipes (MacLure, 2005; forthcoming, 2006).

19. Bob Dylan, 'She Belongs to Me' 1965, Special Rider Music. My comments here are also informed by Jones' (1994) analysis of Marcel Duchamp's notorious installation *Étant donnés* (1946–66), which obliged viewers to look through peepholes in a wooden door.

REFERENCES

Badie, M. F. (nd) Le trompe l'oeil dans l'art baroque. http://www.univ-montp3.fr/recherche/ea738/chercheurs/badie/trompe.pdf. Accessed September 2005.

Bal, M. (1999) *Quoting Caravaggio: Contemporary Art, preposterous history* (Chicago, IL, University of Chicago Press).

Baudrillard, J. (1998) The *trompe l'oeil*, in: N. Bryson (ed.) *Calligram: Essays in new art history from France* (Cambridge, Cambridge University Press).

Benjamin, W. (1968) Theses on the philosophy of history, in: *Illuminations* (New York, Harcourt), pp. 253–264.

Benjamin, W. (1979) *One-Way Street and Other Writings*, E. Jephcott and K. Shorter, trans. (London, New Left Books).

Benjamin, W. (2002) *The Arcades Project*, H. Eiland and K. McLaughlin, trans. (Cambridge, MA, Harvard University Press).

Bhabha, H. (1994) *The Location of Culture* (London, Routledge).

Bryson, N. (1990) *Looking at the Overlooked: Four essays on still life painting* (London, Reaktion).

Buci-Glucksmann, C. (1994) *Baroque Reason: The aesthetics of modernity* (London, Sage).

Buck-Morss, S. (1991) *The Dialectics of Seeing: Walter Benjamin and the Arcades Project* (Cambridge, MA, MIT Press).

Butler, J. (1990) *Gender Trouble: Feminism and the subversion of identity* (London, Routledge).

Butler, J. (2004) *Undoing Gender* (London, Routledge).

Castricano, J. (2001) *Cryptomimesis: The Gothic and Jacques Derrida's ghost writing* (Montreal, McGill-McQueen's University Press).

Caws, M.A (1997) *The Surrealist Look: An erotics of encounter* (Cambridge, MA, MIT Press).

Clifford, J. (1981) On Ethnographic Surrealism, in: *The Predicament of Culture* (Boston, MA, Harvard University Press).

Cohen, M. (1993) *Profane Illumination: Walter Benjamin and the Paris of surrealist revolution* (Berkeley, CA, University of California Press).

Cohen, M. (2004) Benjamin's Phantasmagoria: the *Arcades Project*, in: D. S. Ferris (ed.) *The Cambridge Companion to Walter Benjamin* (Cambridge, Cambridge University Press).

Deleuze, G. (1992) *The Fold: Leibniz and the baroque*, T. Conley, trans. (Minneapolis, MN, University of Minnesota Press).

Derrida, J. (1980) *The Archaeology of the Frivolous: Reading Condillac* (Pittsburgh, PA, Duquesne University Press).

Derrida, J. (1983) Plato's Pharmacy, in: *Dissemination* (Chicago, IL, University of Chicago Press).

Derrida, J. (1990) Some Statements and Truisms about Neologisms, Postisms, Parasitisms, and Other Small Seisisms, in: D. Carroll (ed.) *The States of 'theory': History, art and critical discourse* (New York, Columbia University Press).

Derrida, J. (1994) *Specters of Marx, the State of the Debt, the Work of Mourning and the New International*, P. Kamuf, trans. (New York, Routledge).

Esty, J. D. (1999) Excremental Postcolonialism, *Contemporary Literature*, 40, pp. 22–59.

Fer, B. (1993) Surrealism, Myth and Psychoanalysis, in: B. Fer, D. Batchelor and P. Wood (eds) *Realism, Rationalism, Surrealism: Art between the wars* (New Haven and London, Yale University Press in association with the Open University).

Foster, H. (1993) *Compulsive Beauty* (Cambridge, MA, MIT Press).

Foucault, M. (1970) *The Order of Things: An archaeology of the human sciences* (New York, Vintage Books).

Haraway, D. (1992) Ecce Homo, Ain't (Ar'n't) I a Woman, and Inappropriate/d Others: The human in a post-humanist landscape, in: J. Butler and J. Scott (eds) *Feminists Theorize the Political* (London, Routledge).

Huhtamo, E. (2002) On the Origins of the Virtual Museum. Nobel Symposium (NS 120) 'Virtual Museums and Public Understanding of Science and Culture' May, 26–29, Stockholm, Sweden. Available online at: www.nobelprize.org/nobel/nobelfoundation/symposia/interdisciplinary/ns120/lectures/huhtamo.pdf (Accessed July 2005.)

Jay, M. (1993) *Downcast Eyes: The denigration of vision in twentieth century French thought* (Berkeley, CA, University of California Press).

Johnson, B. (1987) Thresholds of Difference: Structures of address in Zora Neale Hurston, in: *A World of Difference* (Baltimore, MD, Johns Hopkins University Press).

Jones, A. (1994) *Postmodernism and the En-Gendering of Marcel Duchamp* (Cambridge, Cambridge University Press).

Krauss, R. (1993) *The Optical Unconscious* (Cambridge, MA, MIT Press).

Kwa, K. D. (2002) Romantic and Baroque Conceptions of Complex Wholes in the Sciences, in: J. Law and A. Mol (eds) *Complexities: Social studies of knowledge* (Durham, NC and London, Duke University Press), pp. 23–52.

Lather, P. (1996) Troubling Clarity: The politics of accessible language, *Harvard Educational Review*, 66.3, pp. 525–545.

Lather, P. (2005) Science and Scientificity in the Rage for Accountability: A feminist deconstruction. Paper presented at the Annual Meeting of the American Educational Research Association, April 11–15, 2005, Montreal.

Latour, B. (2000) When Things Strike Back: A possible contribution of 'science studies' to the social sciences, *British Journal of Sociology*, 51.1, pp. 107–123.

Law, J. (2003) And if the Global were Small and Non-coherent? Method, complexity and the baroque. Lancaster: Centre for Science Studies, Lancaster University, at http://www.comp.lancs.ac.uk/sociology/papers/Law-And-if-The-Global-Were-Small.pdf. Accessed July 2005.

Lyotard, J.-F. (1984) *The Postmodern Condition: A report on knowledge* (Bennington, G. and Massumi, B. trans. (Manchester, Manchester University Press).

MacClancy, J. (1995) Brief Encounter: The meeting in Mass Observation of British surrealism and popular anthropology, *Journal of the Royal Anthropological Institute*, 1.3, pp. 495–512.

MacLure, M. (2003) *Discourse in Educational and Social Research* (Buckingham, Open University Press).

MacLure, M. (2005) 'Clarity Bordering on Stupidity': Where's the quality in systematic review?, *Journal of Education Policy*, 20.4, pp. 393–416.

MacLure, M. (forthcoming, 2006) Entertaining Doubts: On frivolity as resistance, in: J. Satterthwaite, W. Martin and L. Roberts (eds) *Discourse, Resistance and Identity Formation* (London, Trentham).

Nancy, J.-L. (1996) The Deleuzian Fold of Thought, in: P. Patton (ed.) *Deleuze. A Critical Reader* (Oxford, Blackwell).

Power, M. (1999) *The Audit Society: Rituals of verification* (Oxford, Oxford University Press).

Sayous, P. (nd) History of the Automaton http://www.automates-anciens.com/english_version/frames/english_frames.htm (Accessed September 2005.)

Schaffer, S. (1997) Babbage's Dancer. Hypermedia Research Centre, University of Westminster. http://www.hrc.wmin.ac.uk/theory-babbagesdancer4.html (Accessed September 2005.)

Scheurich, J. J. (2000) A RoUGH, ramBling, strAnGe, muDDy, CONfusing, e1LIPtical Kut: From an archaeology of plain talk, *Qualitative Inquiry*, 6.3, pp. 337–348.

Smith, R. (1995) *Derrida and Autobiography* (Cambridge, Cambridge University Press).

Spivak, G. C. (1976) Translator's Preface, in: J. Derrida (ed.) *Of Grammatology* (Baltimore, MD, Johns Hopkins).

Spiteri, R. and LaCoss, D. (eds) (2003) *Surrealism, Politics and Culture* (Aldershot and Burlington, Ashgate).

St. Pierre, E. A. (2000) The Call for Intelligibility in Postmodern Educational Research, *Educational Researcher*, June–July, pp. 25–28.

St. Pierre, E. A. and Pillow, W. (eds) (2000) *Working the Ruins: Feminist poststructural theory and methods in education* (New York, Routledge).

Stafford, B. (2001) Revealing Technologies/magical Domains, in: B. Stafford and F. Terpak (eds) *Devices of Wonder: From the World in a Box to Images on a Screen* (Los Angeles, CA, Getty Research Institute).

Standage, T. (2004) *The Mechanical Turk: The true story of the chess playing machine that fooled the world* (Harmondsworth, Penguin).

Strathern, M. (2000a) The Tyranny of Transparency, *British Educational Research Journal*, 26.3, pp. 309–201.

Strathern, M. (ed.) (2000b) *Audit Cultures: Studies in accountability, Ethics and the Academy* (London, Routledge).

Stronach, I. and MacLure, M. (1997) *Educational Research Undone: The postmodern embrace* (Milton Keynes, Open University Press).

Taussig, M. (1993) *Mimesis and Alterity* (London, Routledge).

Terpak, F. (2001) Objects and Contexts, in: B. M. Stafford and F. Terpak (ed.) *Devices of Wonder: From the world in a box to images on a screen* (Los Angeles, CA, Getty Publications).

Turner, B. (1994) Introduction, in: C. Buci-Glucksmann (ed.) *Baroque Reason: The Aesthetics of Modernity* (London, Sage).

Visweswaran, K. (1994) *Fictions of Feminist Ethnography* (Minneapolis, MN, University of Minnesota Press).

Zamora, L. P. (nd) *Trompe l'loeil* tricks: Borges' baroque illusionism. University of Houston: http://www.uh.edu/~englmi/BorgesBaroqueIllusionism/ (Accessed September 2005).

5
The Disciplines and Discipline of Educational Research

DAVID BRIDGES

FROM FOUNDATION DISCIPLINES TO POSTDISCIPLINARITY

The organisation of educational theory and research under the 'foundation' disciplines of the philosophy, sociology, psychology and history of education dominated the functioning of teacher education and of the educational research community in the UK and in many other parts of the English speaking world in the 1960s and through to the 1980s (see Tibble, 1966 for a classic example and Bridges, 2003 for a more detailed account of this period). For a while these foundation disciplines appeared to offer: *differentiation* between different kinds of enquiry (R. S. Peters had recently complained of the current condition of educational theory as 'undifferentiated mush'); *coherence* in terms of the internal consistency of any one of these forms; and the '*systematic*' or rigour of enquiry, which raised such enquiry above the level of popular or received opinion—the discipline of the discipline.

However, these foundation disciplines only ever provided provisional forms of coherence, temporary alliances, between what were often radically different traditions. The sociology of education, for example, contained everything from traditional hard data survey people through ethnographers, neo Marxists and critical theorists to postmodernists and social relativists. Psychology spanned neurophysiology, behaviourism, cognitivism and constructivism through to psychoanalysis. The ideological and methodological differences between these communities of scholars were at least as great as anything they might have in common. If philosophy of education retained for a while a slightly greater coherence in the UK around an analytic and Kantian tradition this was at the price of a period of virtual exclusion of some of the more extravagant alternatives available in continental Europe. Increasingly through the eighties and nineties these fault lines in the foundation disciplines became more evident and new, more segmented intellectual communities and practices emerged. New alliances were formed, as the links between some of these research practices were observed and built upon and new hybrids of research developed.

This diversification and hybridisation was encouraged too as the educational research community was enriched by people coming into it with a much wider repertoire of methodologies and informing theory, drawn from literary and cultural studies, ethnography, feminist and post colonial theory, etc., etc. The educational research community seems to have taken to heart Elliott Eisner's observation in his 1993 address to the American Educational Research Association:

> If there are different ways to understand the world, and if there are different forms that make such understanding possible, then it would seem to follow that any comprehensive effort to understand the processes and outcomes of schooling would profit from a pluralistic rather than a monolithic approach to research (Eisner, 1993, p. 8).

In the field of educational research the returns to the 2001 Research Assessment Exercise provided clear evidence of creativeness (or recklessness) in combining, crossing over or perhaps transgressing traditional disciplinary structures in a context of what some have described as 'post-disciplinarity'. Among, admittedly, the less conventional descriptions I noted: 'New Paradigm/heuristic/dialogic methods'; 'historical political sociology'; 'ideological history, curriculum and cultural theory'; 'social constructionism—socio-philosophical analysis'; and 'Narcissus myth and deconstruction'. (The full data set for these Research Assessment Exercise submissions is available on www.hefce.a-c.uk/rae and provides a fascinating insight into the diversity of practice in educational research in the UK.)

Not all of these developments necessarily challenge the idea that educational research is based on 'disciplined' enquiry. Commitment to a view of such enquiry as disciplined is entirely consistent with:

(i)   the desirability of drawing more fine grained distinctions between e.g. different kinds of psychological enquiry into human cognition or between the wide variety of different practices taking place under the umbrella of 'sociology'—this is more accurately to respect the principle of differentiation;

(ii) the drawing into the field of educational enquiry of a wider variety of disciplinary resources (e.g. from anthropology, literary studies, economic theory) whose relevance was previously neglected;

(iii) the combination of different disciplinary traditions in 'multi-disciplinary' or 'inter-disciplinary' enquiry to investigate a particular aspect of educational policy or practice.

These developments do indeed challenge the internal coherence of what were once presented as more or less monolithic disciplines (albeit ones with bitter internal disputes); they challenge the exclusive role of the four foundation disciplines; and they challenge their individual sufficiency. They do not, however, thus far necessarily challenge the requirement for such research to be 'systematic and sustained'; to have its own means (methods?) to assist us in examining ideas which are put forward and judging what confidence to place in them—to be disciplined.

The literature on postdisciplinarity in the humanities and social sciences offers different messages on the place of disciplines or discipline in contemporary research. Some sources appear to use reference to multi-disciplinarity, interdisciplinarity and postdisciplinarity interchangeably, though, as Menand rightly observes 'Interdisciplinarity is the institutional ratification of the logic of disciplinarity. The very term implies respect for the discrete perspectives of different disciplines. You can't have inter-disciplinarity, or multidisciplinarity, unless you have disciplines ... This is not the same phenomenon as postdisciplinarity' (Menand, 2001, p. 11).

Other sources are at pains to insist that the discourse of post-disciplinarity is consistent with continuing respect for the discipline of the discipline. The project is rather to add to what discipline-based enquiry can offer than to replace it. In an editorial introducing the journal *Human Affairs: A Postdisciplinary Journal for Humanities and Social Sciences* Visnovsky and Bianchi explained: 'Postdisciplinarity in our understanding does not mean that traditional disciplines have disappeared or indeed should disappear, but rather that they are changing and should change in order to solve complex issues of human affairs. It is not sufficient to approach such complex issues from any single discipline' (Visnovsky and Bianchi, 2002, p. 2). Giroux was at pains to stress that 'At issue here is neither ignoring the boundaries of discipline-based knowledge nor simply fusing different disciplines, but creating theoretical paradigms, questions and knowledge that cannot be taken up within the policed boundaries of the existing disciplines' (Giroux, 1997, xii). Similarly, 'The problem ... is how to construe and resituate the disciplines in a way that removes their effect as unnecessarily constraining foundational structures, while retaining the vitality of inquiry within them, so that the pursuit of knowledge is expanded, and the range of possibilities for what constitutes legitimate intellectual activity is broadened' (Mourad, 1997, p. 86; see also Smith, 2003).

Some, however, seem bent on the destruction of the disciplinary structure of academic life. When Michael Crow became President of Arizona State University he declared in his inaugural policy paper 'A New American University: The New Gold Standard' that: 'Knowledge does not fall within strict disciplinary categories ... The New American University encourages teaching and research that is interdisciplinary, multidisciplin-ary, transdisciplinary and postdisciplinary, leading, where appropriate, to a convergence of the disciplines, an approach that might more accurately described as intellectual fusion' (Crow, 2002, p. 2. Compare the mission statement of the Lancaster University Institute for Advanced Studies at: www.lancaster.ac.uk/ias/about/mission.htm).

I do not have space in this context to examine this expanding body of literature in detail. At the risk of oversimplification it seems to have a number of targets for critique or attack, and there are a number of these that I would not seek to defend. I am happy to acknowledge, for example, that the organisation of academic institutions into strongly bounded discipline-based departments can be an obstacle to fluid and imaginative intellectual endeavour (though most of the organisational alternatives have their problems too). Even when a university such as the University of East Anglia is founded on an organisational principle of interdisciplinarity, the interdisciplinary units themselves tend to establish new barriers to academic collaboration (e.g. between historians in the School of English and American Studies and those in European Studies) as well as new opportunities for collaboration.

I acknowledge, similarly, that the containment of research programmes within disciplinary boundaries, especially in fields such as education, which requires multiple approaches, is unhelpful (see Bridges, 2003 for illustrations of the role of the philosopher in interdisciplinary research environments).

I acknowledge that the view that any particular disciplinary structures are in some way 'essential' or ahistorical and unchanging is unsustainable. Any historical perspective on the evolution of human understanding can only confirm this evolutionary course. Phenix emphasised that: 'the concept of disciplines as species of knowledge is to be understood dynamically. The disciplines are not an array of fixed traditional ways of knowing that have been ordained at some special creation. They are structures of enquiry and understanding that emerge out of the continuous process of epistemic development' (Phenix, 1964, p. 49). The practice of one community of enquiry may become increasingly contested from within; distinctions within disciplinary frameworks become clearer and more significant; methods and methodologies more refined and new conversational communities established.

This view is also compatible with the idea that discipline and rule governed systems may emerge from practices of enquiry in which they are by no means clearly defined—Schön's 'swampy lowland' of research and practice (Schön, 1983, p. 42). Rule governed systems emerge out of research practice as well as being brought to it. Appignanesi and Garratt describe, for example, their experience of 'working without rules in order to find out the rules of what you've done' (Appignanesi and Garratt, 1995, p. 50). In *The Rise of the Network Society*, Manuel Castells writes of 'the self-organising character of nature and society' but adds: 'Not that there are no rules, but rules are created, and changed, in a relentless process of deliberate actions and unique interactions' (Castells, 2000, p. 74). My only qualification to the literature that describes the evolutionary character of epistemic communities is to warn that one can underestimate the continuities in these communities as well as their capacity for change (see Toulmin, 1972).

Finally, I share the view in some of the literature that to maintain that particular disciplinary structures are in some way reflections of the way reality is ordered is mistaken: rather they play a central role in the way in which we order our experience of reality or order reality itself.

It is not, however, the disciplines as forms of academic organisation that I want to protect (though such organisation just may prove contingently important) but the discipline that they provide to intellectual enquiry. The notion of post-disciplinarity in educational research worries me in so far as it suggests that educational research cannot any longer be thought of as having any discipline. It is worrying because the loss of 'discipline' has two huge consequences. The first is that it totally undermines the basis of the special claim of educational research on our or anyone else's attention; the second is that it renders meaningful conversation within communities of arguers impossible. Let me explain these two consequences more fully.

'SYSTEMATIC AND SUSTAINED ENQUIRY MADE PUBLIC'

Why should we give attention to something claiming to be research? Why, more particularly should we perhaps give it special attention in comparison to e.g. popular belief, rumour, individual opinion or the latest newspaper story? What are the features of research which merit particular credence? The answer has to lie in the particular features of some kinds of enquiry—ones which satisfy the conditions that earn it its status as 'research'—over others. Research is in this sense I think an honorific concept that incorporates certain normative features. Peters and White suggested that the term research in academic communities was used to refer to 'systematic and sustained enquiry carried out by people well versed in some form of thinking in order to answer some specific type of question' (Peters and White, 1969, p. 2). They contrasted this with a broader definition employed by Mace who in his *Psychology of Study* maintained that 'research is, after all, just "search", looking for answers to questions and for solutions to problems' (quoted in Peters and White, 1969, p. 2). Stenhouse took up two of Peters' and White's characteristics and added a third, so that research was defined as 'systematic and sustained enquiry made public' (Stenhouse, 1980).

The requirement that research is *sustained* enquiry draws attention to its seriousness of commitment and has incidentally implications for the intellectual virtues of patience, industriousness, thoroughness and care which it calls into service. But it is the requirement that research is *systematic* which is of particular relevance here. What might this mean? What is the 'system' in enquiry that deserves to be honoured as research?

First there is a fairly ordinary way in which we might talk about enquiry as systematic. Research can be contrasted with other forms of more casual enquiry which may make no demands on the enquirer to have concern for e.g. the comprehensiveness or representativeness of the information collected; the orderliness with which information is collected or stored; the thoroughness of the search; the care and accuracy with which information is translated, transferred or transcribed. Research calls all of these principles into play.

But, secondly, 'systematic' carries suggestions of a system of enquiry, of rule governed activity which embodies requirements about the relationship between evidence, analysis and interpretation; about the way in which inferences are drawn; about the ways in which the results of new enquiry may or may not confirm or refute previous sets of beliefs; about the kinds of claims which particular kinds of evidence or argument can support; and about the level of confidence with which they entitle one to hold certain beliefs. Even in our personal systems of beliefs we dispense with such 'systems', such rules, at some peril; but the notion of research picks out enquiry in which respect for such rules and systems and the discipline that they impose on the enquiry is a *sine qua non*. It is these that merit its honouring as research or, in the sense in which the French use the term, its claims to be '*scientifique*'.

The reason why we might give special attention to research—and urge others to do likewise—lies, on this view, in its claims (i) to be based on sustained enquiry; (ii) to be enquiry characterised by the qualities of care and thoroughness contained in the everyday sense of the systematic; and (iii) in its claims to be systematic in this slightly more technical sense of a rule governed system of enquiry. Such rule government constitutes the discipline of the form of enquiry—and when such discipline is sufficiently well developed and differentiated it enables us to refer to the system as a discipline. Discipline may of course be applied more or less rigorously or vigorously. On the whole in academic circles beliefs are seen to be more deserving of our belief to the extent that they are derived from enquiries that have been conducted with greater rigour. So there is a connection between these considerations of enquiry as systematic, disciplined and rigorous and considerations to do with the quality of the research (though this does not mean that these are the only relevant criteria of quality).

The argument goes further however. For though research may require periods of isolated and individual study, it rests essentially on and in communities of enquirers, and such communities owe their identity to 'commonly understood norms of enquiry' (Shulman 1999, p. 164), a shared discourse, shared discipline, shared 'systematics'. As Hunt argues, 'the discipline of a discipline, by which I mean the rules of conduct governing argument within a discipline, does have a worthy function. Such rules make a community of arguers possible' (Hunt, 1991, p. 104). The conditions for both the production and validation of research require communities of arguers, enquirers and critics—and a condition for the possibility of such communities of arguers is their sharing in a common language and their shared recognition and reference to some common rules of (in this case) intellectual and creative behaviour. Popkewitz emphasises the importance of these rules, not only in allowing communication and argument but also in developing 'standards of enquiry': 'Research exists within communities of discourse which maintain and develop standards of enquiry ... Scientific communities involve commitments to certain lines of reasoning and premises for certifying knowledge. Each scientific field has particular constellations of questions, methods and procedures. These constellations provide shared ways of "seeing" the world, of working, of testing each others' beliefs' (Popkewitz, 1984, pp. 2–3). McCarthy (1982) articulates a Habermasian view of both the epistemological and social conditions for such communities of arguers:

> Communication that is oriented towards reaching understanding inevitably involves reciprocal raising and recognition of validity claims. Claims to truth and rightness, if radically challenged, can be redeemed only through argumentative discourse leading to rationally motivated consensus. Universal-pragmatic analysis of the conditions of discourse and rational consensus show these to rest on the supposition of an 'ideal speech situation' characterised by an effective equality of chances to assume dialogue roles (McCarthy, 1982, pp. 255–6).

The rules that I refer to and the intellectual, moral and institutional props which maintain them, constitute the discipline of the discipline, of the tradition of thought and representation with which they are associated. It is in this sense that I suggest that discipline is a *sine qua non* of research. 'Disciplines,' argues Lenoir with perhaps surprising lack of qualification in a sociological analysis, 'are *essential* structures for systematising, organizing, and embodying the social and institutional practices upon which both coherent discourse and legitimate exercise of power depend' (Lenoir, 1993, p. 73, my italics).

RESEARCH AS A RULE GOVERNED ACTIVITY

It is a common feature of human rule governed practices that the rules are inexplicit, uncodified, tacitly understood. There is no rulebook. Epistemologically functional rules (e.g. governing the relationship between specific cases and general theories) may easily get blurred with social conventions attached to a discipline (e.g. regarding the use or non use of the first person in research reports). They tend to become more explicit when they are transgressed and critics point to the transgression. Eisner argued that: 'When research methods are stable and canonized, the rules of the game are relatively clear. With new games, new rules' (Eisner, 1993, p. 8). I tend to think that it works almost the other way round. The more firmly established a discipline the less explicit is people's awareness of its rules. It is in the formation and development of new patterns of enquiry that people are especially aware of what is distinctive about it. It goes with my acknowledgement of the diversity of the intellectual resources that are today brought to the field of educational research that there are some significantly different rule governed systems in play. But let me at least illustrate the sort of rules that I have in mind—i.e. the kind of rules that shape the shared meaning and understanding that underpins research enquiry and its claims on our credibility.

1. *Rules that link the methods appropriate to the research task or conclusion to particular ontologies and epistemologies and hence shape the character of the truth claims*—so for example someone who employed or offered three case studies as an attempt to answer a

question about the scale of pupil disaffection in a given country would have made a kind of category mistake. Equally, someone offering a set of statistical tables in answer to a question about students' experience of disaffection may (perhaps less obviously) have done the same.

2. *Rules that shape the way in which appropriate inferences can be drawn from the evidence or indicate the impossibility of such inferences.* Part of what defines a disciplined form of enquiry are the rules which govern the movement (or lack of it) between evidence/ data and analysis, generalization, theory building. Examples would include the level of probability one could extract from an analysis of statistical correlations or the kind of movement one might make (or not make) from an individual case study to e.g. grounded theory or general policy.

3. *Rules that indicate what are the analytic and explanatory concepts appropriate to the research task and evidence*—understanding (and reflecting in one's research) e.g. an appropriate perspective on the ways in which questions to do with how certain educational goods are distributed; questions of whether or not such distribution is fair; questions to do with the role of capitalism in shaping this distribution and questions of God's will with respect to such distribution may or may not be distinguished and inter-related. This is not to suppose that these questions are simply resolved or resolvable: it is rather to make the point that part of the discipline of educational enquiry and part of what constitutes the shared understanding of different elements within that community consists in either having a view of this relationship or in sharing a language in which different views of this relationship can be intelligently explored.

Schwab drew these three types of rules together into what he referred to as the 'syntactical structure' of each discipline:

> There is, then, the problem of determining for each discipline what it does by way of discovery and proof, what criteria it uses for measuring the quality of its data, how strictly it can apply its canons of evidence, and, in general, to determine the pathway by which the discipline moves from its raw data to its conclusion. This cluster of problems I shall call the problem of the *syntactical structure* of each discipline (Schwab, 1964, p. 11).

It is the elements of this 'syntactical structure' that provide the rules or systematic nature—the discipline—of a discipline. In principle at least, it is the discipline in research that renders its outcomes especially worthy of our attention and credulity.

This last claim is especially important. The rules that go at least partly to constitute a discipline have a purpose, which is to contribute to the greater illumination and understanding of different aspects of our experience and our world. Phenix asks: 'How ... can we be sure that the concept of a discipline is definite and significant enough to serve as a basis for the organization of knowledge? The answer,' says Phenix, 'is empirical and pragmatic: disciplines prove themselves by their productiveness. They are the visible evidence of ways of thinking that have proven fruitful. They have arisen by the use of concepts and methods that have generative power' (Phenix, 1964, p. 48). There is, perhaps, the risk of either a certain circularity in this position or of an internal contradiction. If we can know the value of beliefs (generated by the disciplines) 'empirically and pragmatically' then presumably we do not need the disciplines as means of discriminating the wheat from the chaff of belief. Alternatively, if it is through the disciplines (alone) that we can distinguish the wheat from the chaff of belief, then we cannot determine their value 'empirically and pragmatically'. Phenix, however, places the onus on the creative function of disciplines as generators of ideas, which could go some way to get round this problem.

Such rule-governed systems are not necessarily obstacles to innovation or creativity. Popkewitz stresses the paradoxical way in which these rule governed systems provide, nevertheless, the conditions for challenge, creativity and dissent: 'Science exists in the preparedness of individuals to think up, explore and criticise new concepts, techniques of representation, and arguments . . . While it may seem paradoxical, the procedures, norms and interactions of the scientific community maintain a form of anarchy which encourages individual creativity' (Popkewitz, 1984, pp. 3 and 6). Such controversy sometimes confronts us with seemingly intractable problems of jurisdiction. Where are the rules or seats of adjudication that enable us to decide between contesting views? Meta-discourses such as philosophy and history provide a resource for such argumentation up to a point, but I do not claim that they can always offer a resolution— especially when they are themselves at the centre of the controversy. Writing with respect to controversy around the rules governing historical enquiry, Spitzer argues that, 'stories about the past will continue to command our assent when they proceed from shared assumptions as to relevant evidence, legitimate inference, and coherent logic. We cannot validate these standards by appealing to them, but there is no need to validate them if the parties to the conversation share them' (Spitzer, 1996, pp. 120–121). Spitzer adopts an interesting and persuasive approach to the question of veridicality in history by examining a number of case studies of debates around attempts at historical deception—and observes the standards to which all parties to these debates are appealing. He concludes 'this is to say not that we can stipulate the universal standards of historical truth but that we can identify the specific standards that are assumed to legitimate a given claim' (Spitzer, 1996, p. 12).

All this movement is, nevertheless, movement around a notion in which the idea of a set of rule governed practices in a community with at least some basis of a shared discourse is pivotal and indispensable. In this sense educational research may fruitfully and creatively reach out to the wealth of intellectual and representational resources available to it inside and outside the academy, but to do so is to grasp and to apply the particular discipline which characterises any of these traditions and whose rigorous application renders their products worthy of greater attention and more confident belief.

To address a possible criticism from a different standpoint, however, neither any conversational community, nor even any rule governed conversation constitutes a discipline for the purposes of educational or any other kind of research. The conversation and the rules have to be constructed in some sense on the basis of their functionality in stronger rather than weaker warrant for belief (or disbelief). A conversation aimed at demonstrating mutual admiration or affection, asserting dominance or achieving reconciliation may be rule governed at least in the anthropological sense or in terms of linguistic moves—it may in this sense be 'disciplined'—but it only becomes disciplined in the academic and epistemological sense of the term if it is constructed to serve this epistemological purpose. It may, as sociologists of knowledge often point out, serve other social functions ('privileging' particular individuals or communities, reinforcing particular social hierarchies) and the need may arise to address these social consequences, but these should not entirely distract attention from the matter of whether or not it does indeed serve its epistemological purpose.

DISCIPLINE AS AN OBSTACLE TO ENQUIRY?

This pragmatic principle of whether or not particular rule governed demands on a conversational community serve their epistemological purpose is a critical one. Rules, of course, both open up possibilities (e.g. enabling the social processes that produce meaning) and close them down e.g. by disallowing discursive forms which do not conform but which may nevertheless have the potential to reveal something interesting. Foucault writes of discourse as 'a stumbling block, a point of resistance and a starting point for an opposing strategy' (Foucault, 1982, p. 101). Stephen Ball explains: 'Discourses constrain the possibilities of thought. They order and combine words in particular ways and exclude or displace other combinations. However, in so far as discourses are constituted by exclusions as well as inclusions, by what cannot be said as well as what can be said, they stand in antagonistic relations to other discourses, other possibilities of meaning, other claims, rights and positions' (Ball, 1990, p. 2).

The notion of 'discourse' that is employed here is in many ways a more substantive one than 'discipline' as I am employing it. I have in mind a system which is primarily procedural, methodological and which frames the form of an enquiry rather than its content. 'Discourse' usually indicates something more heavily ideological characterised by theories and concepts which come to frame how people think about e.g. educational practice—notions like 'educationally disadvantaged'; 'special needs'; 'giftedness'; 'marketisation'; 'inclusive education'; 'under achievement' and their attendant ideological and theoretical baggage. In so far as it is part of the neo-Foucaultian project to examine critically the genealogy of these ideas, the power relations that they serve and the subtle ways in which they support e.g. docility and self-policing compliance under particular regimes, then this presents no threat to the notion of discipline as I have articulated it. Indeed this critical activity might, I assume, require its own discipline if it is to be conducted rigorously and successfully. 'Discourse analysis' has its own place among the range of contemporary disciplined practices in social science and, more narrowly, educational research.

No one imagines the disciplined pursuit of knowledge and understanding to be entirely free from entanglement with structures designed or developed to maintain and legitimate certain orders of power. This is precisely why its more sophisticated practitioners seek to operate under conditions which reduce these influence to a minimum e.g. by defending the autonomy of their institutions against political interference or fighting off institutional attempts to suppress research which might be damaging to the interests of the institution itself; by submitting to ethical codes which govern their rights in relation to the powerful and their obligations in their relations with the weak; by submitting to methodological and epistemological requirements which force critique of their taken-for-granted assumptions, expose the ideological underpinnings of their work and enable non-participants to challenge structural bias in the enquiry or in its conclusions.

In his classic study of the inter-relationships between the social and epistemological practices of 'academic tribes' Becher argues—and evidences on the basis of his empirical work—the claim that 'the ways in which particular groups of academics organise their professional lives are intimately related to the intellectual tasks on which they are engaged. In practice,' he acknowledges, 'the two would seem to be inseparably intertwined; but in attempting to explore the characteristic features of the relationship it is necessary to separate the first analytically from the second' (Becher, 1989, p. 1). Importantly he goes on to describe the way in which epistemological considerations come to drive social and cultural relationships rather than vice versa: 'It is crucial to my argument that, once such a field (of enquiry) becomes identified in terms of certain characteristics ... a whole set of properties inherent in that identification come into play—properties which can profoundly affect the way of life of those engaged in the exploration of the field. *The cultural consequences in these instances have to be seen as closely derived from epistemological considerations*' (ibid, p. 4—my italics).

One response to all this (and perhaps this is the Foucaultian response) is to say that any attempt to separate the epistemic from the political is in vain. Each attempt to escape from or find a position outside the power-knowledge nexus is doomed to fail. One perhaps rather waspish reply to this is to ask what, then, is the point of Foucault's own writing and the intellectual industry that this itself has spawned? Is this not in some sense contributing to our illumination of the conditions under which we engage in our different discourses and of the limitations and dangers which lie in them? Foucault himself would suggest that this is the case:

'Power-knowledge ... is not for me the fundamental problem but an instrument allowing the analysis—in a way which seems to me to be the most exact—of the problem of the relationship between subject and games of truth' (from a 1988 interview cited by Marshall, 1990, p. 23). More sympathetic, however, is the reply that the relationship between intellectual enquiry in its 'disciplined' forms and structures of power is an interminable wrestling match. We can observe over time both (i) challenges to our systems of enquiry by those observing the ways in which these become distorted by structures of power and (ii) challenges to those systems of power and the constructions of the natural and social world they support by those vigorous in deploying forms of enquiry—enquiry which can illuminate both the operation of those 'knowledge-power' systems and the world over which they seek to exercise control. Of course, this last possibility could be a complete conceit, but it is a conceit which stands alongside the possibility that I am alone in the universe or that all my thoughts and actions are pre-determined: it is equally intriguing but provides no basis for the way in which one might actually conduct one's life or that small part of it which is occupied with educational enquiry and research.

CONCLUSION

The last twenty-five years have seen a huge and bewildering enlargement in the intellectual resources from which educational researchers have drawn. They have also seen a preoccupation with the *diversification* of method perhaps over the *development* of method in ways that strengthen its capacity to contribute to the epistemological project that it serves. Developing and refining the discipline of any form of enquiry must surely be a central concern for any research community in so far as this is a project which has to do with (i) *understanding* the credibility and illumination that are associated with the beliefs that issue from the research and (ii) *enhancing* the credibility that we are entitled to attach to the beliefs that issue from the research. So also must the cultivation among novices to the rigours of such enquiry of the understanding, skill and virtue that it demands.[1] For Kuhn (1977) intellectual progress requires a context in which there is relatively close agreement on theories, methods of enquiry and the requirements for the initiation of newcomers into the discipline. Where there is the kind of pluralism and dissension that characterises science discourses and more specifically educational research, 'systematic advances in knowledge' as Becher puts it, 'must await the onset of maturity and the emergence of a developed paradigm' (Becher, 1989, p. 10). The educational research community has taken on board in the last twenty-five years a rich repertoire of forms of enquiry and representation. Perhaps in the next phase of the development of educational enquiry, we should focus on understanding and refining the conditions—the discipline—under which these are conducted.

I may, of course, have reached the wrong conclusion from my own argument, so let me return to the simplest statement of the issue that I have been trying to address to assist in its refutation. The claim of enquiry which is honoured as research is that there are features of the conduct of the enquiry which ought to command greater confidence in the beliefs which issue from it than would be expected, other things being equal, from enquiry which lacked these features.[2] I refer to these features at different times as the 'systematics', the 'rule governed systems' and the 'disciplines' of educational enquiry. Is this right? If not, what construction are we to put on whatever is going on in educational research? And if it is, should we not be seeking their functional and qualitative improvement rather than their displacement?

NOTES

1. The notion that initiation into a research community consists simply in training in methods and techniques seems to me to be a severely limited one. Underlying all this is the cultivation of, among other things, intellectual virtue.
2. Having greater confidence in what *not* to believe is in my terms included in this aspiration.

REFERENCES

Appignanesi, R. and Garratt, C. (1995) *Post-modernism for Beginners* (Cambridge, Icon Books).

Ball, S. J. (1990) Introducing Monsieur Foucault, in: S. J. Ball (ed.) *Foucault and Education: Disciplines and knowledge* (London, Routledge), pp. 1–8.

Becher, T. (1989) *Academic Tribes and Territories: Intellectual enquiry and the culture of disciplines* (Milton Keynes, SRHE and the Open University Press).

Bridges, D. (2003) *Fiction Written Under Oath? Essay in philosophy and educational research* (Dordrecht, Kluwer).

Bridges, D (2003) Six Stories in Search of a Character? 'The philosopher' in an educational research group, in P. Smeyers and M. Depaepe (eds) *Beyond Empiricism: On criteria for educational research* (Leuven, Leuven University Press).

Castells, M. (2000) *The Rise of the Network Society, Volume I: The rise of the network society*, 2nd edn. (Malden and Oxford, Blackwell).

Crow, M. (2002) A New American University: The new gold standard (Arizona State University at www.asu.edu/president/library/whitepapers/designimperatives.doc).

Eisner, E. (1993) Forms of Understanding and the Future of Research, *Educational Researcher*, 22.7, pp. 5–11.

Foucault, M. (1982) The Subject and Power, in: H. L. Dreyfus and P. Rabinow (eds) *Michel Foucault: Beyond structuralism and hermenuetics* (Brighton, Harvester Press).

Giroux, H. (1997) Series Forward, in: R. P. Mourad, *Postmodern Philosophical Critique and the Pursuit of Knowledge in Higher Education* (Westport, CT and London, Bergin and Garvey).

Hunt, L. History as Gesture; or the scandal of history, in: J. Arac and B. Johnston (eds) *Consequences of Theory* (Baltimore, Johns Hopkins University Press).

Lancaster University Institute for Advanced Studies (2005 downloaded) Mission of the Institute of Advanced Studies at www.lancaster.ac.uk/ias/about/mission.htm

Kuhn, T. (1977) *The Essential Tension* (Chicago, University of Chicago Press).

Lenoir, T. (1993) The Discipline of Nature and the Nature of Disciplines, in: E. Messer-Davidow and D. R. Shumway (eds) , *Knowledges: Historical and critical studies of disciplinarity* (Charlottesville, VA, University Press of Virginia), pp. 70–102.

Marshall, J. D. (1990) Foucault and Educational Research, in: S. J. Ball (ed.) Foucault and Education: Disciplines and knowledge (London, Routledge), pp. 11–28.

McCarthy, T. (1982) Rationality and Relativism, in: J. B. Thompson and D. Held (eds) *Habermas—Critical Debates* (London, Macmillan).

Menand, L. (2001) *The Marketplace of Ideas* (American Council of Learned Societies: Occasional Paper no. 49).

Mourad, R. P. (1997) *Postmodern Philosophical Critique and the Pursuit of Knowledge in Higher Education* (Westport, CT and London, Bergin and Garvey).

Peters, R. S. and White, J. P. (1969) The Philosopher's Contribution to Educational Research, *Educational Philosophy and Theory*, 1, pp. 1–15.

Phenix, P. (1964) The Architectonics of Knowledge, in: S. Elam (ed.) *Education and the Structure of Knowledge* (Chicago, IL, Rand McNally).

Popkewitz, T. S. (1984) *Paradigm and Ideology in Educational Research: The social functions of the intellectual* (London and New York, Falmer).

Powell, A. G. (1980) *The Uncertain Profession: Harvard and the search for educational authority* (Cambridge MA, Harvard University Press).

Schön, D. (1983) *The Reflective Practitioner* (New York, Basic Books).

Schwab, J. J. (1964) Problems, Topics and Issues, in: S. Elam (ed.) *Education and the Structure of Knowledge* (Chicago, IL, Rand McNally).

Shulman, L. (1999) Professing Educational Research, in: E. Lageman and L. Shulman (eds) *Issues in Educational Research: Problems and possibilities* (San Francisco, Jossey and Bass), pp. 159–165.

Sizer, T. R. and Powell, A. G. (1969) Changing Conceptions of the Professor of Education, in: J. S. Counelis (ed.) *To Be a Phoenix: the education professoriate* (Bloomington. IN, Phi Delta Kappa) chapter 3.

Smith, M. J. (2003) *Producing and Consuming Knowledge: The relevance of the 'new production of knowledge debate' for disciplinary and transdisciplinary social science* at www.sspp.us/protected-essays/2003-SPEP-Smith.doc

Spitzer, A. B. (1996) *Historical Truth and Lies About the Past: Reflections on Dewey, Dreyfus, De Man and Regan* (Chapel Hill, NC, University of North Carolina Press).

Stenhouse, L. (1980) *What Counts as Research?* Unpublished mimeo, CARE Archive, University of East Anglia.

Tibble, J. W. (ed.) (1966) *The Study of Education* (London, Routledge and Kegan Paul).

Toulmin, S. (1972) *Human Understanding*, Volume 1 (Oxford, Clarendon Press).

Visnovsky, E. and Bianchi, G. (2002) Editorial, *Human Affairs*, vol. 12.

Wilson, J. (1972) *Philosophy and Educational Research* (Slough, National Foundation for Educational Research).

Woods, R. G. (1971) *Education and its Disciplines* (London, University of London Press).

6
Consistency, Understanding and Truth in Educational Research

ANDREW DAVIS

INTRODUCTION

In 1992 Elliot Eisner published a paper about objectivity in educational research. He was especially concerned with the difficulties he took to be inherent in what he called 'ontological objectivity', linking this to 'seeing things as they are' and to the correspondence theory of truth. He wished researchers to countenance a greater variety of modes of inquiry than those 'for which a literal conception of truth is a relevant criterion' (Eisner, 1992, p. 14). He reminded us of the kinds of truth available in novels, history and anthropology, which depend on interpretations, and referred to these as 'literally fictions—things made' (ibid.). He felt that at least some educational research should aspire to truth of this kind. Moreover, Eisner is well known for comparing teaching to an art rather than a science. Robin Alexander comments that 'If it is an art, it makes sense to apply, as did Eisner, the procedures and criteria of artistic appraisal' (Alexander, 2000, p. 275).

This chapter explores some of the philosophical issues provoked by comparing aspects of educational research with the arts. In particular it examines whether the links between *consistency*, on the one hand, and truth and significance, on the other, may be challenged if legitimate analogies between qualitative educational research claims and arts appraisals may be drawn.[1] In the final section I proceed to examine potential parallels between value judgments in the arts and assessing the worth of educational research itself.

Qualitative educational research involving interpretations of classroom interactions or student achievements provides the context for my explorations. It is frequently the case that several researchers will scrutinise the same social event and reach verdicts about what is taking place or has been achieved. Eisner seems to have sought validation of qualitative research claims of this kind in terms of *agreement*. He characterises 'consensual validation' as 'agreement among competent others that the description, interpretation, evaluation and thematics of an education situation are right' (Eisner, 1991, p. 112). One way of achieving this, not be supported by Eisner himself, would be by adopting what he calls 'procedural objectivity'—that is, 'using a method that eliminates, or aspires to eliminate, the scope for personal judgment' (Eisner, 1992, p. 10). However I want to ask whether consensual validation is a necessary condition for the legitimacy of interpretations of social phenomena in qualitative research.

Unlike Eisner with his reference to 'fiction' I attempt to retain a hold on realism. He comments that 'Different ways of seeing give us different worlds' and that 'Different ways of saying allow us to represent different worlds' (Eisner, 1992). What Eisner 'really meant' is beyond the scope of this chapter and does not affect my argument here. *If* he meant to deny that there is a reality out there that exists independently of us, and to assert that people with different ways of seeing are literally in different worlds, then I am assuming that this is simply nonsense. We all inhabit the same world, though undoubtedly our interpretations of it are inescapably structured by our concepts and cultures. We can avoid the positivist dream of just one way of seeing the world as it 'really is' without descending into relativist confusions.

For the purposes of this discussion, and possibly for *any* purposes it is futile to attempt to *define* qualitative research. The activities it covers certainly do not form a natural class. They include ethnographic studies, thick descriptions in the manner of Clifford Geertz (for example, Geertz, 1973), grounded theory, applications of interpretive social science, exercises in connoisseurship and narrative and hermeneutic approaches. (In listing these separately I am not implying that each of them constitutes separable and distinct paradigms—many familiar examples of educational research will fall under more than one of these descriptions.)

Qualitative research typically concerns itself with description and explanation within the framework of 'folk psychology'. People act intentionally, they are motivated, they act or refrain from acting for reasons, they behave rationally or irrationally and they act or fail to act on their desires. Groups may act in concert; they may unite behind a leader, act together in a rational manner or the reverse, and so on. The context for each individual's behaviour is a complex set of interrelated beliefs, some of which are true and justified and hence amount to knowledge. Moreover actions and language have identity and meaning partly because of the sets of social practices in which agents and speakers are embedded. This has the familiar consequence that many categories applied to human behaviour and social phenomena differ radically from the 'natural kinds' prevalent in the traditional sciences. The characterisations of behaviour reflect both features of that behaviour and how it is situated in its social and cultural environment (see Davis, 2005a and 2005b).

Educational research invariably includes both elements of qualitative and non-qualitative inquiry. For example Maria Goulding, Tim Rowland and Patti Barber (2002) report that 56% percent of students successfully answered a certain question about ordering decimals in a test of mathematical subject knowledge. Anyone following the procedures adopted by the writers of this chapter and checking the students' answers to the decimal question should also produce a figure of 56%. If not, and failing easy explanations in terms of temporary errors, for instance, then interest in the figure of 56% would rapidly diminish. It seems to be a straightforward result of quantitative research. Test success is inevitably linked *indirectly* to human behaviour as the subject of folk psychology, but little or no interpretation of such behaviour is required for the production of this figure. The same article offers reports about human thought and action featuring richness, complexity and significant elements of interpretation. Just one example is a judgment about learners: 'problems with fractions, algebraic symbolism and proof were very clear and occasionally accompanied by expressions of inadequacy, fear and even panic'. It is with such reports that much of the following discussion is concerned.

Before proceeding, it is important to note that qualitative researchers of a realist temper may well not welcome my approach. Typical expressions of their views include the following: 'Results are understood to be substantiated where different perspectives converge so that triangulation becomes a process of mutual conformation … The implication is that convergence provides evidence of accuracy and objectivity' (Madill, Jordan and Shirley, 2000, p. 3). Now I readily concede that in many cases such triangulation is a sound procedure and one that deservedly inspires confidence in its results. However, to repeat, I want to investigate whether convergence is a *necessary condition* of accuracy and objectivity in all forms of qualitative research.

Consistency is very obviously a necessary condition for truth and significance in some fundamental domains of inquiry. In natural sciences such as physics and chemistry results must be replicable. If not, they are discredited, or an explanation is required within the terms of the relevant scientific theory to account for the anomaly. If a scientist wants to say something true and objective about the size of a planetary body, the velocity of an object, the voltage in a wire or what happens when iron filings are added to sulphuric acid then it should be clear how the claims are verified. Anyone with the relevant skills, resources and instruments should be able to test the claims and come up with the same results. It is true that scientists are usually concerned with consistency when researching events of the *same kind* rather than consistency of verdicts between researchers investigating one specific event. However, consistency of the former type entails consistency of the latter type. (Kuhn and Feyerabend apparently felt that it was impossible to compare claims made in later scientific theories with those made in earlier theories but for the purpose of the present discussion this complication can be put to one side.)

To sum up: in natural sciences, if consistency, reliability and replicability are not to be had then the results of the so-called research may be safely ignored.

INCONSISTENCY AND AESTHETIC JUDGMENTS

In the history of philosophical debate about values the claim that normative judgements are 'mere' expressions of feeling has been powerfully argued. David Hume is just one representative of this tradition. Those holding that we project our sentiments on a world whose fabric lacks value in principle may take disagreement to be a symptom of this fact. 'If moral facts were reports of "objective" states of affairs, then we should expect in morality the breadth of convergence that emerges in some of the more rigorous empirical and theoretical disciplines' (Shaper-Landau, 1994, p. 331). Note that disagreement is not a *necessary condition* of the validity of Hume's approach to value since socialisation would sometimes constrain the diversity of opinions.

Clearly there are widespread disagreements between those appraising works of art, compositions, musical performances, dance, poetry, drama and novels. A quick response would be to insist that judgments about beauty, elegance, grace and so forth are 'merely' reflections of feelings. This would be to deny the very legitimacy of Kant's 'judgements of taste' that aspire to universal validity:

> he says that the thing is beautiful; and it is not as if he counts on others agreeing with him in his judgment of liking owing to his having found them in such agreement on a number of occasions, but he demands this agreement of them. He blames them if they judge differently, and denies them taste, which he still requires of them as something they ought to have; and to this extent it is not open to men to say: Every one has his own taste. This would be equivalent to saying that there is no such thing as taste, i.e. no aesthetic judgment capable of making a rightful claim upon the assent of all men (Kant, 1928, p. 52).

Now we could simply accept that we are concerned here with subjective responses. Yet we still might contend that the very existence of a range of feelings is important. Would such a contention have any force in selected qualitative educational research contexts?

Suppose educational research involves assessing teaching quality. Goulding *et al.* describe a student teacher as 'experienced a disabling tension between her own pedagogical knowledge, beliefs and practices and those of the class teacher' on her first practice. Later in the course she is reported to be able 'to clarify her own understanding from first principles and identify and build upon the significant points in children's progression' (Goulding *et al.*, 2002, p. 700). It is not clear from the article whether these verdicts were reached by more than one assessor—and for my purposes this is of no consequence. Imagine, simply for the sake of argument, that for research purposes it is held to be *essential* that a reasonable level of consistency between different assessors is achieved. Suppose our assessors of teaching quality to have appropriate levels of subject knowledge and professional experience. If the researchers collaborate over a period of time a reasonable consensus on verdicts should be perfectly possible, and indeed this is a matter of common experience. Yet given the criteria concerned, should we not *expect* a range of verdicts about at least *some* aspects of the teaching performances concerned? For opinions will incorporate normative and interpretive components. Of course, a proportion of the disagreement will stem from everyday human failings such as fatigue, irrational hatred of the clothes worn by the student teacher or his regional accent. But in addition some assessors will differ in their reactions *to his performance as such* and that should not be ignored, or so it might be argued.

However, this is a weak response. It concedes the subjective character of the inconsistent verdicts yet asserts the significance of the appraisers' feelings. I suggest that few would take this seriously. Educational research cannot be credited with significance merely on the basis of professionals' subjective reactions to classroom interactions, however well-informed.

A stronger rejoinder to the crudely subjectivist version of aesthetic judgments floated at the start of this section would point up the complexity and richness of aesthetic disputes. A disagreement about whether a mathematical proof is 'elegant' might stem from differing views of proof itself—one assessor favouring an algebraic approach while another took especial delight in the use of visual representations of various kinds. A range of verdicts about whether the performance of a baroque violin sonata was 'expressive' might reflect a diversity of approaches to the 'meaning' of the piece—one assessor paying much attention to the composer's intentions as far as these could be determined, another attempting to interpret the piece in the context of the particular cultural setting in which it first emerged while yet another focused on the music as a conveyer of meaning to the listener in the twenty-first century. This scenario does not assume that aesthetic appraisals fall neatly into just one of these three categories, nor that the categories exhaust the possibilities. Many appraisers will draw on complex hybrids of these and other approaches. It simply illustrates potential sources of inconsistency.

Scruton (1997) explains one aspect of the complexities inherent in aesthetic judgment in terms of 'aspect perception', an idea he attributes to Wollheim (1987) who calls it 'representational seeing'. When we see one thing in another, such as seeing a face in a picture (which itself is not a picture *of* a face), we have an instance of such aspect perception. Sometimes we entertain the idea that there is, for instance, a man in a picture—we need not be thinking that there is a man there; we may be restricted to an imaginative involvement. In his discussion Scruton refers to ambiguous figures; many readers will associate these with Wittgenstein's treatment of 'seeing as' in *Philosophical Investigations* and his examples of the schematic cube and the duck-rabbit (Wittgenstein, 1958).

Suppose we accept, at least for the sake of argument, that there are possibilities for inconsistency within the field of aesthetic appraisal that are *not* necessarily linked to the 'merely subjective'. Is it plausible to suggest that analogous sources of inconsistency may be found in the interpretive contexts often figuring in educational research? 'Aspect perception' seems a rich and powerful idea to play with in this connection. The 'thick descriptions' to be found in some ethnographic research and the narratives offered about classroom events capture aspects of the relevant phenomena in such a way that sometimes more than one 'story' seems appropriate and even 'true'. I now consider a possible example from Alexander (2000).

Alexander analyses lessons across five countries in many ways, including the elusive feature of 'pace'. Given the complexity of this notion, different observers might well conflict in their judgments about whether a particular lesson features it. Alexander's solution (not that he thought of it in this way) is to offer *five* aspects of pace, characterised as organisational pace, task pace, interactive pace, cognitive or semantic pace and learning pace. It might be thought that this sophisticated analysis could facilitate agreement between different interpreters of a given lesson. Yet Alexander is aware that judgments about these different types of pace need to be referenced to the objectives of the teacher and to the kind of classroom control sought, among other things. Some aspects of pace can be in tension with others. For instance, he identifies a lesson where achieving a desirable pace of exchanges between pupils was not wholly consistent with covering conceptual ground at a good pace.

On the face of it more than one illuminating interpretation of these complex and sometimes conflicting classroom processes might be offered by a range of observers. While we can at least imagine interpretations that unambiguously and damagingly conflict, it is also seems possible that each of a range of interpretations that seem to be in tension with each other could offer valid insights into what is taking place. The view I am defending here rejects 'narrative constructivism' (Fay, 1996, p. 190), according to which narrative structures are imposed on a 'formless flow of events'. Our lives are 'inescapably narratival in form' (p. 197), but this does not mean that there is 'One True Story to be told about any life or historical event' (p. 197).

Many will object at this point that this is obviously unsatisfactory and that researchers would need to work towards excluding the potential inconsistencies I have illustrated here. For within a particular society a level of consensus *can* develop about the quality of novels, paintings, compositions and other expressions of the creative arts. Similarly, participants in educational research in which classroom interactions are being judged can develop a shared culture with converging verdicts.

Although this is perfectly possible, any attempt to *ensure* high levels of consensus arguably damages something at the heart of aesthetic judgments and the arts. It is no accident, no peripheral inconvenience, that the history of Western Art music includes the rejection of tonality by Schoenberg and the Second Viennese School—that Messiaen[2] fails to follow the canons of sonata development and the sense of progression over time that are central to the classical compositions of Haydn and Mozart. When these events occurred they were highly controversial and perhaps still are. Those making aesthetic appraisals of such works of Western Art Music will not achieve convergence in judgment. A sophisticated treatment of issues in the philosophy of music is beyond the scope of this chapter. All that can be said here is that, crudely speaking, some judgments about whether, for instance a piece of music 'has a proper sense of direction' or 'develops appropriate tensions and satisfying resolutions of these' will involve making assumptions about the extent to which music *must* in any sense present a narrative over time. These assumptions will not, and arguably *should* not, be required to be shared universally by those reaching verdicts about quality in this area.

Were musical developments to have been subject to a requirement that they evoked a consistent response from appropriately qualified judges then many events crucial to the continued flourishing of musical culture could not have taken place. It would have been, in effect, to erect a barrier between the appraisers and the essence of that which they were appraising.

Again, any idea that this point is relevant to educational research will be unwelcome to some. Am I implying that judgments involved in educational research could be subject to revolution and radical subversion resembling paradigm shifts in the arts? For this, it might be urged, would be patently absurd. It is precisely this kind of thing that has brought educational research into disrepute (see, for example, Mortimore, 2000 for a rehearsal of typical recent criticisms of educational research).

Such a rejection of the analogy with aesthetic judgment arguably misses the point. It is not being suggested that continuous or even occasional revolution would be a good thing within educational research. Paradigm shifts in the arts are an extreme instance of something that is nevertheless at their very heart: the continuing possibility of value and significance outside practices and sets of criteria developed by particular communities and cultures in any one place and at any one time. The question under consideration is whether this idea is relevant to at least some of the interpretive judgments at the heart of educational research. There *are* parallels between the rich, complex and value laden subject matter of aesthetic judgments, and the social phenomena about which value-laden interpretive judgments are sometimes made in educational research. This does not *establish* that prioritising consistency forces researchers to be *selective* about the truth they capture, but it is at least suggestive.

An unsympathetic critic at this point might demand *examples* of what is excluded by the demands of consistency. However, it is simply not possible to satisfy this demand, for any candidate is just the kind of feature whose presence in any particular social situation would be contested. A putatively robust example would be a feature about which there would be agreement in verdicts, and hence not, after all an example at all.

HOLISM AND PARTICULARISM IN NORMATIVE JUDGMENTS

I now examine the possibility of combining a degree of inconsistency with 'significance' stemming from a type of *holism* inherent in judgments about classroom situations, especially teaching performances, and about student achievements. Some hold that a rigorous approach to such judgments should involve the specification of criteria. The kinds of criterion-referencing prevailing in the National Curriculum in the UK, and the attempts to lay down 'competences' that effective teachers should exhibit, exemplify just such a treatment. The apparent virtues of this way of proceeding are obvious. Researchers and assessors have a clear framework within which they can work. When discussing their impressions with each other they have common guidelines; a developing consensus and consistency of verdicts seem very likely outcomes.

Yet the meaning and significance of many of these criteria cannot be separated from that of their bedfellows. Take just a sample from the list of qualities that we are told researchers take to be essential for good teaching:

> Good teachers encourage learning for understanding and are concerned with developing their students' critical thinking skills, problem-solving skills, and problem-approach behaviours.
> Good teachers demonstrate an ability to transform and extend knowledge, rather than merely transmitting it; they draw on their knowledge of their subject, their knowledge of their learners, and their general pedagogical knowledge to transform the concepts of the discipline into terms that are understandable to their students . . ..
> Good teachers set clear goals, use valid and appropriate assessment methods, and provide high quality feedback to their students.
> Good teachers show respect for their students; they are interested in both their professional and their personal growth, encourage their independence, and sustain high expectations of them (Ramsden *et al.*, 1995, p. 24).

All these qualities exhibit a measure of holism. For instance, what counts as valid and appropriate assessment methods depend at least in part on what counts as showing respect for students, which in turn cannot readily be interpreted apart from how we are going to construe encouraging learning for understanding. Many of the criteria cannot be considered and assessed *on their own*. How they are applied to classroom processes depends on how related criteria are applied, and vice versa. There is a kind of hermeneutic circle here. We cannot understand any one criterion unless we understand others and how that one relates to the others. Yet in turn we cannot understand any one of the others either without understanding the rest and how they fit together. There is no need to exaggerate the position to make the basic point. We must concede that some criteria are more 'atomic' than others. Be that as it may, how does all this relate to our theme of *consistency*?

Perhaps it would be possible for assessors to reach agreement with each other over a period of time about this kind of 'criteria jigsaw'—about how the different elements should be seen as relating to each other when appraising the human and social phenomena concerned. My concern about this is as follows. Might there be a *cost* to securing such an agreement? Might there not be 'aspects' of the phenomena that are excluded? For instance, when reaching a verdict about the clarity of the goals being set by the teacher, if we insist that this criterion is related in specific ways to others, such as showing respect for the students, are we scrutinising the performance in one particular way and excluding other perfectly legitimate approaches? Are we, so to speak, seeing the educational situation as illuminated by a particular kind of lighting when other aspects might become visible under different illumination?

It is instructive to relate this debate to issues that have arisen over the last two or three decades around the approach to meta-ethics known as moral particularism—a debate associated especially with Jonathan Dancy and John McDowell. When considering reasons favouring one action rather than another, for instance, Dancy claims that

1. A feature or part may have one value in one context and a different or opposite value in another.
2. The value of a complex or whole is not necessarily identical with the sum of the values of its elements or parts (Dancy, 2000, p. 139).

Examples are contested by those opposed to particularism, but here are two simply to illustrate the type of thesis Dancy supports. The fact that an action results in pleasure can make it better in some circumstances *and worse* in others. Suppose a possible action of mine results in letting people watch hangings. If the people get pleasure from the spectacle then (it might be claimed) my action is morally worse than it otherwise would have been. A second case: 'That one of the candidates wants the job very much indeed is sometimes a reason for giving it to her and sometimes a reason for doing the opposite' (Dancy, 2000, pp. 132–3).

We need not be in a position to pronounce definitively on the philosophical strengths and weaknesses of moral particularism in order to draw some parallels between examples of these kinds and situations where judgments about student learning are being made. Irony in an essay about postmodernism might be a strength: the same irony in a critical discussion of Frege on sense and reference could be wholly out of place and provide a reason for a lower mark than would otherwise have been earned. Rich imagery and metaphor might enhance a discussion of Keats' poetry, but could well detract from the quality of an analysis of the German economy between the two World Wars. One explanation for this 'particularism' lies in the holism and the 'hermeneutic circle' referred to above. The weight and significance of irony, for instance, simply cannot be appraised outside the context of the writing in which it occurs; its role and contribution depend crucially on other features of the assignment in question. Arguably there can be legitimate disagreement between assessors about the contribution of such features to the overall quality of the essay. If we insist on excluding such disagreement in order to achieve the requisite levels of reliability and to make the assessment process 'work' are we absolutely certain that in so doing we are continuing to examine *all* the significant features of the student products or achievements concerned?

I suggest that similar points could easily be made about contexts where classroom interactions are being interpreted and appraised. Might an insistence on converging judgments in the spirit of objectivity and rigour mean that important aspects of the situations are missed? This question deserves at least serious consideration.

INCOMPARABILITY AND INCOMMENSURABILITY

So far, this chapter has in effect been discussing the attempts to impose the requirements of one kind of educational research on another. Demands for consistency and reliability, most obviously appropriate in the context of quantitative research, are widened to include qualitative research. I have tried to show how comparisons between some kinds of qualitative research and the realm of aesthetics are appropriate, and why this could leave room for a measure of inconsistency. This raises the thorny question of *comparing* different kinds of research. A notorious example of this is well known to UK readers in the form of the Research Assessment Exercise (RAE). In this final section I discuss some of the philosophical issues this raises, again in the light of analogies with aesthetic judgments.

We are concerned here with what has sometimes been called 'incommensurability'. The intellectual background to this is provided by Isaiah Berlin who defends a pluralism of values, as opposed to a monism according to which we can order, compare and contrast values within some kind of overall theory. '... human goals are many, not all of them commensurable. To assume that all values can be graded on one scale, so that it is a mere matter of inspection to determine the highest, seems to me to falsify our knowledge that men are free agents' (Berlin, 1969, p. 171).

Could it be that a measure of disagreement between those attempting to grade the quality of educational research stems from the fact that they are attempting to compare *at least some* features that should not be compared? If, for instance people are asked to compare the Taj Mahal with the Sydney Opera House there will be a range of reactions. These will include sheer bewilderment, verdicts favouring the Opera House, verdicts according them the same value and judgments on the side of the Taj Mahal. The diversity of responses in itself proves nothing. However it might well be symptomatic of the fact that people think that in such examples comparisons are odious. Similarly they may feel that a Mozart opera ought not to be compared with a Coldplay item, and Jane Austen's novel *Emma* ought not to be weighed against Tolkien's *Lord of the Rings*.

Note however that the opening formulation above speaks cautiously of *at least some features* that should not be compared. If we work hard enough we can find 'covering values' (Chang, 1997) against which the items *could* be compared, at least in theory. We cannot compare *Emma* with *Lord of the Rings* in respect of their depictions of the *nouveau riche* or the verbal painting of landscape, but perhaps we can make more progress if we consider them under the heading 'Worth of literature written in English'.

It may be objected that we cannot compare the value of the treatment of the *nouveau riche* in *Emma* and in the *Lord of the Rings* because only *Emma* attempts it. Similarly Tolkien achieves (with consummate skill and artistry) the verbal painting of landscape, while Jane Austen is for the most part otherwise employed. What is needed for the argument are features that are in a sense common to both works yet where comparability is genuinely open to question. Both works deal with *morality*, for instance. So perhaps 'morality' is an ingredient of a 'covering value'. Yet arguably Tolkien's epic portrayal in a fantasy world of the struggle of good against evil should not be considered alongside Jane Austen's subtle and gently ironic treatment of Emma's moral failings. Superficially we are within reach of a covering value but at a deeper level the works are simply not doing the same kind of thing. Insisting that we must reach a verdict on which work does this 'better' seems to involve a fundamental distortion of the distinctive moral qualities to be found in each work.

I suggest that in our treatment of these examples we are moving towards what Lukes calls 'incommensurability'. He explains this as applying where it would be 'inappropriate' to make comparisons. At the same time he denies that such comparisons necessarily would be unintelligible or meaningless. So although a comparison would not be incoherent we nevertheless hold back from making one; 'we do sometimes refuse to commensurate or compare alternatives ... such a refusal can display our understanding of what is involved in certain relationships' (Lukes, 1997, p. 185).

To set Lukes' views in context we need to compare and contrast them with other recent treatments of incomparability and incommensurability. For instance John Broome (2001) thinks of incommensurability as involving alternatives that realise such different values that 'it is impossible to weigh them against each other precisely ... When values are incommensurable, it may not be determinate which of the two alternatives is better. It may be that neither is better than the other, yet we also cannot say they are equally good' (Broome, 2001, p. 12). He goes on to illustrate incommensurability in this sense with the example of God telling Abraham to sacrifice his son, claiming that submitting to God's will *cannot* be weighed against saving Isaac.

Consider this treatment alongside that of Chang who argues that the failure of the trichotomy of possible relations between A and B—that A is neither better nor worse than B and that A and B are not equally good—does not prevent them being what she calls 'on a par': they could still in some sense be comparable. She dubs those prepared to countenance a *fourth* relation between A and B 'tetrachotomists', observing that 'the tetrachotomist thinks that even if one item is neither better nor worse than another and that the items are not equally good, there may nevertheless be an evaluative difference between them' (Chang, 2002, p. 664). Even if she is right about this we are now contemplating comparability of a radically different kind from that in which we can compare A and B according to any kind of common measure.

I suggest that one of the reasons for our refusal to rank certain items on a common scale is our awareness of the *distinctive* quality of the features concerned.[3] It is not a global rejection of ranking procedures, nor yet an obscurantism about the possibility of covering values in the majority of cases. It is rather the appreciation that *some* aspects of morality and the arts resist ordering on a scale in terms of a common value. This is not to claim that 'distinctiveness' is a sufficient condition for significant value.

It is to make the much more modest contention that it is a *necessary* feature of *some* kinds of significant value.

There are yet other conceptions of incommensurability in recent philosophical literature. I briefly draw attention to just one more here. Incommensurability may be seen as involving the possibility of disagreement even given reasonable reflection: 'Incommensurability marks a practical limit on the power of reason alone to decide value conflicts' (Plaw, 2004, p. 113). As stated, this is compatible with a Humean approach to normativity but Plaw likens political judgments involving incommensurability in this sense to aesthetic judgments and he clearly does not think of the latter as merely subjective. His view allows for disagreement that cannot be resolved through reason and yet that is not simply a reflection of differing subjective reactions.

Suppose then that it is an essential feature of certain values that they cannot be weighed against each other on any kind of common scale. (I certainly cannot claim to have established this here—but would contend that the examples cited are at least suggestive.) How ought this to impinge on the kinds of judgements about educational research to which the RAE is committed? Large scale quantitative studies will be weighed not only against other studies of that kind, but against ethnographic case studies, philosophical/conceptual investigations, historical analyses of education, comparisons between the teaching of calculation methods in different cultures and so forth.

If the social phenomena under scrutiny feature at least some qualities that ought not to be captured on a common scale involving ranking and grading then where professionals are in effect attempting to do just this they are likely to disagree. They are going through the motions of a process whose incoherence they at least tacitly appreciate. Suppose relevant assessors underwent some kind of 'training' to improve consistency in judgments in order to strengthen the reliability of the process. Arguably this will tend to exclude the consideration of qualities with 'incommensurability' aspects. Given the well-known 'balkanised' character of current educational research such exclusion might well be a significant issue.

Now in an effort to avoid such problems we may be able to find 'covering values'. Some of these will suffer from the taint of performativity, such as citation indices. Others will be bland, and abstract from the distinctive features of specific types of research in virtue of which their incommensurability arises in the first place. I will give the last word on this particular topic to Bernard Williams. He notes that 'if there are many and competing genuine values, then the greater extent to which a society tends to be single-valued, the more genuine values it neglects or suppresses' (Williams, 1980, p. xix).

CONCLUSION

The approach in this chapter has been deliberately cautious and tentative. I have sought to raise philosophical questions that at least ought to be *considered* in connection with aspirations to high levels of consistency in educational research. I cannot claim to have established robustly that significant features of educational phenomena are excluded by the demands of reliability. At the same time I think that enough has been said to cast doubt on an unreflective adherence to procedural objectivity and high standards of consistency.

NOTES

1. In an interesting discussion Pamela Moss (1994) also questions the closeness of the link between reliability and validity in educational research but not in connection with the arts or Eisner's writings.
2. 'Where a conventional Western composition will seem to unfold as a thread through time, Messiaen's discontinuous music rather provides an environment within which time itself can be observed, "coloured", as he would say, by rhythm; time suspended, in his slow movements, or time racing forwards, in his scherzos and dances, or, most frequently, time changing its rhythmic colour from moment to moment. Instead of affirming the orderly flow of everyday existence, this is music that acknowledges only two essences: the instantaneous and the eternal' (Griffiths, 2006 [Grove online]).
3. If we want to follow Chang, we should not go as far as claiming that items cannot be compared— in her thinking 'evaluative difference' does not imply incomparability.

REFERENCES

Alexander, R. (2000) *Culture and Pedagogy* (Oxford, Blackwell).
Berlin, I. (1969) Two Concepts of Liberty, in: *Four Essays on Liberty* (Oxford, Oxford University Press).
Broome, J. (2001) Are Intentions Reasons? And How Should We Cope with Incommensurable Values?, in: C. Morris and A. Ripstein (eds), *Practical Rationality and Preference: Essays for David Gauthier* (Cambridge, Cambridge University Press), pp. 98–120.
Chang, R. (1997) Introduction, in: R. Chang (ed.) *Incommensurability, Incomparability and Practical Reason* (Cambridge MA, Harvard University Press).
Chang, R. (2002) The Possibility of Parity, *Ethics*, 112.4, pp. 659–688.
Dancy, J. (2000) *The Particularist's Progress*, in: B. Hooker and M. Little (eds), *Moral Particularism* (Oxford, Clarendon Press).
Davis, A. (2005a) Social Externalism and the Ontology of Competence, *Philosophical Explorations*, 8.3, pp. 297–308.
Davis, A. (2005b) Learning and the Social Nature of Mental Powers, *Educational Philosophy and Theory*, 37.5, pp. 635–647.
Eisner, E. (1991) *The Enlightened Eye: Qualitative Inquiry and the Enhancement of Educational Practice* (New York, Merrill).
Eisner, E. (1992) Objectivity in Educational Research, *Curriculum Inquiry*, 22.1, pp. 9–15.
Fay, B. (1996) *Contemporary Philosophy of Social Science* (Oxford, Blackwell).
Griffiths, P. (2006) Messiaen, Grove Music Online ed. L. Macy. Online at: http://www.grovemusic.com (Accessed 7 January 2006).
Geertz, C. (1973) *The Interpretation of Cultures* (New York, Basic Books).
Goulding, M., Rowland, T. and Barber, P. (2002) Does it Matter? Primary Teacher Trainees' Subject Knowledge in Mathematics, *British Educational Research Journal*, 28.5, pp. 689–704.
Kant, I. (1928) *Critique of Judgment* (Oxford, Oxford University Press).
Lukes, S. (1997) Comparing the Incomparable: Trade-offs and Sacrifices, in: Chang Ruth (ed.) *Incommensurability, Incomparability and Practical Reason* (Cambridge MA, Harvard University Press).
Madill, A., Jordan, A. and Shirley, C. (2000) Objectivity and Reliability in Qualitative Analysis: Realist, Contextualist and Radical Constructionist Epistemologies, *British Journal of Psychology*, 91, pp. 1–20.

Mortimore, P. (2000) Does Educational Research Matter? *British Educational Research Journal*, 26.1, pp. 5–24.

Moss, P. (1994) Can There Be Validity without Reliability? *Educational Researcher*, 23.2, pp. 5–12.

Plaw, A. (2004) Why Monist Critiques feed Value Pluralism: Ronald Dworkin's Critique of Isaiah Berlin, *Social Theory and Practice*, 30.1, pp. 105–126.

Ramsden, P., Margetson, D., Martin, E. and Clarke, S. (1995) Recognising and Rewarding Good Teaching, Canberra: AGPS. Online at: http://online.anu.edu.au/caut/commproject/rrgt/Chapter2.html#2.6 (Accessed May 20 2006).

Scruton, R. (1997) *The Aesthetics of Music* (Oxford, Oxford University Press).

Shaper-Landau, R. (1994) Ethical Disagreement, Ethical Objectivism and Moral Indeterminacy, *Philosophy and Phenomenological Research*, 54.2, pp. 331–344.

Williams, B. (1980) Introduction to Isaiah Berlin, in: H. Hardy (ed.) *Concepts and Categories* (Oxford, Oxford University Press).

Wittgenstein, L. (1958) *Philosophical Investigations* (Oxford, Blackwell).

Wollheim, R. (1987) *Painting as an Art* (London, Thames & Hudson).

7
No Harm Done: The Implications for Educational Research of the Rejection of Truth

STEFAN RAMAEKERS

'Objective measurement under controlled conditions subjected to an array of statistical procedures has become *the* method to follow in psychological and educational research'. This could easily be something an educational researcher, or scientist, or philosopher wrote very recently. In reality, it comes from an article in *Educational Theory* by R. D. Bramwell from 1978 (p. 225). Apparently not much has changed over almost three decades. In the latest issue of the same journal, a special issue on (the possibility of) educational research as a science entitled *The Education Science Question: A Symposium*, the same observation as the one made by Bramwell is the main focus of discussion. The authors contributing to this symposium take issue with the US National Research Council's report *Scientific Research in Education* (2002), which is taken as seeking 'to reinstate experimental-quantitative methods as the "gold standard" of educational science' (Howe, 2005, p. 236). At stake is (the possibility of) a 'science-based educational research, and its close cousin, evidence-based practice' (Schwandt, 2005, p. 285). The attractiveness of science-based educational research is as powerful now as it was three decades ago, and as it probably will be three or so decades from now. The science-based approach, so it seems, offers no less than the prospect of objectivity, even the certainty of knowledge, and thus brings truth into the picture as an attainable ideal. This stands in contrast with the supposed subjectivity and uncertainty, and consequently arbitrariness and relativism, of non-scientific approaches. Of course, secure foundations for belief are very appealing in uncertain times. We do not want to educate our children on the basis of beliefs that could be false, or for which there is no solid evidence, do we? What, on a more existential level, seems to be worrying here is the charge that, when researchers and policy-makers turn to enquiry which is merely 'subjective' and hence 'arbitrary', there is no longer a place for truth in the educational picture, and this leaves educational policy and practice without foundation or direction.

There is nothing new, either, in the reaction of those who point to an unjustified narrowness in such a science-based approach. They argue that when educational practice becomes defined by reference to this very narrow conception of what counts as evidence, something which goes to the heart of education is lost; it is almost as if the educational itself seems to be surgically removed from education. The following passage from the special issue just referred to captures the spirit:

> Undeniably [rote learning and memorization measurable on standardized tests] is useful, but educational practice is not simply a matter of a teacher imparting, and a student acquiring, facts and information. To educate is to draw out thought—to develop students who are intellectually liberated, so to speak, and thus capable of acting in intelligent, critical, and healthy ways. Deciding whether one is doing the right thing and doing it well in educating a student requires more than an ability to implement evidence-based curricula for teaching knowledge and skills in maths, science, and reading. It requires decision-making methods that are inescapably characterized by simultaneous attention to the particulars of the situation (that is, the particular student one is facing at this time and in these circumstances) and to a host of considerations having to do with values, interests, habits, beliefs, traditions, and so forth that make decisions about how best to educate (at least in a democracy) inveterately untidy, contested, corrigible, and case-specific. This practical character of deliberating educational means and ends cannot be made to go away by increasing the rigor, pace, or reach of science-based thinking (Schwandt, 2005, p. 296).

Schwandt refers to this practical character as 'the rough texture of educational practice' (ibid.) and adds that it is precisely this 'rough texture' that current dominant paradigms of research seek to overcome. A quest for truth as conceived within the science-based approach to research, i.e. in terms of evidence, sits uneasily with this dimension of education. There is not much sense in asking whether values, interests and traditions (such as a child's trust in her mother's or father's love for her, or her belief in God) are true or false in the sense indicated. There is obviously a sense in which educational research can be conceived as providing a 'true understanding' of these values, interest, habits, traditions, in the sense of accurate insight into them. And there are different kinds of ways in which truth is or might be applied (for example, by way of ethnography or phenomenology). The true understanding provided here is needed, for example, to outline the part these values, interests, etc. play in particular social or educational settings. But this is to be distinguished from the quest for truth as implicated in the currently dominant research paradigm. By contrast, in the 'rough texture' of educational practice, the main point of judgement lies in categories such as appropriateness and inappropriateness, the just and the unjust, the good and the bad, perhaps even the honourable and the dishonourable.[1]

I shall take this up later. Before doing so, I want to give a reconstruction of recent discussion concerning the issue of truth in educational theory and research. Most of the literature to be found on this issue can be structured along the paths of the dualisms truth versus belief, explanation versus interpretation, objectivity versus subjectivity, discovery versus (re)construction, etc., and the problem is not just one of separate discourses but of the difficulty in establishing any rapprochement between them. At times the situation seems to be like the one Wittgenstein describes, when the pupil, after repeated instruction, fails to go on by herself: 'It would now be no use to say: 'But can't you see . . .?'—and repeat the old examples and explanations' (Wittgenstein, 1953, #185). Nonetheless, in the absence of anything better, that is what I'm going to do here. (I do not believe that there is, methodologically speaking, a 'beyond' that reconciles the different approaches, nor do I think that would be desirable. If speaking of a beyond were appropriate, it would not be found in a sense far away and above, or in a 'new' approach, but very near to us, in our interests.) What I will be doing is 'putting things side by side', again. What I wish to show is that the 'non-scientific' approaches to educational research which supposedly or seemingly reject the quest for truth do not so much reject truth as shift the focus to other types of question, displaying different interests. I will draw on the work of Stanley Cavell to explain this.

In view of the dominance of the science-based approach, it is perhaps a bit of a surprise to find so much concern in philosophical educational thinking about those currents which are said to reject or abolish the concept of truth, or at least are identified as arguing, in one way or another that 'the concept of truth has no place anymore in current educational thinking' (Cuypers, 2003, p. 167). What are these currents that are so feared? In general, those defending or restoring or rehabilitating the (or some) concept of truth within educational theory identify these currents under the concept of postmodernism or poststructuralism. For Stefaan Cuypers, for example, it is postmodern philosophy of education, which takes its lead from deconstructionism and which attacks a truth-based or what he calls veritistic epistemology, and hence jeopardizes rationality as an educational ideal (Cuypers, 2003). Along the same lines, David Carr expresses his concern about 'the spread of non-realist or anti-realist conceptions of knowledge and truth' (Carr, 1998, p. 12)—which he takes to be promoted within analytical philosophical movements such as the Wittgensteinian 'meaning as use theory', as well as within postanalytical or postmodernist philosophical currents such as pragmatism and poststructuralism (Carr, 1998, 1999). The following passage aptly illustrates the point:

> . . . it seems to have become almost *de rigueur* to be 'incredulous about metanarratives' and to prefer the relativist—or at least pluralist— language of *rival traditions* or *narratives* to any absolutist talk of objective knowledge and truth (Carr, 1999, p. 442).

In the same spirit Martyn Hammersley undertakes, contra those whom he identifies as postmodernists, a defense of realism (Hammersley, 2004).

Postmodernism is, to give one more example, also Dennis Phillips' target. He is bothered most by the postmodernist's rhetorical style and lack of (rational) argument (Phillips, 1997; Phillips and Burbules, 2000).

Without exception these philosophers of education pinpoint postmodernism's critique of truth-based epistemology, or rationalist educational philosophy, or objective educational research, as being a critique of the foundationalism and infallibilism that underlie (or rather, which they argue postmodernists take to be underlying) such conceptions of educational research and philosophizing. The postmodernist critique is taken to argue that everything is fraught with the subjective and that truth is reducible to linguistic mechanisms, or to the perspective of class or gender. Charges that postmodernism promotes or simply is (a form of) relativism or scepticism are not far away here. Feminism is quite often regarded as a case of such postmodernism and is accordingly criticised— though this is a use and a critique of feminism that completely disregards its ambivalent relationship with postmodernism.

The replies to the postmodernist critique consist, equally invariably, of a reorientation of truth-based epistemology and rationalist educational philosophizing which embraces non-foundationalism and fallibilism. This is a substantive challenge to the postmodernist critique. For if that critique can be characterised as a critique of the epistemic absolutism and dogmatism inherent in classical truth-based epistemology, then this critique is accurately neutralised by emphasising that the quest for knowledge and truth does not amount to the quest for absolute certainty and (so to speak) eternal foundations. (All authors mentioned emphasize this in different but similar ways.) The quest for such foundations and absolute certainty would involve a metaphysical claim that is incompatible with the fallibilist stance. In fact, fallibilism is embraced for the very reason of importing the possibility of criticizing partial viewpoints, correcting biased perspectives, amending dominant perspectives. Knowledge and truth can then be saved as a body of provisional beliefs which are always open to criticism, but which provide, nevertheless, firm grounds upon which to act in the meantime. Accordingly, since the possibility of objective truths—given the best possible evidence and the best possible certainty at a particular moment—is safeguarded, education can be provided with the appropriate grounds for action. Practitioners and policy makers 'want to be guided by reliable answers' to their questions, Phillips argues (Phillips and Burbules, 2000, p. 2). 'Teachers don't want fluff educational theory and ideology. They want to know what works' (Murray, quoted in Schwandt, 2005, p. 286). In order to meet these needs and demands, so the response to the postmodernist critique goes, educational researchers ought to resist the seductive arms of the postmodern embrace and assume an attitude which is orientated towards truth and knowledge construed in these fallibilist terms.

In a way, there is good sense in this particular (re)turn to a quest for truth and knowledge—to (provisional but) firm grounds, to (revisable) certainties—be it in the form of philosophical argument about it, or in the form of a re-emphasis on and reinstatement of experimental-quantitative methods. Currents in philosophy such as feminism, deconstructionism and poststructuralism have, during recent decades, gradually inscribed an indelible sensitivity for difference, otherness and the alien in our postmodern culture and its self-understanding. That this, taken together with the cultural crisis (North versus South, Islam versus West), problematizes our educational questions is apparent, among other things, from the observation that in the wake of these currents and cultural developments 'doing something' (as, for example, initiating into a practice) has all but become synonymous with 'doing (somebody an) injustice' in the sense that the action imposes 'content', or 'shape', or 'substance' on somebody or something. Developments such as these have not so much encouraged the sort of self-reflection which could possibly give rise to positive educational action as promoted what Nietzsche called 'suspicion about ourselves' (*The Gay Science*, section 346). As it achieves self-understanding, our contemporary culture seems to be haunted by what we could call 'postmodern agony', an indefinite, underlying but disturbing suspicion that whatever we do always already involves 'too much of the self' and 'not enough of the other'. This renders problematical our understanding and practice of education as initiation. On the part of the practitioner (parent, teacher) this seems to have intensified what Nietzsche calls her 'impetuous demand for certainty', 'the demand that one *wants* by all means something to be firm ... [a] demand for foothold, support' (ibid., section 347). The recent call (in the US) for more character education is a good example here (see Noddings, 2003, for a critical discussion). The attractiveness of science-based educational research and a post-positivistic approach can be seen in these terms as well. In this sense, the views of Phillips and Murray quoted above are apt expressions of exasperation in the face of postmodernist developments and of contemporary cultural needs.

But let us take a closer look at those currents of thought which are so feared because of their rejection of truth and knowledge, or at least because of their scepticism about these concepts, and which are readily lumped together as postmodernist. I have selected some examples which explicitly focus on educational *research* instead of on educational theory in general or philosophizing more specifically. The reasons for this particular selection are that postmodernist and poststructuralist accounts of educational philosophy, and theory more broadly, have been given elsewhere (to name but two examples: Blake *et al.*, 1998 and 2000), and, more importantly, that I am interested in how concepts such as truth and knowledge are indeed dealt with in (so-called) postmodernist, or let us call them more neutrally *alternative*, accounts of educational research. What is it to be feared here? What is it that is argued for, if indeed this is a matter of argument (for Phillips does not think there is much argument to be found, only rhetoric: see Phillips, 1997)?

In an article titled 'Pursuing Truth in Narrative Research' Jane O'Dea argues for a rapprochement between literature and research. She opposes 'empirical quantitative truth' with what she calls 'artistic literary truth' (1994, p. 162), arguing that this is the type of truth educational researchers, or at least those engaged in narrative research, should pursue. What is so particular to this artistic literary truth is that it conveys, O'Dea argues (quoting Weitz), 'limited and partial claims about certain phenomena' (O'Dea, 1994, p. 163). 'Such partial claims', she continues, 'leave room for the irreducible complexity of the world while yet offering penetrating insights as to our experience of it' (ibid.). What kind of claims O'Dea is referring to is probably clear to readers of novels. These are claims, O'Dea says, 'that strike us as startlingly "true", strike us as accurate, compelling if incomplete renditions of common lived experiences' (1994, p. 164). That she puts 'true' between inverted commas is important. It indicates, I take it, that these claims are not true in the sense of backed up by overwhelming evidence, or truthlike in the Popperian sense, but are true in the sense that not understanding them, not grasping them, is tantamount to not understanding something important about the human condition.

That this is connected to a particular *kind* of writing I take to be a matter of internal relations. When writing, novelists express the way they understand the world, the way they make sense of the world, or the world makes sense to them. In this sense, the novelist, with each stroke of her pen, puts herself at risk, or at least exposes herself, instead of cutting off her own subjectivity, as if that would block a real understanding of the world. In as much as educational researchers are asked to do something similar to this—O'Dea connects the idea of artistic literary truth with a concept of authenticity as truthfulness and honesty—then this is clearly far removed from the contemporary obsession with research *methodology* within which the activity of doing research is made researcher-proof (see Smith, 2003, p. 133). That this seems to abolish disinterested knowledge is not at issue here. As I understand O'Dea, her concern is not so much with an idea of educational research that cultivates the connection between disinterested knowledge and technology (i.e. offering techniques which work), as with the educational researcher who tries to offer insights, tries to offer practitioners a way to probe their deepest concerns.

Robert Stake and Dale Kerr also pursue the analogy between research and art, more particularly the paintings of René Magritte. They draw on Magritte's understanding of his paintings—not so much as expressing ideas but rather as having the power to create them—to suggest that 'Research can be designed so that as much as its power to express conclusions is its power to stimulate thinking' (Stake and Kerr, 1995, p. 56). This is not an open pathway to relativism: rather it is an acknowledgement of the fact that research conclusions are inevitably interpreted in particular ways by particular practitioners. Instead of deploring this (and putting more and more effort into making teaching teacher-proof), Stake and Kerr propose facing this challenge directly and therefore setting educational researchers the task of 'restructuring [the forms of their researches] with the service of meaning-makers in mind: the readers, the practitioners, the policy setters, the people' (ibid., p. 60). In simple terms, educational practitioners do not just mechanically apply techniques based on research findings. Application of research findings involves all the sensitive attunements to a particular context similar to those a child has to appropriate for saying something is a ball, or is difficult, or joyful. And as with O'Dea, the interest here is not primarily 'what is' and its technological derivation 'what works', but, as Stake and Kerr put this, 'what is worth pondering' (ibid., p. 61). Shifting attention to this can be done in many ways. For Stake and Kerr, 'The able researcher draws attention to expectations and assumptions, shocking the reader out of complacency' (ibid., p. 57).

Whereas O'Dea and Stake and Kerr show their divergence from research methodology modelled along the natural sciences without explicitly saying so, Bent Flyvbjerg (2001) explicitly contrasts the place and tasks of social science and its research with those of the natural sciences. In *Making Social Science Matter*, Flyvbjerg goes against the dominant tendency to conceive social science as a science in the way of the natural sciences and reiterates the well-known idea that social science should occupy a place of its own,[2] by trying to show that the current comparison between social and natural sciences in terms of epistemic qualities is misfiring, and that 'the social sciences are strongest where the natural sciences are weakest' (Flyvbjerg, 2001, p. 3). For Flyvbjerg this is the place (or domain, or level) of 'reflexive analysis and discussion of values and interests, which is the prerequisite for an enlightened political, economic, and cultural development in any society' (ibid.). Flyvbjerg's way into this is the Aristotelian notion of *phronesis*, a development and understanding of which will help him 'restore social science to its classical position as a practical, intellectual activity aimed at clarifying the problems, risks, and possibilities we face as humans and societies, and at contributing to social and political practice' (ibid., p. 4)—hence his phrases 'phronetic social science' and 'phronetic research'. That this differs from a search for unequivocally verified knowledge should be clear. Rather, phronetic research should develop answers to questions such as 'Where are we going?', 'Is this desirable?', and 'What should be done?' (see, for example, ibid., p. 61). Phronetic research does not generate techniques which work, but, more modestly and more adapted to social context, it provides 'input to the ongoing social dialogue about the problems and risks we face and how things may be done differently' (see for example, ibid., pp. 61 and 139). As with O'Dea and with Stake and Kerr, we see here the same reflexive move being made, emphasising the relevance of the interests of the practitioner. As I understand Flyvbjerg, conclusions as to what has to be done, or 'what works', are not drawn by social researchers, nor do they make decisions. Such conclusions are drawn and such decisions made (that is, reliable answers are given) in and after the public debate that has (hopefully) been aroused, instigated by what the researcher has had to offer. In terms of educational research, the reliable answers that teachers and policy makers are (said to be) looking for are not (and cannot be) offered ready-to-hand by the educational researcher. Rather, what is offered is the possibility of dialogue; what is delivered is a contribution to dialogue and praxis; what is implied is that reliability is not a straightforward empirical matter.

I take Maggie MacLure's efforts (2003) to propose 'discourse-based educational research' as being work along similar lines: on the boundaries or margins of and between research, literature and reflexivity. For MacLure such discourse-based educational research 'would set itself the work of taking that which offers itself as commonsensical, obvious, natural, given or unquestionable, and trying to unravel it a bit—to *open it up* to further questioning' (MacLure, 2003, p. 9). Her focus is on the discourses employed in education and in educational research, and on how these discourses work. For example, it appears to be the case that an appeal to the real is made when relevance is at issue, or stronger yet, in order to invoke relevance, hence creating an opposition to what is not real, or merely constructed, and hence not relevant. The interest of discourse-oriented educational research is not to determine what is 'really real', for instance by discerning what is real from what is merely constructed or rhetorical. Instead, discourse-based educational research, MacLure argues, 'would be immensely interested in how appeals to "real teachers" and "real worlds" *work* as rhetorical power-plays that try to install some version of reality by disqualifying others' (ibid., p. 12). As I have argued elsewhere (Ramaekers, 2002), it is vital not to close one's investigative gaze too soon, not to close one's eyes to what is not sought by one's investigative procedures. I tend to see such research as a form of consciousness-raising about the discourse used, and hence about the kind of reality evoked by using it. What it demands of the (educational) researcher can be expressed as an ability to adopt a certain distance towards—which is perhaps more aptly put as a cultivating a certain kind of sensibility to—the discourses in which her research is couched.

MacLure draws our attention to, for example, 'the demand ... that research writing should be "lucid", "readily understood", keep to the correct length, renounce style, flourish, and so on' (MacLure, 2003, p. 114). For MacLure this demand is connected to a particular kind of understanding of language and of how it gives us access to the world. 'We have become accustomed', she argues, 'to thinking of the supposedly plainer (puritanical) versions as closer to the truth, more innocent, or at least more appropriate for research purposes' (ibid., p. 115). Going a little further we may well ask why categorisations of educational problems 'work', not least in the sense of giving those confronted with the problems some peace of mind. Undeniably, there is the feeling of being acknowledged in one's personal suffering, but that is only one of the intricate ways in which categorisations and labels operate. For example, learning disabilities such as dyslexia or non-verbal learning disorder are not just discovered 'out there', but are intimately intertwined with a particular kind of society at a particular kind of developmental level, with particular needs and the particular demands it makes of its inhabitants. In this sense, these learning disabilities do a particular kind of work. Drawing attention to the kind of work they do could, for example, reveal that we live in a society that is not able to deal with failure. (This is not to deny the childrens' suffering—undeniably that is real; on the contrary, their suffering is the very point here.)

*

Allow me to make a move familiar in the type of research most celebrated (and granted research funds) today. Let us call these instances of postmodernist, or alternative, educational research my empirical data. I will now try to look through the particularities of these examples, trying to make 'our understanding reach beyond all the examples' (Wittgenstein, 1953, #209), looking for what binds them, as it were a general explanation, and hence to make sense of these cases.

What is quite clear here is that these types of research do not immediately offer answers or solutions, i.e. something which dissolves the problem—in short, the kind of reliable answers post-positivists such as Phillips argue educational research should deliver (see, for example, Phillips and Burbules, 2000). They do not offer anything, or at any rate not much, of the 'what works' sort—which is likely to be true of all philosophical approaches—but, rather, they shift the focus to another set of questions. We might call these questions quite simply existential questions: questions which put the person herself, the institute in which she partakes and which she represents, the community in which she lives, at stake; questions which also bring (again) into focus the most ancient of educational questions: not how, but *why* education? The stakes of education are not primarily technological in nature, but first and foremost existential. Another way of putting this is that, against the contemporary fixation on methodology—with its promise of the redemptive powers of human interference—these 'alternative' accounts (re-)embrace and openly face the 'agony of thinking and all the torment of feeling and understanding' (Wiggins, quoted in Schwandt, 2005, p. 296). The (re)introduction of the subjective, the (re)emphasizing of the researcher's investment, does not signify an abdication of truth and knowledge, but a fuller acknowledgement of human involvement in understanding the world. Drawing on Stanley Cavell, what 'unifies' these cases is that they bring our understanding of educational research and our thinking and philosophizing about education into a region which shows us that the human relation to the world and others in it is 'closer, or more intimate, than the ideas of believing and knowing are made to convey' (Cavell, 1996, p. 257). What this intimacy, or closeness, amounts to is, as I understand Cavell, entailed in Wittgenstein's idea of agreement in judgements.

Famously, Wittgenstein defines truth in terms of human agreement:

'So you are saying that human agreement decides what is true and false?'—It is what human beings *say* that is true and false; and they agree in the *language* they use. That is not agreement in opinions but in form of life.

If language is to be a means of communication there must be agreement not only in definitions but also (queer as this may sound) in judgments (Wittgenstein, 1953, ##241–242).

This is not to be understood as 'mere human' agreement (hence not real, or really true, or objective). In other words, it is a misunderstanding of Wittgenstein to conceive of this as a kind of constructivism, or even as some kind of contractualism. This takes agreement as meaning agreement 'about' something, at the same time implying that what one agrees 'about' can be fairly easily altered. What should not be missed is the importance of what Wittgenstein means when he says that human beings agree *in* forms of life, *in* judgements. Cavell argues that:

> The idea of agreement here is not that of coming to or arriving at an agreement on a given occasion, but of being in agreement throughout, being in harmony, like pitches or tones, or clocks, or weighing scales, or columns of figures. That a group of human beings *stimmen* in their language *überein* says, so to speak, that they are mutually voiced with respect to it, mutually *attuned* top to bottom (Cavell, 1979, p. 32).

Agreement is not a matter of convention, of *mere* convention, for, as Cavell puts this, 'no current idea of "convention" could seem to do the work that words do' (Cavell, 1979, p. 31). Taking Wittgensteinian agreement literally as in 'convention' suggests that people come together, decide on a bunch of issues, and then go their different ways, acting as they have agreed—as if having closed a contract. Rather, what 'agreement' conveys here is that the nature of a human being's initiation into a community is not one of coming to agree about things but one of entering into agreements 'that were in effect before our participation in them' (Cavell, 1988, p. 40). It points to 'a background of pervasive and systematic agreements among us, which we had not realized, or had not known we realize' (Cavell, 1979, p. 30). The normativity, the constitutive force, of these agreements should, therefore, not be underestimated. A group of individuals does not decide or construct what is normative: rather, individuals *grow into* normativity. What should not be confused is the difference between a community collectively sustaining normative practices and a collection of individuals constructing normative procedures. Wittgenstein speaks of this normativity as 'the hardness of the soft' (Wittgenstein, 1961, p. 44e). By this he means to convey that what seems at the outset to be rather 'soft', i.e. merely human agreements, that is cultural and social accretions, linguistic valuations, something which we can (supposedly) oppose to the hard data of biology, of genetic destiny,[3] is in fact deeply constitutive of the way we see, understand, feel about the world. Wittgensteinian agreements are, we could say, embodied. As agreements they are not articulated; rather, they show themselves in what we say and do, in how we speak and act.

The passivity implied here is simultaneously accompanied by a certain kind of activity. That human beings grow into normativity can be put by saying that Wittgensteinian agreements are (already) accepted. This points to the indelible human investment in this agreement in judgements. The latter are collectively *upheld by and in* a particular community of competent language speakers. There is, then, an indispensible human contribution to Wittgensteinian agreements, not in the sense of 'something subjective' tainting (and hence removable from) the objective, or the true, or the real, but in the sense that if this human investment were cut off, there would no longer be something we could call objective, true or real. In terms of the standard definition of truth (S knows that p, if and only if: S believes that p; p is true; and S is justified in believing that p), whatever it is that S believes, p being true is a matter of (non-conventional) agreement in judgements. This is no different for adapted accounts, such as Cuypers' one, which 'invoke[s] the Popperian notion of verisimilitude or truth-likeness in the analysis of knowledge' (Cuypers, 2003, p. 177):

S fallibly knows that h, if and only if:
1. S believes that h is truthlike
2. h is truthlike, and
3. S is justified in believing (i.e. has good reasons for claiming) that h is more truthlike than its rivals on available evidence (Cuypers, 2003, p. 177).

What is 'truthlike', or counts as 'available evidence', falls under the Wittgensteinian account of truth or falsity, i.e. being a matter of agreement in judgements. A good example within this fallibilist, non-foundationalist understanding of knowledge, is Hammersley's account of it. 'We should', he argues, 'treat 'knowledge' as referring to *what we take to be* beyond reasonable doubt' (2004, p. 70, emphasis added). The relevance of 'what we take to be', as opposed to talk of 'what is', should be clear. 'Evidence' does not cut deeper than agreement.

When I said (drawing on Cavell) that those 'alternative' accounts of educational research which supposedly abdicate the search for truth draw our attention to a relation of human being to the world and others that is more intimate or closer than can be captured in terms of 'belief' and 'knowledge', it is this account of Wittgensteinian agreement that I had in mind. We could refer to this, in more familiar terms, as the ethical, epistemological, metaphysical and presuppositions that support our picture of the world. But this way of putting it is slightly misleading since it makes it seem as if it is something that can be easily and lucidly discovered, put into propositions, hence brought under our control. It is also misleading in the sense that it makes it seem as if such a discovery can be seen as an 'increase of learning'[4] (hence, again, controllable, easily teachable, conveyable), whereas what is achieved in becoming aware of our agreements in judgements is probably more aptly put in terms of (or has probably more to do with) what could be called a 'transformation of existence'.[5] It is the sort of transformation that is entailed in an answer to (or a thoughtful pause regarding) the question what happens to us when we have understood those 'artistic literary truths' O'Dea speaks of, or what happens to us when we become aware of the kind of language or discourse that is used to communicate our understanding of the world to others.

Let us take this closer to those non-foundationalist and fallibilist accounts of truth, discussed above. One marked fear here, either expressed or implied, is that when leaving the road of the quest for truth, we enter the domain of mere belief—and beliefs can, as we all know, be false. As Phillips puts it: 'Questing for truth and knowledge about important matters may end in failure, but to give up the quest is knowingly to settle for beliefs that will almost certainly be defective' (Phillips and Burbules, 2000, p. 3). And we do not want to educate our children against the background of beliefs which could be false, or which are not proven to be not defective. (But what about a child's trust in her mother's or father's love for her, or her belief in God?) It should be clear that what is also implied here is that postmodernist and poststructuralist accounts of educational research, by giving up the quest for truth and knowledge, are concerned only with beliefs.

However, even granted that the charge of 'abdication of truth' can be sustained, the implication of a descent to 'embracing (mere) beliefs' is wrong. As previously indicated, the focus shifts. By way of illustration, let us consider briefly the two poetry teachers in the film *Dead Poets Society*, the teacher played by Robin Williams and the one replacing him after he has been fired. The issue turns around how to read poetry. The latter teacher uses the reading method, following it line by line, step by step, as it is printed in the first chapter of the textbook—a reading method, I take it, which is approved by the scientific community (after all, it is printed in a college textbook), most likely has proven its merit (it makes 'knowing poetry' measurable on standardized tests), and which forms the kind of reliable answer teachers want to be guided by during the dangerous undertaking that is called the teaching of poetry. The other teacher, played by Robin Williams, also starts by reading the first lines of that method, then, however, proclaims that method to be rubbish, asks his students to rip the chapter out of the book, and shifts the focus of reading poetry, we could say, from method to feeling, to sensibility, to the heart, to passion— and then exemplifies that by passionately talking about and reading poetry. Is this a better approach? (In the film, of course it is. But that is not the point.) This is the wrong question, because it leads one to ask what the assessment outcomes are with this approach. This is the wrong question, for what has happened here is not primarily something that has to do with the 'method' of reading and being taught poetry and what evidence there is of its effectiveness. This teacher has left the path of truth and established knowledge, so it seems, but he has done so not to embark upon a journey with 'mere beliefs', but to embark upon a journey of inspiration—and that, as seems to be forgotten, is also educational.

The difficulty (at least for those on the post-positivist side) is that inspiration cannot be framed in terms of evidence-based practice. It concerns a type of experience that cannot be put into textbook rules. What Wittgenstein says about expert judgement is illuminating here:

Correcter prognoses will generally issue from the judgments of those with better knowledge of mankind.
Can one learn this knowledge? Yes; some can. Not, however, by taking a course in it, but through *'experience'*.—Can someone else be a man's

teacher in this? Certainly. From time to time he gives him the right *tip*.— This is what 'learning' and 'teaching' are like here.—What one acquires here is not a technique; one learns correct judgments. There are also rules, but they do not form a system, and only experienced people can apply them right. Unlike calculating-rules.
What is most difficult here is to put this indefiniteness, correctly and unfalsified, into words. (Wittgenstein, 1953, p. 227e)

Can we teach, can someone learn, the way that particular teacher teaches poetry? Yes; but not in the sense of techniques. What I wish to add to Wittgenstein's observations here is that it involves something unteachable, i.e. a person's willingness to stop hiding herself behind a textbook method, a person's courage to expose her self in her teaching and reading of poetry. This is not to say the textbook method is necessarily bad, but merely to point to something that is also educational, but forgotten in methodology-driven times. (And, probably, that teacher played by Robin Williams, would, and could, have succeeded in inspiring his students with the standardized textbook method.)

Another fear on the part of non-foundationalists and fallibilists is that of losing track of reality. Postmodernist and poststructuralist accounts of educational research are frequently charged with anti-realism. One of the reasons is that they (supposedly) hold that everything is fraught with the subjective: hence they multiply realities, and deny any distinction with and access to the objective. As already indicated, the reply to this consists in embracing the fallibilist critique. As Phillips puts this, 'To the postpositivist . . . *nothing* is immune to criticism!' (Burbules and Phillips, 2000, p. 42). Or as Cuypers has it, when arguing that the Popperian notion of truth-likeness is 'an essential instrument in the conceptual tool-box of the realist fallibilist': 'there always may be good reasons for claiming that h is superior or more closely similar to the truth than its rivals' (Cuypers, 2003, p. 177). At this point the waters between the two 'traditions' (if I may simplify it in this way) are, I think, the most deep. For those 'alternative' accounts of educational research the distinction between the subjective and objective cannot be made, or cannot be made to be transparent. The very fact that it is argued on the other side that everything can be submitted to critique, or that truth can be approximated, implies the possibility of distinguishing between the one and the other. Here the subjective is treated like some kind of bias, which with sufficient interpersonal effort and reflexivity can be exposed and hence put aside as a falsifying element in our understanding of reality. This does not imply that the existence of bias is not acknowledged in those 'alternative' accounts; rather, removing bias does not dissolve the human investment in upholding what is true, real, objective. In Wittgensteinian terms: language is not an opaque screen, the opacity of which is like a bias, inhibiting our access to the world. The human investment in language—and what other language than the human is there? even so-called other, e.g. animal, languages have to pass through our language if we are to understand them—is no impediment to our understanding of the world.

As a final example, let us take a closer look at so-called evidence-based practices, and what is at issue if not a quest for truth and knowledge. Instead of drawing an example from schooling, I will take the television programme 'Supernanny' as an illustration. The TV programme presents itself as an application of established theory, as an evidence-based practice. The solution to the problem with the child needs to be taken step by step, and in order to do this, Supernanny teaches the parents a number of techniques. During one such episode these included the 'involvement-technique' in which the idea is to involve your child in the kind of things you normally do: e.g. a father had a habit of going shopping without his problem-child, but now he was asked to take her with him and involve her in what he normally did so that she was constantly busy, never feeling the need to behave problematically. The 'sleep-in-your-own-bed-technique', also called the 'sleeping-technique', requires that the child sleeps in her own bed; in particular, the mother was taught to put her child into bed in a specific way, again and again, until she fell asleep, several days in a row until the child stopped getting up by herself. The 'off-the-hip-technique' seeks to detach the child from the mother. (In this particular episode, the child literally hung onto her mother's skirt or was carried around by her mother.) A special kind of technique based on vocal exercises involved the mother practising an 'authoritative voice'. Finally, not really a technique, but nonetheless something fitting very well within the same scheme: 'mom-time', provided for a particular period of time during the weekend in which the mother was allowed to do things, out of the house, that had nothing to do with the household. Quite clearly, the language used—techniques, exercises, time-slots—is appealing and very much in tune with the current *Zeitgeist*. It is the kind of language that promises real learning since it accords with the familiar recipe: 'doing something that works, that's effective'. The following scene is a good example. The mother returns to the home and the father seems to have done the dishes. The mother says: 'What? All by yourself?' Not without a little pride, the father says 'Yes', to which the mother replies: 'Wow! He's learning'. The mother herself phrases what has happened in terms of learning, in terms of, that is, the language of 'what works'. The very fact that she expresses it in this way is important, for it shows how we have become accustomed to a particular mode of addressing reality.

But here we can set to work that ancient philosophical distinction, between surface and depth, between the shallowness of the surface and the insightfulness of the depth, without, to be sure, wishing to subscribe to that distinction's metaphysical implications. Simply put: there is more than meets the eye here, more than the episode (with its particular editing) shows. The change (the improvement) that occurs is not a direct consequence of the application of those techniques. Rather, the change— the true change, if you will—is staged at a different, a deeper, level. This stage can be illustrated by the following expressions, mostly the mother's. 'How can I let my child cry without doing anything?', 'I hate it when he cries' (during the first session of the sleeping-technique), 'I don't understand why this is so hard for me' (as a reaction to the fact that she seems incapable of saying no to her child, of applying the off-the-hip-technique). At some points there are even what could be called flashes of educational insight: 'I need to create a space between X and myself', 'It's hard because I'm used to giving in to him', 'It's hard to break the cycle'. What is crucial to see here is that the mother thus shows that she accounts for the fact that what is changing, what needs changing, is something that affects herself (her self). What is needed, or what she is in the process of doing is, in an expression of Nietzsche's, a 'reversal of one's habitual estimations and esteemed habits' (Nietzsche, 1995, Foreword § 1).[6] Here is it useful to recall the depth of (Wittgensteinian) agreement, its non-conventional character, the hardness of what seems to be only soft, its embodiedness. The difficulty of the task the mother is in the process of undertaking is, then, not to be underestimated, since it amounts to nothing less than attempting 'to feel differently'.[7] (It may be interesting to ponder over the question why David Hume found certainty and peace of mind in something he called 'habits'.) The turning point is indicated by the mother herself, when, somewhere in this episode, she says 'It's really up to me to want things to change'. The educational import of this remark could hardly be underestimated: notwithstanding all the techniques, 'at some point in teaching the pupil must go on—and want to go on—alone' (Cavell, 2005, p. 114). Particularly telling is the first time she is said to enjoy her 'mom-time': upon being asked by Supernanny what she wants to do, she is nonplussed: 'I can't think of anything'. You can almost see her thinking about the household, feeling guilty about the fact that many more things still need to be done. In the end Supernanny sends her off for a walk.

Near the end of the episode, Supernanny is recorded saying: 'It's a wonderful feeling to know that you've helped make a difference'. What is really making a difference? Is it teaching someone to apply techniques? (Though, to be sure, that's exactly the selling package of this television programme's formula: a pressing problem—of the kind about which you can only exclaim 'Oh my God!'—which is to be gone at with clear and distinct techniques.) Isn't helping make a difference helping to bring about a genuine change? Something in the order of having 'one's estimate of the worth of existence' (Cavell, 2005, p. 121) shaken?

What shape can educational research take, then? Or perhaps that is a misleading question—as if educational research should take a completely different shape so as to distinguish it from the dominant strand and mode of doing research in education. What type of questions should be part of educational research? In view of what I have been trying to convey, these are questions that search for what educational practitioners *are willing to accept* as true, as desirable, as good. Contrary to what this might suggest, this is not an open invitation for unbridled relativism. Rather, it brings into view the ethical embeddedness of educational practice, and brings educational research back into the kind of deliberation that Cavell sees as turning around the appropriate and the inappropriate, the just and the unjust, the good and the bad, the honourable and the dishonourable.

Those 'alternative' accounts of educational research, which are said to abolish truth and the search for justified knowledge, and thus to leave education without directives, reliable guidelines, grounds and certainties, are designed to (re)turn educational practitioners and policy makers to a culture of thinking and acting. They try to expose the sort of questions educational researchers and practitioners ask—or are nowadays strongly inclined to ask—as expressions of a longing for the redemption of their educational investments. What these accounts bring to the fore and the way in which this is done fits ill with any attempt at framing in terms of evidence and 'what works'. Our attention is drawn to deeper, i.e. more basic, questions concerning for example society's expectations about education, and our own expectations and demands as parents, teachers, researchers. This (re)turn to the existential level can be taken as an invitation to reorient ourselves as parents, or as teachers, or as researchers. We may well ask what kind of harm is done when such research efforts are no longer made.

NOTES

1. Cf. Cavell, 2005, p. 120.
2. Cf. Peter Winch's *The Idea of a Social Science* for the basic contours of this 'place of its own'.
3. I am drawing on a passage from Sheridan Hough (1997, p. 13) here. Hough uses this line of argument on Nietzsche, but I find it applies equally well to Wittgenstein.
4. Concept adopted from Cavell, 2005, p. 122.
5. Ibid.
6. My attention to this passage has been drawn by Cavell, 2005, p. 117.
7. Phrase borrowed from Nietzsche, 1982, 103.

REFERENCES

Blake, N., Smeyers, P., Smith, R. and Standish, P. (1998) *Thinking Again: Education after postmodernism* (London, Bergin & Garvey).
Blake, N., Smeyers, P., Smith, R. and Standish, P. (2000) *Education in an Age of Nihilism* (London, Routledge/Falmer).
Bramwell, R. D. (1978) Education and the Two Traditions of Science, *Educational Theory*, 28, pp. 223–230.
Carr, D. (1998) Introduction: The post-war rise and fall of educational epistemology, in: D. Carr (ed.) *Education, Knowledge and Truth: Beyond the postmodern impasse* (London, Routledge), pp. 1–15.
Carr, D. (1999) Toward a Re-evaluation of the Role of Educational Epistemology in the Professional Education of Teachers, in: S. Tozer (ed.) *Philosophy of Education 1998* (Urbana, Philosophy of Education Society), pp. 439–447.
Cavell, S. (1979) *The Claim of Reason: Wittgenstein, skepticism, morality, and tragedy* (New York, Oxford University Press).
Cavell, S. (1988) *In Quest of the Ordinary: Lines of skepticism and romanticism* (Chicago, IL, The University of Chicago Press).
Cavell, S. (1996) The Ordinary as the Uneventful, in: S. Mulhall (ed.) *The Cavell Reader* (Oxford, Blackwell Publishers Ltd), pp. 253–259.
Cavell, S. (2005) *Philosophy the Day after Tomorrow* (London, The Belknap Press of Harvard University Press).
Cuypers, S. E. (2003) The Concept of Truth in Educational Theory, in: P. Smeyers and M. Depaepe (eds) *Beyond Empiricism: On criteria for educational research* (Leuven, Leuven University Press), pp. 167–179.
Flyvbjerg, B. (2001) *Making Social Science Matter: Why social inquiry fails and how it can succeed again* (Cambridge, Cambridge University Press).

Hammersley, M. (2004) Get Real! A defense of realism, in: H. Piper and I. Stronach (eds) *Educational Research: Difference and diversity* (Aldershot, Ashgate), pp. 59–78.

Hough, S. (1997) *Nietzsch's Noontide Friend: The self as metaphorical double* (University Park, PA, Pennsylvania State University Press).

Howe, R. K. (2005) The Education Science Question: A symposium, *Educational Theory*, 55, pp. 235–243.

MacLure, M. (2003) *Discourse in Educational and Social Research* (Buckingham, Open University Press).

Nietzsche, F. (1982) *Daybreak: Thoughts on the prejudices of morality*, R. J. Hollingdale, trans. (Cambridge, Cambridge University Press).

Nietzsche, F. [1877] (1995) Human, All Too Human, in: E. Behler (ed.) *The Complete Works of Friedrich Nietzsche, vol. 3* (Palo Alto, CA, Stanford University Press).

Nietzsche, F. [1882] (2001) *The Gay Science. With a prelude in German rhymes and an appendix of songs* (Williams, B. ed., J. Nauckhoff, trans. (Cambridge, Cambridge University Press).

Noddings, N. (2003) *Happiness and Education* (Palo Alto, CA, Stanford University Press).

O'Dea, J. (1994) Pursuing Truth in Narrative Research, *Journal of Philosophy of Education*, 28, pp. 161–171.

Phillips, D. C. (1997) (Re)Inventing Scheffler, or Defending Objective Educational Research, *Studies in Philosophy and Education*, 16, pp. 149–158.

Phillips, D. C. and Burbules, N. (2000) *Postpositivism and Educational Research* (Oxford, Rowman & Littlefield Publishers).

Ramaekers, S. (2002) Postmodernism: A 'sceptical' challenge in educational theory, *Journal of Philosophy of Education*, 36, pp. 629–651.

Schwandt, T. A. (2005) A Diagnostic Reading of Scientifically Based Research for Education, *Educational Theory*, 55, pp. 285–305.

Smith, R. (2003) Research and Revelation: What really works?, in: P. Smeyers and M. Depaepe (eds) *Beyond Empiricism: On criteria for educational research* (Leuven, Leuven University Press), pp. 129–140.

Stake, R. and Kerr, D. (1995) René Magritte, Constructivism, and the Researcher as Interpreter, *Educational Theory*, 45, pp. 55–61.

Winch, P. (1958) *The Idea of a Social science and its Relation to Philosophy* (London, Routledge).

Wittgenstein, L. (1953) *Philosophische Untersuchungen/Philosophical investigations* (G. E. M. Anscombe, trans. (Oxford, Basil Blackwell).

Wittgenstein, L. (1961) *Notebooks, 1914–1916*, G. E. M. Anscombe, trans. (Oxford, Basil Blackwell).

8

The Quantitative-Qualitative Distinction and the Null Hypothesis Significance Testing Procedure

NIMAL RATNESAR AND JIM MACKENZIE

Discussions of research methodology tend to be dominated by a contrast, and often conflict, between two approaches, the quantitative and the qualitative. The first chapter of Burns (2000) is typical.[1] Research is divided, at least in the social science areas, between two competing methods. On the one hand, there is 'the traditional scientific approach' (p. 3), which 'holds that only a systematic, quantitative approach to generating and testing is adequate' (p. 4). Citing Kerlinger (1986), Burns distinguishes four ways of knowing: tenacity (i.e. holding on to what one already believes), authority, intuition, and science, of which only the last is self-correcting (p. 5). 'The four most important characteristics of science are control, operational definition, replication and hypothesis testing' (p. 5). 'Science is based on the form of logic known as deduction. The basic syllogism is: All Ps are Q/This is a P/Therefore this is Q' (p. 8).[2] The strength of the scientific approach is that it 'produces answers which have a much firmer basis than the lay person's common sense or intuition or opinion' (p. 9).[3]

On the other hand, there is 'the qualitative approach' (p. 10). 'The task of the qualitative methodologist is to capture what people say and do as a product of how they interpret the complexity of their world, to understand events from the viewpoints of the participants. It is the lifeworld of the participants that constitutes the investigative field' (p. 11). 'Qualitative descriptions can play the important part of suggesting possible relationship(s), causes, effects, and even dynamic processes in school settings. Qualitative methods can highlight subtleties in pupil behaviour and response, illuminate reasons for action and provide in-depth information on teacher interpretations and teaching style' (p. 13). And qualitative reports are much easier to read and understand than reports of quantitative research (p. 14).

At the end of his discussion, Burns admits 'the practice of dichotomising and polarising social science research into quantitative and qualitative modes is overdone and misleading. . . . The contrast that can be supported is the dichotomy between naturalistic research and experimental research' (p. 14).

As a naturalistic description of the behaviour and lifeworld of people *engaged* in educational research, Burns's chapter has considerable validity. But as an account of research methods, it requires substantial correction. The most staggering point is the parochialness and ignorance of the scope of knowledge and of research implicit in the claim. Despite the invocation of Kerlinger's four ways of knowing, Burns's contrast is inapplicable to most of the vast tracts of knowledge outside the social sciences. Mathematical knowledge, for example, is produced neither by naturalistic nor by experimental methods.[4] The natural sciences do indeed use both naturalistic and experimental methods, but field studies are not narratives about the lifeworlds of rocks or pulsars or different kinds of algae, and experimental studies often do not fit Burns's requirements of controlling ('systematically eliminat[ing] the simultaneous influence of many variables', p. 6), operational definition, replication, and hypothesis testing.[5] Even most of those who study aspects of human society—historians, economists, students of linguistics, legal researchers, lexicographers, clinicians, psephologists, philosophers—use methods which bear little resemblance to either the quantitative/experimental or the qualitative/naturalistic models Burns describes. In Burns's case, the focus is clear. Despite his very general title, he is actually writing about research only in education, and only about certain kinds of research in that field; and his emphasis is heavily on quantitative/experimental studies. He devotes 344 pages to quantitative methods but only 164 pages to qualitative methods—ethnographic research, unstructured interviewing, action research, case studies, and historical research are the kinds described, and 50 of these pages are examples of research reports—and 40 pages to survey methods. These proportions are not unusual in textbooks on educational research.

It is, of course, possible to stipulate that all methods other than statistically analysed experiments are to be called 'qualitative', just as it is possible to divide all mammals into bats and non-bats. In both cases, the second class is so heterogeneous (mice, whales, kangaroos, tigers, and baboons differ greatly from each other) as to leave us wondering why the classification was made in that way. In particular, though some methods that are qualitative according to this definition are less than rigorous and their results are very shaky, others—most obviously proofs in Zermelo-Fraenkel set theory, including of course the formal probability theory underlying any use of statistics—are far more rigorous and have conclusions far more certain than anything in empirical science. The phrase 'qualitative methods' on this suggestion is simply an index of the speaker's narrowness of outlook. The notion that by mentioning both quantitative and qualitative research one is being inclusive and covering all possibilities is a clear indication of ignorance of the scope of research methodology.[6]

Equally striking about the account is its neglect of ideas. If 'Research is a systematic investigation to find answers to a problem' (p. 3), it is surprising that there is no attempt to consider the differences between kinds of problems and the differences between kinds of answers to them (propositions), even at the simplest level. The answer to a clinical problem will commonly be a singular recommendation for what should be done in the existing context; the answer to a theoretical problem may be a context-free generalisation, the answer to another kind of problem may be different again. When Burns gives an example of the Barbara syllogism with singular minor, he remarks that 'the generalisation involved in the first proposition [the major premiss], i.e., all Ps are Qs, is difficult to prove in many cases' (p. 3), but he does not attempt any further taxonomy of propositions into generalisations and non-general propositions, let alone differentiation of each class into subspecies. There is no mention of other forms of traditional syllogism (though Bocardo or Fesapo are more congruent with Popperian methodology.) He describes the statement 'People are poor and starving because God wills it' as metaphysical, and says that such statements cannot be tested (p. 8), but he does not tell us what makes a statement a 'metaphysical' one. Apparently, those that mention God have this characteristic, but that need not be necessary for being metaphysical. There is no discussion of whether any metaphysical propositions however defined are falsifiable, nor of whether any other kinds of propositions are unfalsifiable. Nor is there discussion of whether falsifying propositions may themselves be falsifiable, the immunisation of propositions from falsification by adding conditions, the prospect that propositions may thereby be emptied of empirical consequences, how evaluative or particular or singular or existential or relational propositions fit into this picture with generalisations, and so on.

NULL HYPOTHESIS SIGNIFICANCE TESTING

Burns's fourth requirement for science, hypothesis testing, is the heart of the inferential use of statistics as he and many others understand it. However, statistics and probability are not used as a way of presenting data as relevant evidence for sorting through doubts and uncertainties and for indicating the degree of confidence in inferences warranted by the data. Rather, what is meant is the use of the Null Hypothesis Significance Testing Procedure (henceforth NHSTP). In the 1960s this was presented as the *sine qua non* of scientific research (Gigerenzer, 1993), and still is 'currently the cornerstone of many "quantitative" methods courses' (Gorard, Prandy and Roberts, 2002, p. 36), as indeed Burns's book confirms. The NHSTP is given pride of place as an indispensable tool of quantitative research and treated with such awe and respect that its output the 'p-value' is regarded as more authoritative than a substantial effect size or even the inter-ocular impact of some graphical description of the data. Obtaining a low p-value below some threshold number is termed 'statistical significance' and is often seen not only in terms of *research* success itself but as the ticket to publication in journals (Gigerenzer, 1993; Sohn, 2000); Salsburg says that 'it provides Salvation: Proper invocation of the religious dogmas of Statistics will result in publication in prestigious journals' (1985, p. 220). Frick, though he concedes at least its insufficiency, still defends it on the grounds that it helps categorise findings 'as being acceptable or not to enter the corpus of claims in psychology' (1996, p. 388).

The main steps of the NHSTP are as follows:

- Specify the null hypothesis, H_0, which is to be opposed; no one would go through with the NHSTP unless they wished to oppose the H_0.
- Calculate a p-value (which these days is invariably done by a computer program).
- If the p-value is smaller than the preset level of significance, á (commonly set at 0.05 though some times 0.01—both for historical reasons rather than from any epistemic significance), then reject H_0. Otherwise, rigorously speaking, one *fails to reject* (rather than *accepts*) H_0 at that level of significance. In the event of a rejection of H_0 then the alternative hypothesis, H_A, the one the researcher wishes to put forward, is claimed as acceptable and publishable.

In addition, it is sometimes recommended that *power* (which is the frequentist probability of correctly rejecting a false H_0—i.e. a long run rate as opposed to an epistemically evaluative comment on any single case), should also be calculated.[7] The preset level of significance, α, is also not a comment on the case at hand but the long run error *rate* of wrongly rejecting H_0—but under identical circumstances.

The p-value is the probability, in the frequentist sense, of obtaining a value of the test-statistic that is at least as extreme as that calculated from the data under H_0. (With some computer programs stars replace the p-value, where the smaller the p-value the more stars, implying that some rejections are of higher rank than others.)

The Null Hypothesis Significance Testing Procedure (NHSTP) is presented, taught and practised as an uncontroversial dichotomous decision rule and also as 'the monolithic logic of scientific inference' (Gigerenzer, 1993, p. 324, his emphasis); indeed, it is what *inferential* statistics is taken to be all about: a simple mechanical procedure that almost anyone can perform and use to make a research claim. However, it is not uncontroversial, in its origins or in its continued use. Of the NHSTP, Meehl wrote 'I suggest to you that Sir Ronald [Fisher] has befuddled us, mesmerized us, and led us down the primrose path. I believe that the almost universal reliance on merely refuting the null hypothesis as the standard method for corroborating substantive theories in the soft areas is a terrible mistake, is basically unsound, poor scientific strategy, and one of the worst things that ever happened in the history of psychology' (1978, p. 817), and Wang wrote of it that 'The tyranny of the N-P [Neyman-Pearson] theory in many branches of empirical science is detrimental, not advantageous, to the course of science' (1993, p. 21).[8] However, neither Fisher nor Neyman and Pearson is to blame for the way the NHSTP is used, though it draws from the ideas of both. It is rather textbook writers and social research educators who have put together and perpetuated this hybrid procedure (Gigerenzer, 1993; Hubbard and Bayarri, 2003); and still very few textbooks mention that it is problematic (Gliner, Leech and Morgan, 2002).

Not only would neither Fisher nor Neyman and Pearson have agreed with the NHSTP as currently taught and practised but each accused the other party of the same sin, the mechanical and otherwise thoughtless use of statistics (Gigerenzer, 1993). Neyman (1957) noted that Fisher consistently used 0.01 as a conventional level of significance regardless of the research context and problem (p. 12) even though he [Fisher] opposed the final accept-or-reject outcome of the use of the Neyman-Pearson theory (Gigerenzer, 1993, p. 321). Fisher for his part argued that while the N-P theory was possibly useful with repeated sampling for testing long sequences of hypotheses as in industrial quality control contexts, it was *irrelevant* to scientific advance (Hacking, 1965). While Neyman and Pearson certainly saw their [N-P] theory as meaningfully applicable in such industrial contexts and Neyman referred to the ideas of N-P theory, relating it to the wider context of 'the concluding phase of scientific research' (1957, p. 14), as a matter of inductive behaviour involving 'an act of will to behave ... in a particular manner' (p. 12), nevertheless they clearly recognised the need for judgment: as Pearson wrote: '*Of necessity*, as it seemed to *us*, we left in our mathematical model a gap for the exercise of a more intuitive process of personal judgment in such matters—to use our terminology—as the choice of the most likely class of admissible hypotheses, the appropriate significance level, the magnitude of worthwhile effects and the balance of utilities' (1962, p. 395, emphases added). According to the originators of the N-P theory it is only after the exercise of meaningful judgments that an accept-or-reject decision at some preset level, α, is sensible; and adopting such behaviour over a *long run* of experiments in terms of error *rates* can be used cost-effectively to control quality in some industrial process (such as, for example, ensuring that the diameter of ball bearings on a production line is within acceptable limits). Fisher saw the p-value as an indication or measure of inductive inferential evidence for being able 'to argue from consequences to causes, from observations to hypothesis' (1935, p. 3), but he also said 'no isolated experiment, however significant in itself, can suffice for the experimental demonstration of any natural phenomenon' (p. 13).

The NHSTP as commonly practised, however, dispenses with such niceties as judgment and repeated testing: it matters only whether or not a single experiment produces a statistically significant result. The rigid dichotomous decision to reject or accept (or, more rigorously stated, not to reject) the null hypothesis (which is usually a straw dummy anyway), then follows mechanically, but not by any argument concerning the epistemic state of a research claim. The calculations involved in the NHSTP make no reference whatsoever to any alternative hypotheses nor does the decision, to reject or not, have any epistemic significance of itself. Almost anyone can do it (Gigerenzer, 1993), but the NHSTP procedure rigidly demands that if a significant result is obtained then the null hypothesis, H_0, *must* be rejected—no ifs or buts. There is no room for *almost* significant, though, 'surely, God loves the .06 nearly as much as the .05' (Rosnow and Rosenthal, 1989, p. 1277)—and as for power, 'surely God loves the .79 nearly as much as the .80 recommendation for power' (Ernest and McLean, 1998, p. 60). Neither Fisher nor Neyman and Pearson would have endorsed this rigidity. The N-P theory does not require that a manufacturing process should be rejected outright if a sample is drawn that gives a significant result. One should behave only *as if* the null hypothesis is false and check the machinery, because false alarms are likely in the long run (Gigerenzer, 1993); and in checking the machinery a vast number of collateral premises are then appealed to in judging whether the machinery is in order or is in need of replacement or repair. Fisher, too, not only said no single experiments could suffice for the demonstration of natural phenomena (1935, p. 13), but also held that it was only after 'fundamental thinking has been accomplished' that exercises 'Constructive imagination, together with much knowledge based on experience' that a 'problem be given a mathematical form' and that it was 'nothing but an illusion to think that this process can ever be reduced to a self-contained mathematical theory of tests of significance' (Fisher, 1939, p. 223). Fisher (1939) highly commended 'Student' (the pen-name of W. S. Gossett) for possessing not only these qualities but also the required pertinacity to perceive and solve problems. Indeed such pertinacity or 'good tenacity' is among what Lakatos (1973, p. 95) held as among the essential qualities of a good researcher. As well, Fisher (1933, p. 46) was quite aware that it was necessary that the statistician be appreciative of the limitations of any available data.

However those who use the NHSTP in social and educational research do not follow Fisher's or Neyman's and Pearson's advice; rather the p-value of a single study is routinely treated as sanctifying or damning some hypothesis, and the results are published without replication and without examining the 'machinery' that produced the result to see if the data are anomalous or limited in any way.

Rigidity that does not admit that it may well be more reasonable to suppose it is the data that are anomalous or limited, but requires instant rejection of the null hypothesis upon obtaining statistical significance, together with the view that science progresses through accumulating publicly verifiable empirical facts and through mechanical procedures and experiments which anybody can repeat at will, are of course the characteristics of a kind of positivism (Polanyi, 1962) which disavows the intuitions and judgements of the researcher. And this is characteristic of the practice of the NHSTP. Thankfully physicists in the early 1900s were not bothered with the need for 'rigour' of this sort, or Einstein's theory of relativity might never have caught on (Polanyi, 1962; Carver, 1993). As Rozeboom (1960) has noted with reference to the NHSTP, research does not progress through decision-precipitating rules, but through inferential judgements by which we appropriately adjust our beliefs and opinions. It is quite absurd to make an epistemic claim to a general proposition on the basis of a single experiment, as the NHSTP attempts to do.

It is perhaps along these lines that the real philosophical difference underlying the quantitative-qualitative divide is drawn: positivism as contrasted with rationalistic realism, bats as opposed to non-bats, NHSTPism versus (real) research. Research worthy of the name requires an intellectual commitment (Polanyi, 1962), judgement (Fisher, 1939; Pearson, 1962; Rozeboom, 1960), the necessary kind of pertinacity or good tenacity (Fisher, 1939; Lakatos, 1973), and a constructive imagination (Fisher, 1939). The house of knowledge has many mansions. Even poetry may use numbers and John von Neumann put his faith in 'the influence of men with an exceptionally well-developed taste' to avoid 'degeneration' in mathematics (1947, p. 196).

As for a *probabilistic modus tollens*, claimed as the justifying logic of the NHSTP, that just doesn't work either, (Cohen, 1994; Royall, 1997; Sober, 2002); rare events do happen (Hacking, 1965); a frequentist low probability, a mathematical construct, does not automatically convert to the inferential notion of implausibility; and randomisation is not a cure either because the nice mathematical properties of a random variable do not extend to the given data sample in hand. To maintain the illusion that research, even just within education, is to be thought of as divided between quantitative and qualitative is no longer sustainable.[9]

NOTES

1. There are many textbooks providing introductions to research methods for students of education and the social sciences. Burns (2000) is typical of the genre and is widely used. We have focused our remarks on it for the sake of definiteness.

2. This form is recognisable as the argument schema known in the traditional formal logic of the Middle Ages as Barbara with singular minor. An argument is deductively valid just in case it is logically impossible for all the premises to be true and the conclusion false. Traditional syllogistic can represent some, but not all, valid deductive arguments.

3. Since Burns will later cite Popper with approval for endorsement of the scientific approach, it may be worth noting Popper's own account of this 'firm basis', which differs starkly from Burns's: 'The empirical basis of objective science has thus nothing "absolute" about it. Science does not rest upon solid bedrock. The bold structure of its theories rises, as it were, above a swamp. It is like a building erected on piles. The piles are driven down from above into the swamp, but not down to any natural or "given" base; and if we stop driving the piles deeper, it is not because we have reached firm ground. We simply stop when we are satisfied that the piles are firm enough to carry the structure, at least for the time being' (Popper, 1959, §30, p. 111). Burns does not cite this work, though it is of course the central text for Popper's views on scientific method.

4. Mathematical research is certainly not quantitative in the sense defined.

5. And even when they seem to, this may be a misleading appearance of the conventions for writing up research insisted upon by editors of scientific journals. '[T]he scientific paper is a fraud in the sense that it does give a totally misleading narrative of the processes of thought that go into the making of scientific discoveries' (Medawar, 1963, p. 38).

6. One recalls the boast by a rural radio station that it plays both kinds of music, Country *and* Western.

7. Burns defines: 'power is the ability of a statistic to correctly reject the null hypothesis when it is false' (2000, p. 160).

8. The N-P [Neyman-Pearson] theory refers to the theory developed by Jerzy Neyman and Egon Pearson. The N-P theory departs from Fisher's idea of hypothesis testing (of considering the

probabilistic behaviour of just one hypothesis), in that it also recognises the need to include the alternative hypothesis *together* with the possibility of the errors of wrong decisions about which of the hypotheses could be true. Under the N-P theory the error of rejecting a true null hypothesis is called an error of the first kind (type I error), while the error of accepting or failing to reject a false null hypothesis is called an error of the second kind (type II error). The N-P theory uses the criterion of what it calls the critical region. If the value of the test statistic, as calculated from the sample, falls into that region then the null hypothesis, according to which such an event is deemed improbable or infrequent, is regarded as rejectable—albeit with the possibility of a type I error. In addition the N-P theory also discusses the idea of the *power* of a test, which is the probability or (limiting relative) frequency with which a test would correctly reject a false null hypothesis.

9. Work for this chapter was hindered by the inadequate funding of Australian academic libraries.

REFERENCES

Burns, R. B. (2000) *Introduction to Research Methods*, 4th edn (Sydney, Longmans Pearson Education Australia).

Carver, R. (1993) The Case Against Statistical Significance Testing, Revisited, *Journal of Experimental Education*, 61, pp. 287–292.

Cohen, J. (1994) The Earth is Round ($p < .05$), *American Psychologist*, 49, pp. 997–1003.

Ernest, J. M. and McLean, J. E. (1998) Fight the Good Fight: A Response to Thompson, Knapp, and Levin, *Research in the Schools*, 5.2, pp. 59–62.

Fisher, R. A. (1933) The Contributions of Rothamsted to the Development of the Science of Statistics. Annual Report of the Rothamsted Station, pp. 43–50. (Reprinted in his *Collected Papers*, ed. J. H. Bennett, vol. 3 (Adelaide, University of Adelaide Press), pp. 84–91).

Fisher, R. A. (1935) *The Design of Experiments* (Repr. Edinburgh; Oliver & Boyd, 8th edn, 1966).

Fisher, R. A. (1939) 'Student', *Annals of Eugenics*, 9, pp. 1–9 at ⟨http//www.library.adelaide. edu.au/digitised/fisher/165.pdf⟩ (Reproduced with permission of Cambridge University Press).

Frick, R. W. (1996) The Appropriate Use of Null Hypothesis Testing, *Psychological Methods*, 1.4, pp. 379–390.

Gigerenzer, G. (1993) The Superego, the Ego, and the Id in Statistical Reasoning, in: G. Keren and C. Lewis (eds) *A Handbook for Data Analysis in the Behavioral Sciences: Methodological Issues* (Hillsdale, NJ, Lawrence Erlbaum Associates), pp. 311–339.

Gliner, J. A., Leech, N. L. and Morgan, G. A. (2002) Problems with Null Hypothesis Significance Testing (NHST): What do the Textbooks Say?, *Journal of Experimental Education*, 71.1, pp. 83–92.

Gorard, S., Prandy, K. and Roberts, K. (2002) An Introduction to the Simple Role of Numbers in Social Science Research. ESRC (Economic and Social Research Council) Teaching and Learning Research Programme, Research Capacity Building Network, Occasional Paper Series, Paper 53 at ⟨http://www.cf.ac.uk/socsi/capacity/Papers/roleofnumbers.pdf⟩.

Hacking, I. (1965) *Logic of Statistical Inference* (Cambridge, Cambridge University Press).

Hubbard, R. and Bayarri, M. J. (2003) Confusion Over Measures of Evidence (p's) versus Errors (α's) in Classical Statistical Testing, *The American Statistician*, 57.3, pp. 171–182.

Kerlinger, F. (1986) *Foundations of Behavioral Research* (New York, Holt).

Lakatos, I. (1973) Lectures on Scientific Method, in: M. Motterlini (ed.) *For and Against Method* (Chicago, University of Chicago Press).

Medawar, P. (1963) Is the Scientific Paper a Fraud? Repr. in his *The Strange Case of the Spotted Mice and Other Classic Essays on Science* (Oxford, Oxford University Press), 1996, pp. 33–39.

Meehl, P. E. (1978) Theoretical Risks and Tabular Asterisks: Sir Karl, Sir Ronald, and the Slow Progress of Soft Psychology, *Journal of Consulting and Clinical Psychology*, 46.4, pp. 806–834.

Neumann, J. von (1947) The Mathematician, in: R. B. Heywood (ed.) *The Works of the Mind* (Chicago, University of Chicago Press).

Neyman, J. (1957) Inductive Behavior as a Basic Concept of Philosophy of Science, *International Statistical Review*, 25, pp. 7–22.

Pearson, E. S. (1962) Some Thoughts on Statistical Inference, *Annals of Mathematical Statistics*, 33, pp. 394–403.

Polanyi, M. (1962) *Personal Knowledge: Towards a Post-Critical Philosophy* (London, Routledge & Kegan Paul).

Popper, K. R. (1959) *The Logic of Scientific Discovery* (*Logik der Forschung,* 1934) (London, Hutchinson).

Rosnow, R. L. and Rosenthal, R. (1989) Statistical Procedures and the Justification of Knowledge in Psychological Science, *American Psychologist,* 44, pp. 1276–1284.

Royall, R. (1997) *Statistical Evidence—a Likelihood Paradigm* (Boca Raton, FL, Chapman and Hall).

Rozeboom, W. W. (1960) The Fallacy of the Null-Hypothesis Significance Test, *Psychological Bulletin,* 57, pp. 416–428.

Salsburg, D. S. (1985) The Religion of Statistics as Practiced in Medical Journals, *American Statistician,* 39, pp. 220–223.

Sober, E. (2002) Intelligent Design and Probability Reasoning, *International Journal of Philosophy of Religion,* 52, pp. 65–80.

Sohn, D. (2000) Significance Testing and the Science [Comment], *American Psychologist,* 55.8, pp. 964–965.

Wang, C. (1993) *Sense and Nonsense of Statistical Inference: Controversy, Misuse, and Subtlety* (New York, Marcel Dekker).

9

A View from Somewhere: Explaining the Paradigms of Educational Research

HANAN A. ALEXANDER

INTRODUCTION

For some time now educational researchers have puzzled over the question: How can the subjective perceptions of single participant-observers in particular cases found in qualitative inquiry yield knowledge worthy of the name, given the concern for objectivity and generalisability inherent in the positivist approach to social and behavioral science?[1] Philosophers have long been concerned with questions of this kind. How, they ask, is one thing possible, supposing certain other conflicting or contradictory things? How is it possible for us to have free will, for example, supposing that all actions are causally determined or for evil to be possible, given the existence of an omnipotent omniscient good God? (Nozick, 1981, p. 8) Addressing these sorts of questions requires what Robert Nozick has called a philosophical explanation, which articulates deeper principles that can remove the apparent conflict and put one's beliefs in alignment.

Perhaps the most common explanation offered in response to this question in educational research argues that qualitative inquiry such as phenomenology and ethnography is grounded in constructivism, an alternative epistemology to the positivist orientation of quantitative research (Guba, 1990; Guba and Lincoln, 1985, 1989; Shkedi, 2003). According to this account, positivism is not the only epistemological game in town. We can distinguish at least two conceptions of knowledge, one that aims to discover and explain relations between dependent and independent variables and another that strives to understand human experiences, norms and purposes (Von Wright, 1981; Snow, 1990; Cronbach, 1975). To buttress this approach, some authors refer to Thomas Kuhn's notion of a scientific research paradigm (Kuhn, 1996), suggesting that qualitative inquiry constitutes a new paradigm in social and educational research that is as intellectually legitimate as the quantitative paradigm (Patton, 1980, 1990).

I shall refer to this as the dual (or plural) epistemology thesis. Its chief advantage is that in the so-called methodology wars between quantitative and qualitative methods, this thesis allows for a strategy of mutual appeasement that enables the two orientations to coexist in the professions of social and educational research. Nevertheless, this explanation of the viability of both qualitative and quantitative research methods suffers from a number of serious flaws (Alexander, 1986).

In this chapter I offer an alternative to the dual-epistemology that avoids these difficulties. I argue that something like Dewey's pragmatism may offer a promising way out of the false dichotomies that have so often characterised this debate (Biesta and Burbules, 2003; Johnson and Onwuegbuzie, 2005; Maxcy, 2003). However, avoiding the quagmires of self-defeating relativism to which pragmatism too often succumbs (e.g. Rorty, 1980; 1982) requires appeal to a limited conception of transcendence—higher ideals that are not dependent upon but that govern human activities within space and time—though tied more closely to what Aristotle called practical wisdom than to the sort of abstract theory or pure reason with which ideas of this kind have often been associated. Acknowledging the futility of what Thomas Nagel (1986) called 'the view from nowhere'—a completely neutral account of objective reality— requires admitting the possibility of a view from somewhere, even if we cannot come to agreement concerning where that view is from or what vantage point it allows. I call this alternative, rather provocatively, 'transcendental pragmatism'.[2]

The chapter is divided into five parts. In the first section I discuss the reemergence of the so-called methodology wars between quantitative and qualitative methods in the educational research community. Next I consider some of the difficulties with the dual epistemology thesis as a basis for resolving tensions between the warring camps along with some of the historical debates that led me to search for an alternative. Section four lays out that alternative and the final section addresses some of its consequence for educational research.

I NEW SKIRMISHES IN THE METHODOLOGY WARS

The question of how it is possible to believe the findings of qualitative inquiry, given concerns for causal explanation and generalisation, gained prominence in the educational research community in the last part of the twentieth century. In the US, researchers such as Egon Guba (1990), Yvonna Lincoln (Guba and Lincoln, 1985, 1989), Robert Stake (1995), Michael Patton (1990, 1980), and Elliot Eisner (1991) questioned some of the central assumptions of the positivist orientation against which their emerging interest in qualitative methods was being judged. Interest in this question became more acute as radical scholars of education and those interested in postmodernism gained prominence, such as Henry Giroux (1992), Stanley Aronowitz (Aronowitz and Giroux, 1993), Peter McLaren (1994), Michael Apple (1990, 1982), and Thomas Popkewitz (1984), who challenged not only the ways in which positivist educational researchers collect and analyse data, but the very possibility that knowledge in education (or elsewhere) could be distinguished from power and ideology.

After a quarter century of methodology wars, in which positivists and anti-positivists of different stripes attempted to expose and defeat one another's assumptions, it appeared for a time as though educational researchers had reached a truce that allowed different camps to tolerate if not also respect each other's positions, based at least in part on the doctrine of dual epistemology. That truce was broken, however, in 2001 when an act of the US Congress entitled 'No Child Left Behind' endorsed randomized controlled experimentation as the so-called 'gold standard' of research methodologies. The research branch of the US Department of Education consequently allocated federal funds to support experimental research such as randomised field trials almost exclusively, or in a few instances quasi-experimental approaches such as regression discontinuity methods (Campbell and Stanley, 1963, Shaddish, Cook and Campbell, 2002). The political environment in Washington during the period that led up to this endorsement was characterised by social conservatism and concern about the poor quality of much educational research. It prompted many interested parties in the US educational research community to call upon the National Research Council (NRC) of the National Academy of Sciences to establish an independent group to, as one commentator put it, 'jump the Congressional gun, and offer a less narrow and more reasoned account . . . of what it is to be "rigorously scientific" ' (Phillips, 2005). The NRC report, which on this account was careful to recognise the academic respectability of a variety of disciplines in educational research, including for example, educational anthropology and ethnography, offered the following six criteria as 'guiding principles' for a 'healthy community of scientific researchers'. Scientific research should:

(i) Pose significant questions that can be investigated empirically; (ii) Link research to relevant theory; (iii) Use methods that permit direct investigation of questions; (iv) Provide a coherent and explicit chain of reasoning; (v) Yield findings that replicate, and generalize across studies; and (vi) Disclose research data and methods to enable and encourage professional scrutiny and critique. (Feuer, Towne and Shavelson, 2002)

Yet, as a number of critics point out (Erickson and Guiterrez, 2002; St. Peter, 2002; Eisenhart, 2005), the NRC report does not veer as far as its advocates claimed from the narrow empiricist path set by the revival of what another commentator called 'experimentism' in educational research (Howe, 2005). For example, it continues to hold up replication and generalisation as standards against which most, if not all, educational research ought to be judged. Some critics (e.g. Moss, 2005) point out that the NRC report does not take sufficient account of the epistemological differences between research that seeks to discover causal explanation for purposes of prediction and control, on the one hand, and that which pursues purposive (or intentional) explanation and hermeneutic understanding, on the other (von Wright, 1981). Other commentators offer various forms of pragmatism or post-positivism as an alternative to the scientific positivism inherent in the preference for randomised experiments (Schwandt, 2005; Howe, 2005; Phillips, 2005).

One can only wonder why this debate has reemerged in the educational research community with such vehemence. There are surely many social and political influences that can account for the acrimony and intensity of the discussion. But there are philosophical issues involved here as well, including weaknesses in the doctrine upon which the truce in the methodology wars was, at least in part, founded. For the dual epistemology thesis never adequately addressed the question of how it is possible to embrace the findings of research grounded in a qualitative orientation given the empiricist demand for randomization and generalisability, or conversely, how quantitative results can be meaningful given the hermeneutic critique of positivism and post-positivism.

II DUAL EPISTEMOLOGY AND ITS DISCONTENTS

One difficulty with the dual epistemology thesis is that it tends toward a self-refuting form of relativism that hinders the systematic assessment of merit in social and educational research. Each paradigm has its own assumptions, according to this view, and it is unreasonable to criticise one on the basis of the other. It follows that the only criteria that can be used to evaluate any specific application of a research paradigm are internal; and if an orientation does not prize logical consistency, for example, there is no way to call it to account. As Johnson and Onwuegbuzie wrote recently (2005), 'When it comes to research quality, it is not the case that anyone's opinion about quality is just as good as the next person's, because some people have no training or expertise or even interest in research' (p. 16).[3]

A second problem with dual epistemology is that it tends to discourage mixing qualitative and quantitative methods in single studies by encouraging epistemological and methodological purism among both qualitative and quantitative researchers. However, an increasing number of researchers are looking to integrate quantitative and qualitative methods in mixed research designs (Creswell, 2003; Sieber, 1973; Tashakkori and Teddlie, 1998). These designs 'attempt to legitimate the use of multiple approaches in answering research questions, rather than restricting or constraining researchers' choices'. This form of research is expansive, inclusive, and pluralistic, suggesting that researchers may select their methods eclectically, in accordance with research question being asked (Johnson and Onwuegbuzie, 2005, p. 17).[4]

The third problem with this orientation concerns its interpretation of Kuhn's concept of scientific research paradigms. Setting aside the fact that Kuhn did not hold that scientific paradigms exist in the social or behavioral sciences—a belief probably linked to his positivist past—if the advent of qualitative inquiry is a scientific revolution ala Kuhn, it cannot leave our attitude toward the previous paradigm—positivist social science—unaffected. On Kuhn's view, the new paradigm ought to replace the old one, as Copernican supplanted Ptolemaic astronomy, by accounting for data that were previously unexplained. Alternatively the new paradigm should enable us to view the old one in a new light, as Einstein's relativity thesis contextualized the meaning of Newtonian mechanics (Kuhn, 1996).[5]

Fourth, the qualitative revolution in social and educational research raised hard questions concerning the coherence of such positivist notions as social laws that are generalizable across historical, cultural, or linguistic contexts (Campbell and Stanley, 1963; Hempel, 1966; Nagel, 1961), behavioral facts independent of ethical values or political ideology, or valid and reliable measures that meaningfully capture the dynamic flow of human discourse. Yet, many dual epistemology devotees continue to check for possible errors in qualitative descriptions using softer versions of these very criteria, such as consensual validity, structural corroboration, and referential adequacy (Eisner, 1994, pp. 212–21; 1991), or trustworthiness, authenticity, and accountability (Guba and Lincoln, 1985; Shkedi, 2004). This presents qualitative inquiry as a weak form of empiricism, when according to the constructivists it is grounded in an entirely different and, to their minds, more compelling account of the very nature of knowledge itself. Although some have also recognized that standards of this kind are unduly influenced by positivism and misrepresent qualitative inquiry as a weak form of empiricism (Guba and Lincoln, 1989; Richardson, 1994), few have acknowledged the impact of these criticisms on how we ought to view measurement-based research in its own right, as well as how it ought to connect to emergent trends in qualitative inquiry (Onwuegbuzie, 2002).

In contrast to the methodological purism mentioned above, one consequence of this weak empirical attitude is a tendency to embrace forms of eclecticism that do not take adequate account of conceptual and epistemological differences between alternative accounts of the research process. For instance, Madhabi Chatterji refers to longitudinal studies of class-size that involve randomized field trials in a large number of elementary schools to show that evaluation conditions violate the assumptions of textbook field experiments, and so require a mixture of qualitative and quantitative methods. It is difficult for researchers to properly manipulate independent variables (IV) in such cases, since they are 'rarely, if ever, single, discrete, narrowly scripted and easily identifiable' conditions in field settings.

In most studies of 'class-size reduction', the definition of the IV becomes complicated by the presence or absence of volunteers, para-professionals, teacher interns, or other teachers who along with regular teachers in the classroom, provide different degrees of instructional support to a given number of students. This alters the ratio of instructional staff to pupils and the operational definition of the field 'treatment' condition. Often field treatment conditions may vary across classrooms and schools studied, and sometimes, even in the same classroom at different times of the day. Without adequate documentation of these *qualitative variables* (emphasis in the original), the effects are hard to interpret, let alone replicate (Chatterji, 2005, p. 14).

No doubt some form of observation would be useful in such cases to assist evaluators in developing empirically valid operational definitions of class-size and teacher-student ratios. However, as we shall see below, the very idea of a 'qualitative variable', the identification of which can assist in the proper manipulation of 'quantitative variables', misconstrues the heart of qualitative inquiry, which aims to understand the meanings and purposes of human activity not the causes of human behaviour. More importantly, this example underestimates the conceptual difficulties inherent in randomised field-testing, even when its weaknesses are overcome by the addition of supplemental methodologies.

For the qualitative revolution in educational research joins a philosophical debate unresolved since Hume challenged the very idea of causal explanation and undermined the modern departure from conceptions of knowledge descendent from Plato and Aristotle (Hume, 2000). Of the responses to Hume, two have been especially influential, and both are problematic. One followed Kant in understanding knowledge as a rational approximation of reality grounded in universal cognitive structures (Kant, 1998, 2004). This approach leaves the methods of empirical science intact, but vests their epistemological authority in the structure of mind. On this view, knowledge is objective, universal and generalisable. Positivists and post-positivists have generally taken this route. The other response followed Hegel in challenging Kant and reviving Platonic and Aristotelian transcendentalism (Hegel, 1978, 1953; Taylor, 1975). In this view, knowledge is contextual, subjective and particular—a product of embodied agents living in concrete historical and linguistic communities. Phenomenologists and hermeneutic theorists have generally followed this path.[6]

Positivism is probably the most influential movement to apply the principles of empiricism, developed originally by the likes of Bacon (2002) and Locke (2000) to transform the study of nature, to the investigations of people and societies (Comte, 2001). It did so, however, with a certain naiveté about the possibility of resolving the Humean predicament by means of the emerging statistical sciences. Recall that Hume argued that we can never know, in an apodictic or indubitable sense, that empirical consequences 'Ci ... Cn' will necessarily follow from initial conditions, 'Ii ... In', but only that at best they may probably follow. Our acceptance of so-called scientific laws based on such notions as cause and effect, Hume concluded, is more a matter of psychological need and cultural custom than epistemological warrant (Hume, 2000). Yet even the exact extent of this probability cannot be measured, since we have no way of accurately judging the number of possible cases in which these conditions or consequences might apply (Lesnoff, 1974).

Popper responded to Hume's critique by claiming that we may not be able to verify that consequences 'Ci ... Cn' follow from initial conditions

'Ii ... In', but we can say with certainty when this is not the case. Falsification should replace verification, therefore, as the primary aim of science (Popper, 1992, 1972). This view, which became known as post-positivism, has become especially influential in educational research (Phillips and Burbules, 2000), but it turns out to be overstated. Popper's disciple Imrre Lakatos (1978) pointed out that scientific researchers do not falsify single statements or even more complex theories one at a time. Rather they extend the core assumptions of larger research programmes, until such time as there is sufficient evidence to contravene those assumptions, which are then rejected for a new core and concomitant programme of research. In other words scientific research programmes may vary according to the judgments of distinct knowing subjects. The threat that this sort of subjective judgment poses to the objectivity of scientific knowledge may be offset by appeal to an inter-subjective community of researchers that decides when to abandon one research programme for another. However, at the end of the day, post-positivism does not succeed in salvaging the objectivity of scientific knowledge from Hume's critique.

Edmund Husserl may have offered the clearest account of the epistemological underpinnings of what later became known as constructivism. If there ever was a paradigm shift in the history of epistemology that sought to replace its predecessor it was this. Husserl argued that empiricism got off to a false start at the outset, when Descartes challenged the veracity of his very existence; perhaps life is a mere dream or grand deception (Descartes, 1996, 1999). Husserl objected to the comprehensiveness of Descartes' famous response, 'I think therefore I exist'. That someone doubts his own reality, Husserl reasoned, shows only the existence of a questioning subject, not of a person with a physical presence. We can only know indubitably that which presents itself within consciousness, concluded Husserl; we can say nothing at all with certainty about life beyond our own thoughts and experiences. To achieve knowledge that cannot be doubted, a new science called 'phenomenology' would need to bracket all references to reality outside of consciousness, and focus our attention on life as it is experienced internally (Husserl, 1960, 1967). Unfortunately, Husserl's brackets leave the questioning subject alone in his own solipsistic universe, since Husserl allows no reference whatsoever to anything other than that which presents itself in consciousness.

Not only does phenomenology bracket objective reality, it embraces Nietzsche's critique of every other form of external transcendence as well, leaving for analysis only that constructed within consciousness (Nietzsche, 2001). But if ideals independent of consciousness are ruled out of court as well as objects, then there is nothing independent of the self to which one could possibly appeal as a criterion for judging the merit of a phenomenological depiction. Narcissism and nihilism must necessarily result. Of course, like the post-positivists, Husserl and disciples do refer to inter-subjective tests for phenomenological studies (Schutz,, 1982; Schutz and Luckman, 1983). Yet given the ontological isolation that follows from

Husserl's critique of Descartes, it is hard to know what such an inter-subjectivity could possibly mean, since the only subjects that can be accounted for within this orientation are those that present themselves in consciousness, and there is no way of knowing, according to Husserl's account, whether these other subjects exist beyond the self.

III AN ALTERNATIVE: TRANSCENDENTAL PRAGMATISM

How, then, might we conceive deeper principles that can explain how it is possible to believe qualitative descriptions in the face of the demands of positivism, or to embrace experimental results given the phenomenological critique? To answer we require an account of inquiry that is pluralistic in that it allows for different methods to coexist, but that also defines the conditions under which it makes sense to speak of them as agents of some notion of truth. This was essentially Kant's project in which he followed an interpretation of Aristotle that emphasized theory over practice, although not without acknowledging a deep connection between the two.

Aristotle distinguished between the practical wisdom suitable for understanding how personal and political affairs ought to be conducted, *Phronesis*, and theories about how the world works, *Sophia*. Phronesis consists of ethical and civic virtues required for living a good life and creating a just society. Though alluding to higher ideals, the virtues are always expressed in terms of local cultures and customs. Sophia, on the other hand, attempts to grasp physical and metaphysical reality by means of two sorts of reasoning, *techne*, designed to reveal what he called the efficient or mechanical causes of events and *episteme*, which focuses on teleological or final causes. Efficient causes precede events, 'pushing' them into being as it were, by disrupting or intervening in a state of affairs in a random or chance manner. Teleological causes, on the other hand, 'pull' an event toward a natural or intrinsic state, one that is part of the very design of things. Since events cannot be explained without reference to a larger order in which they are set; the whole possesses a greater degree of reality than the parts. Teleological explanations are more fundamental than mechanical explanations, in Aristotle's view, because they tie physical to metaphysical reality (Aristotle, 1994; Smith, 2002, pp. 35–41).

Perhaps the problems with both post-positivism and phenomenology originate in just such a naïve distinction between theory and practice—description and prescription—that can not withstand criticism. It was American pragmatism, John Dewey in particular, that emphasized the incoherence of the theory-practice distinction. An opponent of what he called 'false dualisms', Dewey avoided a harsh dichotomy between the inner lives of human beings and a so-called 'objective' reality that exists outside of them. However, rather than expressing his views in the terms of German idealism, he chose what has sometimes been called a naïve naturalism. What exists, on Dewey's view, are not objects but events that like Heidegger's notion of 'Being' entail the interaction between organisms and their environments (Heidegger, 1996). Dewey called the amalgamation of these events experience. All inquiry, whether in the natural or human sciences, is about resolving problems that present themselves in experience (Dewey, 1938). We confront a problem, formulate a hypothesis about how to address it, and test out our hypothesis in experience to see if it works. A hypothesis is said to be true, on this view, not if it corresponds to an uncritical conception of external reality, but rather only if it resolves the dilemma or difficulty for which it was formulated. Inquiry, then, is a practice designed to solve problems encountered in experience (Dewey, 1910). Practice, not theory, is the driving force of all scientific endeavors, or to reverse the motto attributed to social psychologist Kurt Lewin that there is nothing so practical as a good theory; in Dewey's view there is nothing so theoretical as intelligent practice (see Biesta and Burbules, 2003; Maxey, 2003).

Whatever the merits of this position, however, one cannot avoid its tendency toward radical relativism or subjectivism (Popper 1996). How, one might ask, is it possible to decipher the degree to which one account of events is better than another, since each person brings her own conception of what it might mean to solve the problem at hand? An answer may be found by applying Aristotle's analysis of efficient and final causes to this Deweyan synthesis of theory with practice as least as its appears in the human sciences.

Charles Taylor argues that even if some behaviors can be explained by statistical laws over which actors can exercise no influence, many if not most human activity is governed by norms or purposes over which people can exercise control. If one wants to understand why someone took an umbrella from the umbrella stand today, when he failed to do so yesterday, or covers or uncovers his head when entering a house of worship, one must inquire into the norms that govern the culture in which that person lives and the reasons why he chooses to behave in this way and not that. Humans are purposeful beings; and to understand their actions we are compelled to reference teleological explanations that articulate the purposes that move people to act. Although many such purposes are imminent in existence or experience, such as the desire to fit in with a particular group, or to please (or displease) one's family, or to meet basic needs for survival, they will always be subordinate to higher ideals, such as friendship, loyalty, solidarity, respect or the sanctity of life. Taylor calls these ideal strong values (Taylor, 1964, 1984; Smith, 2002, pp. 33–57).[7] In short, the ends of inquiry into human activity are first ethical and political, concerning the worthwhile life and the just society, and only secondarily epistemological, relating to such issues as objectivity and subjectivity (Kant, 1997, 2002; Murdoch, 1970; Scheffler, 1991).[8]

But how can ethical and political ideals serve as a basis for criticism in educational research when they are often contested? One answer lies in the fact that the very idea of critique implies standards of assessment grounded in competing traditions or conceptions of the good. Of course, some traditions embrace ideals dogmatically. They are resistant to changing circumstances, counter-arguments or contrary experience. They also tend to discourage independent ideas and choices, and understand human behaviour as under the control or authority of an external agent or force. Traditions of this kind often appear to provide clear ethical standards against which to judge social policies and programmes. But in fact, these dogmatic standards tend to undermine a key condition for ethical discussions or debates to be meaningful altogether—that within reasonable limits people are the agents of their own beliefs, behaviours, and desires. Only if we can effect a change in these matters, does it make any sense at all to call upon us to do so. But if I am the agent of my own actions, then it follows that it must be possible for me to be wrong about even my most fundamental commitments. Were this not the case, if I was right for example because it is in my very nature to be correct, then it would be my nature, not me, choosing my commitments. For ideals to be ethical, in other words, they *must* be fallible. Ethical traditions that provide genuine standards of assessment must therefore be dynamic not dogmatic, embracing ideas that represent the best available formulation of the good, at least as we are given to understand it for now, but assuming that there could always be a better way or a more compelling perspective (Alexander, 2001; Phenix, 1972).[9]

Viewed in this light, knowledge—at least in education—is always the possession of an embodied agent, constrained by language, culture and history, who grasps, albeit imperfectly, the contours of an entity or the meaning of an idea that transcends—exists independently or outside of—his or her limited experience. And this requires—as a regulative principle—the existence of ideals beyond our own contextualised experience whose ultimate content remains shrouded in culture, history, language, and tradition. To recognize the futility of a view from nowhere we must acknowledge the possibility of a view from somewhere.

Contrary to the No Child Left Behind legislation, it would appear that before we can decipher what might count as a significant causal link in education we must first unwrap the meanings, identify the purposes, or grasp the concepts embedded in traditions created by historical communities, devise new ways to extend or understand those traditions, and even occasionally create new traditions of understanding altogether (Gadamer, 1989; Moss, 2005).[10] Knowledge of the human condition, in short, is first qualitative in nature—and to the extent that measurement comes into play, it is for the sake of making more precise the qualities that we seek to clarify, understand and distinguish.

Such a view, as Plato (2002) long ago observed, is mediated through the logic of illustration rather than generalisation (Bourdieu, 1990) that communicates enduring truths by means of discursive descriptions and non-discursive symbols. We understand and create meaning out of experience, in other words through examples communicated in narratives, allegories and parables. However, in contrast to Plato (1987) for whom illustrations facilitate communication of absolute truth, the position emerging here suggests that concrete cases are a good but imperfect means to articulate very limited understandings of what we can only assume lies beyond our complete grasp (Alexander, 2004). Truth is conceived in this view not as correspondence to objective reality, or as serving some theoretical function or purpose, but in the way descriptions embody and enable us to grasp the nuanced and dynamic form of transcendent ideals (Langer, 1954), the capacity of texts, symbols and stories to capture the contours of feelings in forms. Viewed from this perspective, even a large, random statistical sample is but an extended and elaborate case that outlines the conceptual shape of experiences common to a significant population of people (Feyerabend, 1996).[11]

Consider intelligence testing, among the paradigm cases of measurement-based research in the behavioural and social sciences. Walter Feinberg (1983) has demonstrated the degree to which tests of this kind reflect strong socio-economic, cultural and linguistic biases, rather than the capacities of a given cognitive structure. In other words, these sorts of tests actually measure the degree to which a person has the ability to realize certain cultural, social or ethical ideals. Though ideals about an aspect of human flourishing, the constructs measured by tests of this kind are by no means absolute or unchanging. On the contrary, the very contextualisation of these measures brought about by critiques such as Feinberg's has itself led to reevaluation of views about the personal qualities that enable scholastic, educational, or social achievement, which in turn entails a reassessment of the sorts of societies in which one should want to live and what it could mean to prosper in those societies.

IV SOME CONSEQUENCES FOR EDUCATIONAL RESEARCH

At least three consequences for educational research emerging from this essay deserve emphasis.

First, educational research worthy of the name must be conducted within the context of explicit and adequately defended visions of the good in which non-dogmatic ideals are adumbrated to govern policies, practices, and pedagogies. The task of both quantitative and qualitative research in such contexts is to interpret and elaborate the traditions of thought and practice that inform the relevant visions, and to explore ways in which these ideals can be transmitted and transformed across the generations. To this end philosophy, especially substantive ethics and the analysis of educational aims and aspirations, has a much more significant role to play in educational research than it has heretofore been afforded by the educational research community. One of the most salient problems with the emphasis on randomised experimentation as gold standard in educational research is that the No Child Left Behind legislation makes a host of assumptions about the meaning of education and the social and political ends it set out to serve without adequately clarifying or defending them.

Second, it follows that randomised experiments cannot be the gold standard of educational research. Nor does the post-positivism of the NRC report offer a sufficiently robust alternative to the naïve empiricism of the

No Child Left Behind legislation. Both fail to take adequate account of the sustained difficulties within philosophy of science to respond convincingly to both Hume's and Husserl's critique of empiricism; and neither demonstrates sufficient understanding of the key role purposive action plays in educational practice. This is not to say of course that quantitative designs have no contribution to make to our understanding of education; but rather that their role can be properly determined only within the context of a social and educational vision of the sort mentioned above.

Finally, the logic of illustration in educational research precedes the logic of generalisation. We come to understand ideals first through detailed examples of concrete cases, and only secondarily by means of abstract and universal covering laws. We have yet to articulate adequate cannons of rigor to govern this logic. But it is undoubtedly a category mistake of the first order to model these canons on weak forms of empirical standards such as reliability, validity, and generalisability. D. C. Phillips' (2005) reference to the legal analogy is especially apt in this connection. The task of a legal advocate, he reminds us, is to present the 'facts' of a case to those who sit in judgment with sufficient corroborative evidence as to warrant their assertability, a term he borrows from Dewey (1938). This evidence might come from a variety of witnesses, descriptions, documents, and measures. Yet a case based on 'warranted facts' will be meaningless without a strong argument concerning application and interpretation of the law in relation to those 'facts'. If there is an ideal form of inquiry to inform and enhance educational policy and practice, in other words, it is more likely to resemble the practice of law than the discovery of statistical laws. Law involves the prescription of norms that actors must learn to follow based on proper reasoning, whereas statistical laws state regularities that control behavior regardless of human choices.

This account may be a disappointment to those whose preferred epistemology seeks control on the basis of explanation and prediction. But the fact that we can sometimes predict does not authorise us to control, and in all events we control much less than the positivists may have once supposed. It follows that we should be wary about what we think inquiry enables us to predict, since what we take to be true or right today may turn out to false or troubled tomorrow. Inquiry at its best endows us with insights to better control ourselves, not generalisations to more efficiently dominate others; and the surest path to self-governance lies in reaffirming Socrates realisation that genuine wisdom begins with the recognition of how little we really know.[12]

NOTES

1. The term 'positivism' is usually used in a sweeping sense among educational researchers to refer to the epistemological orientation most commonly associated with empirical research in the natural or exact sciences. This view affirms with scientific positivists that empirical truth is to be discovered by means of controlled experiments alone, and with the logical positivists that the aim of the experimentation is to verify causal laws for the purposes of explanation, prediction, and

control. Qualitative researchers differ as to whether they follow the Anglo-American distinction between the sciences and humanities and so cede the term 'scientific' to the exact sciences, or the German distinction between *Naturwissenschaften* and *Geisteswissenschaften*, and so refer to qualitative research as scientific only in a different sense.

2. This essay can be viewed as an attempt to articulate a version of pragmatism that embraces a less radical form of relativism than Rorty's (see Bernstein, 1983, pp. 197–206).

3. Ken Howe makes a similar argument against what he calls the 'incompatibility thesis'. However, not all dual epistemology advocates hold quantitative and qualitative inquiry to be incompatible. Indeed, some hold that qualitative inquiry in some sense compliments the quantitative. Both versions of the thesis, however, are flawed for the reasons mentioned (see Howe, 1988, 1992).

4. This is part of a wider tendency in the natural and human sciences toward what Clifford Geertz has called 'blurred genres' (see Geertz, 1983, pp. 19–35).

5. Jerome Bruner appears to make a similar point when he distinguishes between paradigmatic and narrative forms of inquiry, a distinction that parallels the German differentiation between *Naturwissenschaften* and *Geisteswissenschaften* as opposed to the Anglo-American natural science, social science, and the humanities. Ironically, most commentators on Kuhn, both pro and con, interpret *The Structure of Scientific Revolutions* as a relativistic tract, which undermines the very foundational account of empirical science that constructivists who propose to complement rather than challenge positivism appear to protect (Lakatos and Musgrave, 1970). Yet, the human sciences turn out to be paradigmatic in a much deeper sense than Kuhn allowed for the natural sciences, in that they entail the documentation and creation of examples and illustrations of transcendental ideals to which all academic inquiry alludes in one form or another, even though they may lie beyond our direct grasp (see Bruner, 1986).

6. Isaiah Berlin (1998, pp. 243–435) traces the origin of this tradition to Vico and Herder.

7. Taylor directed this critique at the human sciences alone; but if natural science is itself a cultural phenomenon, then it too must be understood as bound up with human purpose and meaning (Geertz, 1994).

8. In this connection, Mill (1987) was not far off the mark in referring to social and human studies as moral sciences, even if his account of the nature of those studies may have been overly enamored with positivist conceptions of the physical sciences.

9. I have argued that dogmatic ideals are essentially amoral or non-ethical in the sense that they flatten possibilities for the exercise of human agency (see Alexander, 2005).

10. David Bridges (2003) has called this 'fiction written under oath', which entails as I understand it, a commitment to express to the best of one's ability ideals that transcend human existence or experience.

11. Thus, among today's most compelling reconstructions of scientific explanation after Hume is Peter Lipton's (1991) notion of 'inference to the best possible explanation'.

12. I am grateful to the students in my seminar on Methodological Issues in Education Research at the University of Haifa, where some of these ideas were first presented, to my mentor Denis Phillips for pointing out the importance of Dewey's thought to the historical sketch presented here, and to my colleagues Rivka Eisikovits and David Bridges for comments on the manuscript.

REFERENCES

Alexander, H. A. (1986) Cognitive Relativism in Evaluation, *Evaluation Review*, 10.3, pp. 259–280.

Alexander, H. A. (2005) Education in Ideology, *Journal of Moral Education*, 34.1, pp. 1–18.

Alexander, H. A. (2004) Moral Education and Liberal Democracy: Spirituality, community, and character in an open society, *Educational Theory*, 53.4, pp. 367–387.

Alexander, H. A. (2001) *Reclaiming Goodness: Education and the spiritual quest* (Notre Dame, ID, University of Notre Dame Press).

Apple, M. W. (1990) *Ideology and Curriculum* (New York, Routledge).

Apple, M. W. (1982) *Education and Power* (Boston, MA, Routledge and Kegan Paul).

Aranowitz, S. and Giroux, H. (1993) *Postmodern Education: Politics, culture and criticism* (Minneapolis, MN, University of Minnesota Press).

Aristotle (1994) *Metaphysics*, D. Bostock, trans. (Oxford, Clarendon Press).

Bacon, F. (2002) *The New Organon*, L. Jardine and M. Silverthorne, eds. (Cambridge, Cambridge University Press).

Berlin, I. (1998) *The Proper Study of Mankind* (London, Pimlico).

Berliner, D. C. (2002) Educational Research: The hardest science of all, *Educational Researcher*, 31.8, pp. 21–24.

Bernstein, R. J. (1983) *Beyond Objectivism and Relativism: Science, hermeneutics, and praxis* (Philadelphia, PA, University of Pennsylvania Press).

Biesta, G. and Burbules, N. C. (2003) *Pragmatism and Educational Research* (Lanham, MD, Rowman and Littlefield).

Bourdieu, P. (1990) *The Logic of Practice*, R. Nice, trans. (Cambridge, Polity Press).

Bridges, D. (2003) *Fiction Written Under Oath: Essays in philosophy and educational research* (Dordrecht, Kluwer).

Bruner, J. S. (1986) *Actual Minds, Possible Worlds* (Cambridge, MA, Harvard University Press).

Campbell, D. T. and Stanley, J. (1963) *Experimental and Quasi-experimental Design for Research* (Chicago, IL, Rand McNally).

Chatterji, M. (2005) Evidence on 'What Works': An argument for extended-term mixed-method (ETMM) evaluation designs, *Educational Researcher*, 34.5, pp. 25–31.

Cronbach, L. J. (1975) Beyond the Two Disciplines of Scientific Psychology, *American Psychologist*, 30, pp. 116–126.

Creswell, J. W. (2003) *Research Design: Qualitative, quantitative, and mixed approaches* (Thousand Oaks, CA, Sage).

Comte, A. (2001) *The Positivist Philosophy of Auguste Comte*, H. Martineau trans. (Bristol, Thoemmes).

Descartes, R (1999) *Discourse on Method*, D. M. Clark, trans. (London, Penguin).

Descartes, R. (1996) *Meditations on First Philosophy*, J. Cottingham, trans. (Cambridge, Cambridge University Press).

Dewey, J. (1938) *Logic: A theory of inquiry* (New York, Henry Holt).

Dewey, J. (1910) *How We Think* (Boston, MA, Heath).

Eisner, E. W. (1994) *The Educational Imagination*, 3rd edn. (Saddle River, NJ, Prentice-Hall).

Eisner, E. W. (1991) *The Enlightened Eye: Qualitative inquiry and the enhancement of educational practice* (New York, Macmillan).

Eisenhart, M. (2005) Hammers and Saws for the Improvement of Educational Research, *Educational Theory*, 55.3, pp. 245–261.

Erickson, F. and Guiterrez (2002) Culture, Rigor, and Science in Educational Research, *Educational Researcher*, 31.8, pp. 21–25.

Feinberg, W. (1983) *Understanding Education: Toward a reconstruction of educational inquiry* (Cambridge, Cambridge University Press).

Feyerabend, P. K. (1996) *Against Method* (London, Verso).

Feuer, M. J., Towne, L. and Shavelson, R. J. (2002) Scientific Culture and Educational Research, *Educational Researcher*, 31.8, pp. 4–14.

Gadamer, H. G. (1989) *Truth and Method* (New York, Crossroad).

Geertz, C. (1983) *Local Knowledge: Further essays in interpretative anthropology* (New York, Basic Books).

Geertz, C. (1994) The Strange Estrangement: Taylor and the natural sciences, in: J. Tulley (ed.) *Philosophy in an Age of Pluralism*, pp. 83–95.

Giroux, H. (1991) *Border Crossings: Cultural work and the politics of education* (New York, Routledge).

Guba, E. (1990) The Alternative Paradigm Dialogue, in: E. Guba (ed.) *The Paradigm Dialogue* (Newbury Park, CA, Sage).

Guba, E. and Lincoln, Y. (1989) *Fourth Generation Evaluation* (Newbury Park, CA, Sage).

Guba, E. and Lincoln, Y. (1985) *Naturalistic Inquiry* (Beverly Hills, CA, Sage).

Husserl, E. (1970) *The Crisis of the European Science and Transcendental Phenomenology*, D. Carr, trans. (Evanston, IL, Northwestern University Press).

Husserl, E. (1967) *Ideas: A general introduction to pure phenomenology*, W. R. Boyce Gribson, trans. (London, Allen and Unwin).

Husserl, E. (1960) *Cartesian Meditation: An introduction to phenomenology*, D. Cairns trans. (The Hague, M. Nijhoff).

Hegel, G. W. F. (1978) *The Phenomenology of Spirit*, A. V. Miller trans. (Oxford, Clarendon Press).

Hegel, G. W. F. (1953) *Reason in History*, R. S. Hartman trans. (Minneapolis, MN, Bobbs-Merrill).

Heidegger, M. (1996) *Being and Time*, J. Stambaugh, trans. (New York, SUNY Press).

Hempel, C. G. (1966) *The Philosophy of Natural Science* (Englewood Cliffs, NJ, Prentice-Hall).

Howe, K. R. (1988) Against the Quantitative-qualitative Incompatibility Thesis, or, Dogmas Die Hard, *Educational Researcher*, 17, pp. 10–16.

Howe, K. R. (1992) Getting Over the Quantitative-qualitative Debate, *American Journal of Education*, 100, pp. 236–256.

Howe, K. R. (2005) The Question of Educational Science: Experimentism vs. experimentalism, *Educational Theory*, 55.3, pp. 307–321.

Hume, D. (2000) *An Enquiry Concerning Human Understanding* (Oxford, Clarendon Press).

Johnson, R. B. and Onwuegbuzie, A. J. (2005) Mixed Method Research: A research paradigm whose time has come, *Educational Researcher*, 33.7, pp. 14–26.

Kant, I. (2004) *A Prolegomenon to Any Future Metaphysics*, G. Hatfield trans. (Cambridge, Cambridge University Press).

Kant, I. (2002) *Groundwork for the Metaphysics of Morals*, A. Zweig trans. (Oxford, Oxford University Press).

Kant, I. (1998) *Critique of Pure Reason*, P. Guyer and A. W. Wood, trans. (Cambridge, Cambridge University Press).

Kant, I. (1997) *Critique of Practical Reason*, M. Gregor, trans. (Cambridge, Cambridge University Press).

Kuhn, T. S. (1996) *The Structure of Scientific Revolutions* (Chicago, IL, University of Chicago Press).

Lakatos, I. (1978) *The Methodology of Scientific Research Programs* (Cambridge, Cambridge University Press).

Lakatos, I. and Musgrave, A. eds. (1970) *Criticism and the Growth of Knowledge* (Cambridge, Cambridge University Press).

Langer, S (1954) *Problems of Art* (New York, Scribners).

Lesnoff, M. H. (1974) *The Structure of Social Science* (London, Allen and Unwin).

Lipton, P. (1991) *Inference to the Best Explanation* (London, Routledge).

Locke, J. (2003) *An Essay Concerning Human Understanding* (Bristol, Thoemmes).

McLaren, P. (1994) *Life in Schools: An introduction to critical pedagogy in the foundations of education*, 2nd edn. (White Plains, NY, Longman).

Maxcy, S. J. (2003) Pragmatic Threads in Mixed Methods Research in the Social Sciences: The search for multiple modes of inquiry and the end of philosophical formalism, in: A. Tashakkori and C. Teddlie (eds) *Handbook of Mixed Methods in Social and Behavioral Research* (Thousand Oaks, CA, Sage).

Mill, J. S. (1987) *The Logic of the Moral Sciences* (London, Duckworth).

Moss, P. A. (2005) Understanding the Other/Understanding Ourselves: Toward a constructive dialogue about 'principles' in educational research, *Educational Theory*, 55.3, pp. 268–283.

Murdoch, I. (1970) *The Sovereignty of Good* (London, Routledge and Kegan Paul).

Nagel, E. (1961) *The Structure of Science: Problems in the logic of scientific explanation* (London, Routledge and Kegan Paul).

Nagel, T. (1986) *The View from Nowhere* (Oxford, Oxford University Press).

Nietzsche, F. (2001) *The Birth of Tragedy, The Gay Science, Thus Spoke Zarathustra, and On the Genealogy of Morals*, D. B. Allison ed. (Lanham, MD, Rowman and Littlefield).

Nozick, R. (1981) *Philosophical Explanations* (Cambridge, MA, Harvard University Press).

Onwuegbuzie, A. J. (2002) Positivists, Post-positivists, Post-structuralists, and Post-moderns: Why can't we all get along. Towards a framework for unifying research paradigms, *Education*, 122.3, pp. 518–530.

Patton, M. Q. (1990) *Qualitative Evaluation and Research Methods* (Newbury Park, CA, Sage).

Patton, M. Q. (1980) *Qualitative Evaluation Methods* (Beverly Hills, CA, Sage).

Pellegrino, J. W. and Goldman, S. R. (2002) Be Careful What You Wish For—You May Get It: Educational research in the spotlight, *Educational Researcher*, 31.8, pp. 15–17.

Phenix, P. H. (1972) Transcendence and the Curriculum, *Teachers College Record*, 73.2, pp. 271–283.

Phillips, D. C. (2005) A Guide for the Perplexed: Scientific educational research, methodolatry, and the gold versus platinum standards, keynote address to the annual meeting of the European Association of Learning and Instruction, Cyprus.

Phillips, D. C. and Burbules, N. C. (2000) *Postpositivism and Educational Research* (New York, Roman and Littlefield).

Plato (2002) *Phaedrus*, R. Waterfield, trans. (Oxford, Oxford University Press).

Plato (1987) *The Republic*, D. Lee, trans. (London, Penguin).

Popkewitz, T. (1984) *Paradigm and Ideology in Educational Research: The social functions of the intellectual* (London, Falmer).

Popper, K. R. (1996) *The Myth of Framework: In defense of science and rationality*, M. A. Natturno, ed. (London, Routledge).

Popper, K. R. (1992) *The Logic of Scientific Discovery* (London, Routledge).

Popper, K. R. (1972) *Objective Knowledge* (Oxford, Clarendon Press).

Richardson, L. (1994) Writing: A method of inquiry, in: N. K. Denzin and Y. S. Lincoln (eds) *Handbook of Qualitative Research* (Thousand Oaks, CA, Sage).

Rorty, R. (1982) *Consequences of Pragmatism* (Minneapolis, MN, University of Minnesota Press).

Rorty, R. (1980) *Philosophy and the Mirror of Nature* (Princeton, NJ, Princeton University Press).

Scheffler, I. (1991) *In Praise of the Cognitive Emotions* (London, Routledge).

Schutz, A. (1982) *Life Forms and Meaning Structure*, H. R. Wagner trans. (London, Routledge and Kegan Paul).

Schutz, A. and Luckman, T. (1983) *The Structure of the Life World*, R. M. Zaner and H. Tristram Engelhardt trans. (Evanston, IL, Northwestern University Press).

Schwandt, T. A. (2005) A Diagnostic Reading of Scientifically-based Educational Research, *Educational Theory*, 55.3, pp. 285–305.

Shaddish, W. R., Cook, T. D. and Campbell, D. T. (2002) *Experimental and Quasi-experimental Designs for Generalized Causal Inference* (Boston, MA, Houghton Mifflin).

Shkedi, A. (2003) *Words That Try to Touch: Qualitative research, theory and practice* (Tel Aviv, Tel Aviv University Press) (Hebrew).

Sieber, S. D. (1973) The Integration of Fieldwork and Survey Methods, *American Journal of Sociology*, 73, pp. 1335–1359.

Smith, N. H. (2002) *Charles Taylor: Meaning, morals, and modernity* (Cambridge, Polity).

Snow, C. P. (1990) *The Two Cultures* (Cambridge, Cambridge University Press).

St. Peter, E. (2002) 'Science' Rejects Postmodernism, *Educational Researcher*, 31.8, pp. 25–28.

Stake, R. E. (1995) *The Art of Case Study Research* (Thousand Oaks, CA, Sage).

Tashakkori, A. and Teddlie, C. (1998) *Mixed Methodology: Combining qualitative and quantitative approaches* (Thousand Oaks, CA, Sage).

Taylor, C. (1985) *Philosophy and the Human Sciences* (Cambridge, Cambridge University Press).

Taylor, C. (1975) *Hegel* (Cambridge, Cambridge University Press).

Taylor, C. (1964) *The Explanation of Behavior* (London, Routledge and Kegan Paul).

von Wright, G-H. (1981) *Explanation and Understanding* (Ithaca, NY, Cornell University Press).

10
Philosophy, Methodology and Action Research

WILFRED CARR

> If natural giftedness for speaking is lacking, it can scarcely be made up for by methodological doctrine ... This has significance for the theory of science. What kind of science is it that presents itself more as a cultivation of a natural gift and as a theoretically heightened awareness of it? ... Inquiry into the history of science ... indicates that the notion of method, fundamental to modern sciences, brought into dissolution a notion of science that was open precisely in the direction of such a natural human capacity ... This is the practical philosophy established by Aristotle (Hans-Georg Gadamer, 1981, pp. 114–5).

INTRODUCTION

'This book', writes Bridget Somekh on the opening page of *Action Research: a Methodology for Change and Development*, 'is about the many ways in which social science researchers can use action research methodology to overcome the limitations of traditional methodologies' (Somekh, 2006, p. 1). After identifying 'eight methodological principles for action research' (p. 6), Somekh lists 'a range of methodological issues that are problematic for action researchers' (p. 11). Some of these issues—the nature of human action, the status and validity of the knowledge produced through action research—are indeed those that are at the forefront of action research's methodological debates. But one issue that is never debated or discussed is why it is felt necessary to define action research by reference to something called a 'methodology'. Some writers on action research seem to think that without a 'methodology' action research would lack the norms and standards that safeguard its claim to the status of 'real' research. But researchers in the natural sciences do not find it necessary to legitimise their inquiries by invoking something called 'methodology'. Nor do philosophers or historians. So why is it needed in action research? What is methodology? What purpose does it serve?

Strictly speaking 'methodology' refers to the theoretical rationale or, to use Somekh's term, 'principles' that justify the research methods appropriate to a field of study. So understood, a methodology cannot be derived from research but instead has to be grounded in that form of *a priori* theoretical knowledge usually referred to as 'philosophy'. Thus in action research, as in any of the other social sciences, 'methodology' stands in a particular relationship to 'philosophy' such that research methods are justified by the former which is in turn justified by knowledge derived from the latter. What action research methodology derives from philosophy is a theoretical account of the distinctive nature of the 'action' that constitutes its object of study and an epistemological justification for the kind of knowledge it seeks to generate. It is thus unsurprising that, in elaborating on her 'eight methodological principles for action research', Somekh draws heavily on a range of philosophical theories of human action as well as those epistemological theories which recognise the 'personal' and 'contextualised' nature of knowledge (pp. 27–30). Nor is it surprising that many of action research's methodological debates replicate the general debate about what constitutes valid knowledge of human action that was initiated by the two opposing methodological perspectives articulated in Emile Durkheim's *Rules of Sociological Method* (Durkheim, 1982) and Max Weber's *The Methodology of the Social Sciences* (Weber, 1949).

But why do we assume that the need for an intellectual justification for action research can only be met by articulating its methodological rationale? Why is it felt necessary to import the methodological discourse of the social sciences into debates about the nature and conduct of action research? Since these are questions about the origins of our current understanding of 'what action research is', it follows that a necessary prerequisite to adequately answering them is to produce an account of how this self-understanding emerged and why it has come to take the form that it now does. In other words, the necessary starting point to any explanation of why action research is now understood as a social scientific research methodology is to show how this understanding is deeply ingrained in the way in which action research interprets its own past.

THE HISTORY OF ACTION RESEARCH

The conventional way of writing the history of action research is to divide it into two stages (Wallace, 1987; Kemmis, 1988; McTaggart, 1991). The first of these covers the period between the 1920s and 1950s and is intended to show how 'action research originated in the United States where, from the 1920s onwards, there was a growing interest in the application of scientific methods to the study of social and educational problems' (Wallace, 1987, p. 99). The most cited figure of this period is Kurt Lewin (Adelman, 1993) who is generally attributed with introducing the phrase 'action research' to describe a form of inquiry that would enable 'the significantly established laws of social life to be tried and tested in practice' (Lewin, 1952, p. 564). It is also Lewin who is credited with devising 'the action research method' which he portrayed as a spiral of steps, each of which is composed of 'a circle of "planning", "action" and "fact finding" about the result of the action' (Lewin, 1946, p. 205). Thus, in its initial formulation, 'action research' was defined as a method that enabled theories produced by the social sciences to be applied in practice and tested on the basis of their practical effectiveness.

Although the original impulse for the emergence of action research was the widespread failure to translate the findings of social scientific research into practical action, it remained firmly wedded to the 'applied science' view of the relationship between social science and social change embedded in the epistemological assumptions endemic to the positivistic culture that dominated American social sciences in the 1940s. In this culture, action research could only legitimise its claim to be a genuine social science by conforming to the methodological principles prescribed by the epistemology of positivism. It is thus hardly surprising that the eventual rejection of action research by the American social scientific community in the 1950s was not so much due to its failure to relate social research to social action as to its inability to conform to the positivist insistence that it should, like any other social science, produce empirical generalisations by employing quantitative methods for the collection and analysis of data. It was because of this failure to meet the methodological requirements of positivism that action research become marginalised and went into rapid decline (Sanford, 1970).

The second stage in the historical evolution of action research invariably takes as its starting point the 'resurgence' or 'revival' of interest that occurred in the context of educational and curriculum research in the UK in the early 1970s. The reasons that have been given for this revival include a growing conviction of the irrelevance of conventional educational research to the practical concerns of teachers and schools (Kemmis, 1988), the claim that teacher professionalism could best be enhanced by giving them a research role (Stenhouse, 1975), and the view that a reformulated version of Lewin's action research method would, by enabling teachers to test curriculum policies and proposals in their own classrooms, lead to improvements in pedagogical practice and stimulate innovative curriculum change (Elliott, 1998).

The British version of action research that emerged during this period differed from its American predecessor in several ways. One of these was its rejection of a positivistic research methodology in favour of the kind of 'interpretive' methodologies that were increasingly being employed in the social sciences. As a result action research was increasingly seen as a form of inquiry that utilised 'qualitative' rather than 'quantitative' research methods, that focused on the perspectives of participants and social actors (Kemmis, 1988) and that generally took the form of case studies of specific situations that would be useful to practitioners (Wallace, 1987).

What also distinguished this revised version of action research was a radically different conception of its object of study. Whereas Lewin and his followers had construed 'action' as little more than a practical skill or technique to be assessed in terms of its instrumental effectiveness, its principle exponents now insisted that, in education, 'action' referred to an educational practice which, in turn, was understood as ethically informed 'action' through which educational values were pursued (Elliott, 1991). As Kemmis put it, 'The objects of educational action research are educational practices . . . Practice as it is understood by action researchers is informed committed action' (Kemmis, 1988, pp. 44–45). As a result, action research was no longer seen as a method for assessing the practical utility of social scientific theories but as a means whereby practitioners could test the 'educational theories' implicit in their own practice by treating them as experimental hypotheses to be systematically assessed in specific educational contexts. Reviewed and revised in this way, Lewin's action research cycle was transformed from a method by which practitioners applied social scientific theories to their practice into a method which allowed practitioners to assess the practical adequacy of their own tacit theories 'in action' (Elliott, 1991, 1998).

This brief account of the origins and evolution of twentieth century action research obviously leaves a lot to be desired. Nevertheless it should be sufficient to indicate how our contemporary understanding of action research relies on a narrative which portrays its history as a story of methodological progress and advance—a story of how, by conceptualising 'action' as a species of morally informed practice and by construing 'research' in accordance with post-positivistic research methodologies, action research has been able to liberate itself from the errors and confusions of its historical predecessor and develop a more intellectually sophisticated understanding of its task. But what it also shows is that the history of action research is, like any other history, a history of continuity as well as change. So although this history reveals how action research has changed in accordance with the developments that have occurred in the social sciences, the original assumption that action research is a form of social scientific research has remained unchallenged and unopposed. Similarly, although 'action' is now construed as a species of 'practice', this has not disturbed the assumption that action research can only contribute to the improvement of practice by conforming to the norms and standards prescribed by some research methodology. So while this way of writing the history of action research undoubtedly shows why we now debate questions about the kind of methodology on which action research should be erected, it does nothing to illuminate the logically prior question of why we now assume that a mode of inquiry concerned with the development of practice needs to be erected on the basis of a research methodology at all.

How is this question to be answered? Clearly it is not itself a methodological question and any suggestion that it can be answered from within the confines of action research's own methodological debate simply begs the very question at issue. Moreover, since this is essentially a question about the way in which action research now understands its own historical ancestry, the only way in which it can adequately be answered is by displaying a willingness to construct the history of action research in a radically different way. And one obvious way of rewriting action research's twentieth century history is to treat it as a recent episode in a much longer, more complex, and still continuing, process of historical and cultural change. Looked at from this much longer and larger historical perspective, action research will no longer be seen as a peculiarly twentieth century phenomenon. Instead it will be seen to be nothing other than a modern manifestation of the pre-modern tradition of practical philosophy through which our understanding of the study of practice was originally articulated and expressed.

THE PRE-MODERN TRADITION OF PRACTICAL PHILOSOPHY

In ancient Greece the word 'philosophy' referred to virtually all forms of serious intellectual inquiry and its modern separation from 'science' would make little sense. Also, the conceptual structures within which the concept of action was understood were very different from our own. Within these structures, the important conceptual distinctions were not between 'theory' and 'practice' or 'knowledge' and 'action', but between different kinds of human activities and the type of knowledge that guides and informs them. Thus theory (*theoria*) was essentially construed as an activity engaged in by those who pursued knowledge 'for its own sake' and 'theoretical philosophy' referred to those contemplative forms of enquiry that used *a priori* reasoning to achieve knowledge of eternal truths. Since the whole point of theoretical philosophy was to transcend the particularities and contingencies of ordinary human life, it was deemed to have no relevance whatsoever to the conduct of everyday practical activities. However, a theoretical task to which the Greeks did attach some importance was that of articulating the mode of reasoning, the form of knowledge and the kind of 'philosophy' appropriate to different types of human action. It is this task which was so brilliantly accomplished by Aristotle who, in the *Nicomachean Ethics*, provided a detailed philosophical analysis of different forms of human action and the different types of reasoning they employ (Aristotle, 1955).

For Aristotle, the most important conceptual distinction to draw when considering human action is between the two forms of human action which the Greeks called *poiesis* and *praxis*. *Poiesis* refers to the numerous productive activities that form the basis of economic life. Because it is a form of 'making action' whose end is known prior to the practical means taken to achieve it, *poiesis* is guided by the form of reasoning that the Greeks called *techne* and that we would today call instrumental 'means-end' reasoning. *Poiesis* is thus a form of instrumental action that requires a mastery of the knowledge, methods and skills that together constitute technical expertise. For the Greeks, the activities of craftsmen and artisans were paradigm cases of *poiesis* guided by *techne*. And, as such, they were guided by 'productive philosophy'—what we would today call 'applied science'—which provide the principles, procedures and operational methods which together constitute the most effective means for achieving some pre-determined end.

Although, for Aristotle, *praxis* is also a form of action directed towards the achievement of some end, it differs from *poiesis* in several crucial respects. First, the 'end' of *praxis* is not to make or produce some object or artefact, but progressively to realise the idea of the 'good' constitutive of a morally worthwhile form of human life. But *praxis* is not ethically neutral action by means of which the good life can be achieved. The good of *praxis* cannot be 'made': it can only be 'done'. It follows from this that *praxis* is a form of 'doing' action precisely because its 'end'—to promote the good life—only exists, and can only be realised, in and through *praxis* itself. *Praxis* also differs from *poiesis* in that knowledge of its end cannot be theoretically specified in advance and can only be acquired on the basis of an understanding of how, in a particular concrete situation, this knowledge is being interpreted and applied. *Praxis* is thus nothing other than a practical manifestation of how the idea of the good is being understood, just as knowledge of the good is nothing other than an abstract way of specifying the mode of human conduct through which this idea is given practical expression. In *praxis*, acquiring knowledge of what the good is and knowing how to apply it in particular situations are thus not two separate processes but two mutually supportive constitutive elements within a single dialectical process of practical reasoning.

The name Aristotle gives to this form of reasoning is *phronesis*. But, although *phronesis*, like *technē*, involves subsuming particular cases under general principles, it is not a deductive form of reasoning which issues in a prescription for action. Nor is it a form of reasoning that can be learned in isolation from practice. Rather it can only be acquired by practitioners who, in seeking to achieve the standards of excellence inherent in their practice, develop the capacity to make wise and prudent judgements about what, in a particular situation, would constitute an appropriate expression of the good. Thus, for Aristotle, *phronesis* is not a method of reasoning, but a moral and intellectual virtue that is inseparable from practice and constitutive of the moral consciousness of those whose actions are rooted in a disposition to do 'the right thing in the right place at the right time in the right way' (MacIntyre, 1981, p. 141). As such, *phronesis* is a mode of ethical reasoning in which the notions of deliberation, reflection and judgement play a central part. 'Deliberation' is necessary because, unlike *technē*, *phronesis* is not a methodical form of reasoning about how to achieve some specific end, but a deliberative process in which both means and ends are open to question. Such reasoning is reflective because the means are always modified by reflecting on the end just as an understanding of the end is always modified by reflecting on the means. And *judgement* is an essential element of *phronesis* because its outcome is a reasoned decision about what to do in a particular situation, that can be defended discursively and justified as appropriate to the circumstances in which it is being applied.[1]

Since, for Aristotle, *phronesis* is inseparable from, and can only be acquired in, practice, it cannot be developed or improved by appealing to theoretical philosophy which provides a purely abstract and intellectual understanding of the idea of the good. Similarly, to assume that *phronesis* can be informed and guided by 'productive philosophy' would simply be to transform *praxis* into a form of *poiesis*. Indeed, for Aristotle, the peculiarities of *phronesis*—its embeddedness in *praxis* and the way in which it is inseparable from the concrete situations in which it is applied— mean that it can only be advanced by a form of 'practical philosophy' that is exclusively concerned with sustaining and developing the kind of practical knowledge that guides *praxis*.

What emerged from Aristotle's analysis of *phronesis* and *praxis* was, of course, the mode of inquiry that was to constitute the pre-modern tradition of 'practical philosophy'—a tradition that permeated western intellectual culture until the seventeenth century and that has only been finally discarded in our own modern times (Toulmin, 1988, 1990). Within this tradition, it was always recognised that the indeterminate and imprecise nature of *praxis* unavoidably entails that practical philosophy is an 'inexact' science which yields a form of knowledge that cannot be applied universally and unconditionally. But, although it was readily conceded that practical philosophy does not provide a body of knowledge that practitioners can simply apply, this did not undermine its claim to be the 'science' that enables practitioners progressively to improve their practical knowledge and develop their understanding of how the good internal to their practice may, in their own particular situation, be more appropriately pursued. But what it did imply is that this claim could only be made good by a science that was concerned to defend and preserve, rather than supplant or replace, the reasoning already implicit in *praxis*. And the only kind of science that could coherently make this claim was a 'practical science': a science that sought to advance *praxis* by promoting the kind of reflectively acquired self-knowledge that would allow practitioners to identify and eliminate the inadequacies and limitations of the practical knowledge sustaining their practice. So understood, practical philosophy is 'practical' in that it recognises that the knowledge that guides *praxis* always arises from and must always relate back to practice. And it is 'philosophical' in the sense that it seeks to raise the unreflectively acquired knowledge of the good embedded in *praxis* to the level of self-conscious awareness in order that practitioners may subject their pre-philosophical understanding of their practice to critical examination.

Interpreted in this way, practical philosophy does not at all resemble that peculiarly twentieth century discipline of 'applied ethics' which separates 'first order' practical and moral questions from the 'second order' philosophical justification of the ethical principles on which these 'first order' questions depend. Rather, it is nothing other than a pre-modern version of twentieth century action research. Like action research, it takes ethically informed human practice as its unique object domain. Like action research, it can be defined as 'a form of reflective enquiry undertaken by practitioners in order to improve their own practices, their understanding of these practices and the situation in which these practices are carried out' (Kemmis, 1988, p. 42). And, like action research, it accepts that the knowledge that informs and guides practice is 'contextualised knowledge that cannot be separated from the practical context in which it is embedded' (Somekh, 2006, p. 28).

But, although action research represents a twentieth century embodiment of practical philosophy, it nevertheless differs from it in several crucial respects. For example, while in practical philosophy an understanding of the distinctive nature of practice is allowed to determine the kind of 'science' appropriate to its development, action research emerged in response to the need for a new social scientific research paradigm that would eliminate the gap between theory and practice. So while practical philosophy 'was designed precisely to protect practice against unwarranted theoretical incursions' (Dunne, 1993, p. 216), action research was designed to provide a research methodology that would integrate theory and practice by drawing on theoretical knowledge 'from psychology, philosophy, sociology and other fields of social science in order to test its explanatory power and practical usefulness' (Somekh, 2006, p. 8).

What also distinguish practical philosophy from action research are the radical differences in the historical contexts in which they emerged and the background assumptions and beliefs shaping the perspectives in terms of which they were made intelligible. It is therefore only to be expected that, when viewed from the historical perspective informing our contemporary understanding of action research, practical philosophy will tend to be regarded as an outmoded and methodologically naïve mode of inquiry that can contribute nothing to action research's current methodological debates. But should the Aristotelian tradition of practical philosophy be dismissed as having nothing more than antiquarian interest? Or does it provide us with an external vantage point which, by transcending the boundaries of action research's internal methodological debate, may help us to discover why action research has been so keen to embrace the idea of 'methodology' and whether it was misguided to do so? Fortunately, the intellectual resources needed to answer this question are provided by Hans-Georg Gadamer's powerful re-affirmation of the Aristotelian tradition of practical philosophy and his ambitious attempt to show how it can be rehabilitated in a way that would make it appropriate to the modern world.

THE CONTEMPORARY REHABILITATION OF PRACTICAL PHILOSOPHY

In his seminal text *Truth and Method* (1975a) Gadamer provides a compelling account of how the modern preoccupation with 'method' has led the social sciences to adopt 'a methodologically alienated form of self-understanding' (Gadamer, 1975b, p. 312) that conceals the conditions that make human understanding possible and thereby distorts the character of human understanding itself. For Gadamer, the principal cause of this state of affairs is the modern social sciences' 'prejudice against prejudice'—their presumption that it is only by eliminating the distorting effects of bias and subjectivity from their inquiries that they can legitimise their claim to be rational sciences, uncontaminated by irrational presuppositions and beliefs. But what Gadamer clearly demonstrates is that the aspiration to achieve a purely rational understanding is illusory, that human understanding is never simply 'given' in any perception or observation but is always 'prejudiced' by an interpretive element that determines how perceptions and observations are understood. Moreover, just as the act of understanding is always an act of interpretation, so it also has an inescapably historical character. This is so because the particular prejudices that are brought to bear in any act of understanding are not the irrational or idiosyncratic biases of individuals but are embedded in the historical and cultural traditions to which individuals unavoidably belong. But although the fact that we can never transcend or deny the authority of tradition—although we can never escape the hold of what Gadamer calls 'effective history'—means that we can never evaluate our prejudices by appealing to some tradition-independent criteria of rationality, it does not entail the impossibility of rational understanding. For Gadamer 'there is no unconditional antithesis between tradition and reason' (p. 250): just as reason can only be sustained from within a tradition, so a tradition can only be sustained through the active use of reason. As Gadamer puts it, 'even the most genuine and solid tradition does not persist by nature ... it needs to be affirmed, embraced and cultivated. It is essentially preservation ... but preservation is an act of reason' (ibid.).

But, if reason is itself always embedded in tradition, how can it contribute to the cultivation of tradition? Gadamer's response is first to show that, just as all understanding involved 'interpretation', so it also involves 'application' in the sense that it is always affected by the particular historical situation to which it is being applied. It is when the practical demands of the present cannot be adequately met on the basis of a mode of understanding inherited from the past that adherents to a tradition are confronted with the need to reflectively expose and rationally revise their understanding so as to transcend the limitations of what, within this tradition, has hitherto been thought, said and done. So although there can be no unprejudiced criteria of rationality, participants to a tradition can nevertheless rationally revise the prejudices inherent in their self-understanding by achieving that level of self-reflective awareness that Gadamer calls 'effective historical consciousness': an explicit awareness of the 'effective history' that is sustaining their prejudices and shaping their understanding of their own historical situation. For Gadamer, it is only this kind of historical understanding that enables us to identify the inadequacies of the prejudices at work in our understanding, recognise their questionableness and 'distinguish the true prejudices by which we understand from the false ones by which we misunderstand' (Gadamer, 1975a, p. 266). And it is by so allowing us to bring the inadequacy of our inherited understanding into dialectical confrontation with the practical demands of the current situation to which it is being applied that historical consciousness promotes the rational development and evolution of the tradition within which this understanding is embedded. Thus, for Gadamer, the relationship between reason and tradition is dialectical: each transforms and is transformed by the other.

How is 'effective historical consciousness' acquired? It is not acquired by employing any method or technique but by engaging in an open conversation in which participants strive to come to a true understanding of their historical situation. It is thus achieved by individuals displaying a willingness to put their own assumptions and beliefs at risk by participating in a genuine dialogue in which they allow the partiality and particularity of their own perspectives and understandings to be exposed to, and amended on the basis of, the perspectives and understandings of others. By engaging in such conversation, adherents to a tradition learn to recognise the historically contingent and culturally situated nature of their own understanding and hence the parochial nature of what Gadamer calls their 'historical horizons'. Thus, the outcome of conversation is not an 'objective' understanding of a situation, but a 'fusion of horizons'—an achievement of shared understanding in which the inadequacies and limitations of each participant's initial understanding become transparent and what is valid and valuable is retained within a more integrated and more comprehensive understanding of the situation under discussion.

Gadamer's account of the historical structure of human understanding is, of course, entirely applicable to an understanding of the social sciences and in a collection of essays published under the title *Reason in the Age of Science* (Gadamer, 1981) he shows how modern social science has its own 'effective history', how its concepts of 'rationality' and 'objectivity' are internal to a tradition and, hence, how social scientific knowledge is only as 'rational' or 'objective' as the historically rooted prejudices that this tradition has bequeathed. What this reveals is that the assumption of a wholly ahistorical concept of reason that is independent of tradition is nothing other than a definitive 'prejudice' of the tradition of modernity and hence that modernity—which for Gadamer 'can be defined quite unequivocally as a new notion of science and method' (Gadamer, 1981, p. 6)—has led to a view of the social sciences in which prejudice and tradition are treated as adversary notions and the concept of methodology is assigned a central role. But once we recognise that the social sciences' aspiration to transcend the distorting influence of prejudice and tradition is one of the illusions of modernity—once we acknowledge that 'there is no understanding that is free of all prejudice' (Gadamer, 1975a, p. 465)—then we cannot avoid the need to articulate 'an understanding of social science that is no longer based on the idea of method' (Gadamer, 1980, p. 74). And for Gadamer the search for a non-methodical understanding of social science inevitably leads to a re-understanding of 'the remote and no longer vital tradition of Aristotelian philosophy' (p. 78). 'But how', he asks, 'does the philosophy of Aristotle lead itself to this discussion? How can the philosophical analysis of human life and human attitudes and human actions and human institutions by the ancient thinker contribute to a better understanding of what we are doing?' (p. 76).

Gadamer responds to these questions by engaging in a dialogical encounter with Aristotelian philosophy in which Aristotle's analysis of *phronesis* and *technē* is allowed to expose the prejudices of our contemporary understanding of social science and thereby enable us to forge a better understanding of 'what social science is'. What emerges from this 'conversation' is a 'fusion of horizons' whereby our understanding of what is important and significant in Aristotle's practical philosophy is modified and transformed by the perspective formed by our modern historical situation, and our understanding of our modern historical situation is in turn modified and transformed by the perspective afforded by Aristotle's practical philosophy. What we learn from this 'appropriation' of Aristotle is that the kind of reasoning appropriate to the development of human understanding is analogous to the non-technical mode of situated and contextual practical reasoning that Aristotle called *phronesis*. But what we then also begin to recognise is how, in the culture of modernity, the Aristotelian notion of *phronesis* has been rendered obsolete, dialogue has been replaced by technical expertise and historical consciousness has been supplanted by a rigid conformity to methodological rules. As Gadamer puts it,

> The great merit of Aristotle was that he anticipated the *impasse* of our scientific culture by his description of the structure of practical reason as distinct from theoretical knowledge and technical skill ... In a scientific culture such as ours the fields of *technē* are much more expanded. The crucial change is that practical wisdom can no longer be promoted by personal contact and the mutual exchange of views ... Consequently the concept of *praxis* which we developed in the last two centuries is an awful deformation of what practice really is ... The debate of the last century ... degrades practical reason to technical control (Gadamer, 1975a, p. 107).

For Gadamer, one of the major consequences of this deformation of *praxis* is that it has led to the demise of practical philosophy and its replacement by a collection of value-free 'social sciences' exclusively reserved for those who possess the necessary methodological sophistication and technical expertise. In these circumstances, argues Gadamer, the chief task of philosophy is to repudiate the assumptions on which this view of social science has been erected and to develop a non-methodical, dialogical model of the social sciences in which the role of practical reason in the formation of human purposes and social ends is given full recognition. And, for Gadamer, the only way for philosophy to achieve this task is by reasserting the value and validity of the science of practical philosophy in a way that would make it appropriate for the modern world. As he puts it, 'the scientific character of practical philosophy is, as far as I can see, the only model for the self-understanding of the social sciences if they are to be liberated from the spurious narrowing imposed ... by the modern notion of method' (Gadamer, 1979, p. 107).[2]

PRACTICAL PHILOSOPHY, METHODOLOGY AND
ACTION RESEARCH

The implications of Gadamer's rehabilitation of the Aristotelian tradition of practical philosophy for our understanding of the social sciences are obviously far-reaching.[3] But what is equally obvious is how it enables us to provide answers to questions about the role of methodology in action research that are not available from within the confines of action research's own methodological debate.[4] For what it clearly demonstrates is how the very notion of a 'methodological debate' is itself rooted in action research's acceptance of certain historically rooted prejudices concerning the nature of practice and how practical knowledge can be developed. And what this implies is that it is only by displaying a willingness to bring our self-understanding of action research into dialogical encounter with Gadamer's analysis of the Aristotelian tradition of practical philosophy that we will be in a position to achieve that level of 'effective historical consciousness' which would allow us to appreciate the extent to which our conception of action research as a form of methodologically principled social scientific inquiry has been contaminated by the prejudices of modernity and how these prejudices continue to exercise a distorting influence on the way in which action research is now conducted and understood. But once we are prepared to give this kind of historical depth to our understanding of 'what action research is', some important insights begin to emerge.

What immediately emerges is a realisation not only of how twentieth century action research represents the starting point for a new social scientific 'research paradigm', but also of how practical philosophy has been transposed into a cultural context in which the pre-modern meanings attached to the concepts of 'action', 'practice', 'knowledge' and 'philosophy' have been radically transformed. Deprived of the conceptual and cultural resources necessary for its continuing existence, it is hardly surprising that practical philosophy has been rendered obsolete and replaced by an 'action research paradigm' which was based not on a philosophical analysis of the role of human reason in the development of practical knowledge, but on the need to develop a research methodology appropriate to the social scientific study of 'action'. It was of course only by so embracing the notion of 'methodology' that action research could be vindicated in terms of the prejudices that shaped the dominant culture of modernity. But in doing this, action research itself became deeply implicated in depriving *praxis* of the tradition of inquiry through which it had hitherto been articulated and sustained.

Thus, what also emerges is an understanding of how, in the course of the transition from practical philosophy to action research, the concept of *praxis* has been distorted and how such distortions could only have been avoided by developing a form of action research which acknowledged that *praxis* cannot be developed or improved by a mode of inquiry that is based on methodological principles or rules. This second insight implies another. One of the ways in which action research methodology functions to communicate a distorted concept of *praxis* is by concealing both its historical and cultural embeddedness and the non-methodical mode of practical reasoning through which it develops and evolves. But, by doing this, it deprives us of any understanding of why it is that action research can only contribute to the improvement of practice by meeting the need of practitioners to develop those forms of philosophical reflection and historical consciousness that the development of their *praxis* requires. Moreover, in so far as an initiation into the methodology of action research has now replaced philosophy and history in the study of practice, practitioners are thereby denied access to precisely those kind of inquiries that would allow them to understand why their practice cannot be improved on the basis of knowledge derived from a form of action research conducted on the basis of a methodology.[5]

Thus, what finally emerges is a realisation of how action research has itself contributed to the erosion of the intellectual and cultural conditions that are necessary if its avowed commitment to the development of practice is to be fulfilled. However, once action research is prepared to expand its own 'historical horizons'—once, that is, it is prepared to make its own implicit acceptance of the dominant beliefs of modernity explicit—then it should become increasingly apparent why action research can only be made intelligible as a mode of inquiry that aspires to create and nurture the kind of dialogical communities within which *phronesis* can be embedded and which the development of *praxis* presupposes and requires. If it were to be understood in this way, action research would no longer feel it necessary to demonstrate its legitimacy by appealing to a methodology. Instead, it would be a form of inquiry that recognised that practical knowledge and understanding can only be developed and advanced by practitioners engaging in the kind of dialogue and conversation through which the tradition-embedded nature of the assumptions implicit in their practice can be made explicit and their collective understanding of their *praxis* can be transformed. It would therefore retain its claim to be a form of 'practitioner research' that enables practitioners to test the assumptions implicit in their practice, but would now insist that since these assumptions are always historically and culturally embedded, they can only be tested through a form of research concerned to promote historical consciousness. It would thus be a form of research that recognised that history is the domain in which practical reasoning is constituted and cultivated and that the power of history is something that a research methodology can never eliminate or transcend.

Interpreted in this way, action research would no longer be understood as a social science 'research paradigm' that can achieve what conventional social scientific research has conspicuously failed to achieve. Rather it would be regarded as nothing other than a post-modern manifestation of the pre-modern Aristotelian tradition of practical philosophy. As such, it would be a mode of inquiry whose chief task was to reclaim the sphere of *praxis* from its modern assimilation to the sphere of *technē* by fostering the kind of dialogical communities in which open conversation can be protected from the domination of a research methodology. This is not an easy task to achieve. Within the dominant culture of modernity, the concepts of *phronesis* and *praxis* have been rendered marginal and now face something approaching total obliteration. But it is only by seeking to ensure that the void created by the demise of practical philosophy will not be filled by a research methodology that action research will be able to defend the integrity of *praxis* against all those cultural tendencies that now undermine and degrade it.[6]

NOTES

1. My account of Aristotle's distinction between *phronesis* and *technē* draws heavily on the second part of Dunne (1993).
2. For a detailed exposition and analysis of Gadamer's theory of understanding, see Bleicher, 1980; Bernstein, 1983; Warnke, 1987; Dunne, 1993.
3. Some of these implications are developed as part of Bent Flyvbjerg's argument for creating a 'phronetic social science' explicitly committed to contributing 'to the ongoing social dialogue' concerning the questions 'Where are we going?' 'Is this desirable?' 'What should be done?' (Flyvbjerg, 2001, pp. 60–61). For an attempt to articulate the idea of a 'post-paradigmatic phronetic political science', see Schram (2004).
4. The significance of Gadamer's appropriation of Aristotelian practical philosophy for our understanding of action research was noted many years ago by John Elliott (Elliott, 1987).
5. For a discussion of the ideological role that the notion of 'methodology' plays in the social sciences see MacIntyre (1979).
6. This is an expanded version of a paper originally presented at the 2005 *International Conference on Practitioner Research/Action Research* in Utrecht, Holland.

REFERENCES

Adelman, C. (1993) Kurt Lewin and the Origins of Action Research, *Educational Action Research*, 1.1, pp. 7–24.
Aristotle (1955) *The Nicomachean Ethics*, J. A. K. Thompson, trans. (London, Penguin).
Bernstein, R. J. (1983) *Beyond Objectivism and Subjectivism: Science, Hermeneutics and Praxis* (Oxford, Blackwell).
Bleicher, J. (1980) *Contemporary Hermeneutics* (London, Routledge & Kegan Paul).
Durkheim, E. (1982) *The Rules of Sociological Method* (Macmillan, London).
Dunne, J. (1993) *Back to the Rough Ground: 'Phronesis' and 'Technē' in Modern Philosophy and in Aristotle* (London, University of Notre Dame Press).
Elliott, J. (1987) Educational Theory, Practical Philosophy and Action Research, *British Journal of Educational Studies*, 35.2, pp. 149–169.
Elliott, J. (1991) *Action Research for Educational Change* (Milton Keynes, Open University Press).
Elliott, J. (1998) *The Curriculum Experiment: Meeting the Challenge of Social Change* (Buckingham, Open University Press).
Flyvbjerg, B. (2001) *Making Social Science Matter* (Cambridge, Cambridge University Press).
Gadamer, H-G. (1975a) *Truth and Method*, G. Barden and J. Cummings, trans. and ed. (New York, Seabury Press).
Gadamer, H-G. (1975b) Hermeneutics and Social Science, *Cultural Hermeneutics*, 2, pp. 307–316.
Gadamer, H-G. (1979) The Problem of Historical Consciousness, in: P. Rabinow and W. M. Sullivan (eds) *Interpretive Social Sciences: a Reader* (Berkeley, University of California Press).
Gadamer, H-G. (1980) Practical Philosophy as a Model of the Human Sciences, *Research in Phenomenology*, 9, pp. 74–85.
Gadamer, H-G. (1981) *Reason in the Age of Science*, F. G. Lawrence, trans. (Cambridge, MA, MIT Press).

Kemmis, S. (1988) Action Research, in: J. P. Keeves (ed.) *Educational Research, Methodology and Measurement: An International Handbook* (Oxford, Pergamon Press).

Lewin, K. (1946) Action Research and Minority Problems, *Journal of Social Issues*, 2.4, pp. 34–46.

Lewin, K. (1952) Group Decision and Social Change, in: G. E. Swanson, T. M. Newcomb and E. L. Hartley (eds) *Readings in Social Psychology* (New York, Holt).

MacIntyre, A. C. (1979) Social Science Methodology as the Ideology of Bureaucratic Authority, in: M. J. Falco (ed.) *Through the Looking Glass: Epistemology and the Conduct of Inquiry* (Tulsa, University Press of America).

MacIntyre, A. C. (1981) *After Virtue: A Study in Moral Philosophy* (London, Duckworth).

McTaggart, R. (1991) *Action Research: A Short Modern History* (Geelong, Australia, Deakin University Press).

Sanford, N. (1970) Whatever Happened to Action Research?, *Journal of Social Issues*, 26.4, pp. 3–23.

Schram, S. F. (2004) Beyond Paradigm: Resisting the Assimilation of Phronetic Social Science, *Politics and Society*, 32.3, pp. 417–433.

Somekh, B. (2006) *Action Research: A Methodology for Change and Development* (Maidenhead, Open University Press).

Stenhouse, L. (1975) *An Introduction to Curriculum Research and Development* (London, Heinemann).

Toulmin, S. (1988) The Recovery of Practical Philosophy, *The American Scholar*, 57.3, p. 354.

Toulmin, S. (1990) *Cosmopolis: The Hidden Agenda of Modernity* (New York, The Free Press).

Wallace, M. (1987) A Historical Review of Action Research: Some Implications for the Education of Teachers in their Management Role, *Journal of Education for Teaching*, 13.2, pp. 97–115.

Warnke, G. (1987) *Gadamer: Hermeneutics, Tradition and Reason* (Cambridge, Polity Press).

Weber, M. (1949) *The Methodology of the Social Sciences* (New York, Free Press).

11

Educational Research as a Form of Democratic Rationality

JOHN ELLIOTT

I RE-DESCRIBING 'EDUCATIONAL RESEARCH': A TASK FOR A PRACTICAL PHILOSOPHY OF EDUCATION

There is a strong case (cp. Elliott, 1978) for making a distinction between 'educational research' and 'research on education'. What makes research *educational* is its practical intention to realise educational values in action. It addresses practical questions and in doing so cannot avoid taking an evaluative stance on the aims of education. On this view, it is a form of inquiry aimed at the formation of practical insights and judgments. Since these are rooted in the everyday experiences of education practitioners educational research constitutes a form of commonsense inquiry rather than a science. On the other hand, 'research on education' aspires to produce 'objective knowledge' about practice in classrooms and schools by adopting the position of an impartial spectator who transcends the evaluative perspectives of education practitioners. Such a position is presumed to be a condition of describing and explaining what is *really* going on in institutions of learning. 'Research on education' assumes that theoretical questions about education could can only arise, be addressed and answered from a position that transcends the common experience of the practitioners operating inside classrooms and schools.

My original and primary intention in coining this distinction was a very practical one. In the UK from the late 1960s onwards I and some other academics had been working collaboratively and dialogically with teachers through projects and courses to effect educationally worthwhile changes in their classrooms. This involved a process of gathering and interpreting evidence about the problems teachers experienced in realising their pedagogical aims, and developing and testing action hypotheses about problem solutions. We came to describe this process as a form of action research, and in doing so increasingly encountered opposition from within the educational research community, and indeed from some education practitioners. The opposition argued that while we were engaged in good professional development activities with teachers, it was not proper research. It simply lacked the scientific rigour expected of educational research. My response to such opposition was to embark on the project of redefining the terms in which educational research as a practice had been cast. I cast 'educational research' as a form of action research in the hope of opening up new practical possibilities for creating a better link between research and educational practice than that provided by what I called 'research on education'.

In this chapter I will argue that my project of re-describing educational research—a project I have come to regard as 'practical philosophy' of the kind depicted by Wilfred Carr (2004, pp. 55–73)—is as relevant now as it was a quarter of a century ago, and perhaps more so. It is philosophy with the very practical aim of changing over time the practice of educational research. Doing philosophy is not for me a matter of fixing the meaning of terms for all time. In re-describing educational research there is an important sense in which I am not claiming to provide a truer picture of that process than the picture embedded in what I call 'research on education'. Such a claim would imply that my picture puts researchers in touch with the realities of life in classrooms and schools in a way that the more conventional picture cannot. I regard the two pictures as simply sitting alongside each other. However, this does not imply a kind of relativism, such that there are no good reasons for preferring one picture to another. I will argue that there are practical and indeed political reasons for preferring my picture of educational research, albeit one that is continuously changing, to the one embedded in 'research on education'.

For example, I have been particularly concerned over the years with the problem of linking 'theory' and 'practice'. I have experienced it first and foremost as a practical problem that has arisen in the context of my own research practice. Teachers tend to ignore the theories produced by researchers on the grounds that they are practically irrelevant. They cannot connect them with their ordinary commonsense experience. I came to the conclusion that this problem largely stemmed from the context in which researchers tend to generate theory, one that is distanced and divorced from the practical context of teachers work. One possible solution lay in effecting a marriage between the processes of theoretical reasoning (research) and making practical judgments by giving the former a home within the context of practice. For many researchers such a solution was inconceivable. So I became interested in how they pictured the conditions under which it became possible to generate theory and in offering an alternative picture of such conditions. I found myself engaged in what I can only describe as 'practical philosophy' inasmuch as the philosophical questions I addressed about the relationship between educational theory and practice stemmed directly from a practical problem I experienced as an educational researcher.

II EDUCATIONAL RESEARCH, COMMONSENSE AND SCIENCE

The distinction I make between 'educational research' and 'research on education', as research aimed at the production of a body of knowledge and shaped by the concepts, procedures and methods that are definitive of the empirical sciences, involves conceiving 'educational research' as the development of *educational* insights and judgment, with regard to everyday situations in classrooms and schools. It is connected with the Aristotelian concept of *phronesis* as a matter of the formation of good practical ethical judgments. I interpret Aristotle as saying that this process involves a distinctive kind of practical reasoning. Aristotle argues that *phronesis* is shaped by value-laden conceptions of practical ends that have no fixed and antecedent meaning. Their meaning is defined through judgments about how best to realise the ends in a practical form in particular circumstances. *Phronesis* presumes that our conceptions of ends are embedded in our practices, and therefore inseparable from our practical judgments about means. I argued that conceptions of *educational* ends are of this kind. They refer to values that are regarded as internal qualities of *educational* practice. As such, they cannot be clearly specified in advance of the means selected to instantiate them. Practical reasoning about how to realise *educational* ends is not a form of instrumental/ technical rationality, which Aristotle calls *techne*.

For example, I have worked with teachers whose pedagogical aims were couched in terms of values that referred to qualities of the learning process they wished to engage students in rather than to the specific learning outcomes—knowledge and skills—that might desirably result from such a process. Hence, the teachers articulated their aims in terms of value-laden conceptions of a worthwhile educational process such as 'learning through inquiry or discussion', 'autonomous or self-directed learning', 'critical and creative thinking', 'collaborative learning', 'democratic learning', etc. Such concepts are inevitably vague. Their meaning can only be clarified by studying examples of attempts to realise the values they signify in practice.

Aristotle's concept of *phronesis* appears to support my view of educational inquiry as a form of commonsense reasoning, by contrast perhaps with Richard Pring's view (1976, ch. 5) that 'commonsense' simply covers judgments based on taken-for-granted beliefs. For the fact that many people base their practical judgments on taken-for-granted assumptions does not imply that they have to. More recently Wilfred Carr (2004, pp. 61–62) has argued, contrary to my view, that Aristotle's concept of *phronesis* does not name a reasoned state of practical judgment, but rather a process grounded in taken-for-granted beliefs that are embodied in a practical tradition. He contends that *phronesis* is not always sufficient to determine good practice in some situations. Problems arise that cannot be resolved on the basis of traditional understandings of good practice. They challenge practitioners to call these existing understandings into question in order to discern new ways of expressing the values or ends that are inherent in the tradition. He points out that thinking of this kind is the process by which established practical knowledge gets reconceived to develop the tradition. It will entail a rigorous examination of the biases (pre-understandings, even prejudices) about good practice that the practitioner brings to the situation and a systematic gathering of evidence around the problem(s) it presents. Carr concludes that although this form of practical reasoning depends on *phronesis* it reflexively transcends it. Indeed he is depicting the same process that I had made central to my re-description of 'educational research', but this implies that I was wrong to view it as synonymous with *phronesis*. I am inclined to persist with my interpretation of the concept and in this respect draw support from Joseph Dunne's meticulous scholarship on Aristotle's concepts of practical knowledge (see 1993, p. 244). He cites textual evidence that makes it clear that *phronesis* picks out a rational capacity for action.

Where my 1978 account of 'educational research' differed significantly from Aristotle's conception of *phronesis* is that I attempted to depict educational research as a form of commonsense theorising (pp. 15–19). Aristotle himself regarded *phronesis* as a non-theoretical form of judgment and reasoning that was quite distinct from theoretical knowledge and reason, which he called *episteme*. As Dunne points out, for Aristotle the spheres of theory and practice are incommensurable, the former being 'emphatically distinguished from any knowledge that might have practical import' (Dunne, 1993, p. 238). Theoretical knowledge consisted in a contemplative grasp of the principles that governed an unchanging and eternal cosmic order transcending the contingencies of everyday living. I wished to see, for reasons explained earlier, the term 'theory' freed from the essentialist assumptions—assumptions based on the nature of the world, or the human mind or language—that shaped its meaning in Greek thought, and put to the service of practice. Concepts should rather be seen as characterising value-laden conceptions of ends (cp. Blumer, 1970, ch. 4). They constitute concrete universals inasmuch as their meaning can only be determined through concrete practical experience. Moreover, their meaning changes over time and with experience. This process of continuously constructing and reconstructing the meaning of our value concepts in practice can usefully be depicted as a form of commonsense theorising, in which case educational theories are generated in the context of practice through the judgments and actions of teachers. This provides a very different picture of educational theory from the one that has come to dominate relationships between academics and the teaching profession. I hoped that it might open up new possibilities of engaging teachers with educational research.

The notion of 'situational understanding', comparable to that of *aesthesis*, which Aristotle sees as a key component of *phronesis*, characterises 'theories' expressed in practical judgment. Good judgments in the context of educational practice will depend on the quality of the 'situational understanding' that underpins them. They are to be described in terms of capacities to discern the educationally relevant features of a situation and then to discriminate those that are critical for *educational* practice. The validity of such understanding can only be tested in action, by the extent to which it enables practitioners to effect changes that are experienced as more educationally worthwhile than the previous state of affairs. Indeed such changes will expose problematic features of the situation that were previously hidden from view and thereby open up new challenges for practitioners. The development of 'situational under-standing', therefore, proceeds interactively with the development of educational practice. It constitutes a form of action research.

Over the years I qualified and revised the terms in which I originally drew the distinction in 1978 between 'educational research' and 'research on education' (see Introduction to Selected Papers, Elliott, in press). I became more reluctant to draw a boundary between these descriptions in terms of 'commonsense' and 'scientific' reasoning. 'Educational Research' became increasingly depicted as a 'practical science'. This was because in casting it as a form of research in which teachers played a significant role many of my fellow educational researchers felt that it must, therefore, lack the rigour they associated with scientific research. I concluded that any attempt to re-contextualise the use of the term 'rigour' must also be accompanied by a re-contextualisation of the meaning of 'science'. Increasingly I presented the distinction between 'educational research' and 'research on education' as providing two different pictures of scientific research. However, scientific reasoning and the kind of commonsense reasoning that I depicted stood in a different relation to each other in each picture.

The assumption made by many scientists that their findings transcend and frequently conflict with commonsense understandings of the world has been recently questioned by the scientific journalist John Horgan in both the *New York Times* and *The Guardian* newspapers (18 August, 2005). Horgan argues that the non-specialised knowledge and judgment that is rooted in everyday experience and 'helps ordinary people to get through ordinary days' (commonsense) is often needed to discipline scientific theorising. He regards the scientists' contempt for commonsense judgment and insight as having two unfortunate consequences. One is that scientists tend to measure the profundity of their theories, however flimsy their evidential basis, in terms of how preposterous they appear from the standpoint of commonsense. The other is that scientists only regard other scientists as qualified to judge their work. However, Horgan is careful not to convey the message that commonsense is always the best test of scientific theories. What is critical in this respect is the extent to which theories are ultimately supported by sound empirical evidence. He argues that some of the most profound (well-evidenced) insights of science can violate our commonsense intuitions. By way of example he cites Einstein's stubborn refusal to accept one implication of the quantum mechanics he prepared the groundwork for—that is, that at small scales reality dissolves into a cloud of probabilities. This refusal was based on his commonsense belief that specific causes yield specific effects.

Horgan appears to define 'commonsense' in terms I discussed earlier: as intuitive (taken-for-granted) non-rational belief. 'Science', on the other hand, provides at its best, he claims, a rational basis for belief. At its worst, however, it peddles irrational theories. Hence, the need for science to be disciplined by commonsense. Although Horgan leaves little space for my original notion of educational research as a form of commonsense rationality, he does, I feel, leave room for the idea of a 'practical science' of education. His view that sound evidence is the ultimate test of a scientific theory does not, in my view, make him an empiricist. He is generally sceptical about 'scientific' quests for unifying theories and cites the attempt to find a theory that unifies quantum mechanics and general relativity. He points out that each of these theories employs a different language from the other and, therefore, describes different worlds. This nominalist stance of Horgan's implies that the standards of judgment that define what counts as sound empirical evidence in support of theories will themselves vary according to the particular language of description employed, there being no linguistically neutral standpoint from which to observe the facts. What makes him sceptical of any claim to provide a single unifying theory, he contends, is that no conceivable experiment could confirm it evidentially. I take him to be saying that it is impossible to specify a universal standard for judging what would count as evidence for such a theory. This is entirely consistent with what I called his nominalist stance. However, from his point of view his scepticism towards grand theory stems directly from his commonsense intuition and the history of science.

I would suggest that 'nominalism' as a philosophical theory is rooted in ordinary people's experience of the complexities of contemporary living in these postmodern times. Given that experience, the belief that the things and events it consists of can be explained in terms of a single cause defies 'commonsense', as Horgan uses the term. So does the belief that there is only one 'true way' of describing the complexities of human experience. It is currently commonsense to believe that they can be validly described from different angles and points of view.

Horgan's account, of the positive role of commonsense belief in relation to the claims of scientists, may explain why many educational practitioners are sceptical about the grand theories generated by researchers in the field of education and beyond. Such theories attempt explanations that tend to reduce everything that happens in schools and classrooms to a single cause. Hence, some researchers have claimed that the performance of pupils as measured by standardised tests is the direct effect of the teaching methods employed or school culture. From a practitioner's point of view, such reductionist findings defy commonsense and are of little value in helping them to cope with the complexities of the everyday situations they experience in classrooms and schools, such as coping with disruptive and disaffected students. In order to cope they need theories of a different kind: those that enable them to discern the practically relevant features of the complex situations they have to handle on a day-to-day basis. Such theories I would claim provide insights, not by being applied to practical situations, but by being situated in them. I tend to think that Horgan might accept this view, for the major reason he wants to bring science into an alliance with the commonsense intuitions of ordinary people is that it should serve the practical purpose of helping them to cope with the complexities of everyday living. How, from his nominalist outlook, could scientific descriptions (theories) of the world serve such a purpose if they were not situated in the practical problems and complexities of everyday life? In his article Horgan is basically offering us a picture of science that is not detached from ordinary people's practical purposes. This is not unlike my attempt to depict educational research as a practical science.

One familiar objection to such a depiction is that scientific theories refer to general features of a class of objects, whereas in my account of educational research as a form of action research, 'theories' refer only to the particular features of instances. Therefore, such research does not qualify as 'science'. This objection often takes the form of a currently fashionable contrast between 'Big Science' educational research and 'Practitioner Research' (see Bassey, 2003, pp. 12–18). The former is viewed as large-scale in scope and aimed at producing generalisable knowledge, whereas the latter is regarded as small-scale inquiry that teachers carry out within the confines of their particular classrooms. In the 1978 paper I argued that 'educational research' can be a source of generalisation but of a different kind from the kinds of predictive generalisations generated through 'research on education' (p. 22). In this respect I made use of Stake's distinction between formalistic and naturalistic generalisation (1978, pp. 5–7). The latter is grounded in practitioners' insights into their particular situations. In sharing these insights they become capable of recognising commonalities in their experience that can be cast in the form of generalisations.

Both Alasdair MacIntyre and Martha Nussbaum have cast further light for me on this issue of generalisability. MacIntyre (1990, pp. 59–61) argues that standards of practical reasoning are embedded in *traditions* that represent the best standards developed to date about how to realise the values that constitute the ends of a social practice. He has pointed out that the fact that there are no fixed standards for practical judgments of a non-instrumental kind does not imply that such judgments cannot be rationally justified. Best standards are those that have stood the test of time and accommodated the challenges of changing circumstances. Although, for McIntyre, such traditions guide practices in particular circumstances they are always open to revision in the light of new contingencies that challenge practitioners to find new ways of embodying their values in practice. What I called 'situational theories' now seem to me to be standards of this kind. They possess not only concrete significance in a particular context of practice but also *universal* significance for communities of practice. This is because they not only draw on the general insights embedded in tradition but also reconstitute the tradition itself.

MacIntyre's argument is echoed by a fellow neo-Aristotelian, Martha Nussbaum, in her distinction between general and universal principles (1990, pp. 67–68). A general principle, Nussbaum argues, not only covers many cases, but 'applies to them in virtue of some rather non-concrete characteristics' (ibid.). In other words it originates in the process of abstracting elements of the case from the particularities of time and circumstance. Generalisations based on random controlled and experimental trials in the field of education are currently attractive because they promise to yield the kind of general principles (generalisations) Nussbaum refers to as a way of rationally ordering educational practice. In contrast universal principles, according to Nussbaum, apply to all particular cases ' that are in the relevant ways similar' (ibid.). She argues that principles of this kind play an important role in practical reasoning without being prior to particular perceptions of situations of choice. She views them as summaries of good concrete judgements in situations that are discerned to be similar in all practically relevant respects. As such, they are useful as guides to perception: to discerning the practically/ethically relevant features of particular concrete and complex situations that tend to repeat themselves from one situation to another. This is quite different from the normative function of general principles as 'the ultimate authorities against which the correctness of particular choices is assessed' (ibid.). Universal principles, captured in summaries of good concrete judgements in similar situations, represent the 'voice of concrete practical experience' (ibid.). Yet at the same time they are open to the experience of surprise. Our capacity to recognise the unique and novel features of a case that are nevertheless ethically significant depends on our use of these universal 'rules of thumb'. Being capable of recognising the unanticipated when it occurs depends on the anticipations provided by such universal principles.

Educational research, which involves teachers sharing and developing their practical insights into the problems of realising their educational values in concrete teaching situations and their judgments about how these are best resolved, can yield useful summaries of the universal significance of insights and judgments to guide further reflection and action. The diagnostic and action hypotheses developed in the contexts of the Humanities Curriculum and Ford Teaching Projects in the UK can be regarded as having this form and function (see Elliott, 1976, pp. 2–22 and 1983, pp. 105–123). I now feel that we can make a useful distinction between the 'generalisabilty' and 'universalisability' of research findings and that both can justifiably count as scientific knowledge, for reasons I will explain later.

III EMANCIPATING EDUCATIONAL RESEARCH FROM METHODOLOGY

The distinction between 'educational research' and 'research on education' can appear coterminous with the distinction between the kinds of data gathered and the methods used for doing so (cp. Elliott, 1978, p. 21). The latter deploys quantitative data gathering methods while the former deploys qualitative methods. This is because 'research on education' aims to produce reliable predictive generalisations while 'educational research' aims to develop an understanding of the practically relevant features of particular situations (p. 13). But since many researchers use qualitative methods to carve out forms of inquiry that look very much like another version of 'research on education', there is reason to be dissatisfied with depicting it in terms of employing quantitative as opposed to qualitative methods. The manner in which qualitative methods were used often appeared like an attempt to produce an alternative form of *episteme* to the one provided by quantitative methods. Although many qualitative researchers in education focused on situations and events from the standpoint of their meaning for those involved, they employed second-order theoretical constructs to explain these meanings. Their research findings tended to suggest that things were not how they appeared to participants because they were unaware of the social, economic and political factors that inevitably condition their commonsense constructions of meaning. With varying degrees of explicitness a great deal of qualitative research in the education field claims to have penetrated to a level of reality that is hidden from the view of participants. Qualitative methods have been used to illuminate practice in the field of education on the assumption that such illumination can only stem from a methodological standpoint that transcends the commonsense standpoint from which those engaged in practical pursuits like education construct meaning. One might depict this standpoint in terms of a transcendental phenomenology (Husserl) in which, after describing the contents of consciousness, the researcher places them in *brackets* to focus on their *essential* features.

What is far from clear, as David Hargreaves (1997, p. 412) has pointed out, is how the illumination provided by the use of qualitative methods yields actionable knowledge. Hargreaves, however, believes that such knowledge can be guaranteed by employing a particular quantitative method in the form of random controlled experiments. This is partly because he views actionable knowledge in instrumental terms, as *techne*. In doing so he leaves no room for an account of actionable knowledge that co-determines the means and ends of *educational action*. Hargreaves is operating with a different view of practical reasoning in education and its relationship to research. It is a view cast in terms of a logic that is both objectivist and instrumentalist. In the former respect he has something in common with some of the qualitative researchers he is critical of. Both appear to embrace a view of knowledge cast in essentialist terms as a grasp of the principles that order things in themselves. They simply differ on what such knowledge consists of, whether it is of things that exist independently of the mind (an objectivist *episteme*) or of things of the mind (a subjectivist *episteme*). The different kinds of research methods proposed by each directly flow from these different conceptions of knowledge.

I no longer wish to draw a boundary between 'educational research' and 'research on education' in terms of the kinds of research methods employed. Much qualitative research is as much 'research on education' as a lot of quantitative research, insofar as it shares with the latter a certain picture of research. This is a picture of an activity aimed at discovering essential truths about a reality that lies beyond how the world appears to those engaged in the practical pursuits of everyday life. I must confess to no longer being interested in methodological questions, as they presuppose that there is a method or group of methods that is necessary for discovering essential truths about the objects of inquiry. With respect to research methods I now see 'educational research' as an eclectic and heuristic form of inquiry. It is not necessary to justify such methods 'methodologically', in the sense of providing access to the 'truth'. There is, I would now argue, no particular method or group of methods that 'educational research' must necessarily employ. Whatever helps practitioners to develop a reasoned capacity for action in the service of their educational values will do. Methods will be selected in the context of practice as the situation unfolds. At times questions will arise that call for the gathering of certain kinds of qualitative data, while at other times the gathering of certain kinds of quantitative data may be more appropriate.

IV DEMOCRATISING EDUCATIONAL RESEARCH AND THE QUESTION OF RIGOUR

In continuously qualifying and revising the terms of my distinction between 'educational research' and 'research on education', I have found myself increasingly following in the footsteps of John Dewey and more recent advocates of philosophical pragmatism, particularly Richard Rorty. Dewey extended what he believed to be characteristic of 'scientific method' beyond the substantive focus of its traditional subject matter to cover all inquiry (see Dewey, 1974, pp. 182–192). He thought of scientific method, not so much as a subject specific procedure, but as a manifestation of certain general attitudes and virtues in all forms of inquiry (including ethics, aesthetics and philosophy). These included curiosity, objectivity, honesty, open-mindedness and a commitment to freedom of thought and discussion. For Dewey such attitudes and virtues constituted a democratic way of life. Science on this conception is not a method or procedure for accessing a reality that exists independently of a community of inquirers. What is to count as warranted or justified belief in contrast to mere opinion, dogma and guesswork is solely determined by a democratic discussion aimed at achieving an unforced consensus.

Rorty (1999, p. xxi) has questioned whether the term 'method' is the best way of describing the democratic process of inquiry that Dewey depicted. He suspects that Dewey's use of the term 'method' conveys the kind of empiricist assumptions that he was attempting to free scientific inquiry from. Rorty wants our picture of science to be purged of all essentialist assumptions. All methodological discourses, he believes, are inevitably grounded in such assumptions and presume a spectator theory of knowledge. There are no wholesale constraints on inquiry, Rorty argues (1982, p. 165), 'derived from the nature of objects, or of the mind, or of language'. The only constraints are conversational ones, 'those retail constraints provided by the remarks of our fellow inquirers'. He argues that those of us engaged in inquiry 'have a duty to talk to each other, to converse about our views of the world, to use persuasion rather than force, to be tolerant of diversity, to be contritely fallibist' (1991, p. 67). Such are the democratic virtues that Dewey associated with the scientific method but that Rorty wishes to dissociate from the essentialist connotations of the term 'method'. In this sense he gives us an account of inquiry without method. It is one that supports my account of 'educational research' as it has evolved. However, I would want to distinguish 'methodology' from 'method'. The former term may be used to refer to a universal procedure for accessing essential truths about the objects of inquiry. This is what Rorty appears to be referring to when he talks about method. However, I would want to use the term 'method' to refer to a specific technique for gathering a certain kind of data. My account of 'educational research' is an account of inquiry without a methodology, but this does not imply that it does not make use of data gathering techniques. I would, therefore, disagree with those who depict action research as a methodology.

Rorty's, and to a large extent Dewey's, account of inquiry implies that there is no standpoint from which to describe the world, whether natural or social, other than one that is conditioned by the practical purposes and interests of human beings. What a democratic process of inquiry determines is which descriptions of the human environment, natural as well as social, best enable human beings effectively to interact with it to satisfy their needs and desires. Such an account of inquiry leaves little room for a conception of science as a distinctive form of theoretical reasoning that is discontinuous from practical reasoning focused on the conduct of human affairs. This, I believe, is why Horgan believes that it is important for ordinary people to get involved with professional scientists in the process of determining what counts as a good theory.

There is no need to characterise educational research as deploying a particular methodology in order to depict it as a rigorous and disciplined process. Educational research on my account derives its discipline from the exercise of certain capabilities that are best depicted as democratic virtues. Although specific techniques of data gathering and analysis will be heuristically employed to enhance the exercise and development of such capabilities in particular contexts of inquiry, they require no justification as features of a methodology. Rorty himself views rigour as something 'you can have only after entering into an agreement with some other people to subordinate your imagination to their consensus' (1998, p. 339). I interpret him as saying that rigour is the quality of reasoning that emerges in the course of a good conversation; namely, one that is disciplined by the democratic virtues.

V PRACTICAL RATIONALITY AND EDUCATIONAL RESEARCH

I was particularly concerned in 1978 to distinguish educational research from a form of research that is cast in the form of a positivistic science, and the need to make this distinction has not diminished since. From the standpoint of positivism, science provides us with empirical knowledge of causal laws that are beyond speculation and in doing so constitutes a sure and certain foundation on which to reshape and modernise our social practices.

When positivism's picture of science dominates what counts as an educational science, then it will take the form of 'research on education', for this implies that researchers adopt the standpoint of an impartial spectator as a condition of getting in touch with empirical reality. However, this also implies that such a stance is in the interest of social practitioners, for it is a condition of practical rationality, conceived in instrumentalist terms. Positivism, therefore, links theory and practice in terms of a logic that marries an objectivist view of knowledge, an *episteme*, with an instrumentalist view of practical reason. Such a marriage defines practical rationality in terms of what Nussbaum (1990, pp. 56–57) has called 'the science of measurement'. She breaks this 'scientific' conception of rationality into four constitutive claims. First, there is the claim of *Metricity*: that ' in a particular choice situation there is some one value, varying only in quantity, that is common to all the alternatives'. The rational chooser is one who uses this single standard as a metric to weigh each alternative and thereby determine which will yield the greatest quantity of value. Secondly, there is the claim of *Singularity*: that one and the same metric or standard applies in all situations of choice. Thirdly, there is the claim of *Consequentialism*: that the chosen actions only have instrumental value as a means of producing good consequences. Fourthly, by combining each of these claims we have the principle of *Maximisation*: 'that there is some one value, that it is the point of rational choice, in every case, to maximize'.

Policy-making and research in the field of education has become increasingly shaped by this so-called 'scientific' picture of practical reasoning (see Schwandt, 2005, pp. 294–295, and Elliott and Doherty, 2001, pp. 209–221, in relation to the US and the UK respectively). Hence, the educational reforms initiated by many governments are viewed as devices for 'driving up standards', conceived in terms of *metricity* and *singularity*. Research increasingly takes the form of school and teacher effectiveness research aimed at determining how schools and teachers can 'add value' to students' learning. The *maximisation principle* is embedded in the idea of 'value added', which presumes that the practices of schools and teachers only have value if they produce good *consequences* and that these can be quantified in terms of a single metric that applies generally across the system. Hence, the widespread use of standardised testing in school and teacher effectiveness research. The findings from such research are now widely regarded as furnishing the rational basis for modernising educational practice in schools and classrooms. Hence, the currently fashionable, widely circulating notion in many policy contexts of 'evidence-based practice'.

Nussbaum (1990, p. 55) claims that contemporary conceptions of practical rationality in 'almost every area of social life' are so dominated by the 'science of measurement' that we are in danger of losing sight of the Aristotelian conception of practical rationality as *phronesis*. I agree. The inroads the evidence-based practice movement has made within the field of education in western countries, and even more globally, are testimony to this. However, this 'scientific' picture of rationality is also making it increasingly difficult to imagine any other relationship between science and practical reasoning. For example, Schwandt (see above) depicts the growing dominance of a 'science of measurement' in the US educational system and, while wanting to see more space for a deliberative form of practical inquiry, appears reluctant to call it 'scientific' on the grounds that it is too messy for that. I believe that we need to construct a different picture of scientific inquiry in the field of education. This is why it more and more seems useful to marry Aristotle's concept of *phronesis* with a pragmatist account of 'science' in re-describing educational research.

As the development economist Amartya Sen has pointed out, in relation to public choice theory (see 2002, pp. 39–42), a principle of practical reasoning couched in terms of the maximization of utility leaves no space for the rational scrutiny of goals and values. Opening up one's choices to rational scrutiny is simply to have their instrumentality and efficiency in maximising the desired end assessed. The possibility of a reasoned self–scrutiny of our goals and values is pre-empted by the principle of maximisation. The ends themselves are simply taken for granted. Sen argues that 'rationality cannot be just an instrumental requirement for the pursuit of some given—and unscrutinized—set of objectives and values'. Moreover, Sen also points out that the maximisation of utility principle imposes another limit on our view of practical rationality. Not all our values, he contends, are goals. Some may rule out the pursuit of certain kinds of goals or at least impose restrictions on the means we adopt to bring them about. Hence our choice behaviour may be based on reasons that qualify the maximisation of utility principle. We may choose certain behaviours not to maximise utility but to act in ways that are ethically consistent with our non-goal values. In this respect Sen appears to want to open up a space for *phronesis* in any account of practical rationality.

All this leads Sen to conclude that we need a broader conception of practical rationality that reaches beyond the maximisation principle to include a 'critical scrutiny of the objectives and values that underlie any maximizing behaviour' and an acknowledgement of values that constitute '*self-imposed* constraints on that behaviour'. He casts such a conception in terms of a democratic process of *rational scrutiny* that is based on discussion of the reasons people might offer for their choice of actions. Such reasons will be various. They will include non-instrumental as well as instrumental considerations, and considerations of ends as well as the means of bringing them about. Sen argues, along similar lines to Rorty, that values are rationally established and validated through free and open discussion alone (2002, p. 287) and, like Rorty, claims that rationality in the sphere of values does not require some set of Kantian-like transcendental rational principles for ordering people's values. He also shares with Rorty, the view that the process of reasoning about values through discussion is a disciplined affair, and it is discussion itself that provides this rather than 'a favored formula, or an essentialist doctrine' (p. 46). Rorty argues that there is a use of the term 'rationality' that is synonymous with *tolerance* of difference and a willingness to engage in free and open conversation with each other about our goals and values in order 'to put together new, syncretic, compromise ways of life' (Rorty, 1998, p. 187). What both he and Sen do is to offer us a picture of rational inquiry in which instrumental reasoning is not dissociated from a rational scrutiny of ends and from the question of whether some ends restrict and limit our pursuit of others.

VI DEMOCRATIC RATIONALITY IN EDUCATIONAL RESEARCH: THE MARRIAGE BETWEEN *PHRONESIS* AND *TECHNE*, AND THE BANISHMENT OF *EPISTEME*

Sen's points are particularly pertinent to the limited conception of practical rationality provided by the 'science of measurement' that is increasingly embedded in contemporary educational policy-making and research in OECD countries and beyond in the developing world. My account of 'educational research' to date can be regarded as an attempt to acknowledge a realm of *educational* values that imposes limits on the extent to which educational practice should be shaped by the maximisation principle, as this is embedded in the 'science of measurement'. However, it can be criticised on the grounds that it draws too tight a boundary between two forms of practical reasoning in education, namely, *techne* and *phronesis*. Although, some will argue, 'educational research' should acknowledge the limits that specifically *educational ends* place on the means of bringing more utilitarian ends about, it should surely not ignore questions of an instrumental kind entirely. I would now accept such criticisms and argue that both forms of practical reasoning—*techne* and *phronesis*—need to be set alongside each other within a broad conception of educational research as a discursive and democratic process. Such a process will engage teachers, policy-makers and other stakeholders in society, at both national and regional/local levels, in a reasoned consideration of:

- the extrinsic goals and values that education is expected to serve;
- the consequences of alternative courses of action for realising both intrinsic and extrinsic ends of education;
- how to realise *educational* values in particular forms of practice;
- the limits this sets on selecting means to bringing about ends that are extrinsic to education.

This picture of a unified educational research process would leave room for gathering evidence that supports a degree of instrumental reasoning. For example, the kind of democratically constituted and discursive research forum outlined above may articulate a need for evidence about the problems of realising values that have been traditionally regarded as internal to education in a context where schools and teachers are required to maximise the human capital—knowledge and skills— deemed to be necessary for economic progress. The requirement for education to serve such utilitarian goals is often perceived to be a constraining feature of the situations in which teachers are attempting to realise values they regard as specifically educational, such as developing students' powers of reasoning and judgment. Understanding what is at stake in such situations will require a gathering of evidence both about the consequences of particular practices and about how the values and goals they are intended to serve are interpreted. Such evidence would then be fed back into the forum to support further analysis of the problem and the search for possible solutions that can be tested in practice. This means that the agendas for research and the processing of research evidence would be controlled by the information needs of such forums. In this context the determination of what kinds of evidence are required and its significance for practice would be shaped by a democratic process of inquiry.

The problem with that form of 'research on education' that is shaped by a 'science of measurement' is that it is profoundly undemocratic and in this sense irrational. Even though in the UK it increasingly has to engage 'user-groups' at all stages in the research process, such engagement is necessarily restricted and constrained by the use of methodological dogma. We need instead a picture of educational research that enables teachers to subject their practical judgments about educational means and ends to reasoned scrutiny by their peers, their students, parents and other stakeholders in society. Such research will, following Sen:

1. Refrain from shaping teachers' judgments in compliance with pre-selected, context-independent axioms or canonical specifications of proper objectives and values.
2. Accommodate a diversity of reasons for valuing education.
3. Respect participants' freedom, within the context of disciplined discussion, to make their own decisions about what ends and means should be valued in the field of education.

This picture of educational research may enable the teaching profession to put together with members of the wider society a new, syncretic, compromise (Rorty's words, above) vision of education that accommo-dates those values that are internal to education in any genuine democracy, while acknowledging utilitarian ends, such as developing human capital for a competitive 'knowledge economy'.

Although my account of 'educational research' would now leave space for it to serve the interests of instrumental reasoning in the education field, it does not leave room for a 'science of measurement' in the terms depicted by Nussbaum. For research to count as 'educational research' it would need to be free from objectivist assumptions and the standpoint of the impartial spectator. It would also need to acknowledge that instrumental reasoning alone does not justify educational practice. From the nominalist and pragmatist perspective outlined earlier we can still call 'educational research' of this kind 'scientific'. This is simply because it will aim to produce well-evidenced descriptions of practice in education systems that enable educators to better realise the practical ends of education, whether intrinsic or extrinsic ones, as these become articulated, orchestrated, syncretised and transformed in the course of a democrati-cally constituted and discursive process of educational inquiry. Such a process need be no less scientific than research in the natural sciences.

Rorty (1999, pp. xx and 5) contends that whether we are arguing for a theory concerning the microstructure of material bodies or for one about the proper balance of powers between branches of government, we are arguing about what we should do to make progress. In this respect he argues that there is no sharp break between science and social science. Although the first argument, as Rorty points out, is about what we should do to make technological progress and will, therefore, take the form of instrumental reason, I would suggest that the second argument is likely to involve a blend of *techne* and *phronesis*. In the sphere of social practices, such as education, scientific descriptions will need to accommodate *phronesis* as well as *techne*, and to show how the two might be integrated in practical judgment and action.

VII CONCLUDING REMARKS

Scientific descriptions of the world of education require no justification in terms of getting closer to what is *really* happening. The professional researchers who help to generate them through evidence-gathering activities, therefore, require no methodological justification for their activities. What justifies them is that they enable us to describe educational situations in ways that open up new and interesting possibilities for educational practice. For the sake of progress, educational practice needs to become more evidence-based, but not in the terms depicted by a 'science of measurement'. Yes, there will be room for the gathering of quantitative data and measurement, but also for the gathering of qualitative data and qualitative judgment. The project of re-describing educational research is necessary for political reasons, since it can provide an alternative account of what is involved in modernising the educational system to realise our social hope of a better, more democratic and just society.

REFERENCES

Dewey, J. (1974) Science as Subject-Matter and as Method, in: R. D. Archambault (ed.) *John Dewey on Education: Selected Writings* (Chicago and London, University of Chicago Press).
Bassey, M. (2003) A Vision for the Future of Educational Research, *Research Intelligence*, 84, pp. 12–15.
Blumer, H. (1970) What is Wrong with Social Theory?, in: W. J. Filstead (ed.) *Qualitative Methodology* (London, Rand McNally).
Carr, W. (2004) Philosophy and Education, *Journal of the Philosophy of Education*, 38.1, pp. 55–73.
Dunne, J. (1993) *Back to the Rough Ground: Practical Judgment and the Lure of Technique* (Notre Dame, IN, University of Notre Dame Press).
Elliott, J. (1976) Developing Hypotheses about Classrooms from Teachers' Practical Constructs: An Account of the Work of the Ford Teaching Project, *Interchange*, 7.2, pp. 2–22.
Elliott, J. (1978) Classroom Research: Science or Commonsense, in: R. McAleese and D. Hamilton (eds) *Understanding Classroom Life* (Windsor, NFER Publishing Company).
Elliott, J. (1983) A Curriculum for the Study of Human Affairs: the Contribution of Lawrence Stenhouse, *Journal of Curriculum Studies*, 15.2, pp. 105–123.
Elliott, J. (In Press) Reflecting where the Action Is: The Selected Writings of John Elliott on Pedagogy and Action Research (London, Routledge).

Elliott, J. and Doherty, P. (2001) Restructuring Educational Research for the 'Third Way'?, in: M. Fielding (ed.) *Taking Education Really Seriously, Four Years' Hard Labour* (London and New York, RoutledgeFalmer).

Horgan, J. (2005) Come On, Use Your Commonsense, in: *The Guardian*, 18. 08. 05.

Hargreaves, D. (1997) In Defence of Research for Evidence-based Teaching: A Rejoinder to Martyn Hammersley, *British Educational Research Journal*, 23.4, pp. 405–419.

MacIntyre, A. (1990) *Three Rival Versions of Moral Enquiry* (London, Duckworth).

Nagel, T. (1986) *The View from Nowhere* (Oxford, Clarendon Press).

Nussbaum, M. (1990) An Aristotelian Conception of Rationality, in: *Love's Knowledge* (Oxford, Oxford University Press).

Pring, R. (1976) *Knowledge and Schooling* (London, Open Books).

Rorty, R. (1982) *Consequences of Pragmatism* (Minneapolis, MN, University of Minnesota Press).

Rorty, R. (1991) Pragmatism without Method, in: *Objectivity, Relativism and Truth: Philosophical Papers Volume 1* (Cambridge, Cambridge University Press).

Rorty, R. (1998) Derrida and the Philosophical Tradition, in: *Truth and Progress, Philosophical Papers* (Cambridge, Cambridge University Press).

Rorty, R. (1999) *Philosophy and Social Hope* (London, Penguin Books).

Schwandt, T. (2005) A Diagnostic Reading of Scientifically Based Research for Education, *Educational Theory*, 55.3, pp. 285–305.

Sen, A. (2002) *Rationality and Freedom* (Cambridge, MA, Harvard University Press/Belknap), Chs. 1 and 8.

Stake, R. (1978) The Case Study Method in Social Inquiry, *Educational Researcher*, 7.2, pp. 5–8.

12
Philosophical Research and Educational Action Research

MARIANNA PAPASTEPHANOU

INTRODUCTION

Educational action research has emerged as a challenge to traditional academic research in education. It aims to empower the practitioner and effect change in multiple ways. The explicit philosophical influence and the implicit philosophical assumptions that are reflected in action research are very rich and diverse. Mostly, however, the kind of philosophy that grounds action research aspires to be most critical and circumspect regarding the role of philosophy and theory as such. It rehabilitates practice and emphasizes the possibility that active engagement with everyday professional life, rather than antecedent contemplation, may be productive of sound theoretical conclusions. Theory is valued, but for the most part only as a democratically testable outcome of practical endeavour through trial and error. Theory has no privileged access to objective truths, because there is neither epistemic privilege nor supra-social validity.

Pragmatism as the broader philosophical framework of educational action research tends to treat theory and practice in a way that results in critical social science gaining precedence over philosophy precisely where philosophy has been considered to be at its strongest: critical vision. Within a pragmatist outlook, 'general theories are best seen as practical proposals whose critical purchase is not moral and epistemic independence but practical and public testing according to criteria of interpretive adequacy' (Bohman, 1999, p. 472).

At first glance, theory and practice find in this formulation their much-desired unity, safely protected from master-narrative philosophies of the past. But a closer look reveals an inflation of practice to the point that the critical is forgone for the explanatory: what sets the criteria for the appraisal of general theories? The answer is their capacity to interpret the lifeworld; yet, is this solely what a theory is supposed to do? Proponents of this account would retort that within their approach there is much room for normativity too, that is, for going beyond the mere interpretation of the lifeworld so as to change it. General theories do not only inform societies about how they function; they also inform them about how to proceed. Thus, theories can be tested according to their practical success in leading societies to better prospects. This consequentialism, which is debatable and problematic for many other reasons that cannot be run through here, connects progress to the yardstick of further everyday practice alone. Something is fruitful and worth pursuing when it makes life easier and makes practice more effective.

Approaches of this sort rightly question the self-bestowed prerogative of theorists to claim access to truth through isolated reflection. But when they merely replace the academic with the lifeworld agent as the subject of reflection, they preserve quasi-Platonic, anamnesiac—the assumption that knowledge is already available and must be drawn from one's own soul— or even solipsistic implicit assumptions about knowledge. More explicitly, this is how the subjectivist framework is rescued once again in those approaches. The unnoticed assumption that seems to slip in is that, if one thinks about something, the truth about it will be revealed automatically in the wake of one's internal tensions and critical impasses or practical failures. As Feldman argues, however, reflective practitioners as situated beings confront the danger of having a distorted or inauthentic image of themselves and adopt a way of attending to their reflection and inquiry that reinforces the status quo instead of transforming it (Feldman, 2002, p. 235). Thus a simple reversal of the position of the academic and the practitioner does not solve the problems of the relationship between theory and practice. Having said that, there can be no return to the philosopher as a self-appointed prophet, I suggest that the theory and practice relation be recast and a new connection between philosophical and other kinds of research be established.

That theory and practice are not divided from an action research point of view (Somekh, 2003, p. 256) is no proof that their relation is not one of unresolved competition. For some theorists, the tension disappears, so it seems, when the two poles are internally connected. By establishing thus that the polar opposites are internally connected, they jump to the conclusion that what is achieved is a non-conflictive relation. However, avoiding external imposition of the one pole on the other and accor- ding equal weight to each secures only a brittle balance: deeper-laid qualitative differentiations perpetuate the tension. Symmetrical roles do not necessarily entail tension-free coordination or maximum activation of the potentialities of both poles. Such an activation could possibly be approximated through redefinitions of theory and practice that undo qualitative differentiations.

The need for a renegotiation of the role of philosophy and theory and their relation to practice and social science is not a new idea. The relevant literature abounds in such examples and the bearing on education generally and educational action research in particular is well documen- ted. Here I wish to show the need for reformulations as this need emerges from the course of action research in different philosophical-historical contexts and the role of polemics in the shaping of the priorities and self-understanding of action research. I examine the philosophical bases of Germanic[1] and Anglophone[2] action research in order to exemplify how ill defined or lopsided accounts of theory and practice affect action research. Pluralism is often presented as a way out of hegemonic unifying philosophies but it is accompanied, I argue, with polemical side effects that can trap thought instead of redeeming it. The critical springboards that philosophy can offer cannot be simply derived directly from the flow of lifeworldly immediate experience, no matter how enriched it becomes. This will assist me to discuss the theory versus practice dilemmas, the challenges and risks, in a light that brings to the fore but also problematizes existing responses to the role of philosophy.

THE GERMANIC AND ANGLOPHONE CONTEXTS OF EDUCATIONAL ACTION RESEARCH

If the integrity of science is endangered by the over-estimation of the a priori [...] it is no less true that philosophy is crippled by its underestimation: by mistaking conceptual enquiries into what it makes sense to say for empirical enquiries which must wait upon experience for their solution (Winch 1977, p. 16).

The Central European context that preceded and indirectly accelerated the emergence of action research in Germany relied on philosophical, historical and conceptual pedagogical frameworks and avoided engagement with practical educational issues. The overt prioritization of theory over practice further cemented the dichotomy between academic research and technological research (Posch, 2003, pp. 233–4). The academia that emerged from a neo-humanist educational ideal soon degenerated into an intellectually 'elitist, apolitical, conformist self-conception of an internally autonomous institution that remained far removed from practice while intensively conducting research' (Habermas, 1987, p. 13). As positivism grew and joined forces with technical and societal transformation and development in practice, and also due to the exasperation caused by the aforementioned failure of humanism,[3] the context shifted toward instrumental rationality. The source of knowledge for education remained the academic sphere but now not in its more 'humanistic' version but rather in its 'scientistic' one, enriched with the 'solid knowledge' emerging from laboratories, technological institutions and administrative centres. The so-called 'realistic turn' that educational research underwent in German-speaking countries can be described as a culmination of the causal-nomological model of thought. 'Empirical analytical and reductionist research following the methodological principles of natural sciences gained attention and promised to produce relatively context-free laws (e.g. on teaching and learning) to be applied in educational practice' (Posch, 2003, p. 234).

Action research (*Handlungsforschung*) in central Europe can be theorized as a reaction to both extremes that shaped the course of educational practice contemporaneously or later. Some researchers saw action research 'as offering points of departure for overcoming alleged or real shortcomings in traditional hermeneutical education' (Altrichter and Gstettner, 1993, p. 334). Others introduced it as an attack on two fronts: 'against impractical hermeneutics caught in old-fashioned ideologies and against a new wave of social technologists propagating seemingly more modern concepts which, on closer examination, turned out to reiterate ideologies of dependence and oppression in a slicker outfit' (ibid.). Thus, German action researchers joined efforts to bridge the gap between theory and practice, undo the sedimented research hierarchies, show the interdependence of scientific truth and practical change and establish a constant intervention in the lifeworld.[4] *Handlungsforschung* was meant to address and remedy 'old social fault lines' that were (re)emerging, 'such as the separation of manual and brain work, of theory and practice, of academic knowledge and everyday experience, of "objective" results and "subjective" insights, of expert and lay competency, and of the researcher and the researched' (Altrichter and Gstettner, 1993, p. 334).

The philosophical tendency that inspired the new sense of critical social science underlying those efforts was one that favoured the combination of explanation and criticism. Works in critical social science that were regarded as emblematic of efforts beyond the false dilemmas of traditional hermeneutics and positivism (e.g. works by Marx, Horkheimer or Habermas) and that inspired action research did not use a distinctive explanatory form or special and unique methodology. Rather, as Bohman remarks, they employed various methods and explanatory styles and were often 'cooperative and interdisciplinary in their mode of research' (1999, p. 460). Pioneering works on action research in Germany started 'from a *critique of traditional social research*, its reification of persons, its "occult techniques" and its lack of both social theory and influence upon practice' (Altrichter and Gstettner, 1993, p. 331, their italics). The thread that united them was the aspiration to a comprehensive theory that would make separate social sciences converge 'and underwrite the superiority of the critic' (Bohman, 1999, p. 460). A fundamental feature of the comprehensive theory was its partisanship. 'The German tradition of *Handlungsforschung* has been regarded as cooperative research of academic researchers and teachers in order to produce "emancipatory" knowledge. The philosophical background was critical theory, with its strong opposition against the status quo in society' (Posch, 2003, p. 236).[5] Converging social scientific theories should be embedded in a liberating form of politics that would also supply the method of verification of the theories (Bohman, 1999, p. 460). That is, the validity of the theories lay in their capacity to effect change, to have desirable practical consequences. What is very significant here, however, is that the desirability of the consequences was judged on normative theoretical grounds and not on some populist celebration of the social currency of various ideas.

The Anglophone equivalent to the Germanic reaction against positivism similarly objects to the technical rationality that has informed educational research (Weiner, 2004). According to Elliott, action research is 'a questioning of the terms and conditions that shape practice' (2003, p. 172). Kurt Lewin's ideas, the Stenhouse tradition (Posch, 236; Elliott, 1993 and 2003), Elliott's emphasis on pragmatism and Carr and Kemmis's (1986) employment of Habermasian ideas are some constitutive moves in the Anglophone line of action research. The concept of truth that corresponded to the spirit of Kurt Lewin's pioneering work on action research was the pragmatist one of William James (Heikkinen *et al.*, 2001, pp. 14–5). In the case of the Stenhouse tradition and Elliott's path-breaking development of action research, the connection of emancipation and the empowerment of the teacher also resonates with a pragmatist notion of truth and not an *Ideologiekritik* of a Marxist origin.[6] The influence of a continental emancipatory ideal is more apparent in Carr and Kemmis. The Elliott side of the English version of action research was not only influenced by pragmatism, MacIntyre and Aristotelian thought but also by Habermas (Rué, 2003, p. 203) albeit in varying degrees and quite selectively.

The differences between German and English action research can be summarized as follows. German action researchers 'were keen on theories, systematic thought, and wanted to get their objectives and ideas right *before* they were to be realised in practice' (Altrichter and Gstettner, 1993, p. 351). On the other hand, 'English action researchers seem to have more entelechistic confidence in processes, dynamics, evolution, and hypotheses even if they might turn out to be wrong. They are also interested in the clarification of aims or values, although they tend to see it as a task which has to be solved in practice again and again' (ibid.). German action research insisted on radical notions of emancipation and critique of social reality whereas the Anglophone equivalent toned those notions down. As I see it, Anglophone action research displays a more introvert tendency to solve matters within the school and its particular context[7] (e.g. about the researcher's profile, about how to proceed methodologically and how to change school reality or become more effective and contribute to 'higher standards'). Under the influence of a pragmatic account of knowledge and experience, 'for the action researcher the test for the truth or validity of a belief is whether it "works" in practice, and the best way to find out what works is to try it out' (Bridges, 2003, p. 184).[8] Within the Anglophone version, there has arguably been an excessive trust in the theory-generative element in action research methodology such that external sources of critique recede and evaluative judgments on processes, means and ends seem like insiders' talk. There have also been strong voices arguing, despite their convergence with the former version,[9] for a more active engagement in critical theory and connecting emancipation with a transcendent critique of educational practice. By no accident, both positions within English action research reflect solid but diverging philosophical foundations proving unintentionally the non-circumventible presence and influence of discourses and critical reflections that have not been produced by practice as such.

Action research went into decline in Germany but it has been reintroduced in the Germanic world (especially in Austria) since the mid-1980s. However,

Austrian action research is hardly a revival of the German version. On the contrary, it emerged through the influence of the Anglophone tradition of Elliott and Stenhouse (Altrichter and Gstettner, 1993, pp. 348–9). Compared with the earlier German position, the Anglophone tradition and the Germanic new version appear less unsuspecting and more disillusioned. For one thing, their protagonists seem aware of the need to critique not just positivism but also the whole scientific enterprise (Altrichter and Gstettner, 1993, p. 350). In this way, their approach becomes more radical and more amenable to the vigilance recommended in recent philosophical literature (Standish, 2001; Smith, 2003). But, simultaneously, a sense of too much free-floating and perhaps political abdication is evident when what works becomes the watchword and justifies the non-generalizability of practice in the name of context-dependence and situatedness. The content that theory, practice and their relation take in different reconstructions, being so flexible, determines the endless shifts of emphasis and the variety of political implications they generate.

Why *Handlungsforschung* in Germany was so short-lived is often explained as a result of a supposed conservative tendency within it towards a cooperation of academic researchers and teachers instead of encouraging the empowerment and independence of teachers as researchers. The historical materialist direction that critical social science took is often identified as the source of many intractable problems and failures—a major one being the blockage of a pragmatist pluralism that would elevate practice to the role of the arbiter of conflicting theoretical claims. The idea of a comprehensive theory provided 'the critic with an epistemically superior status over and above the limits of the participants' perspectives'. Further, it underwrote 'the claims that such criticisms are "scientifically justified"' (Bohman, 1999, p. 460). There were also criticisms that 'the basic objectives were characterized by "vague terms, unclarified preconditions and contradictions"' (Altrichter and Gstettner, 1993, p. 342). Critics had the impression that 'otherwise disunited German action researchers merely agreed in their "socio-political orientation"' (ibid.). To many observers, action research did not represent 'a new research strategy but rather a more or less disguised method of politico-pedagogical manipulation'. The fact that the fundamental criticism of society 'soon got into conflict with the conservative ideology of educational administration' (Posch, 2003, p. 236) was registered as another important reason for the failure. Promoting progressive educational and socio-political aims branded action research as too leftist. 'Its pronounced activism and admitted partiality was a scientific flaw for some and a political provocation for others' (Altrichter and Gstettner, 1993, p. 346).

I sympathize with the criticisms regarding the empirical side of the matter, that is, the faulty way in which action research was conducted, and I agree that German action research had a deflationist stance toward practice in its optimist confidence in theory. The ideal of cooperation no doubt degenerated to a biased view 'in which the teachers tended to provide the data and the academics produced the publications' (Posch, 2003, p. 236). However, I take issue with theorists who limit their interpretation of the abandonment of action research in Germany to this account alone. In addition to it, we must take into consideration the fact that the excessive reliance of German action research on theory could not be easily revisited by the disheartened proponents themselves. That was the case because a general polemical conservative philosophical backlash surfaced, one that was external to the action research project as such but ran counter to its radicalism nevertheless. Further elaboration on this will reveal also what I identify as an opposite deflationism in the English and the new Germanic action research.

If we contrast the five paradigms that, according to Lenhart (1994, pp. 16–17), could be found in West German educational theory since the end of the 1960s with the three new ones that gained precedence in the 1980s,[10] we realize the extent to which critical anti-capitalist trends lost their cultural influence. Within the span of 20 years they surrendered to trends that are more compatible with a neo-liberalist agenda: for instance the mutual support and compatibility of evolutionism and versions of liberalism is well explained in the relevant literature (Munn-Giddings, 2001). Also, given that in East Germany the official paradigm informing educational research was specifically Marxist-Leninist, the growing disappointment with and, finally, the collapse of, communism affected the support for Marxist theory in the West. Hence, in the educational theory of United Germany, 'Marxism is in a more marginal position than it used to be in old West Germany' (Lenhart, 1994, pp. 16–17). Since variations of Marxist themes functioned as the basic material of critical social science for the promotion of a comprehensive regulative ideal, what was also swept along was the belief in philosophy's liberating partisanship. In this context, deflationism is, this time in relation to theory, noticed in the underestimation of the potential to open new paths and fight for them theoretically first rather than subject them to the touchstone of 'realistic' practical concerns.

Marxism can no longer convince about its supposed superiority as a 'unique fit between critical explanation and the goals of a particular political practice' (Bohman, 1999, p. 461) in its master narrative self-immurement. But this does not mean that any critical demand for a shared view treating or curing the symptoms and pathologies of neo-liberalism is expendable. As Richard Smith argues, a therapeutic conception of philosophy may revivify 'that sharing of ideas which stands in opposition to the various forms of fragmentation that increasingly threaten [...] the possibility of thinking fruitfully and creatively about the values and purposes of higher education' (2003, p. 322). Far from expressing nostalgia for a Marxist approach, I believe that its fall contributed to an adulteration and a domestication of the commitment to critique. The Ought is now adapted to the Is, whereas in the past the Is was to be modeled (in the utmost possible proximity) after the Ought. For sure, the old German action research failed due to the ossification of the theoretical tenets of the day and the deflation of the significance of practice. But that was not a defeat inflicted due to the emergence of a better theory, one that would be truly more compatible with human realities; ultimately, theory as such gave way, under the pressure of a technocratic and 'modernizing' ideal, to imperatives of performativity and applicability. If German *Handlungsforschung* failed because of an undeserved and self-deceptive fascination with its own radicalism, action research survived and flourished in the Austrian and Anglophone contexts by conceding or relinquishing most of the political radical spirit. As we shall see in the next section, this can be explained to some extent by the polemics among theories and the pressures for systemic adaptation.

Before that, I shall conclude this section by highlighting the reasons for opting for a comparative 'diachronic' tackling of the issue of action research rather than a 'synchronic' head-on discussion focusing only on the English version. A revival of *Handlungsforschung* as such is hardly possible or even desirable. Yet, its hasty and wholesale condemnation by many commentators (or the total overlooking of it in the Anglophone context) and the concomitant celebration of newer versions of action research block the possibility of learning something from it. 'Why, for a start, should the latest be the best, as if time inevitably devalued and truth reached its expiry date? Why should the latest necessarily be appropriate to our concerns? Perhaps what is more distant is precisely what we most need, to gain perspective on our problems and to resist their parochial preoccupations' (Standish, 2001, p. 500). Counterfactual possibilities of the past could be mobilized again in different frameworks, divested of the old metaphysics that entrapped them. After all, it is possible that the more daunting and refined an ideal, the more difficult it is to be attained and, conversely, the more tenuous or undemanding it is, the easier it gains applicability.

THE POLEMICS

> The monstrous [Auschwitz] occurred without interrupting the smooth breathing of everyday life. Since then a conscious life is no longer possible without mistrust for continuities that assert themselves without question and also want to draw their validity out of their questionlessness. (Habermas, 1990, p. 208).

It has been a philosophical fashion lately to hold that conflict, and not just critique or controversy, is the force that disrupts the homogenizing regularities that silence, or delay, the new and the unknown. In the context of action research, this could be translated as an increased pragmatist trust in polemics among diverse theories competing for explanatory space. It may be true that there is no meta-narrative under the aegis of which to expect to find theory- or action- coordination. But it is equally plausible that the protests of otherwise disunited constructions may fail to challenge question-less continuities in a coherent and consistent way and they may ultimately play a negative 'pacifying' role. The polemical set up of enemies creates convergence amongst a plurality of voices and establishes tensions that hinder any attention to possible merits of the opponent's insights. In so doing, it may simultaneously obscure subtler and unwitting forms of making common cause with the polemical opponent or it may push in directions that would have been less extreme, had polemics been less vociferous.

The trends representing major philosophical influences on Anglophone action research, namely, critical theory and pragmatism, converge in some minimal assumptions despite their differing origins (Anglo-American and continental philosophy respectively) and their different emphases on the meaning of truth, critique and emancipation. For both of them the enemy is too much technicism and intellectual vacuity. 'Social inquiry that only develops optimal problem-solving strategies in light of objective knowledge of the consequences of all available courses of action is rightly called "technocratic" by Habermas and other critical theorists and rejected by pragmatists from Mead to Dewey' (Bohman, 1999, p. 463). In educational action research, this leads to valuing theory, avoiding narrow definitions of practice and keeping at bay unduly anti-intellectual stances. As Elliott explains his own position, 'people can denounce theoretical discourse, but I have always thought that the American pragmatic tradition of George Herbert Mead, John Dewey and others articulated a kind of view of knowledge and action that seemed to be embedded in action research' (2003, p. 176). Indeed, pragmatism suggests that the greater the variety of theoretical perspectives (having the epistemic resources for testing developing policies for achieving socially valuable ends), 'the better the public testing of such policies and problem-solving strategies' (Bohman, 1999, p. 464).

Yet we should not mistake this accommodation of theory for a full-blown retrieval of theory's critical force. Who or what determines the socially valuable end or the acquisition of useful knowledge? Many critics react to the pragmatist reliance on human choice and stress that 'decisions and choices can in fact be passive, routine or mechanical, rather than conscious, interested or committed' (Feldman, 2002, p. 239). Further, others diagnose that the pragmatist notion of truth and knowledge presupposes the criteria of usefulness and better practice and is thus in no position to validate change (Heikkinen, 2001, p. 15). Against inflationist treatments of theory, pragmatism questions any priority of theory over practice on the issue of critique and emancipation. But in so doing, it narrows the province of theory and attenuates its critique. This can be better illustrated first through the following brief discussion of a discrepancy within Anglophone action research and secondly through a parallel contradistinction of the prescriptivism of old German action research and the polemical attacks against it.

First: when Carr and Kemmis (1986) make emancipation conditional on the overcoming of subjective meaning, the influence of German critical theory of the Habermasian kind is apparent and invites Elliott's criticisms. Elliott attributes precisely to the Habermasian influence what he sees as a false distinction within Carr and Kemmis's work between a 'practical' and an 'emancipatory' paradigm of action research (Elliott, 1993, p. 117). To Elliott, there is a 'possibility that teachers' self-understandings of their practices can alone constitute a source of critical self-reflection and emancipatory action' (Elliott, 1993, p. 116). He favours self-generating critical pedagogy over external sources for theory generation.

Yet, *contra* the academic as a self-appointed prophet, but in an act of mere substitution or reversal, the reflective practitioner seems to gain a similar status that ultimately occludes openness and receptivity. For Elliott, teachers' self-understandings contain tensions, ambiguities and conflicts that fuel reflexivity and criticality. But if it holds true that, for instance, at least in some cases, critical action researchers represent a predominantly white, male value standpoint (Weiner, 2004, p. 632), their self-understandings of their practices do not suffice to alter their standpoint. Thinking that one's own standpoint is self-reflective enough may minimize the permeability of the subjective sphere. Elliott's position is compatible with a largely justified impression that some practitioners are often more self-conscious and committed to better ideals than some academics due to the formers' undergoing societal challenges and criticisms which leave the protected authority of the latter unaffected. But, in its polemical impetus to recuperate the role of the teacher, this position simply reinforces the 'practice versus theory' dichotomy. As Bridges explains, in some of Elliott's arguments theory is coupled with abstraction and practice acquires further legitimation by being characterized reflective thereby becoming privileged (2003, p. 191).

Secondly, let us now see why German action research held too simplistic a concept of the theory-practice relationship. The hasty personalization of theory through the professional researcher and of practice through the practitioner added to an already existing academic elitism. Theoretical issues had to be settled once and for all, so as to provide solid grounds for shaping reality along their guidelines. As Altrichter and Gstettner describe it, theory was meant to become practical so as to improve practice, thus totally overlooking the possibility that theory could be the *outcome* of a process of problem solving. Whilst, as mentioned above, the exaggeration of this possibility has dangerous implications, the failure of German action research to concede a fair share of reflexivity in lifeworldly affairs ossified the dialectic of theory and practice. Practice and practical consequences nourish thought, even if sometimes effects have to be foreseen. As Bridges states, 'we probably do not even fully understand our educational values until we have seen them implemented or seen the conflicts which arise in practice between different principles to which we ascribe in general abstract terms' (2003, p. 190). Overall, German action research preserved the priority of theory over practice due to an exaggeration of the extent of the lifeworld's systemic corrosion and of the immunizing or therapeutic force of academic reflection.

German action researchers are also said to have held rather naïve expectations about the force of the rational argument, thus losing sight of the force of societal power mechanisms. Thereby they neglected or dismissed the possibility of cementing strategic alliances with societal powers and educational or scientific systems (Altrichter and Gstettner,

1993, p. 344). Yet what critics miss here, in my view, is that strategic duplicity usually backfires because it eventually dilutes the initial political aims of the whole enterprise. Ironically, English action research (largely praised for achieving what its German equivalent failed to display, that is, flexibility) seems to have fallen prey to this elasticity and adaptability. 'Action research has become domesticated as a tool offered to teachers for the purpose of realising government policy intentions'—a reality that has worried Elliott and caused Carr and Kemmis's distinction between practical and emancipatory action research (Bridges, 2003, p. 186). Alliances may be helpful for the preservation of the whole operation but they lead to a polemical prioritization of piecemeal politics and a susceptibility to systemic assimilation. It is no wonder that 'many contemporary action researchers are cautious in making claims for the societal impact of their work', stressing rather its 'localised relevance' (Munn-Giddings, 2001, p. 157).

We have seen at the beginning of this section that, to determine successful practice, pragmatism (especially in some versions) conjures up pluralism and its democratic dispersal of power. But the mere existence of a variety of theoretical perspectives does not suffice for accomplishing this validation, since theories may differ on a number of unimportant matters but agree precisely on an issue where divergence would be necessary. Action research often eschews dealing with the difference between social currency and validity by resorting to an enlarged notion of accountability (based on the consensual authorization of truth), for example that implied, or taken to be implied, by democratic pluralism. Yet, despite its being a most cherished regulative political ideal, if it is granted an enlarged epistemological province, democratic pluralism may cause an unshaken legitimation of stabilized meanings.

For Derrida, theory (not as a mere outcome of immediate subjective experience but in a postmetaphysical *a priori* sense) still remains the critical force that undermines the stabilizing order to which other human cognitive endeavours may lead. Drawing from Kant's metaphor of philosophy as a *hypomochlium*, he states that in its leaps to an always shifting and unrealizable fulfillment, academic research finds in philosophy a motivating and activating force. In Kant's words, 'Prussian infantrymen are trained to *start out* with the left foot [. . .]. [T]hey put this foot in front, as on a *hypomochlium*, in order to use the right side for the impetus of the attack, which they execute with the right foot against the left' (in Derrida, 1992, p. 32). Philosophy is depicted as a lever, a left foot moving first in order to allow to the right one to perform the leap, to give the opportunity to the empirical sciences, the government, the community—what lies 'inside' and 'outside' the university—to reflectively address their orthodoxies (Papastephanou, 1997, p. 167). Philosophical insights are summoned to negotiate a compromise with traditional and sedimented meanings. The latter should provide, on their 'own foundational soil, a support for leaping to another place of founding, or, if you prefer another metaphor to that of the jumper planting a foot before leaping—of "taking the call on one foot"'. Then we might say 'that the difficulty will consist, as always, in determining the best lever, what the Greeks would call the best *mochlos'* (Derrida, 1992, p. 31).

The main concern, of course, should be precisely about this act of determining. Theory and philosophy cannot perform the tasks we expect them to without qualifications. They are not exactly the answer to the problem; historically they have been part of it either by committing themselves to the worst consolidations of interest or by tarnishing utopian vision through predetermined ends and contents that pretended to be atemporal. What is a further requirement then? A self-evident one is openness, receptivity manifested in the avoidance of hasty recruitment in one camp of thought. Despite his parallelism of philosophy with the Prussian infantrymen and their attacks, we may take Kant's assertion that 'the antagonism of the conflict of the faculties is not a war' (Papastephanou, 1997, p. 166) as an early cautioning against polemics.

Still, openness and receptivity do not suffice on their own to illuminate empirical research or professional practice (after all, quite what is one open and receptive to?). What are the preconditions for philosophical research that can claim to jump ahead instead of lagging behind? 'Teachers' professional knowledge will be restricting and enclosed if it is not informed at least in some measure by the wider intellectual currents of the society within which they practice' (Bridges, 2003, p. 191). True, but the force of philosophy is at its peak when it turns to intellectual *under*currents, to the counterintuitive and the counterfactual, not in order to establish them as a new fashion but to seriously bring them into academic play. Philosophy is at its critical best when it helps people kick over the traces of intellectual hegemonic convergence.

PHILOSOPHICAL RESEARCH

The thing is, I'm desperate. You see, I'm wearing that horse's head myself. That's the feeling. All reined up in old language and old assumptions, straining to jump clean-hoofed on to a whole new track of being I only suspect is there. I can't see it, because my educated, average head is being held at the wrong angle. I can't jump because the bit forbids it, and my own basic force—my horse-power, if you like—is too little. The only thing I know for sure is this: a horse's head is finally unknowable to me. Yet I handle children's heads—which I must presume to be more complicated, at least in the area of my chief concern (Peter Shaffer 1977, p. 18).

Shaffer's *Equus*, written at a time when the theoretical questioning of the binarism 'reason versus feelings' was common in literary production and criticism, pointed to an unrelenting critique of scientific method and its impact on people. Despite the arguably romanticist or escapist overtones in parts, the play (and the above extract in particular) describes everyday normalcy in its most forceful implications and urges emancipation from it.

Emancipation need not signify redemption of a metaphysical original and authentic self that will be released as soon as we follow a particular philosophical prescription—as the old German action research attachment to teleology assumed. Nor is it the view that change comes out of the effort to catch up with immediate reality and its internal contradictions. The role of education and the teacher cannot be researched and reconsidered exclusively within the school environment. The latter is extensively framed by hegemonic discourses that have to be targeted and unmasked in advance. Because 'some of our dominant "rationalities" — the scientistic, the performative, the managerial—have the characteristics of compulsions', philosophy needs to be therapeutic and seen 'as engaging not just with mistaken opinions but with motivated ones' (Smith, 2003, p. 321). Theory plays a more emancipatory role when it makes felt the *Angst* of the chains, the longing for a radical imagination, the *jouissance* of the unexpected. Philosophical research is indispensable to educational action research not only because it can bring conceptual clarification, but also because it promises the reintroduction of normative enthusiasm and the belief in radical social transformation—the denouncement of the present and the announcement of a possible future. In a harmonious play of reason and feelings, it may unleash new energies, give free rein and make the constraining forces knowable.

However, the renegotiation of the amount of philosophy in action research or of the intensity of the analysis of the philosophy of action research are insufficient for the activation of these possibilities. Philosophy itself must be recast: under the pressure of its own past faults, philosophy is circumspect about any sense of critical *a priori*, as if the latter could be theorized only in undesirable metaphysical rationalist terms. When attempting to cross divides separating various rationalities, it recoils in fear from the chasm gaping underfoot and cedes its critical task to pluralism. But pluralism and the underlying assumption that dispersals of power and voice generative activities are by definition coercion-free or critical can easily become accomplices with the system. Totalitarianism as theorized by Hannah Arendt concerns anonymous and impersonal forces operating in such a way that 'individuals—including rulers—disappear' and are replaced by a system (Coulter, 2002, p. 198). Yet, pluralism on its own is inadequate to combat systemic coercion because it may simply embody many similar voices echoing variations of one received view and thus defusing systemic crises.

If philosophy can prepare the ground for life-forms and meanings yet to come by its appraisal of current reality, then it requires more than mere engagement with educational contexts and activities. Educational theory can 'rely on four kinds of educational research: philosophical, interpretive (which includes historical and qualitative research), quantitative (statistical) and causal' (Smeyers, 2001, p. 491). This may be extended to cover the methodology of educational action research, but what is perhaps equally urgent is to revisit the methodology of philosophical research, that is, its ways of asking philosophical questions, of searching and appraising sources and of conducting dialogue while controlling the excesses of polemics. Philosophy, therefore, must be vigilant and self-critical first and foremost.

The positivist legacy in education has equated research with data or, at best, with a process of a selective and expedient approach to theoretical resources in order to find textual support for what one already believes. To remedy this, philosophy of education has to claim a more active and self-reflective role in order to encourage the philosophical critical impulse that is needed if one is to scrutinize established meanings or practices. This is conducive to educational action research especially when the latter tends to forget that one is a student prior to becoming a teacher and that the academic conditioning that the empowerment of the reflective practitioner seeks to combat has already occurred beforehand. As Standish writes, 'students schooled in what has become orthodox educational research methodology may find it difficult to read in any other way, and hence innumerable paths of thought will be closed off to them' (2001, p. 498). The remedy is more reading and deeper theoretical research that attends to a pluralism that is relationally differential with particular emphasis on the other voice, not always or necessarily on controversy but on the unexpected, on the shock effect. Research not only needs freedom from external imposition but also another kind of reflective freedom, one that heightens awareness of alternative possibilities or 'of the constraints that limit possibilities' (Feldman, 2002, p. 240).

CONCLUSION

It is quite irrelevant whether any empirical evidence suggests that these plans, which are founded only on hope, may be unsuccessful. For the idea that something which has hitherto been unsuccessful will therefore never be successful does not justify anyone in abandoning even a pragmatic or technical aim (for example, that of flights with aerostatic balloons) (Kant 1992, p. 89).

My focus has been on the need to make the intervention of philosophy in action research stronger in critical power. Yet, the critique of the *status quo* should not be limited to the problematic case. It must be complemented with an aporetic stance toward the taken for granted. 'Action research is indeed a process engaged in for the purpose of realising one's educational values, though it will also be a process which constantly throws those values into question and makes us reconsider them' (Bridges, 2003, p. 190). Even then, philosophy's task remains incomplete when alternatives are not implied or provided, when thought experiments and imagination are excluded as too elusive or unrealistic. The aporetic in philosophy requires a moment of new sensibilities injected into a topic in an unprecedented way and educational action research requires pause for philosophical thought of futurity, for 'determining the best leap'.

Evidently, many educationists might consider this account of action research's attunement with philosophy needlessly intricate. Worries of that sort, however, have already been met philosophically. As Standish writes, 'the empiricist can very reasonably retort at this point that there is much important research that needs to be done that manifestly does not require the greater wisdom that is here implied. Up to a point this is surely true. Undoubtedly there is in some cases straightforward information that we need. But the theorisation and practice of educational research rarely stays within such modest bounds' (2001, p. 505). If teachers employ action research to realize their educational visions (Elliott, 2003, p. 171), issues about the realizability as well as the normative acceptability of those visions are not only inescapable but also unmanageable within a concept of theory that is weak in critical, aporetic and imaginative power.

'This may be true in theory, but it does not apply in practice' was a common objection to vision—one that miscast current reality as the arbiter of normativity and incited Kant to defend the regulative role of ideals (1992, p. 61). However, even now, when Occidental thought recovers its capacity for imagination and a sense of futurity, it imposes on them the limits and qualifications of realism. Despite its apparent coupling of thought with human possibility, MacIntyre's advice to practical reasoners 'to imagine alternative realistic futures' (2001, p. 96), for instance, may sound like a throwback to pre-Kantian concerns about philosophy being an idle pursuit of chimeras. If the word 'realistic' implies, as it might, a neo-liberalist conception of the limits of the human self, it may even chime with well-rehearsed and cliché justifications of performativity as the ideal of human praxis that is most compatible with and conducive to the deepest human needs. All in all, the question remains: who or what determines the content of 'realism' and the limits it is meant to impose on imagination? What if these limits are merely products of unimaginative mindsets within everyday normalcy? Educational action research, to the extent that it concerns vision, cannot sidestep this question and, to confront it, it has to treat the theory versus practice controversy critically, aporetically and imaginatively.

NOTES

1. When we use the term 'German-speaking countries' it should be borne in mind that the Federal Republic of Germany, Austria and the German-speaking parts of Switzerland—in terms of the 'scientific community', its fashions and careers—make up a fairly coherent region in the 'geography of academic learning and research'. This academic homogeneity does not apply to the same degree to the school systems and educational policies, due to changing governments and different bureaucratic traditions. Nevertheless, it is fair to say that in most educational matters these three countries are more similar to each other than, for example, to England or France (Altrichter and Gstettner, 1993, p. 330).

2. On the particularities of the specifically North American style of action research and its tendency to include mostly qualitative research see Elliott, 2003, p. 177.

3. In the field of education, as Altrichter and Gstettner write, a 'long-standing hermeneutic tradition was still dominant at German universities and was just in the process of being

severely challenged by "more modern" empirical approaches'. 'One argument among others was that hermeneutic educational science was merely contemplative and did not constitute a practical force for the improvement of education' (1993, p. 334). There were also significant material reasons for reactions to the humanist tradition and later to action research itself but I cannot go over them here since my focus is on the theoretical dimension.

4. German action research 'criticized the dominant approach in disciplines, like education, psychology and sociology, on the grounds that it was multiplying a bad social reality since it was imitating and stabilizing a constitutive moment of social reality by strictly separating the roles of "researcher" and "test persons"'. In this traditional approach, 'the researcher controls the conditions for relevant behaviour; test persons are kept in relative ignorance and must adapt themselves to an externally set context' (Altrichter and Gstettner, 1993, p. 335).

5. Critical social theories 'seek to "liberate human beings from the circumstances that enslave them"' (Horkheimer quoted in Bohman, 1999, p. 459).

6. Joan Rué explicitly recollects Elliott's statement that he did not hold a Marxist point of view (Rué, 2003, p. 198).

7. The knowledge action research starts from is personally-constructed, local knowledge underlying the practitioners' action instead of general knowledge generated in some discourse of social science (Altrichter and Gstettner, 1993, p. 351).

8. Heikkinen *et al.* (2001, p. 14) also explain that 'the quality criterion of action research is pragmatic'. Despite several refinements, the pragmatic influence on action research leads it to search for what works and aim at successful effects. Heikkinen *et al.* use a very convincing example of action research in an Indian reservation in order to show that 'a narrative of a successful action research project could easily be turned into a story of effective colonization and oppression' (2001, p. 10).

9. Elliott explains that both he and Carr 'view action research as a process that breaks down the boundaries between empirical and philosophical inquiry. Following Dewey, we have both argued against separating means and ends in teaching as objects of reflection' (2003, 179).

10. The five paradigms of the 1960s were '(1) a normative approach (e.g. conservative value position); (2) a historic-philosophical position (*geisteswissenschaftliche Pädagogik*); (3) a critical rationalist approach (following K. Popper); (4) a critical theory (e.g. Habermas); (5) a Marxist position'. In the 1980s the new approaches were '(1) systems theory (following Luhmann in the tradition of Parsons); (2) evolutionist perspective; (3) feminist perspective' (Lenhart, 1994, p. 17).

REFERENCES

Altrichter, H. and Gstettner, P. (1993) Action Research: A closed chapter in the history of German social science?, *Educational Action Research*, 1.3, pp. 329–360.

Bohman, J. (1999) Theories, Practices, and Pluralism: A pragmatic interpretation of critical social science, *Philosophy of the Social Sciences*, 29.4, pp. 459–480.

Bridges, D. (2003) A Philosopher in the Classroom, *Educational Action Research*, 11.2, pp. 181–195.

Carr, W. and Kemmis, S. (1986) *Becoming Critical: Education, knowledge and action research* (London, Falmer Press).

Coulter, D. (2002) What Counts as Action in Educational Action Research?, *Educational Action Research*, 10.2, pp. 189–206.

Derrida, J. (1992) Mochlos or the Conflict of the Faculties, in: R. Rand (ed.) *Logomachia: The conflict of the faculties* (Lincoln, NE, University of Nebraska Press).

Elliott, J. (1993) *Action Research for Educational Change* (Philadelphia, PA, Open University Press).

Elliott, J. (2003) Interview with John Elliott, 6 December 2002, *Educational Action Research*, 11.2, pp. 169–180.

Feldman, A. (2002) Existential Approaches to Action Research, *Educational Action Research*, 10.2, pp. 233–251.

Habermas, J. (1987) The Idea of the University, *New German Critique*, 41, pp. 3–23.

Habermas, J. (1990) In D. Rasmussen (ed.) *Universalism versus Communitarianism: Contemporary debates* (Cambridge, MA, MIT Press).

Heikkinen, H., Kakkori, L. and Huttunen, R. (2001) This is My Truth, Tell Me Yours: Some aspects of action research quality in the light of truth theories, *Educational Action Research*, 9.1, pp. 9–24.

Kant, I. (1992) On the Common Saying: 'This May be True in Theory, but it does not Apply in Practice', in: Hans Reiss (ed.) *Kant: Political Writings* (Cambridge, Cambridge University Press).

Lenhart, V. (1994) Educational Research in United Germany, in: J. Calderhead (ed.) *Educational Research in Europe* (Clevedon, Multilingual Matters).

MacIntyre, A. (2001) *Dependent Rational Animals* (Chicago, IL, Open Court).

Munn-Giddings, C. (2001) Links between Kropotkin's Theory of 'Mutual Aid' and the Values and Practices of Action Research, *Educational Action Research*, 9.1, pp. 149–158.

Papastephanou, M. (1997) University or Multiversity? What is *left* of German Idealism?, in: T. Belghazi (ed.) *The Idea of the University* (Rabat, Faculty of Letters).

Posch, P. (2003) Action Research in Austria: A review, *Educational Action Research*, 11.2, pp. 233–246.

Rué, J. (2003) Action Research in Education, in the Era of *Liquid Modernity*, *Educational Action Research*, 11.2, pp. 197–212.

Shaffer, P. (1977) *Equus* (London, Penguin Books).

Smeyers, P. (2001) Qualitative Versus Quantitative Research Design: A plea for paradigmatic tolerance in educational research, *Journal of Philosophy of Education*, 35.3, pp. 477–495.

Somekh, B. (2003) Theory and Passion in Action Research, *Educational Action Research*, 11.2, pp. 247–264.

Smith, R. (2003) Thinking With Each Other: The peculiar practice of the university, *Journal of Philosophy of Education*, 37.2, pp. 309–323.

Standish, P. (2001) Data Return: The sense of the given in educational research, *Journal of Philosophy of Education*, 35.3, pp. 497–518.

Weiner, G. (2004) Critical Action Research and Third Wave Feminism: A meeting of paradigms, *Educational Action Research*, 12.4, pp. 631–643.

Winch, P. (1977) *The Idea of a Social Science and its Relation to Philosophy* (London, Routledge & Kegan Paul).

13
Why Generalisability is not Generalisable

LYNN FENDLER

In the United States, the current federal standards for educational research are found in publications of the *What Works Clearinghouse* (US Department of Education, http://www.whatworks.ed.gov/; hereafter, WWC). These research standards are based almost exclusively on the book *Experimental and Quasi-experimental Designs for Research* by Campbell and Stanley (1963). According to WWC, the only educational research worthy of federal funding is that which can establish causality, in particular, the degree to which an educational intervention (curricular or pedagogical) causes improvement in 'student achievement' as measured by standardised test scores.

In order to be able to establish a basis for causality, the research designs that are acceptable by the WWC are 'a randomized controlled experiment (RCT), a quasi-experiment with matching (QED), or a regression discontinuity design (RD)' (WWC, Criteria for Evaluation). In each case, the basis for making causal claims must be established by statistical tests designed to eliminate confounding variables from the analysis. When research designs meet these standards, they are called 'scientific' by the WWC. This is a particular, and historically specific, definition of science. The type of educational research supported by the WWC is not 'scientific' in the sense of seeking a deeper and more complex intellectual understanding of educational phenomena. Rather, WWC research is 'scientific' in the sense of establishing policy and efficient management of people and resources.

In the WWC definition of acceptable research, there must be randomised control of participants. The purpose of this design is that its findings are supposed to be generalisable to a larger number of people that have demographic characteristics similar to those 'represented' in the study. In that sense, the findings derived from one research setting are supposed to have some relevance in other settings. These standards for research design are gaining favour among funding agencies internationally. Since the publication of these US federal mandates, some university researchers have criticised the standards for being antiquated and narrow in scope, as well for being both methodologically and ethically inappropriate for research in education.[1]

This chapter extends previous critiques of the WWC research standards by pointing out the problems in their assumptions about what is 'scientific'. In this examination of generalisability, I explain the ways that the WWC standards for research:

- confound induction and prediction;
- confuse probability with certainty;
- conflate science with social management.

These problems with WWC standards emerge from the assumption that educational research findings are generalisable. On that basis, I argue in this chapter that generalisability is:

- an example of inductive reasoning and therefore subject to longstanding analytic critiques of induction;
- a form of stochastic, not deterministic, logic;
- a way of thinking that is historically specific to modernity and linked to modern projects of social governance.

In order to examine generalisability from different perspectives, I have compiled critical arguments from three disparate traditions: classical analytic philosophy, statistical modelling and histories of social science. I explicate each of these perspectives in turn and then conclude by suggesting that generalisability is a limited and local phenomenon, not generalisable to other times and places.

ANALYTIC CRITIQUES OF INDUCTION

In educational research, generalisation is an example of inductive thinking because it is a process that seeks to find an overall pattern across an array of specific examples. Analytic philosophers have examined induction in ways that provide insight about the processes of generalisation. In this section, I summarise classical critiques of induction by David Hume, John Stuart Mill and Bertrand Russell and draw connections between their analyses and current assumptions about generalisability.

David Hume's sceptical doubts about human understanding provide us with a curious insight into the meaning of induction. Hume characterises induction in a particular way by using the verb in a passive sense. Describing our understanding of patterns in nature, Hume writes, 'we are induced to expect effects similar to those, which we have found to follow from such objects' (Hume, 1777/1977, p. 23; § IV, Part 2). Hume's argument has two major points: 1) we can experience objects, but the relations between objects are inferred, not experienced; 2) reason always renders the same conclusions from the same premises, and reason cannot account for changes in historical circumstances. From those points, Hume characterises induction as a product of custom or habit and distinguishes that from reason or logic. In making this distinction, Hume does not diminish the value of induction-by-custom, but he does say that such induction is not a kind of reason: 'Custom, then, is the great guide of human life. It is that principle alone, which renders our experience useful to us, and makes us expect, for the future, a similar train of events with those which have appeared in the past' (p. 29, § V, Part 1). Hume's contribution to a critique of generalisability is his explanation that generalisations are derived from habit or custom, rather than from reason. According to Hume's famous example, we become accustomed to the idea that the sun rises every morning; however, our belief that the sun will rise tomorrow is based on our customary experience of the world, not on any abstract principle like the commutative property of addition. The customary nature of generalisation becomes salient when we consider the degree to which generalisation may or may not be able to produce any new ideas or concepts.

John Stuart Mill (1843/1964) argues that the grounds for induction are themselves inductive: 'To test a generalisation, by showing that it either follows from, or conflicts with, some stronger induction, some general-isation resting on a broader foundation of experience is the beginning and end of the logic of Induction' (p. 284). Mill's contribution to a critique of generalisability is his observation that individual facts and general truths are not different in kind, and we derive both in the same way: 'the process of indirectly ascertaining individual facts is as truly inductive as that by which we establish general truths. But it is not a different kind of induction; it is a form of the very same process' (p. 275). Mill characterises both data and generalisations as products of induction, and his analysis provides us with a basis for recognising the recursive or reiterative relationship between facts and generalisations.

Bertrand Russell (1914/1964) calls induction a principle and in his explication reiterates Hume's example of the sun rising every day. But Russell's critique of induction includes appeals to historical occurrences (synthetic premises). For example, when describing the problem with regarding the rising of the sun as a law of nature, Russell raises the possibility that the earth may one day collide with a large body. In that case, as Russell demonstrates, the prediction of the rising sun is not based on reason, but rather on experience, which proves nothing. In another earthy example, Russell writes: 'The man who has fed the chicken every day throughout its life at last wrings its neck instead, showing that more refined views as to the uniformity of nature would have been useful to the chicken' (Russell, 1914/1964, p. 307). Russell's analysis provides us with a compelling distinction between the probability that induction offers and the certainty of a law of nature: 'the fact that two things have been found often together and never apart does not, by itself, suffice to *prove* demonstratively that they will be found together in the next case we examine . . . if they have been found together often enough, the probability will amount to *almost* certainty' (p. 308, italics in original).

The WWC research standards rest on the assumption that prediction is based on induction. Granted, inductive findings have some *probability* for predictive value. However, educational policy is generally not articulated in terms of conditional probability. Policy language attempts to be clearly directive; it is the function of policy to tell people what to do and not to outline conditional alternatives in a philosophical sense. In discourse, there is high predictive value associated with research findings that purport to establish causality. When experimental and quasi-experimental research designs in education are used to inform policy—that is, when research findings are held to be generalisable from one setting to another—that practice confuses induction with prediction. There is also the related problem of certainty—the focus of the next section.

STATISTICAL MODELING AND CLINICAL APPLICATIONS

In the conduct of educational research, the logic of generalisation is made explicit in the mechanisms of statistical analysis. For some insight into these mechanisms, I turn to discussions of statistical modelling, which include both theory (including mathematics and logic) and application (including computer programming and clinical research). Literature on statistical modelling makes careful distinctions among different kinds of generalisability. These distinctions are formulated around problems of contextual differences (sometimes called facets, factors or variables) and around conditions of purpose or application. The following examples will accentuate the importance of understanding generalisability as a stochastic (that is, probabilistic or conjectural) system.

Some theories of statistical modelling include critiques quite similar to Russell's example of the chicken:

> For example, if you want to forecast the price of a stock, a historical record of the stock's prices is rarely sufficient input; you need detailed information on the financial state of the company as well as general economic conditions, and to avoid nasty surprises, you should also include inputs that can accurately predict wars in the Middle East and earthquakes in Japan (http://www.faqs.org/faqs/ai-faq/neural-nets/part3/section-1.html).

In many cases, the methodological discussions about statistical modelling are those that try to explain—and hopefully account for—finer and finer degrees of error. Across a wide range of discussions about statistical modelling, the probabilistic, and therefore undependable, nature of statistical generalisation is emphasised. The stochastic nature of statistical testing is highlighted on several dimensions. For example, study design has been called an art because of the complexities involved in balancing the trade off between good fit and generalisability (see, for example, Myung, Balasubramanian and Pitt, 2000; Koopman, 1999). Thompson (1989) calls attention to the fact that statistical significance, result importance and result generalisability are three different issues, and he cautions us against confounding these three things. Shavelson (1976; 2003) is famous for promoting statistics-based research in education precisely by emphasising the ways in which activities like teaching are notoriously slippery and difficult to quantify. Citing high-powered research studies, Shavelson and Dempsey-Atwood write: 'Consistent conclusions from research on teaching are that teacher effects on pupil outcomes are unstable . . . , that teaching acts themselves may be unstable . . . , and that most teaching acts are unrelated to student outcomes' (Shavelson and Dempsey-Atwood, 1976, p. 554).

Generalisability theory in education was formalised by Lee Cronbach *et al.* (1963; 1972) as a way to address the conflict in classical statistical theory between reliability and validity. In classical statistical theory, there is a tension between a good fitting explanation and a generalisable explanation. Myung, Balasubramanian and Pitt (2000) put it this way: 'The trademark of a good model selection procedure is its ability to satisfy these two opposing goals. We desire a model that is complex enough to describe the data sample accurately but without overfitting and thus losing generalizability' (online version).

Similarly, Koopman (1999), working in the field of epidemiology, emphasises that there are two different types of generalisability:

Scientific generalizability refers to the validity of applying parameter estimates made in a particular statistical target population to other populations. This must be distinguished from statistical generalizability which refers to the validity with which estimates made in a sample population can be applied to the statistical target population. Statistical generalizability so defined relates to what epidemiologists most often call validity. When epidemiologists talk with statisticians, miscommunication is likely because when epidemiologists speak of generalizability they are usually thinking about scientific generalizability while when statisticians speak of generalizability, they are much more likely to be referring to statistical generalizability (online version, §24).

Koopman's distinction between scientific generalisability and statistical generalisability is indicative of a more general confusion between statisticians' discourse and practitioners' discourse. Statistical probability can be strictly valid and yet not address the concerns of practitioners. The parameters of the study may not fit with practitioners' clinical/classroom parameters, and historical facets may not pertain. Another way to say this is that generalizability is not generalizable from the field of statistics to the field of clinical practice.

However, in the current educational research climate, research is meant to provide direction for policy. For the WWC, 'scientific' means useful for informing educational policy. 'Scientific' is conflated with administrative or managerial. In a policy discourse, then, the climate is not favourable for intellectual nuance, conceptual subtlety or accommodation of contextual variations. Educational policy discourse converts probability to certainty in the process of decision-making. This managerial feature of educational research is characteristic of modern social science projects (see, for example, Heilbron, 1995; Porter, 1986; Wagner, 1994).

In sum, within statistical theory, generalisation is unquestionably a stochastic process. Therefore, within statistical modelling, there is no basis for trust or certainty in the generalisability of findings; probability is precisely not certainty. However, in the mandates of the What Works Clearinghouse, an assumption of generalisability underlies the requirements for experimental studies that lead to causal explanations and generalisable findings. That assumption is an unfortunate and misguided attempt to generalize from statistical theory to practical application, an attempt that is not warranted by the standards of statistical theory itself. An experimental form of study design has become a required basis for funding research in education. Although statistical modeling is fundamentally probabilistic, the uptake in educational policy endows the findings with a sense of certainty. When educational policy makers base their decisions on the evidence provided by WWC-accepted studies, findings are converted from probabilities to policies; the conversion entails a transformation from statistical generalizability to scientific generalizability. In those conversions, pedagogical practices like *Reading First* are rendered the 'gold standard' of educational practice.

The mobilisation of probabilistic findings as if they were certainties is, ironically, an irrational and unscientific thing to do. As the previous sections show, analytic philosophers have repeatedly emphasised that generalisation is shaped by habit and convention; and statistical theory draws a clear distinction between certainty and probability. Statistical modelling is done in order to obtain progressively closer approximations of causal determination, but statistical tests are stochastic, not deterministic. For both analytic philosophers and statisticians, then, generalisation is an uncertain foundation upon which to base decisions about educational practice (practice of any kind). It is clear that treating probabilities as certainties is an unscientific thing to do. Therefore, the interesting historical question is to figure out how probability-in-theory got converted into certainty-in-practice. In other words, what historical conditions have supported trust in numbers[2] and the use of statistical evidence for research in education to the extent that no other kind of educational research is fundable by the US government?

HISTORY OF THE SOCIAL SCIENCES[3]

The histories of the social sciences provide analyses of the conditions under which generalisability became fashionable (from about the middle of the 19th century).[4] Generalisability was supported and nourished by several historical factors that characterise modernity. Some of these conditions include the popularity of measurement as a technology of governing society, invention of statistics, the proliferation of law-like thinking in social sciences, the conflation of objectivity and generalisability, and examples of cases in which statistics (=state arithmetic) were deployed as justifications for ways of managing people.

The history of statistics, compiled by the statistician Pearson (1978) is illuminating in this respect. *Statistik* was nothing more than knowledge of statecraft, completely devoid of any trace of mathematics, in the times of Gauss, the writer of normal distribution:

> Gottfried A. Achenwall in 1752, for the first time . . . introduced the word 'Statistik' as the name of a distinct branch of knowledge. That branch was not concerned with numbers, nor with mathematical theory; it was concerned with statecraft and to a less extent with political economy. . . . From Achenwall sprang the German school of statisticians at Götingen who in our modern sense were rather political economists (Pearson, 1978).

Meanwhile a concomitant development in the United Kingdom was the founding of the English school of 'Political Arithmetic' by John Graunt (1620–1674) and Sir William Petty. They never used the word 'statistik' nor called their data 'statistics'. 'A hundred years or more later . . . a Scotsman, Sir John Sinclair 'stole' the words 'Statistics' and 'Statistik' and applied them to the data and methods of Political Arithmetic' (Pearson, 1978). Pearson calls this a 'bold, barefooted act of robbery'. The normal curve, part and parcel of this bold and barefooted act of robbery, was available then to Adolphe Quetelet to ground his idea of the 'average man'.

It is Adolphe Quetelet, the Astronomer-Royal of Belgium in the 1830s-40s, who accomplished the inscription of a bell curve in the budding discourse of social theory that objectified man as its object. We can see in Quetelet's work an example of the kind of thinking that was characteristic of the mid-19th century and that coalesced to comprise the emerging discipline (or disciplines that fell under the rubric of social sciences) of social science (Heilbron, 1995; Hilts, 1981). Hacking tells the story this way:

> Quetelet changed the game. He applied the same curve to biological and social phenomena where the mean is not a real quantity at all, or rather: *he transformed the mean into a real quantity*. It began innocently enough. In a series of works of the early 1830s he gave us 'the average man'. This did not of itself turn averages—mere arithmetical constructions—into real quantities like the position of a star. But it was a first step (Hacking, 1990, pp. 106–107).

After Quetelet, the history of the statistics is a story of how a strictly mathematical representation of numerical probability got appropriated by social scientists who then began generating numerical descriptions of populations. Data proliferated as more things about people got counted, numerical descriptions of the 'average man' were formulated and revised, immigration and industrialisation increased in complexity and statistics increasingly served as a technology by which government offices could rationalise systems of population management, diagnosis and intervention. The 'long baking process of history' has gradually obliterated the debates by early social scientists about the questionable value of applying mathematical formulae to an understanding of human society. When statistical representations made the concept of an 'average man' thinkable, that was a necessary step in making the notion of generalisability possible.

At this stage, the relationship of the statistics to expectations of human behaviour was still innovative and debatable as a goal for social science. In fact, in a notable irony of history, one of the strongest arguments against the use of statistics to talk about human society was launched by Auguste Comte, French sociologist and political philosopher and the founder of positivism. Comte's opposition to statistics was voiced at the same time by the French mathematician Louis Poinsot and also on the other side of the English Channel by John Stuart Mill. Poinsot wrote: 'the application of this calculus to matters of morality is repugnant to the soul. It amounts, for example, to representing the *truth* of a verdict by a *number*, to thus treat men as if they were dice, each with many faces, some for error, some for truth' (quoted in Stigler, 1986, p. 194, italics in original). Mill's description was even more damning when he referred to statistical work as, 'the real opprobrium of mathematics' (quoted in Stigler, 1986, p. 195). Comte expressed his own disgust with the whole idea of a mathematical basis for social science by calling the enterprise 'irrational':

> It is impossible to imagine a more radically irrational conception than that which takes for its philosophical base, or for its principal method of extension to the whole of the social sciences, a supposed mathematical theory, where, symbols being taken for ideas (as is usual in purely metaphysical speculation), we strain to subject the necessarily complicated idea of numerical probability to calculation, in a way that amounts to offering our own ignorance as a natural measure of the degree of likelihood of our various opinions? (Comte, quoted in Stigler, 1986, pp. 194–195).

The application of the normal curve to human sciences was not free of trouble. Careful examinations of Quetelet's 'average man' yielded the observation that the whole statistical exercise was circular. In order to count and compare human characteristics, it is first necessary to specify a characteristic in discrete terms, and second, it is necessary to regard the particular group from whom data were collected as somehow homogeneous—there cannot be too many variables. Quetelet's first studies entailed fairly unambiguously discrete items including births, deaths, heights and weights. However, it is easy to see that the characteristics themselves are based on preconceived perceptions of differences. In other words, Quetelet's statistical analyses had no means of testing or questioning the existing characteristics. The analysis is bound by its original categories:

> the tool he [Quetelet] had created was too successful to be of use for its original purpose. The fitted distributions gave such deceptively powerful evidence of a stable homogeneity that he could not look beyond them to discover that further subclassification could produce other distributions of the same kind, that some normal distributions are susceptible to dissection into normal components. The method was lacking in discriminatory

power; too many data sets yielded evidence of normality. Few new classifications were uncovered; the primary use of the method was as a *device for validating already determined classification schemes* (Stigler, 1986, p. 215, italics added).

Here, J. S. Mill's analytic arguments about the recursive nature of induction can be seen in their historical context. Mill was a fan of Comte, and together they deplored the use of statistics to represent human characteristics.

Given the strength of the opposition, it was certainly not inevitable that statistical constructions would eventually be transformed into real and essential populational attributes. But the historical conditions in the latter part of the 19th century were strong enough to overcome the earlier tendencies against describing human characteristics in terms of symbolic entities. The confluence of developments in government, industry, statistics and social sciences fostered yet another transformation:

It was Quetelet's less-noticed next step, of 1844, that counted far more than the average man. He transformed the theory of measuring unknown physical quantities, with a definite probable error, into the theory of measuring ideal or abstract properties of a population. Because these could be subjected to the same formal techniques they became real quantities. This is a crucial step in the taming of chance. It began to turn statistical laws that were merely descriptive of large-scale regularities into laws of nature and society that dealt in underlying truths and causes (Hacking, 1990, p. 108).

It is the invention of psychology that served as the vehicle by which statistical analyses became acceptable as tools to study human beings. Before the 1880s, researchers regarded various towns and villages as being so idiosyncratic that generalisations across them would be meaningless; there were simply too many extenuating circumstances— from weather, to religion, to custom, language and local history—for it to be possible to apply principles across various cases. But conceptual innovations in statistical theory contributed to overcoming these methodological roadblocks. From Quetelet onward, most statisticians accepted this distinction, even though 'the distinction was blurred and somewhat circular' (Stigler, 1986, p. 256). But the distinction became further blurred as mathematicians developed methodological surrogates for experimental control. Francis Galton's innovation in 1869, which he called 'statistics by intercomparison' claimed to be able to measure talent as easily as height, and the argument rested entirely on the logic of analogy:

Galton turned Quetelet's phenomenon to novel use. If data from the same species arrayed themselves according to this curve and if the unity of the species could be demonstrated by showing that measurable quantities such as stature or examination scores followed the curve, then, once such a species was identified on the basis of measurable quantities, the process could be inverted with respect to qualities that eluded direct measurement! ... the use to which the scale was put was clear and somewhat ironic. Where Quetelet had used the occurrence of a normal curve to demonstrate homogeneity, Galton based a dissection of the population upon it. Using this inferred scale, he could distinguish between men's abilities on a numerical scale rather than claim that they were indistinguishable (Stigler, 1986, p. 271).

Galton's argument by analogy helped to make it possible to consider previously immeasurable qualities as discrete entities that could be counted and graphed. As qualities such as cleverness, morality, wit and civility were appropriated into statistical arrays, these qualities gradually became standardised and reified. As they become more essentialised in discourse, it made more sense to regard those qualities as natural. In that way, the qualities of morality and humour were no longer problematic, but rather they became the categorical bases by which the preconceived classifications of race and gender could be validated.

So it is the 19th century doubling of man into a subject and object of scientific reflection that saw a transformation in the understanding of normal distribution from a statement about the regularities of arithmetical probability to an insight into the workings of society. This transformation is part of a large-scale modernisation that includes the invention of the social sciences and the advent of the common school.

One consequence of the 'doubling of man into subject and object' has been what Hacking (1995) calls the 'looping effect' of human kinds. Hacking introduces his concept of looping in the context of a book about causal reasoning. By looping, Hacking means that as categories get constructed from generalisations, causal connections are made to 'explain' the categorical phenomenon. In discourse, these categories and causes about human kinds become part of knowledge, of which we humans are both subject and object. Hacking provides examples from psychiatry and paediatrics to illustrate that the relationship between classification and the attribution of cause is a chicken-and-egg loop:

Which comes first, the classification or the causal connections between kinds? ... to acquire and use a name for any kind is, among other things, to be willing to make generalizations and form expectations about things of that kind. ... The kind and the knowledge grow together ... [in the case of paediatric X-rays and child abuse] cause, classification, and intervention were of a piece (Hacking, 1995, p. 361).

Hacking's historical treatment of looping introduces another level—a discursive level—of reiteration to processes of generalisation. That is, not only is generalisation reiterative in an analytic sense, it is also reiterative in a discursive/historical sense. Induction is shaped by habit and custom, and now generalisability has itself become a habitual expectation that continues to validate belief in itself.

CONCLUSION

Educational research standards such as those stipulated by the What Works Clearinghouse are based on theoretical premises that confound induction and prediction, confuse probability with certainty and conflate science with social management. These specific tendencies characterise generalisability in educational research as a modernist project. Another indication of the historical specificity of generalisability is that it is currently being replaced by other approaches. More recent literature on research theory is indicating the emergence of scientific approaches to studies that are not focused on generalisability. These newer approaches have been called Bayesian[5] (by Hacking, 2001) and design studies (by Shavelson *et al.*, 2003). Both of these approaches reject the static and algorithmic science of generalisability and replace that approach with a dynamic and reiterative scientific approach. For example, design studies were showcased in a recent issue of the *Educational Researcher*: 'Design studies have been characterized, with varying emphasis depending on the study, as iterative, process focused, interventionist, collaborative, multi-leveled, utility oriented, and theory driven' (Shavelson, *et al.*, 2003, p. 26). Similarly, Hacking describes Bayesian probability saying, 'The Bayesian did not claim that premises give sound reasons for an inductive conclusion. Instead, it was claimed that there are sound reasons for modifying one's opinions in the light of new evidence' (Hacking, 2001, p. 262). These newer approaches to research abandon the presumption of generalisability as a desirable criterion for scientific study. The newer approaches are historically commensurate with post-analytical, post-empiricist and more pragmatic intellectual endeavors.

By analysing and historicising generalisability, this chapter has sought to problematise the assumptions upon which the vast majority of fundable research standards are based. The array of analytic, statistical, and historical critiques combine to suggest that generalisability is an historically specific phenomenon that was invented under particular circumstances and became an indispensable feature of educational research in spite of rational and logical arguments against such over-reliance. One of the effects of an overweening belief in the generalisability of research findings has been to narrow the scope of intellectual and scientific inquiry. Another effect has been to reinforce the 'looping' effects of categorising human behaviour. Finally, since generalisation is part of a reiterative process, generalisability in educational research seems more likely to provide us with validation of our preconceived notions and is less likely to contribute anything new for us to learn.

NOTES

1. See, for example, St. Pierre (2004); Shavelson, Phillips, Towne and Feuer (2003); Shavelson and Dempsey-Atwood (1976).
2. See, for example, Porter, 1995.
3. My thanks to Irfan Muzaffar for his research contributions in this section.

4. For this discussion I draw from several histories of statistics and histories of social sciences, for example, Daston, 1988; Hacking, 1990; Heilbron, 1995; Hilts, 1981; Popkewitz, 2001; Porter, 1986 and 1995; Stigler, 1986.
5. So named after Rev. Thomas Bayes (1702-1761) who published essays on probability and induction.

REFERENCES

Campbell, D. T. and Stanley, J. C. (1963) *Experimental and Quasi-Experimental Designs for Research* (Boston, Houghton Mifflin).
Cronbach, Lee J., Nageswari, R. and Gleser, G. C. (1963) Theory of Generalizability: A Liberation of Reliability Theory, *The British Journal of Statistical Psychology*, 16, pp. 137–163.
Cronbach, Lee J., Gleser, G. C., Nanda, H. and Rajaratnam, N. (1972) *The Dependability of Behavioral Measurements: Theory of Generalizability for Scores and Profiles* (New York, John Wiley).
Daston, L. (1988) *Classical Probability in the Enlightenment* (Princeton, NJ, Princeton University Press).
Hacking, I. (1990) *The Taming of Chance* (Cambridge, Cambridge University Press).
Hacking, I. (1995) The Looping Effects of Human Kinds, in: D. Sperber, D. Premack and A. J. Premack (eds) *Causal Cognition: A Multidisciplinary Debate* (Oxford, Clarendon Press), pp. 351–394.
Hacking, I. (2001) *An Introduction to Probability and Inductive Logic* (Cambridge, Cambridge University Press).
Heilbron, J. (1995) *The Rise of Social Theory*. S. Gogol, trans. (Minneapolis, MN, University of Minnesota Press).
Hilts, V. L. (1981) *Statist and Statistician* (New York, Arno Press).
Hume, D. (1777/1964) *An Enquiry Concerning Human Understanding*, E. Steinberg, ed. (Indianapolis, IN, Hackett Publishing).
Koopman, J. (1999) Balancing Validity, Precision, Generalizability and Importance in the Design of Epidemiological Investigations, Epid655 Lecture of 1–22–99, http://www.sph.umich.edu/epid/epid655/TradeOffNotes.htm. (Accessed August 21, 2005)
Mill, J. S. (1843/1964) Inductive Grounds for Induction (from *A System of Logic*), in: I. M. Copi and J. A. Gould (eds) *Readings on Logic* (New York, Macmillan), pp. 275–286.
Myung, J., Balasubramanian, V. and Pitt, M. A. (2000 October 10) Counting Probability Distributions: Differential Geometry and Model Selection, *Proceedings of the National Academy of Sciences, 97.21*, pp. 11170–11175. Published online 2000 September 26. Accessed August 20, 2005.
Pearson, K. (1978) *The History of Statistics in the 17th and 18th Centuries Against the changing Background of Intellectual, Scientific and Religious Thought: Lectures by Karl Pearson given at the University College London during the Academic Sessions 1921–1933* (New York, Macmillan Publishing).
Popkewitz, T. S. (2001). *Educational Statistics as a System of Reason: On Governing Education and Social Inclusion and Exclusion*. Conference Proceedings: Philosophy and History of the Discipline of Education: Evaluation and Evolution of the Criteria for Educational Research. Onderzoeksgemeenschap Research Community. P. Smeyers and M. DePaepe, directors (Leuven, Belgium October 24–26, 2001).
Porter, T. M. (1986) *The Rise of Statistical Thinking 1820–1900* (Princeton, NJ, Princeton University Press).
Porter, T. M. (1995) *Trust in Numbers: The Pursuit of Objectivity in Science and Public Life* (Princeton, NJ, Princeton University Press).
Russell, B. (1914/1964) The Principle of Induction (from *The Problems of Philosophy*), in: I. M. Copi and J. A. Gould (eds) *Readings on Logic* (New York, Macmillan), pp. 306–310.
Shavelson, R. and Dempsey-Atwood, N. (1976) Generalizability of Measures of Teaching Behavior, *Review of Educational Research*, 46.4, pp. 553–611.
Shavelson, R., Phillips, D. C., Towne, L. and Feuer, M. J. (2003) On the Science of Education Design Studies, *Educational Researcher*, 32.1, pp. 25–28.

Stigler, S. M. (1986) *The History of Statistics: The Measurement of Uncertainty before 1900* (Cambridge, MA, The Belknap Press of Harvard University Press).

Thompson, B. (1989) Statistical Significance, Result Importance, and Result Generalizability: Three Noteworthy but Somewhat Different Issues, *Measurement and Evaluation in Counseling and Development*, 22 April, pp. 2–6.

Wagner, P. (1994) *A Sociology of Modernity: Liberty and Discipline* (New York, Routledge).

What Works, Criteria for Evaluation. http://www.whatworks.ed.gov/reviewprocess/standards.html

14
On Generalising from Single Case Studies: Epistemological Reflections

COLIN W. EVERS AND ECHO H. WU

I INTRODUCTION

It is a commonplace that the techniques, research practices and inferential procedures of different research methodologies are shaped by background, or presumed, theories of knowledge. This is certainly so with case study methodology. The aim of this chapter is to examine one aspect of the interplay between epistemology and methodology: the conditions under which generalisation from a single case, in the sense of inferring claims about a wider class of phenomena beyond that particular case, can be defended. After some preliminary canvassing of issues and problems, the main line of argument proceeds as follows:

(1) It is argued that a great deal of empirical knowledge is brought to case studies or is available to researchers in advance, from outside the evidence within the case itself and informs both the description of the case and any analysis of the case. This is one expression of a more general thesis, namely that all our observations are laden with theory.

(2) Three sources of empirical evidence for generalisation from prior theory are distinguished. The first, which we call 'empirical generalisation', arises from the fact that many of the terms used in the description of particular phenomena or events, are general terms. Thus when we observe or report that there is a glass of water on the table, the terms 'glass', 'water' and 'table' are all general terms applying to an arbitrarily large number of objects. These terms are located in sentences that are in turn located in a network of claims that enjoys all the empirical support accruing to this network, or theory, a theory that itself often specifies the precise scope of legitimate generalisation. The scientific theory that informs our understanding of water may say that all water is made up of oxygen and hydrogen molecules but that only some particular

substances will dissolve in it. Similarly, much work in educational research helps to imbue its theoretical terms with broad empirical content; terms such as 'teacher leadership', 'authentic assessment', 'giftedness', 'childhood' or 'teacher'.

The second source of empirical evidence for generalisation, one that is particularly appropriate in social science, is what we call 'regulative generalisation'. Based on a distinction drawn by Searle (1969, pp. 33–35) between 'regulative rules' and 'constitutive rules', the central idea is that many forms of behaviour can occur in the way they do only if we suppose them to be regulated, either implicitly or explicitly. Thus, being able to drive safely on busy roads presumes the regulative rule, or principle, that everyone drive on the left, or perhaps the right, but never by choosing sides randomly. One does not need to see too many examples of oncoming vehicles in order to reach the necessary regulative generalisation concerning which side of the road is safest to drive on. Thus, in so far as we construe certain behaviours as conforming to regulative rules, we can make inferences from a relatively small number of instances to a general rule. Implicit and explicit regulative rules are also often required for educational practices. For example, a variety of school coordination problems need to be solved requiring, say, division into classes, timetables, patterns of progression through the curriculum and organisational roles for staff. Although these problems may admit of different solutions, a further constraining factor can be the matter of consistency of practice across the unit of educational jurisdiction in order to facilitate mobility of students and equity.

The third source of empirical evidence for generalisation, which concerns the other half of Searle's distinction, and is more directly related to jurisdictional matters, is something we call 'constitutive generalisation'. This draws on the fact that many social practices are not merely regulated by rules; they are also defined by rules. That is, the practice cannot exist without the relevant defining rules. For example, if we know the constitutive rules that define a game of chess then we do not have to observe much chess in order to infer that in every such game, the bishop can only move diagonally. Many features of roles in education are defined constitutively, for example, in employment contracts.

Our claim is that this kind of empirically grounded understanding of regularities in human behaviour provides social science case study research in general and educational case study research in particular with support for making generalisations.

(3) One way in which a generalisation can be defended is by abductive inference. Neither a deductive nor an inductive form of inference, it is sometimes known as inference to the best explanation. In this type of reasoning, the justification of a generalisation relies on the fact that it explains the observed empirical data and no other alternative hypothesis offers a better explanation of what has been observed.

(Walton, 2004; Josephson and Josephson, 1994; Lycan, 1988, pp. 128–156; Evers, 1999)

This overall pattern of argument is later illustrated with the aid of a case study of perceptions of giftedness in Chinese education, and because abductive inference, in common with other forms of empirical justification, is fallible, the discussion concludes with a model for iteratively further improving knowledge of generalisations.

II CASES AND GENERALISATION

A single case study is, roughly speaking, an inquiry concerning a particular event, process, object, phenomenon or state of affairs. Once we move into the detail, however, complexities crowd in. For example, concerning the papers contained in Ragin and Becker's *What is a Case?* (1992), Ragin (1992, p. 8) observes that the contributors 'agreed that individual social scientists answer the question 'What is a case?' in remarkably different ways and that answers to this question affect the conduct and results of research'. His own analysis as to why there is little consensus, at least in sociology, the disciplinary home of all his contributors, involves two factors. First, cases can be conceived as lying along a realist/nominalist axis, ranging from being 'out there' and empirically verifiable (more or less) to being 'theoretical constructs that exist primarily to serve the interests of investigators' (Ragin, 1992, p. 8). Second, he thinks that the various descriptive categories for cases can range from being case specific and generated out of a particular piece of case research, to general, applying across many cases and arising out of prior theory.

For some writers, the question of generalisation intrudes more directly into the classification of cases. Stake (2000) defines case study as a choice of study objects rather than a choice of methods, suggesting that no matter what method we employ, we ultimately choose the case to study. While admitting that researchers may attempt to understand more general phenomena from individual cases and that it is in fact hardly possible to comprehend one case without any knowledge of other cases, Stake insists that case study should focus on the understanding of a specific case rather than on generalising from it. Stake categorises three types of case studies: intrinsic, instrumental and collective. Intrinsic case study is a study in which the researchers have a purpose and an interest in understanding a specific case, rather than trying to make broad generalisation from the study. Instrumental case study is normally conducted with a goal of providing 'insight into an issue or to redraw a generalization' (p. 437), and researchers choose their cases with a purpose to develop and/or test a theory (see Johnson and Christensen, 2000). Collective case study is a product of several instrumental case studies and, according to Stake, it can be used to generalise and construct theories.

Stake (2000) points out that even an atypical case may provide readers with the opportunity to identify a specific aspect of the case that will reshape their existing knowledge about other cases. He argues that 'single or a few cases are poor representation of a population of cases and questionable grounds for advancing grand generalization' (p. 448). Nonetheless, he agrees that case study can be valuable in clarification of theory and can also have some implications for generalisation. These implications come about through what Stake and Trumbull (1982) call 'naturalistic generalization'. What this means is that we bring to a case much prior knowledge to which the new case is added 'thus making a slightly new group from which to generalise, a new opportunity to modify old generalizations' (Stake, 1995, p. 85). Hence, 'sometimes you find that what is true of that one case is true about other cases ' (Stake, 1999, p. 401).

In common with the range of opinion over what counts as a case, controversy exists as to the nature and scope of possible inferences.

> The bulk of the controversy surrounding it has been concerned with the question of generalization: how can the study of a single case (or even two or three cases) be representative of other cases so that it is possible to generalize findings to those other cases? (Bryman and Burgess, 1999, p. xiv)

The difficulty can be seen if we examine the problem of making statistical inductive inferences (or enumerative inferences) from a sample to a population. In order for such an inference to be reasonable, we need to know that the sample is representative of the population. But, in order to know that, we appear to need to know enough about the population to make sampling unnecessary. Fortunately, this 'paradox of sampling' (Kaplan, 1964, p. 239) is easily resolved by requiring that the sample be obtained in an unbiased way, which usually means randomly or, if more is known about the population, randomly within some stratification. However, the concept of enumerative inference from a randomly selected sample to a population only makes sense where the sample size is large enough relative to a network of further conditions concerning, for example, estimates about population variability, the sort of error we can tolerate arising from the sample and the level of confidence we are wanting to impose on the inference. The basic idea is that if we pick enough examples, in an unbiased way, from a larger population, the resulting sample can reasonably be expected to approximate the features of the population. For a sample size of $N = 1$, this kind of inferential machinery cannot get started.

In his earlier work, the methodologist Donald Campbell was scathing about designs 'in which a single group is studied only once . . . [S]uch studies have such a total absence of control as to be of almost no scientific value' (Campbell and Stanley, 1966, p. 6). His main point was that these designs fail to offer a procedure for ruling out alternative hypotheses, or explanations, of the phenomena under investigation. For reasons that we shall consider later Campbell (1975, p. 181), famously, changed his mind, describing his earlier view as a '. . . caricature of the single case study . . .' Nevertheless, his criticisms expressed a widely held view at the time, so much so that researchers were prompted to see alternative virtues in single case studies.

III FOR GENERALISATION

A General Terms, Theory and Observation

Although generalising from single cases is often thought to be a problem, it needs to be appreciated that the specification of the particular in the absence of generalisation is also problematic. Thus, consider our earlier introductory discussion of general terms that made use of Popper's (1972, p. 95) example: 'here is a glass of water'. Popper points out that terms like 'glass' and 'water' are general terms or universals, whose scope of application far outruns any empirical evidence. For denoting something by the word 'glass' is to attribute to it 'certain law-like behaviour' (Popper, 1972, p. 95) that can be captured by a theory or a hypothesis. And the same is true for the term 'water', where the substance it denotes in the glass is an instance of something that has certain properties possessed by all examples of water. In this case, the specification of the particular thing or event—the glass of water being here—is achieved partly by use of an intersecting set of universals.

It is difficult to see how particulars can be identified in any other way. For if there is a potentially infinite number of events and individual things (or 'tokens'), if the world can be carved in an arbitrarily large variety of ways, and if these are to be described by limited cognitive creatures using a finite vocabulary, then apart from the use of names in the vocabulary for denoting particulars, the vast remainder of these events or individual tokens will be grouped in some way into 'types' by the linguistic/symbolic apparatus of description. So instead of every single chair in the world having its own denoting expression token, we use the one token 'chair' to denote the entire class or type, with the burden of unique individuation being borne by intersection of universals.

The upshot is that the scope of inferences is now shaped by terms whose meaning is partly determined by the conceptual role they play in a wider theoretical and empirical context. For example, a case study involving Popper's glass of water may show both that it is located to the left of the nearest person and that the water dissolves sugar. But while there is nothing within the theory of water to imply that every glass of it must always be on the left of the nearest person, the theory does imply that all water, at least in its liquid form, will dissolve sugar. So it would seem that generalisation is difficult to avoid. Of course, the generalisations may be only as warranted as the background theory, but this will be quite problematic when we move to the general terms of educational studies such as 'learner', 'student', 'teacher', 'principal', 'curriculum', 'school' and the like because these background theories are often much more contested than their natural science counterparts.

One well-known approach to qualitative research that does seek to limit the role of possibly mistaken theory prior to some account of what the data may imply, is that proposed by Glaser and Strauss, in their landmark *Discovery of Grounded Theory* (1967). There they insist that the focus of their methodology is not the testing or verifying of hypotheses, but the generating of theory from data, although they 'take special pains not to divorce those two activities' (Glaser and Strauss, 1967, p. viii). Nevertheless, the advantages they see for their theory-generating methodology are often formulated by way of contrast with the disadvantages of 'theory generated by logical deduction from *a priori* assumptions' (Glaser and Strauss, 1967, p. 3). According to Glaser (1978, pp. 2–3), in order to be 'theoretically sensitive' or open to the best possible ways of interpreting data, one should 'enter the research setting with as few predetermined ideas as possible—especially logically deduced, a priori hypotheses'. This is in order to reduce the effect of pre-existing biases that will prevent theory from truly emerging from the data (Glaser and Strauss, 1967, p. 46).

In expressing scepticism about the possibility of approaching research settings without guiding theories, Sturman (1999, p. 104) draws attention to another of Popper's arguments. The context is Popper's (1963, pp. 56–61) criticism of Hume's belief that habits, used to make inductions, are formed out of the constant repetition of events. Popper points out that for repetition to be possible, a later event must be similar to an earlier one. However, if by calling two objects or events, 'similar' we mean that they have many properties in common, then, strictly speaking there is no such thing as a class of similar objects or events. (See Watanabe, 1969, pp. 376–9, for a formal proof, and Goodman, 1972, pp. 437–46, for informal elaboration.) Logically, a swan and a duck have as many properties in common as two swans. For the swans to be grouped, classified or perceived to be more similar, the observer must be weighting some properties as more significant than others. Hence Popper's (1963, p. 61) claim that similarity is always similarity-for–us, that it is always a judgment made relative to a point of view and that 'the belief that we can start with pure observations alone, without anything in the nature of a theory, is absurd'.

Glaser and Strauss (1967, p. 3) realise this, at one point remarking that 'Of course, the researcher does not approach reality as a *tabula rasa*. He must have a perspective that will help him see relevant data and abstract significant categories from his scrutiny of the data'. But in construing grounded theory as a methodology in opposition to hypothesis testing, they end up with a fundamental tension in their view of the role of theory in research, namely: How is it possible to approach data in a theoretically sensitive way so that patterns are able to emerge unforced without the antecedent theory functioning either as a preconception that imposes an interpretation on the data or as a set of hypotheses that the data may confirm of disconfirm?

The goal of trying to minimise theoretical bias in generating theory from data, by trying to minimise the role of theory, is a mistake. All observation, whether made by infants learning or made in the context of 'big science' is theoretically biased, grounded in prior hypotheses, whether biologically encoded (Quine, 1960, p. 83) or symbolically formulated. As Znaniecki (1934, p. 254) remarked a long time ago in the context of explaining analytic induction 'whether we want it or not, every classification is already a theory and involves theoretic conclusions about reality which are the result of previous study'. Even for Glaser's version of grounded theory, the hypotheses must come first. Case study research is therefore best served by approaching data with good biases (those deriving from good theory) rather than with bad biases (those deriving from bad theory). If this analysis is correct, then Glaser and Strauss's real concern, particularly Glaser's in his later work, is not theoretical bias. It is confirmation bias. And this exists when a theory is reckoned to be confirmed, regardless of what the data show. Hence the worry that:

> Potential theoretical sensitivity is lost when the sociologist commits himself exclusively to one specific preconceived theory ... For then he becomes doctrinaire and can no longer 'see around' either his pet theory or any other. He becomes insensitive, or even defensive, towards the kinds of questions that cast doubt on his theory ... (Glaser and Strauss, 1967, p. 46).

Fortunately, just as statistical inference from samples can be improved by dealing with sampling bias through the use of random selection, so inference from case studies can be improved by adopting certain epistemological techniques for reducing confirmation bias. These will be discussed in the last section.

B Social Reality, Social Facts and Generalisation

The task of making generalisations about the social world can be defended more easily if we recognise the rule-based nature of much individual and social behaviour. Searle's (1995) account of the nature of social reality provides a useful point of entry into this set of ideas. Take a single case study of a game of cricket. From observation, let us suppose that two conclusions are reached: first, that when a fast bowler is in action, there are always at least four players in the slip position; and second, that when the wicket is broken, the batsman leaves the field 'out'. In the case of field settings for the bowler, what we are observing is a piece of strategy, a judgment by the captain as to how best to get the batsman out using a fast bowler. A study of more games of cricket will reveal that strategy varies on this point, so a generalisation will be unfounded.

On the other hand, within the rules of cricket, if the batsman's wicket is broken by a validly bowled ball, then by definition, the batsman is out. Rules that define or constitute the game are called constitutive rules. Being 'out' is defined constitutively by the rules of cricket. If, during our case study, we are able to discover the constitutive rules of the game, then we can generalise to all games of cricket that the batsman will be out when the wicket is broken. Now Searle's key point is that the vast bulk of our social life is enmeshed in entities created or constituted by rules and that these rules have the general form 'X counts as Y in C' (Searle, 1995, p. 43). Thus 'having your wicket broken counts as out in cricket' is a constitutive rule of cricket. Or, 'being trained, certified, and employed in a certain capacity in a school counts as being a teacher in the state of Victoria' constitutes being a teacher in that place. Or 'uttering certain words counts as getting married under certain circumstances that include the presence of an authorised person' constitutively defines marriage. The same point can be made for such practices as buying and selling, owning property, voting, making a promise, offering an apology or a greeting, or working in an occupation such as being a teacher, or a student, or a doctor or a lawyer. The reason why classrooms are so similar the world over is not only because the empirical conditions of collective instruction converge on a particular form. It is also a matter of the similarity of the constitutive rules under which the pedagogy of mass education is defined.

Many practices that exist independently of constitutive rules nevertheless require some form of regulation in order to be successfully accomplished. Classroom instruction is a good example of this as it presumes a certain amount of coordination in order to proceed. Indeed, many forms of communication require implicit regulative rules that govern such things as turn-taking, response times, listening and confidentiality. Similarly, much of the administration of education can only proceed on the assumption of a vast amount of implicit and explicit regulation. In recognising the empirical conditions that underwrite the sort of coordination that makes possible a vast range of collective actions, we can strengthen the basis for generalisation beyond what may be an instantiation of these conditions.

C Inference to the Best Explanation

Making use of generalisations embedded in the prior theory that we, as researchers, necessarily bring to a case study is only part of the process of justifying generalisations from a case. It is important to link this theory to the data of the case by an appropriate inferential process. We take this process to be abductive inference which, following Josephson and Josephson (1994, p. 5), we regard as having (mostly) the following pattern:

> D is a collection of data (facts, observations, givens).
> H explains D (would, if true, explain D).
> No other hypothesis can explain D as well as H does.
> Therefore, H is probably true.

Here is an example of how it operates. You observe that someone is walking behind you and suspect that you are being followed. You change direction. The person behind makes corresponding changes. Perhaps, by coincidence, you are both going to the same place. You change direction radically and head back in the opposite direction. So does the person behind. On the strength of these data, you conclude with the hypothesis that you are being followed. In this process of reasoning, hypothesis generation, criticism and acceptance all occur together. (Josephson and Josephson, 1994, p. 9. See also Walton, 2004, pp. 2–22.)

Or consider our earlier example of a regulative rule: driving on one side of the road only. You arrive in a foreign land and observe one or two cars driving on the left. Although various hypotheses may come to mind, background theory suggests a premium be placed on avoiding collisions between fast moving vehicles. A simple rule, or set of rules, that regulates driving behaviour, will achieve this goal. Since this rule coheres well with plausible background theory that helps to render other hypotheses less plausible and since the hypothesis explains the data, the most likely explanation is that all cars in that land are driven on the left.

Notice the role of background theory in helping to adjudicate the matter of the best explanation. Strictly speaking, for inferential purposes hypotheses never occur in isolation but rather as embedded in some theoretical context. We may therefore suppose that the favoured hypothesis, H1 coheres with a body of theory T1, while a rival hypothesis, H2 coheres with a different body of theory, T2. Then, following Lycan (1988, p. 130) we would claim that the sorts of considerations enabling us to choose T1 over T2 as the better theory (and hence H1 as the better hypothesis over H2) are such matters as T1's greater simplicity, consistency, testability, fecundity, coherence and its capacity to leave fewer observations unexplained. (Evers, 1999)

IV A CASE STUDY IN CHINA

In order to see how these criteria for adjudicating the merits of possible abductive inferences might work in practice, consider their application in a particular case study. Actually, there is insufficient space to provide the kind of thick description or rich contextualisation that one normally associates with case study research, but the relatively modest account that is given here should be sufficient to illustrate key logical and epistemological features of making inferences from apparently limited data. This study is about how a small group of Chinese teachers perceived talented performance (TP) and giftedness.

A significant feature of the Chinese literature on this matter, which distinguishes it from a number of influential models to be found in the North American literature, is the greater emphasis it places upon TP and the correspondingly lesser emphasis it places on giftedness as innate ability. In order to check this finding against the perceptions of teachers in China, a preliminary case study was carried out involving eight teachers from a secondary school in Shenzhen, a city abutting Hong Kong. The aim of this case study (which was conducted as part of a broader research project) was to obtain data and reach conclusions relating to Chinese teachers' perceptions about how students achieve or fail to achieve high performance (see Wu, 2005).

A school in Shenzhen was selected for this study because, as is well known in Southern China, a number of schools in Shenzhen, including the school of this study, have programs and activities for gifted and talented students. Secondary school teachers rather than primary school teachers were chosen to participate because many secondary schools in China stream students into different classes according to their achievements. Therefore, secondary school teachers were assumed to have more experience in teaching students who are labelled gifted than do their primary school counterparts.

With the help of the school director of Learning and Research Unit, eight teachers were selected for the focus group interviews: four female and four male. These teachers had a minimum of eleven and a maximum of twenty-two years teaching experience, with an average of sixteen years. Four of them taught Chinese and English language, and another four taught mathematics and chemistry. They were all fluent Putonghua (Mandarin) speakers. Indeed, all teaching in the school was conducted in Putonghua. As the author who conducted the study speaks Putonghua as a first language, there was no problem in communication between the interviewer and the interviewees. The English terms such as 'giftedness' and 'talented performance' were carefully translated into Chinese in order to avoid misunderstanding. 'Giftedness' was rendered as 'tian cai', and 'obtaining talented performance' was translated as 'cheng cai'.

In order to allow respondents the freedom to talk about matters of central significance to them, as well as to ensure complete coverage of topics crucial to this study, the focus group interview was conducted in a semi-structured format. Open-ended probing questions followed three types of enquiry, exemplified as follows: (1) what are your concepts of giftedness and TP; (2) what do you think the origins of TP should be; and (3) what do you believe is the best way for educators to nurture TP among students in China. These questions were derived mainly from the literature on TP and giftedness, especially the Chinese literature, which was assumed to diverge culturally and linguistically from the corresponding literature in the West.

The results obtained concerned mainly two areas. The first was related to teachers' conceptions of TP and giftedness. Although at the beginning of the interview two of the teachers wondered about the distinction between giftedness and TP, most of them had clear views on this point. They thought that giftedness meant high innate ability, and TP referred to high achievement. In their view, giftedness was not a prerequisite for TP. One teacher said clearly, 'we cannot choose to be gifted, but we can choose to be talented' (as translated).

The second area was about the major factors contributing to TP. The teachers' responses covered a range of important issues, including five main areas of controversy: basic innate ability to learn, teacher and school influence, parental and familial influence, specific training, and self-effort and motivation. Most teachers believed that giftedness was not the most important determinant of TP; more than half of the teachers agreed that parents and families could strongly influence students' performance; some of them thought that parenting was the most crucial factor in determining their children's direction and performance, especially in early childhood; and some teachers agreed that, with similar natural abilities, students who were more perseverant, more diligent or had higher motivation would certainly achieve better than the others.

These results are in accord with both the Chinese literature on TP and giftedness, and the long and substantial Confucian cultural tradition in China of viewing TP largely in terms of nurture.

V MAKING GENERALISATIONS

To what extent can the findings of this small case study be generalised to claims about teacher perceptions of talented performance and giftedness across China? As we have been suggesting, a key part of the answer to this question involves how best to exploit the often huge empirical reach of theories that both researchers and participants bring to the case. Since empirical beliefs can arise not only from an experience of some phenomenon but also from an experience of representations of that phenomenon—words, sentences, equations, diagrams—we can begin with the theoretical terms that function within the theories embedded in natural language. So when participants are asked for their views on giftedness and talented performance, then inasmuch as they can be said to understand the language, their answers will be shaped by the multitude of inferential links that these terms enjoy.

In the case of the Chinese expression used to denote giftedness, 'tian cai', the first term, 'tian', means 'The God' and the second term, 'cai', means 'abilities', literally signifying God given abilities which are naturally construed as innate abilities. (But see Shi and Zha, 2000, p. 758, who, in discussing this translation add: 'Chinese psychologists do not think that high ability is totally inborn'.) However, the Chinese term used to denote talented performance, 'cheng cai' always carries the inference that it is the result of a process of development. 'Cheng' means 'to become, to achieve, or to fulfil'. And 'cai' in this context means 'someone who is very able'. Thus the inferential network that characterises the conceptual role of 'cheng cai' within the folk-theory of giftedness and talented performance embedded in Chinese language implies developmental origins of TP. Thus in order to explain the case study data about these teachers' beliefs concerning the nature and origin of TP and giftedness, we invoke the general hypothesis that almost all teachers who understand and speak this same language would embrace similar notions in thinking and using these terms. Of course, for this to be defensible as the best hypothesis depends upon the merits of the background theory into which it is embedded, theory that might cohere with claims about the importance of Confucian culture and its assumptions on the value of hard work in achievement.

A second source of inferential material for generalisation concerns the theory by which we might judge other schools and their educational practices as similar to the case being studied. Here we can take advantage of the fact that much educational practice in China, and elsewhere for that matter, is both constitutively defined and subject to regulation by policy. In the first instance we can look to the more formal machinery of education law and associated administrative regulation (as Sun, 2003, does in his extensive study of the constitutive nature of Chinese education). Let us suppose it turns out to be the case that the sort of gifted and talented education programs conducted in Chinese schools are based on developmental conceptions of talented performance, as captured in the single case study and that the use of standardised intelligence tests to identify and select gifted students for special programs is relatively rare, though again, constitutively defined within the system's administrative documentation (Shi and Zha, 2000, pp. 759–762). The generalisation would thus enjoy the epistemic advantage of both cohering very well with the required constitutive and regulative evidence and being part of a theory that is better than rival accounts by virtue of its inclusion of this evidence.

Although this abductive inferential machinery confers its epistemic support for generalisations in a tentative and provisional way, the process is iterative and can be used to strengthen findings and reduce the problem of confirmation bias over time.

VI IMPROVING KNOWLEDGE OF GENERALISATIONS

Earlier, we remarked that a major concern expressed over the role of prior theory in case studies was the problem of confirmation bias; of seeing in the case only whatever is brought to it in the prior theory. Although the problem requires an extended treatment, an outline of some useful epistemological strategies for dealing with it can be given here.

Recall Campbell's change of mind about the scientific value of single case studies. Here is the core of his argument:

> In a case study done by an alert social scientist who has thorough local acquaintance, the theory he uses to explain the focal difference also generates predictions or expectations on dozens of other aspects of culture, and he does not retain the theory unless most of these are confirmed. In some sense, he has tested the theory with degrees of freedom coming from the multiple implications of any one theory. The process is a kind of pattern-matching . . . in which there are many aspects of the pattern demanded by the theory that are available for matching with his observations on the local setting (Campbell, 1975, p. 181).

The reality that Campbell was responding to, which was contrary to the sort of confirmation bias outcome he earlier expected, was the fact that single case study researchers do find their theories falsified by their case data and do sometimes have difficulty finding a particular theory to explain the phenomena of the case.

Our own proposal for dealing with the relationship between theory and evidence in single case studies is captured in outline in Figure 1.

Let us suppose the case study researcher has a favoured antecedent theory in which, among many other hypotheses, is a generalisation hypothesis, included in T_1. This most favoured theory implies more than just a single observable outcome; it implies a variety of observable outcomes that we can call a pattern of expectations. Moreover, the case

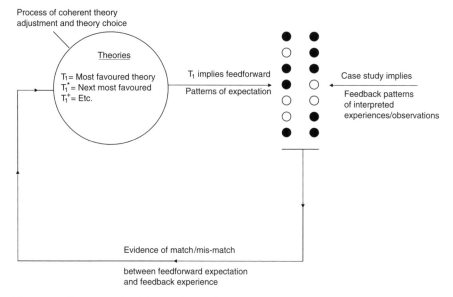

Figure 1. Theory and evidence from single case studies.

itself is a complex of phenomena that also presents to the researcher as a pattern or, over time, a succession of patterns. Now if T_1, when functioning as a guide to the world of the case, is really offering guidance that is no better than coin-tossing, then persistent matching of whole patterns over time and circumstance would indeed be a remarkable coincidence. The persistent matching of feedforward patterns of expectation with feedback patterns of experience, where patterns are large is, like our earlier case of the person concluding they are being followed, more reasonably assumed to be evidence of the truth of T_1.

Given that the social world is complex and truth is going to be hard to come by, researchers will often be faced with mismatches. Here the two most obvious epistemological alternatives are either to amend T_1, the most favoured theory, perhaps by altering some auxiliary hypotheses (Lakatos, 1974, pp. 134–138) or to look to the next most favoured theory T_1^* as a source of feedforward patterns. If the former, then we will have a succession of theories, T_1, T_2, T_3, ... united by similar core assumptions that hopefully will result in convergence of expectation with experience. If the latter, then we will have a number of theories from alternative conceptual schemes, T_1, T_1^*, T_1^+, that will be trialled in the hope of producing a match. Or we will have a combination of these approaches. In any event, through the processes of iterated theory revision and theory competition, the task is to come up with the most coherent theory that can account for the case, subject to the pattern matching constraint.

The demand for coherence in addition to empirical adequacy is meant to add extra epistemic constraints to further limit the possibility of confirmation bias in view of the fact that empirical evidence is theory laden, theories are always underdetermined by empirical evidence and test situations are

212 C. W. Evers and E. H. Wu

sufficiently complex that even extended pattern matching may turn out to be an artifact of, say, ad hoc theory adjustment. Such requirements as simplicity, comprehensiveness, explanatory unity, coherence with other established bodies of knowledge and fecundity reduce the possibility of this consequence (Evers, 1999, pp. 272–275). Following an earlier view of BonJour's, we hold that 'If a system of beliefs remains coherent (and stable) over the long run while continuing to satisfy the Observation Requirement, then it is highly likely that there is some explanation (other than mere chance) for this fact' (BonJour, 1985, p. 171).

Being able to generalise reasonably from a single case is a complex and difficult matter. But, as we have seen, the task is abetted by three important factors. First, cases possess considerably more structure than is commonly supposed, being shaped by such external factors as culture, language, theory, practices of coordination and communication, and a network of constitutive and regulative rules. All of these can apply well beyond the case, thus funding a basis for similarity judgments. Second, researchers bring to a case much more knowledge than is often supposed, being bearers of some knowledge of these external factors, and therefore an idea of what observations might provide the most stringent tests for their presuppositions of inquiry. Finally, an ongoing trajectory of inquiry through time and changing circumstances makes it less likely that a stable match between patterns of researcher expectations and what is observed is sheer coincidence. In these respects, case study research is not different in kind in its use of the epistemic resources we regularly employ to successfully understand and navigate our way around in the world.

BonJour, L. (1985) *The Structure of Empirical Knowledge* (Cambridge, MA, Harvard University Press).
Bryman, A. and Burgess, R. (eds) (1999) *Qualitative Research*, Vol. I (Thousand Oaks, CA, Sage Publications).
Campbell, D. and Stanley, J. (1966) *Experimental and Quasi-Experimental Designs for Research* (Chicago, IL, Rand McNally).
Campbell, D. (1975) Degrees of Freedom and the Case Study, *Comparative Political Studies*, 8.2, pp. 178–193.
Evers, C. W. (1999) From Foundations to Coherence in Educational Research, in: J. P. Keeves and G. Lakomski (eds) *Issues in Educational Research* (Oxford, Pergamon).
Glaser, B. G. (1978) *Theoretical Sensitivity: Advances in the Methodology of Grounded Theory* (Mill Valley, CA, Sociology Press).
Glaser, B. G. and Strauss, A.L (1967) *The Discovery of Grounded Theory: Strategies for Qualitative Research* (New York, NY, Aldine De Gruyter).
Goodman, N. (1972) *Problems and Projects* (Indianapolis and New York, The Bobbs-Merrill Company, Inc).
Johnson, B. and Christensen, L. (2000) *Educational Research: Quantitative and Qualitative Approaches* (Boston, MA, Allyn and Bacon).
Josephson, J. and Josephson, S. (1994) *Abductive Inference: Computation, Philosophy, Technology* (Cambridge, Cambridge University Press).
Kaplan, A. (1964) *The Conduct of Inquiry: Methodology for Behavioral Science* (San Francisco, CA, Chandler Publishing Company).

Lakatos, I. (1974) Falsification and the Methodology of Scientific Research Programs, in: I. Lakatos and A. Musgrave (eds) *Criticism and the Growth of Knowledge* (London, Cambridge University Press).

Lycan, W. G. (1988) *Judgement and Justification* (Cambridge, Cambridge University Press).

Popper, K. (1963) *Conjectures and Refutations: The Growth of Scientific Knowledge* (London and New York, Routledge).

Popper, K. R. (1972) *The Logic of Scientific Discovery* (London, Hutchinson).

Quine, W. V. (1960) *Word and Object* (Cambridge, MA, M.I.T. Press).

Ragin, C. C. (1992) Introduction: Cases of 'What is a Case?', in: C. C. Ragin and H. S. Becker (eds) *What is a Case?: Exploring the Foundations of Social Inquiry* (Cambridge, Cambridge University Press).

Ragin, C. C. and Becker, H. S. (eds) (1992) *What is a Case?: Exploring the Foundations of Social Inquiry* (Cambridge, Cambridge University Press).

Searle, J. (1969) *Speech Acts: An Essay in the Philosophy of Language* (Cambridge, Cambridge University Press).

Searle, J. (1995) *The Construction of Social Reality* (New York, The Free Press).

Shi, J. and Zha, Z. (2000) Psychological Research on and Education of Gifted and Talented Children in China, in: K. A. Heller, F. J. Monks, R. J. Sternberg and R. F. Subotnik (eds) *International Handbook of Giftedness and Talent*, (2nd edn.) (Amsterdam, Elsevier).

Stake, R. E. (1995) *The Art of Case Study Research* (Thousand Oaks, CA, Sage Publications).

Stake, R. E. (1999) Case Study Methodology in Educational Research: Seeking Sweet Water, in: R. M. Jaeger (ed.) *Complementary Methods for Research in Education*, (2nd edn.) (Washington, DC, American Educational Research Association).

Stake, R. E. (2000) Case Studies, in: N. K. Denzin and Y. S. Lincoln (eds) *Handbook of Qualitative Research* (Thousand Oaks, CA, Sage Publications).

Stake, R. E. and Trumbull, D. J. (1982) Naturalistic Generalizations, in: M. Belok and N. Haggerson (eds) *Review Journal of Philosophy & Social Science, VII*, Nos. 1 & 2.

Sturman, A. (1999) Case Study Method, in: J. P. Keeves and G. Lakomski (eds) *Issues in Educational Research* (Oxford, Pergamon).

Sun, M. (2003) *The Concept of System (Tizhi) in Chinese Education* Unpublished PhD dissertation, The University of Hong Kong.

Walton, D. (2004) *Abductive Reasoning* (Tuscaloosa, AL, The University of Alabama Press).

Watanabe, S. (1969) *Knowing and Guessing* (New York, John Wiley).

Wu, E. H. (2005) Factors that Contribute to Talented Performance: A Theoretical Model from a Chinese Perspective, *Gifted Child Quarterly*, 49.3, pp. 231–246.

Znaniecki, F. (1934) *The Method of Sociology* (New York, Rinehart & Company, Inc).

15
Epistemological Issues in Phenomenological Research: How Authoritative Are People's Accounts of their own Perceptions?

BAS LEVERING

THE PRIMACY OF PERCEPTIONS AND BEYOND

For science the unreliability of human perception has always been a problem. At the beginning of the modern era, this unreliability was for Descartes, in his search after a sound path towards truth, sufficient reason to abandon perception altogether. In this day and age, testimonies are increasingly becoming discredited in the administration of justice. In this case the unreliability of perception is exacerbated by the unreliability of memory. Broadly speaking, subjectivity is seen as a major methodological problem. In those cases in which objectivity is considered to be of paramount importance, it is often qualified as an absence of subjectivity. This form of objectivity is generally achieved by using methods of knowledge acquisition that try to rule out subjectivity as much as possible.

No method so consistently identifies the ordinary human being as a subject with the epistemological subject as phenomenology does. Therefore we had better start from the epistemological angle in order to answer the question to what extent we will be able to have implicit faith in people's accounts of their own perceptions. In phenomenology subjectivity is far more a starting point than a problem. The question is not how to separate the subject from the object as much as possible, for subject and object are inseparable. 'I' and 'world'—the terms phenomenologists prefer to use—are inextricably entwined. The I makes meaning and can do no differently. It is logically impossible to detach the I from the world. It is no use asking for a world without I, if only because the search for a world without I already presupposes an I. An I is needed to pose the question. This theme was once clearly illustrated by Jean-Paul Sartre by having a young girl in a beautiful garden wonder whether the garden would be as beautiful without her presence. She decides to leave the garden with a lot of stamping of feet so that the garden is well aware she is leaving, in order to sneak back in to the garden as quietly as possible so that the garden will be unaware of her return, but she does not realize she brings herself in, in full dimension (Sartre, 1964). The so-called 'moment of intelligibility' of phenomenology is called intentionality. We know the world because we give meaning to it.

Placing interpretation at the base of the process of knowledge acquisition may convey the impression that phenomenological epistemology is coupled with an idealistic ontology. This impression is incorrect. Apart from interpretation there is also a derivation of meaning. If a child discovers that a round object can roll, he will realize that he has discovered a property of the world, even though he got the object rolling himself. Interpretation does not create the world even though it opens it up. By emphasizing the significance of embodiment, phenomenology has solved an epistemological problem philosophy has been struggling with since Aristotle: how is it possible for a non-spatial soul to be aware of a spatial body? Descartes made such an issue of this problem that it became virtually insoluble: how is it possible for a non-spatial body to put a spatial body in motion? How is it possible for something immaterial to touch something material? The ghost in the machine had been born. The solutions Descartes attempted to find to the soul–body division were all spurious solutions, whether it concerned indicating the pineal gland as the place in which contact was to be effected or calling on God's help to restore unity.

Maurice Merleau-Ponty has been the one to allot the human body the place in the process of knowledge acquisition it deserves. Embodiment bridges the gap between subject and object, since the body is both subject and object. This is easy to elucidate. I can objectify my hand by looking at my hand. I can count the five fingers and examine the palm and the back. But I can also reach for something with my hand without my eyes seeing this. If I touch objects, my hand functions as a subject. That is what Merleau-Ponty (1976) calls the body-subject (*corps-sujet*): I am the hand that reaches. This is also what defines the typically human manner of being in the world. By having a body I am in the world and by having a finite body I am part of the world.

As soon as we realize the place embodiment occupies in perception, it will immediately be clear how inadequate empirical theories of perception really are. It never happens that images of whole objects fall on retinas. We usually see things halfway; usually something is halfway in front—of us. We generally only see the top and if we see the front, we do not see the back. It is really quite odd that we can live in a world full of half and less-than-half objects. But it is not at all true that we live in a world of half objects, for each of them is made whole by embodiment. Embodiment sees to it that, so to speak, we continually have a glimpse. If I walk around the object I will be able to really see the far side as well. What does not fall on our retinas—the bottom side, the far side—is basically visible. Visibility is a property of the world. Visuality is the property of the subject which brings it about that I see those parts that are beyond my scope (Merleau-Ponty, 1964).

There are many views that are generally ascribed to later phenomenologists, because they were the ones who lucidly discussed the views that, on reflection, are already to be found in Edmund Husserl's voluminous early work. For the father of phenomenology 'consciousness' is already 'awareness of something' and there is already the experience of the distance to the things we perceive. The things we perceive are not in our heads, but, for instance, at a distance of twenty metres or somewhere on the horizon. This is how we experience it. For that reason Husserl calls consciousness transcendental. In his *Phenomenology of Perception* Merleau-Ponty continually struggles against empiricism, on the one hand, and intellectualism, on the other, and constantly reveals the flaws of both of them. The empiricist sees observation as a combination of perception and interpretation, but observation does not elapse in two steps. Observation is immediate. The intellectualist reduces all observation to (the contents of) judgement. If this were true, however, we would, for instance, make no distinction between feeling, seeing and hearing, and this is precisely what we do.

For another interesting characterization of human ontology we may refer to the works of Martin Heidegger. As regards this subject, Heidegger, in his philosophy, turned the ontological issue upside down. If we wish to understand the essence of truth, we will have to look for the truth of essence (Heidegger, 1954). And where man is concerned, essence is preceded by existence. Human existence implies that man is not only bodily in-the-world, but is also projected in time. Man is not only 'now', but he is a unity of past, present and future. Human existence can only be understood from the existential notion of time. The physical time or time of the clock, which cuts time into measures of hours, minutes and seconds, does not suffice to grasp the human perception of time. For waiting can last an eternity, and pleasant hours fly fast. Sometimes an hour is no hour at all; sometimes one hour is significantly longer than another hour.

It is easy to misunderstand the concept of man as a unity of past, present and future. It is true that occurrences in the past can have significance for the present and the future, but that is not the point. The point is that the past, the present and the future are the theme of all human phenomena of experience, which cannot be understood without this dimension (Heidegger, 1978). Thus remorse stands for an unpleasant feeling I am experiencing *now* about an occurrence that took place *in the past* and the sincere intention to avoid such a thing *in future*. Phenomenology often makes its view of human existence clear by reacting against the scientific attitude in social sciences. 'Fear' cannot be understood if we limit ourselves to measuring the amount of current cold sweat.

Not only are people characterized as a unity of present, past and future; they are also capable of retrieving the past. If we think about an occurrence of long ago, we make this occurrence present. We relive the past in our impression and, in a sense, really go back in time. For another person, this going back in time unmistakably manifests itself as a moment of absence. Whether I am lost in thought or thinking about the future, I am not there for the time being: for a while I am somewhere else. In some cases the emotion of those days can return with the same intensity. If, at the time, I did something stupid that I was terribly ashamed of, this same shame will often return to the present with full intensity. But however vivid this memory of the past may be, we usually realize that it is to do with an occurrence of the past. Here, too, the consciousness is transcendental and the distance between now and then is not cancelled.

Phenomenology distinguishes itself from other methodological approaches by concentrating on the phenomena. The so-called phenomenological reduction used to rank as a temporary abandonment of an interpretation of these phenomena. At first it was Husserl's intention to push out into the world behind the phenomena at a later stage. In the so-called transcendental reduction the point is a permanent abandonment of the idea of the existence of an actual reality behind the phenomenal reality. The significance of a phenomenon should not be sought in the relation between the phenomenal world and the actual reality behind it, but in the inter-relationships between the phenomena in the phenomenal field. Speaking of the reliability of persons, it is not the case that reliability only has a meaning if we have traced a characteristic or even a gene. Reliability reveals itself in the consistency between utterance and deed at different moments in time.

Is it not odd that the idea of a 'reality behind the reality' seems more familiar to us than the restriction to the phenomenal reality we are confronted with by phenomenology? Philosophers from Plato to Kant and long after have been able to convince us of this image. In this respect phenomenology can be seen as a reaction to Kant who presupposed a *Ding an sich* behind the thing as a phenomenon. It is this so-called naturalistic disposition which is criticized by Husserl. Husserl (1954) considered the *Ding an sich* (the 'thing in itself') to be a product of substruction. We do not know the reality behind the reality, but it is hypothesized by us. We have our doubts about the phenomenological reality, but what are these doubts founded on? Every scientist will have to deal with the reality he encounters in his everyday experience. No other is available. Laymen often think psychologists have a special sense or a professional eye giving them direct access to other people's inner self, but even psychologists will have to make do with the exterior. This is not to say that it is impossible to make sensible observations on the reliability of, for instance, testimonies, but these opinions are formed, for example, on account of a confrontation of judgements with the facts and established inconsistencies between the judgements among themselves and specifically not on account of the knowledge of 'inner nature' as such.

From a phenomenological point of view the 'inner self' of another person is problematic. Whatever this 'inner self' may be, we have no direct access to it in any way. In this connection the concepts of visuality and visibility, linked to embodiment as introduced by Merleau-Ponty, may be of some use. We observe all kinds of things. The red which, under certain circumstances, suddenly colours the face is perceived as shame. In the eyes which are focused on us while we are talking with someone we read attention. We can even perceive irony or condescension—and these are very complex intentions—and we see it all at once. Whatever the 'inner self' may be, it shows on the *outside*.

THE VOICE OF THE INDIVIDUAL AND THE VOICE OF CULTURE

Subjectivity is the first epistemological starting point of phenomenology. Subjectivity stands for granting personal meaning, acknowledging that each human individual has his own outlook on reality. This individual perspective goes with the prejudices and preferences we have gained in our individual, personal history. Apart from this subjectivity, there is a second epistemological starting point, intersubjectivity: the whole consisting of a common giving of meaning. These shared meanings are laid down in social rituals and customs and the common meanings that are embodied in a language, and these are the products of their time and culture.

Subjectivity is not only an epistemological point of departure, but it is also a methodical problem. In his analysis the phenomenologist will take his personal experience as a starting point, but he is concerned about saying something about reality 'as such'. The phenomenological reduction serves the purpose of his abandoning his personal prejudices. If you analyse 'regret', you do not give an account of your own personal experiences with regret, even though having had regrets yourself does, up to a point, illuminate the phenomenon. The phenomenological reduction is rather an attitude conducive to an open mind than a strict methodical procedure. In the final analysis, the phenomenological reduction is really an impossible operation. If you really abandoned your own interpretation, this would, after all, cause reality to disappear.

The so-called eidetic reduction is in keeping with the epistemological principle of intersubjectivity. Through systematic variation it attempts to make the meaning of the phenomenon, which has to be described, circumscribed. The eidetic reduction can take place both by means of a concrete comparison and through imaginary manipulation. Thus it can be made clear which characteristic can be counted as belonging to a certain phenomenon and which characteristic cannot. It is said that it will really be impossible for the eidetic reduction to yield any new information. It relies, after all, on the meanings we already have at our disposal and which are partly incorporated in the language we have been taught in a particular cultural sphere. If, however, we make the pre-reflexive reflexive, put into words what has never been put into words, then we will have to ask ourselves if we can maintain that which we actually already knew.

It is a common reproach that scientific research only confirms what we already knew. The results from quantitative research are indeed more interesting if they dismiss biases than if they confirm them, but it is also important to 'really' know. In the case of qualitative research in general, and phenomenological research in particular, the reproach that the so-called new knowledge is nothing new but already known is indeed debatable. Phenomenological knowledge strongly appeals to recognition, but the question presents itself whether this is a case of recognition (knowing again what you knew before) in its literal sense. People are easily persuaded by the plausible, but the same goes for the contrary, and in both cases people only too often think they already knew. Recognition is of great importance, but it is not for recognition to decide on what is true or untrue.

In some cases conceptual knowledge is sold as empirical knowledge; in other words, in supposedly empirical research knowledge is gathered about the characteristics of concepts that could just as well have been formulated in an armchair. Bullying, for example, is a big problem among schoolchildren and a lot of empirical research has been done on the subject. Mieke de Waal studied children in groups five and six (9 and 10 year olds) of a non-denominational school in Geldermalsen (an average provincial town in Holland). She mentions the difficult distinction between *bullying* and *teasing*. This distinction is important 'because, if it is a matter of bullying, the bully will have to change. But if it is a matter of teasing, the victim should not be so childish' (de Waal, quoted by Levering, 2002). Arguments can also be settled, in an informal setting, by establishing which concept applies. Language usage provides no information on the issue of which action counts as bullying and which as teasing. That is what the verbal controversy is about, and the dispute can only be settled by making inquiries *post hoc*. I am only concerned with what the distinction between bullying and teasing *presupposes*. The fact that there are forms of interaction that are morally acceptable and ones that are not, and the fact that whether an action counts as bullying or teasing influences children's behaviour, are not the findings of empirical research—in this case observation and interviewing as conducted by de Waal. These were already contained in and accessible in the language itself before de Waal even started her research. For understanding the relevant differences between bullying and teasing, the conceptual analysis of 'thick concepts' suffices (adapted from Levering, 2002).

We seem to have made the switch from phenomenological analysis to conceptual analysis without noticing. The resemblance between phenomenological analysis and conceptual analysis urges itself in a self-evident way by emphasizing the meanings that are embodied in language. Conceptual analysis, interpreted as everyday language analysis, does indeed come very close to phenomenology. Where phenomenology has its beginning in everyday experience, conceptual analysis has its beginning in ordinary language. There are even philosophers who claim that the difference is minimal, since the results of phenomenological analysis have to be reported in words. Phenomenologists will disagree, since they do not see language as the most fundamental carrier of the relation between 'I' and world. Embodiment—and also existential time—precede language. So many scientific concepts have now entered everyday speech that the original connection between language and embodiment seems partly to be lost. Before the metal standard measure was laid down in Paris, people used measurements that traced their origin back to parts of the body, such as feet. We proportion the world as seen from our own corporal size. The old teaching chart at school measures five and a half kilometres as 'one hour's walk', the time you generally needed in the 1930s to move your own body over that distance. Before abstract scientific concepts such as 'authoritarian' and 'extrovert' were introduced in order to describe characteristics or frames of mind, we used to use metaphors related to postures, such as 'headstrong'.

The Husserlian dictum 'Back to things themselves' (*Zurück zu den Sachen selbst*) really stands for 'back to the original experience'. That is why in the phenomenological reduction the endeavour is to abandon not only personal prejudice, but also scientific concepts.

KNOWING ONE'S OWN MIND: THE REAL CHALLENGE TO THE AUTHORITY OF THE FIRST PERSON

The call for reliability of human perception is, seen from the phenomenological point, a special question in a very different way. The phenomenologist can do no other but take what people say and think very seriously. It is, for instance, no use contradicting people who say they are afraid with the argument that they see things the wrong way, that the mice which frighten them are really very sweet little animals and that you can let them run over your hand without any problem. You do not change their reality with these words. Phenomenological research is expressly interested in people's experiences and particularly in the experiences of those people who are usually ignored. In the phenomenological perspective the idea of objectivity has actually disappeared from sight. The things people experience to be true are true. What is more, if the things people call reality have consequences for what they do, then the call for 'objective reality' has become absurd. 'Objectivity' has been replaced by 'intersubjectivity'.

Yet it is important to emphasize once more that the unity of 'I' and world is a matter of unity even where there is distinction: 'I' and world do not coincide. In everyday life we ask for 'some objectivity' from our fellow human beings if, for instance, we are trying to calm down someone who is in an emotional state by saying: first tell me what happened and then what you think of it. The demand for a matter-of-fact account is a sensible demand. This is not to say that facts and values can be separated. Reality as a whole is a product of its time and culture, and what counts as extremely relevant in one place is not 50 in another, and you will be faced by this whether you wish to be or not. For example, the process of secularisation is entirely separated from the objective feasibility of answering the question as to God's existence, but it undeniably pushes the social significance of religion to the background. The extent of church attendance is noticeably declining, but whoever wants to understand the reality of education in the western world should not ignore the position of religion in this world, for otherwise an entirely incorrect picture would be presented.

To doubt the authority of people's accounts of their own perceptions is one thing; to doubt the authority of people's accounts of their own thoughts seems inconceivable at first sight. It is quite common to feel that access to our own thoughts is different from access to other people's thinking. This is indeed the usual idea of 'asymmetry' that is accepted among philosophers. And so it appears that philosophical thought and everyday thought are in agreement. We need to deduce the thoughts of others from their behaviour or facial expressions, in other words indirectly. In contrast, I know my own feelings and emotions directly, through introspection. The claim 'I know better what I myself am thinking than you do', is an appeal to what is called 'first person authority' in philosophy. While we can imagine that, in a sense, we can be a secret to ourselves just as others can be a secret to us, that idea goes against the grain of our basic intuition. Asymmetry and first person authority seem more plausible. However, Gilbert Ryle criticizes Descartes by arguing somewhat provocatively that we know our own inner thoughts not directly but only indirectly from our behaviour, in the same way that everyone else knows us. The inner life of a person is only accessible through externals, Ryle suggests. In other words, we do not have privileged access to our own inner self; there is no first person authority (Ryle, 1973).

Ryle turned Descartes upside down by doubting not the existence of the external world but precisely the existence of the internal world. Wittgenstein has also questioned the nature of the internal world, and by implication the possibility of private thought. Wittgenstein does not deny that our access to our inner self is different from that of others, but, like Ryle, he does not feel that our inner world is essentially private and hidden—as if we would constantly have to determine what we want to show and what we want to hide. He asks:

> Under what circumstances, on what occasions, then, does one say: 'Only I know my thoughts?'—When one might also have said: 'I am not going to tell my thoughts' or 'I am keeping my thoughts secret', or 'You people could not guess my thoughts' (Wittgenstein, 1980, p. 571).

We only make use of first person authority when we want to protect our thoughts from others; then we seclude ourselves from others. Wittgenstein says that this is roughly the same sort of thing as pretending. Normally we are more or less an open book for each other, or rather: we are not constantly trying to hide things.

Sometimes our companion is absent-minded and so lost in thought that we say: 'A penny for your thoughts'. Usually it is not so much that we want to know what it is that the other person is thinking, but rather we want 'to bring the person back to the real world'. To be 'absent' (lost in thought) can sometimes seem to be the wrong kind of 'presence' for our companion. Wittgenstein says:

And yet we do say: 'I'd like to know what he is thinking to himself now', quite as we might say: 'I'd like to know what he is writing in his notebook now'. Indeed, one might say that and so to speak see it as obvious that he is thinking to himself what he enters in his notebook (Wittgenstein, 1980, p. 577).

Still it would be inappropriate to conceptualize knowledge of the self as some kind of inner process. The philosopher Donald Davidson goes a step further than Wittgenstein by suggesting that psychological states are not just 'in the head' but that we get to know our inner self by virtue of the general knowledge we have accumulated about the way in which we tend to (inter)act in the world. He says, 'intersubjectivity is the sphere where each of us uses his own thoughts to make sense of other people's thoughts' (Davidson, 1994, p. 58). One finds out what is in one's own mind by simultaneously finding out what is in the mind of others. Davidson points out that communication between people is actually quite imperfect and that we must continually adjust our interpretations in a charitable manner, assuming that the other person does in fact make sense. As a rule people understand each other reasonably well, and we seem to know, more or less, what goes on inside the other person. But good communication depends upon an adequate self-understanding of the person him- or herself. Davidson would say that the first person does not have privileged access to his or her inner thoughts. And yet one can only make oneself understandable to others to the extent that one is understandable to oneself (Davidson, 1994, p. 64). In other words, an asymmetry continues to exist in the way that the self and the other relate to one's own inner life. This also means that complete openness is quite impossible, since it would presuppose that we know others and ourselves completely. Understanding of self and others is an incomplete, dynamic, ongoing and developing communicational experience.

NARRATIVITY AND THE PRIMACY OF INTERPRETATION

The discussion of first person authority in Anglo-Saxon philosophy has put great pressure on the phenomenological point of departure in that what people say should be taken quite seriously. If people have no privileged access to what is in their own minds, why should we ever consult them? Of course there are situations in which we remain interested in what people think they are thinking, but this is probably more a fundamental political matter than an epistemological one. In education we want the pupil's voice to be heard. We still build new housing estates in which the children's playgrounds are not only at the bottom of the list of priorities, but in which the children have not been able to inform us of their wishes in the preparatory plans either, and this is surely not right. But if we listen to the parties involved and are interested in what they think and feel, we will be taking the risk that they are mistaken.

Yet there are ways to considerably reduce the risk of people making mistakes. If the account we ask for from people can be expressed in a narrative structure, there will be a much greater chance of precluding mistakes. The problem is that not every subject can be couched in a narrative form. The research on which *Childhood's Secrets*, which I coauthored with Max Van Manen, was based was very successful in this respect (Van Manen and Levering, 1996). We asked hundreds of people to describe their first secret and to pay attention to certain aspects of this description. Whether the secret described was really the first secret was not so important. It was more important whether people thought they remembered the story of the secret in every detail. In these accounts of 'the first secret' the point is that the stories have a beginning—somebody decides to keep something secret or is faced with a secret; a middle section—if you have a secret you often have a problem; and an ending— the secret is disclosed or you decide to reveal it or to keep it forever. The story of the secret keeps the narrator alert as to the development of the events. The narrator reports what happened to him and the successive decisions he took and how he felt. There are many subjects that are worth investigating but that cannot be couched in a narrative structure. There are also subjects, however, that are much harder to investigate in this manner. If it is a question of knowledge of successful forms of learning and teaching, this approach can produce good results. But it is, for instance, much harder if it is a matter of fundamental experience, such as a feeling of recognition, which we assume also plays an important part in learning processes. You can, of course, ask people to describe a situation in which, for example, they felt not recognized, but in that case the narrator will inevitably start theorizing about what 'recognition' really means and the story will come to nothing. It may happen that the story proper is completely hidden from sight by the narrator's added theories and explanations. As far as research is concerned, it should really be a matter of striking a balance between the researcher and the researched. The story is up to the research subject; the analysis and theorizing is up to the researcher.

An account in the form of a story has the advantage that the problem of subjectivity is minimized. People can, of course, fabricate a story from beginning to end, but even then it is likely to tell us something interesting. And even when people regard themselves as the authors of their own life stories, they still often note that they do not have the final say in everything.

Narrative analysis fits well into the phenomenological tradition and can, as far as research is concerned, be seen as its completion in some respects. Paul Ricoeur has laid a firm foundation for narrative analysis and has, *en passant*, offered a solution to the philosophical problem of 'personal identity' (Ricoeur, 1984–1988, 1992). The problem of personal identity lies in how it can be possible for people to change and yet remain the same. If personal identity is regarded as a continuous process of reinterpretation of one's own personal history, this changing and yet remaining the same does indeed become understandable. Heidegger's unity of past, present and future is now confronted in a special way. The past, even the personal past, is not simply what happened then and is destined to remain always the same: the past, too, is subject to change. In who I am now I carry my adolescent past with me, but at sixty this adolescent in me will be other than he was when I was forty, and will be other than he was when I was twenty. In self-perception, too, it is not a matter of fixed, unchangeable data that are being interpreted: self-perception *is* interpretation and identity *is* self-interpretation. Narrative analysis has become the fashion in educational research in the extensive use of biographical method and, in some cases, it cannot be distinguished from therapy.

The primacy of interpretation that, at closer inspection, can be traced in the entire history of phenomenology, remains a tricky matter for many researchers. Dolph Kohnstamm, a Dutch developmental psychologist, investigated extraordinary identity experiences among children. Most people have the feeling that self-awareness grows gradually. Kohnstamm's research concerns the more restricted group of people who suddenly had the feeling of 'being a self' as a young child. Kohnstamm put the results of his study in his book *Ik ben ik (I am I)* (Kohnstamm, 2003). Sudden 'I am me' experiences are often associated with vivid and positively experienced memories that have an important function in one's sense of identity well into later life. It is striking that these experiences occur at very different points in people's lives. Not only the experience itself is clear, but also the recollection of the circumstances in which the experience took place. It seems that the discovery of the self is associated with an enhanced degree of consciousness of one's surroundings. Not only can the person still identify the place and time of the experience precisely, but also he or she can still accurately describe particular circumstances such as the play of sunlight and the clock standing still.

Since 'I am me' experiences are not generally made public, Kohnstamm invited people, through radio and newspapers, to share their memories with him. Often these memories had been tidied away. Perhaps nobody else had been interested in the experience at the time, or perhaps the individual concerned thought it too silly to talk about and so they kept silent. Some had not thought the 'I am me, I am not another person' experience interesting, supposing it was too ordinary to waste words on. They did not see what was special about it. Others again did not have any such experience or if they did they had forgotten it. Kohnstamm notes that appreciation of the experience often dawns gradually and is afterwards seen as something so very obvious that people do not see what is special about it.

Kohnstamm makes an important methodological issue of the question whether the stories told to him had been veridical. By posing this question Kohnstamm clearly shows himself as an empirical analyst entering the field of interpretative research. However unlikely it may seem, it is entirely irrelevant to the value of stories as a source of scientific research whether the stories are made up or real. Kohnstamm gives examples of 'I am me' experiences in novel-writing. These examples invariably appear to go back to the author's actual experiences. Of the stories people tell about these experiences, it cannot be decided whether they have been told 'truthfully', though there may be cases where it is abundantly clear that it is a matter of deceit. Since such accounts are essentially *interpretations* of experience, the question whether the experience is true or not is unhelpful. We do not ask whether stories are true or untrue, but whether they are convincing or unconvincing. And this is as true of stories told in real life as of fictional stories. If a novel is unconvincing, it risks not being read to the end. Even the writer of science-fiction, who seems to have a licence to invent at will, cannot go too far if he wants to keep in touch with his readers. At best, phenomenological research does not hand us knowledge of factual human lives, but of possible human lives. The question is whether it is fiction or 'actual' reality that gives us more of such knowledge.

REFERENCES

Davidson, D. (1994) Knowing One's Own Mind, in: Q. Cassam (ed.) *Self Knowledge* (Oxford, Oxford University Press, pp. 43–64.
Heidegger, M. (1954) *Vom Wesen der Wahrheit/On the Essence of Truth* (Frankfurt, Klostermann).
Heidegger, M. (1978) *Being and Time* (Oxford, Blackwell).
Husserl, E. (1954) *Die Krisis der europäischen Wissenschaften und die transzendentale Phänomenologie* (Den Haag, Martinus Nijhoff).
Kohnstamm, G. A. (2003) *Ik ben ik. De ontdekking van het zelf* (Amsterdam, De bezige bij).
(2004). *Und plötzlich wurde mir klar: Ich bin ich. Die Entdeckung des Selbst im Kindesalter* (Bern, Hans Huber Verlag).
Levering, B. (2002) Concept Analysis as Empirical Method, *International Journal of Qualitative Methods*, 1.1, Article 2. Retrieved 20 June 2006 from http://www.ualberta.ca/ ~ ijqm/
Merleau-Ponty, M. (1976) *Phenomenology of Perception* (London, Routledge and Kegan Paul).
Merleau-Ponty, M. (1964) *Le visible et l'invisible* (Paris, Éditions Gallimard).
Sartre, J.-P. (1964) *Situations. Tome III* (Paris, Éditions Gallimard).
Ricoeur, P. (1984–1988) *Time and Narrative. Volume I, II, II* (Chicago, IL, University of Chicago Press).
Ricoeur, P. (1992) *Oneself as Another* (Chicago, IL, University of Chicago Press).
Ryle, G. (1973) *The Concept of Mind* (London, Hutchinson).
Van Manen, M. and Levering, B. (1996) *Childhood's Secrets. Privacy, Intimacy, and the Self Reconsidered* (New York, Teachers College Press).
Wittgenstein, L. (1980) *Remarks on the Philosophy of Psychology. Vol. 1*, G. E. M. Anscombe and G. H. von Wright (trans.) (Oxford, Basil Blackwell).

16
Reasons and Causes in Educational Research: Overcoming Dichotomies and Other Conceptual Confusions

PAUL SMEYERS

> A *picture* held us captive.
> And we could not get outside it,
> For it lay in our language
> and language seemed to repeat it to us inexorably.
> (Wittgenstein, 1953, # 115)

When Peter Winch published his *Idea of a Social Science and its Relation to Philosophy* in 1958 he dealt with many issues that profoundly engage the nature of the social sciences. In focusing on meaningful behaviour he was offering not only a criticism of positivism and naturalism, but also an elaboration of the legacy of the later Wittgenstein's philosophy for the *Geisteswissenschaften* (the human sciences). It is hardly a surprise that the first chapter, which deals with meaning in the context of language, offers a general introduction to the Wittgensteinian stance. After all, Wittgenstein's work, i.e. the *Philosophical Investigations*, was only published in 1953. In the following chapters Winch's focus is on actions, social relations and institutions and how these ought to be studied. Though his position was taken up by some sociologists, it never had the impact on the social sciences that other authors working in the same field such as Alasdair MacIntyre or Charles Taylor had. An exception to this is his later study *Understanding a Primitive Society* (1964) which provoked many responses, especially in the area of philosophy.

In the context of educational research itself, attention to more 'interpretive' stances had to await the increased use of qualitative research methods starting in the 1980s, but here again Winch is hardly mentioned.[1] As argued elsewhere (Smeyers and Marshall, 1995), Wittgenstein's influence in philosophy of education, as opposed to the general philosophical scene, has never been very strong, and his insights are virtually absent in discussions about research. So it is unsurprising not to find references to Winch either. Yet what he argues for, following Wittgenstein, was and still is highly relevant for educational research. It can help to disentangle some of the knots in the debate about the kind of educational research we need (quantitative or qualitative), and of course it may on its own strength give some direction about how to proceed. The on-going discussion itself, about the proper nature of educational research, is as lively as ever. In the American context it has been given new ammunition by some initiatives of the federal government,[2] and in Britain and the rest of Europe its influence is felt wherever the quality of research output is evaluated and, even more generally, in the pressure more philosophical approaches and subjects experience to defend their place in a particular university curriculum.

The debate about the nature of educational research can be introduced in various ways. Most handbooks of qualitative research set out the principles on which they base their alternative, i.e. 'interpretive', approach. Yet for some reason or other, it seems that the arguments that are offered do not have the strength to convince their opponents. Though the two camps hardly ever fail to argue that the two approaches are valid and that one needs both, it seems that in the end it is the quantitative strand that wins when people decide whether something is scientifically validated or not. There is more going on than some leftovers of positivism to be dealt with here. So what is it that prevents the interpretive tradition from being adequately convincing?

Starting from the recent revival of the debate about the nature of educational research, this chapter outlines the central ideas and concepts of Winch's position concerning the social sciences. Its potential for educational research is reappraised in view of recent comments on his work and more broadly on the Wittgensteinian interpretive tradition. The chapter diagnoses that the dichotomy between 'reasons' and 'causes' has done much harm, and that there has been a related tendency to neglect just what an understanding of 'what is real for us' comes down to. In revisiting a number of Winchean key ideas a more adequate framework for educational research is developed. Thus the chapter argues for a pluralistic interpretive position, accommodating various methods and various kinds of understanding of the social, and for an educational science which is part of a political educational debate. The latter, however, as part of a political debate about education, involves a degree of distance from the world of practice and opportunity for reflection. A number of characteristics will be identified that have the potential to overcome the many confusions and distortions which the debate about the nature of educational research has created.

A NEW 'GOLD STANDARD': SCIENTIFIC RESEARCH IN EDUCATION

A recent issue of *Educational Theory* (2005, number 3) published four papers that are of interest to those who want to understand the deadlock in which we seem to have landed. In her study Margaret Eisenhart discusses several research designs for pursuing questions about causation in education. She opens with the observation that determining causation is a fixation in US society: 'Educational researchers are no exception. We are desperate to know what events and processes lead to what educational outcomes, so that we can promote the outcomes we want and eliminate the ones we do not want' (Eisenhart, 2005, p. 245). Her interest has to be understood in the context of the recent report of the National Research Council of the USA, *Scientific Research in Education* (2002). According to a host of critics this report embraces too limited a view of causation and causal explanation and thus advances a position on educational research methodology that differs little from the previously described retrograde view that seeks to reinstate experimental-quantitative methods as the 'gold standard' of educational science. Thus she welcomes for instance approaches that insist on descriptive knowledge as essential if causal analysis is to succeed and on the fact that causal mechanisms cannot be isolated but instead have to be understood as specific to context and intentions if they are not to lose their causal power. One should build on shared commitments and work collaboratively from a variety of perspectives to improve student learning, especially for those who are struggling in school and society. In a similar vain Pamela Moss (2005), following Gadamer, argues that the value of general principles does not lie in serving as a guide for action, bur rather in becoming a guide for reflection. Competing principles can be productively and instructively brought to bear on and challenged by a given case where a decision needs to be made. What we need is open debate and criticism, she concludes.

Thomas Schwandt too rejects the dichotomous thinking that drives a wedge between quantitative and qualitative methods. He also draws attention to some potentially worrying developments: first, that educational reform will become little more than managing the challenges of implementing proven practices; second, he observes an absorption of the practical by the technical; third, he indicates that in the name of scientific integrity the focus is all on what schools do (or fail to) and not on the systemic social injustices and inequalities that are largely responsible for the inequalities seen in school performance. He deplores that in the present market model of educational research hardly any attention is paid to leading a meaningful life and that the 'examined' life[3] is equated with the life that is governed by scientific and technical rationality. To educate is for him to draw out thought, to develop students who are intellectually liberated and thus capable of acting in intelligent, critical and healthy ways. Therefore, so he argues, '. . . educational researchers must begin to think of themselves not simply as scholars within a discipline but as professionals who engage in practical action and bring their knowledge to bear on the complex, at times ambiguous, and often contested issues of practice' (Schwandt, 2005, p. 297). He is sympathetic to those who argue that there is at the present time more at stake than the discourse of scientism, but that this is inseparable for instance from the discourses of performance management, effectiveness and accountability, marketization and vocationalization of education, all of which are constructing our sense of sociality as consumers (ibid., p. 299). It is therefore time to engage in questions such as: who does an educational science serve and how? Who stands to gain and who to lose? And how is all this implicated in the political agenda?

Finally, Kenneth Howe (2005, 2005a), in the same issue, laments the 'unity of science' idea of which the core principles are best exemplified by the physical sciences with randomized experiments, ignoring the interpretive turn and the associated concept of intentional causation and embracing the idea that politics is external to educational science. *Experimentism*, so he argues, 'is conservative because it must investigate "what works" within the maneuver space permitted by the social, political, and economic status quo' (Howe, 2005, p. 242). The alternative he offers, *experimentalism*, begins with the aims and subject matter of a given area of research and develops methodology accordingly. It thus takes a more fallibilist and pluralist view of methodology, incorporates intentionality and looks to the conditions in which people find themselves. In order to achieve a just and effective educational system, it is prepared to criticize and advocate changing these conditions and has in turn to stand up to criticism, including of its own politics.

In some sense, by indicating the different aspects that educational research needs to address according to these authors, all has been said. But this will surely not be the end of the debate. What we really need is a framework that gives a proper place to the various ways to study education and that properly respects the strengths of the various research traditions. The task therefore is to reveal the kind of confusion that lies at the basis of this debate. It is my contention that an amended version of Winch's idea of a social science can do this job. But first, what is it that makes his position powerful and worth investigating?

PETER WINCH'S IDEA OF A SOCIAL SCIENCE

Social science has, according to Winch, taken the wrong turn. Aspiring to be an empirical study, it exemplifies what is characteristic of a positivist approach. It should rather in his view engage itself with understanding human practices and not so much with predictions of social behaviour, for the central concepts that belong to our understanding of social life are, according to him, incompatible with the concepts central to the activity of scientific prediction. In order to argue this Winch needs to develop not only a particular stance concerning the nature of philosophy and social science, but also about human nature. In doing this he draws from the later Wittgenstein such ideas as 'following a rule', 'human shared practices' and 'what it makes sense to say'. But he also devotes a lot of attention to the place of 'reasons' and 'causes' and their respective roles in natural and social sciences. The result is a particular view on the task and method of social science as distinct from an empiricist social study. Though sophisticated and subtle, his view will be criticised later in the chapter for the excesses and for the one-sidedness it may give occasion to. To appreciate fully his argument it is necessary to go into some detail about where he starts from, what is crucial to him and how he develops his stance. Thus the discussion has been organized around four key ideas.

A Any Worthwhile Study of Society Must be Philosophical in Character

The attack that Winch launches in the opening paragraph of *The Idea of a Social Science* is as well directed against a particular conception of philosophy as of social science itself: 'to be clear about the nature of philosophy and to be clear about the nature of the social studies amount to the same thing. For any worthwhile study of society must be philosophical in character and any worthwhile philosophy must be concerned with the nature of human society' (Winch, 1958, p. 3). Clearly this bold claim has two targets. The first is what Winch labels the underlabourer conception of philosophy, which holds that philosophy cannot contribute any positive understanding of the world on its own account: here philosophy is seen as a technique in the course of essentially non-philosophical investigations. The second is a conception of sociology and of the social studies generally which argues that social life should be explained not by the notions of those who participate in it, but by underlying causes of which the agents themselves are not consciously aware (this is often a matter of explaining in the terms of the various groups to which the agents belong).

Philosophy, according to Winch, is not only concerned with eliminating linguistic confusions; and by no means is genuine new knowledge only acquired by scientists by experimental and observational techniques. The philosopher is concerned with the nature of reality as such and in general and thus deals with the question 'What is real?' The answer to it cannot be grasped in terms of the preconceptions of experimental science: 'It cannot be answered by generalizing from particular instances since a particular answer to the philosophical question is already implied in the acceptance of those instances as "real"' (ibid., p. 9). The philosopher reminds her audience of the way in which particular concepts are used and thus offers an elucidation of a particular concept. Invoking Wittgenstein, Winch draws attention to the fact that one cannot make a sharp distinction between 'the world' and 'the language in which we try to describe the world', and argues that it is therefore wrong to say that the problems of philosophy arise out of language rather than out of the world: 'Because in discussing language philosophically we are in fact discussing *what counts as belonging to the world*. Our idea of what belongs to the realm of reality is given for us in the language that we use. The concepts we have settle for us the form of the experience we have of the world' (ibid., p. 15). The relevance of conceptual enquiries into what it makes sense to say should therefore not be underestimated. In this vein he argues that 'the question of what constitutes social behaviour is a demand for an elucidation of the *concept* of social behaviour. In dealing with questions of this sort there should be no question of "waiting to see" what empirical research will show us; it is a matter of tracing the implications of the concepts we use' (ibid., p. 18).

B Understanding Human Practices

Starting from the claim that what is really fundamental to philosophy is the question of the nature and intelligibility of reality, Winch then goes on to consider what is involved in the concept of intelligibility. In order to grasp how an understanding of 'reality' is possible, it is necessary to show the central role which the concept of understanding plays in the activities which are characteristic of human societies. Referring for example to the life of monks, who have certain characteristic social relations with their fellow monks and with people outside the monastery, Winch argues that it would be impossible to give more than a superficial account of those relations without taking into account the religious ideas around which the monks' lives revolve. Thus he writes: 'A man's social relations with his fellows are permeated with his ideas about reality. Indeed "permeated" is hardly a strong enough word: social relations are expressions of ideas about reality' (ibid., p. 23).

In order to give a more detailed picture of the way in which the epistemological discussion of man's understanding of reality throws light on the nature of human society and of social relations between men, he again turns to Wittgenstein's discussion of the concept of *following a rule*. To use a word in its correct meaning as laid down by its definition implies using it in the same way. But it is only in terms of a 'given rule' that we can attach a specific sense to the words 'the same'. The problem thus repeats itself in the circularity of the solution suggested, and it is clear that a formula will not help us to indicate in what sense the rule has to be followed, hence '. . . we must always come to a point at which we have to give an account of the application of the formula' (ibid., p. 29). It is not only the actions of the person whose behaviour is in question as a candidate for the category of 'rule-following' that have to be considered, but also the reactions of other people to what she does. Thus the core concept of the language-game (expressions and activities, the use of a word in a particular social intercourse) or 'practice' is established.[4] Winch holds that any rule that may govern the activities of any person must be in principle learnable or discoverable by any other person and furthermore that a person will in principle not be able to develop the ability to follow rules without the benefit of interaction with other people. Moreover, characteristic for rule-following is that a rule can be misapplied, that the individual rule-follower must understand what she is doing, and that she may reflect on the application given novel circumstances.

In answering the question what it is for something to be real, the empirical observational methods used in the natural sciences and in everyday life cannot possibly be the only yardstick. If so, whole areas of human practice would be excluded (such as ethics or aesthetics), but one would also be confronted with a logical problem. If what is real is a matter of what can be determined by the methods of empirical sciences, this is not a statement from within science but about science. Answering the question requires us to go back to the issue of what is real *for us*, which sets it back in a social practice. We should always pay attention to the subtleness of the distinctions we make in using language, and not give in to the temptation to overlook the varieties of our various modes of expression and to take one of them as central. We must always consider the way words are actually used (and not just talked and theorised about).

Here is a view of language where words are to be understood in terms of their use in the lives of those who deploy them. Language is socially founded and the possibility of communication rests on the fact that we agree in the use of our terms. Having a language, and the notions that go along with that, such as meaning and intelligibility, are logically dependent for their sense on social interaction between people. Evidently this treatment will shed light on other forms of human interaction besides speech (such as praying, the use of gestures), those of which we can sensibly say that they have a meaning, which Winch calls a 'symbolic character'.

C Reasons and Causes and the Task of Social Science

Winch starts with an example of an action performed for a reason, the case of a subject who voted for Labour at the last General Election because she thought that a Labour government would be the most likely to preserve industrial peace. He immediately observes that to say that the subject performed an action for a reason is not to deny that in some cases, even when she has gone through an explicit process of reasoning, it may be possible to dispute whether the reason she has given is in fact the real reason for her behaviour: 'But there is very often no room for doubt; and if this were not so, the idea of *a reason for an action* would be in danger of completely losing its sense' (ibid., p. 46). He then points out that the concepts which appear in that action must be grasped not only by an observer and her hearers, but also by the subject herself. Following this, he discusses what he calls intermediate examples, not formulating a reason prior to casting a vote and a case even farther removed from the paradigmatic one, i.e. Freud's example of 'forgetting' to post a letter. For both he argues that they too are cases of meaningful behaviour. This category also extends to actions such as purely traditional behaviour, for which the agent has no 'reason' or 'motive' in any of the previous meanings. Thus meaningful action is seen by him as symbolic and goes together with certain other actions: it commits the agent to behaving in one way rather than another in the future.

> The notion of being committed by what I do now to doing something else in the future is identical in form with the connection between a definition and the subsequent use of the word defined ... It follows that I can only be committed in the future by what I do now if my present act is the application of a rule ... this is possible only where the act in question has a relation to a social context: this must be true even of the most private acts, if, that is, they are meaningful (ibid., p. 50).

All behaviour which is meaningful is *ipso facto* rule-governed in the above indicated sense, in other words it refers to a human (i.e. shared) practice. Moreover, the nature of human intelligence and rationality may not be interpreted in a rationalistic way: human activity can never be summed up in a set of explicit precepts but has everything to do with 'going on' and thus presupposes 'learning to do something and how to go on'. Therefore, so he argues, the test of whether a person's actions are the application of a rule is not whether he can formulate the rule, but whether it makes sense to distinguish between a right and a wrong way of doing things. He opposes this to a dog's acquisition of a habit, a type of case of which he says that it fits reasonably well into the behaviourist's cherished category of stimulus and response, which does not involve any understanding of what is meant by 'doing the same thing on the same kind of occasion': 'It is only because human actions exemplify rules that we can speak of past experience as relevant to our current behaviour. If it were merely a question of habits, then our current behaviour might certainly be *influenced* by the way in which we had acted in the past: but that would be just a causal influence' (ibid., p. 62). Human actions are therefore not just very much more complex, they are logically different. For Winch the possibility of reflection is essential: thus human history is not just an account of changing habits, but is the story of how people have tried to carry over what they regard as important in their modes of behaviour into new situations which they have had to face. Thus he concludes:

> An honest man may refrain from stealing money, though he could do so easily and needs it badly; the thought of acting otherwise need never occur to him. Nevertheless, he has the alternative of acting differently because he understands the situation he is in and the nature of what he is doing (or refraining from doing). Understanding something involves understanding the contradictory too: I understand what it is to act honestly just so far as and no farther than I understand what it is not to act honestly. That is why conduct which is the product of understanding, and only that, is conduct to which there is an alternative (ibid., p. 65).

D *Understanding Social Life and Scientific Prediction*

Discovering the motives of an action that puzzles us may increase our understanding of that action, but this is something that we discover without any significant knowledge about people's physiological states. For example, we do not need to know about someone's adrenaline level to be able to come to the conclusion that he is agitated. Similarly, dispositional just as much as causal statements are based on generalizations from what has been observed to happen. Both of them are different from an agent's motives, which are better understood as analogous to setting out the agent's reasons for acting which require a reference to the accepted standards of reasonable behaviour current in her society. For example, surveys and statistical information may be helpful when we are trying to understand why some groups suffer more than others from 'burn out', and hence why the propensity to this trait is characteristic of a particular individual, but they are only of limited value in explaining why someone behaved as she did on a particular occasion and why we find it acceptable or not. Reasons are to be distinguished from causes and the foundational task of social study, i.e. to understand social action, is to be done in terms of the reasons of social agents. Therefore, unlike the natural scientist who only deals with one set of rules, to understand social institutions the scholar has to deal with two sets of rules: those governing the scientist's investigation as well as the rules of the human activities themselves specifying what is to count as 'doing the same kind of thing' in relation to that kind of activity. Genuine understanding on the researcher's part thus presupposes the agent's unreflective understanding, and though technical concepts may be used, these will imply a previous understanding of those other concepts which belong to the activities under investigation. It follows that the central concepts which belong to our understanding of social life are incompatible with concepts central to the activity of scientific prediction. Comparing an act of command or obedience to our response to natural events (such as thunder, electrical storms), Winch observes that though human beings can think of the occurrences in question only in terms of the concepts they do in fact have of them, the natural events themselves have an existence independent of those concepts. But issuing commands and obeying them before human beings came to form the concept of command and obedience does not make sense. Therefore Winch also criticises Karl Popper, who holds that social institutions are just explanatory models introduced by the social scientist for his own purposes. For Winch, however, 'The ways of thinking embodied in institutions govern the way the members of the societies studied by the social scientist behave' (ibid., p. 127). The task of social science is not to note regularities but to *explain* them, which implies looking for reasons. The concept of rule-following, i.e. the hallmark of specifically human behaviour, for Winch exemplifies *par excellence* the social nature of human action. At the same time the inappropriateness of causal explanations for the human sciences, and the epistemological and hermeneutic autonomy of social practices, become clear.

PROBLEMS WITH WINCH'S 'IDEA OF A SOCIAL SCIENCE'

The debate concerning the way the social sciences should proceed, begun in the second half of the 19th century, has still not yet reached unambiguous conclusions. In summary, this debate has been between those who argue that the so-called 'scientific method' of the 'empirical' natural sciences (mainly quantitative approaches) should be mimicked, and those who emphasize the role of interpretation in all understanding and enquiry (mainly qualitative approaches). An astronomer, recently interviewed about the 'storms' on the sun said without hesitation: 'We don't understand what is happening there in the sense that we can't predict it'. Whether one looks for causes and presents an argument (a logical structure with premises and conclusions governed by some rule of acceptance) or offers an explanation in terms of a total set of relevant conditions for the event to be explained and the probability of that event in the presence of these conditions, in both cases the Achilles' heel is prediction. Such is the case as well in natural as in social sciences; that is, if one is looking for regularities or causal explanations.[5] But in social sciences there is another option: one may be interested in understanding and thus focus on 'what happened'. Here the object of reference is also to be found in the past. But, though such understanding may help us for future cases, if it does not do so, it is not necessarily ruled out as deficient, i.e. not-scientific.

In this context one finds numerous references to the insights of writers such as Hans-Georg Gadamer, Paul Ricoeur, Alasdair MacIntyre and Charles Taylor amongst others, including, but to a far lesser extent, Wittgenstein and Winch. They all hold that human lives are necessarily to be understood in interpretive (*Verstehen*) and sometimes narrative terms. Such research promises to correct—through its reference to lived experience, through its emphasis on gaining a better understanding of ourselves—the positivistic research still dominant in many educational and other professional contexts. Evidently, it also aspires to providing findings that are in one sense or another useful for practitioners—in other words, to improve practice. But qualitative research in its many variations (such as ethnographic research, participatory observation, action research, qualitative research interviews, the analysis of policy documents etc.) embraces moreover the idea that the paradigm of objectivity of the natural sciences conceals the fact that we always and inevitably bring our pre-understandings with us into any situation. Winch's position is yet another exposition of this interpretive tradition, developing the Wittgensteinian stance into the area of social science research. Here the scholar will start from the problem as formulated by practitioners themselves, as they are in some sense the only ones who can correct her in terms of the problem she is confronted with. Evidently, the researcher will take into account relevant theories and insights from the practitioners' domain, including use of their own technical jargon, and will subsequently offer her findings to the scientific community for consideration and possibly corroboration. But in the end, as there is no objective point of reference, one that can serve as a yardstick to determine the successfulness of a theory—after all, the criteria will always involve normative elements about the kind of practice one wants and a position concerning when it can be said that the problems are adequately dealt with—a lot will depend on the acceptability for practitioners and the research community of the particular insights and 'solutions' that the researcher comes up with. In other words, it is subject to the test of whether what she offers is interesting, convincing, helpful. It goes without saying that this is of a different kind than the test that scientific explanation in the natural sciences is subjected to. This may tempt some to doubt the interpretive stance as a valid position for the social sciences. Even more radically, if one takes seriously into account what this position argues for, it questions whether scientific social research is possible at all—which, as argued above, Winch seems to doubt. A closer look at some of his crucial concepts might prompt us however to amend the Winchean position in some ways, and thus to overcome the conceptual confusions and the dichotomised thinking for which it provides ammunition. I will now go into some of these criticisms as they are helpful in understanding the nature of educational research.

Berel Dov Lerner argues that the typical goal of a Winchean social-scientific project will be 'to understand the conceptual basis of some group's relation to reality, especially as it is expressed in their language, and to clarify the importance of these concepts for the lives of the people involved' (Lerner, 2002, p. 10). This knowledge is to be pursued for its own sake but it is, in Lerner's interpretation, first and foremost an object of moral contemplation for Winch. The results of social research play the same role as do exemplary texts drawn from great works of fiction. The issue we are confronted with here is whether we expect more than this from the social sciences: in other words, whether it is enough for the social sciences to enrich us with a deeper appreciation of how people make sense of their lives. We might for example think of the need for informed guidance in the formulation of public policy, that is, not just an appreciation of the diversity of moral experience but also indications of ways to avoid conflict and mutual harm and to improve the chances of cooperation. Evidently, Winch would not rule that out, but he hardly touches upon it.

Furthermore, Winch's discussion of rule-following behaviour, which he identifies with meaningful behaviour, is meant to support a particular view of the social or human sciences. Quoting Weber, he writes that he is concerned with human behaviour if and in so far as the agent or agents associate a subjective sense with it (Winch, 1958, p. 45). But as Williamson argues (quoted in Lerner, 2002, p. 30), it is not clear whether he is discussing the nature of meaningful behaviour or the nature of human behaviour. Thus he seems, so Lerner argues (ibid., p. 30), to entertain a much stronger claim, i.e. that all human behaviour is meaningful. He avoids, Lerner continues, citing interesting examples of meaningless behaviour 'in order to create the impression that nothing of importance to human life will be missed by a social-scientific program that is devoted solely to the study of meaningful action' (ibid., p. 30). Is 'going for a walk' a case of rule-following? It seems that here the activity has to be distinguished from speaking about it, which latter is evidently rule-governed. But is the activity itself rule-governed? Another problem is to what extent I have to know the rules to be able to perform a particular activity or for someone else to know the rule to identify it as such— consider for example the case of flute playing. Does this imply 'knowledge' of the technical skills, and/or of music, and at what level? Linked to this is the problem of the relationship of concepts to actions. Winch speaks of an internal relationship and sees interactions between people as relations of ideas, but this seems to presuppose that actors are applying concepts in all their interactions. Now there are cases where this is not appropriate, such as where there is a threat of force, something which Winch admits in the introduction to the second edition of his book. But, as Lerner observes, this matter should be pushed further. He gives the example of the parties of a caring relationship such as marriage, who may interact and cooperate for years without ever really establishing common ground as to the goals, best interests and communicative intent that guide their actions.

Winch limits the study of meaningful behaviour to the explication of meaning, thus excluding statistical or causal analysis. Though he stresses that the thoughts and meaningful actions of individuals are guided by the rules and aims of socially founded modes of life, he proposes a strongly psychological (in the sense of *Erlebnis*) view of meaning and associates the idea of meaningful action with 'action performed for a reason'. He rejects the notion of purely hermeneutic meaning where action is concerned. For instance, if someone had been conditioned to act in accordance with some socially established rule as a matter of blind habit, there would, according to Winch, be no reason to say that he followed a rule freely. That a rule-follower understands the rule means that he or she understands how the rule may be broken and that he or she freely decides on how to apply the rule in a novel situation. But what if the application has become ambiguous: can we still say that the individual knows the rule? And is such behaviour then rule-following behaviour? Winch is of course concerned with demonstrating that rules of meaningful behaviour cannot be treated as predictive social-scientific laws. But what stops the social scientist from proposing explanatory laws that are not analogous to the social rules known to the individual in question, Lerner asks (ibid., p. 49). He gives the example of people who can competently categorize line drawings of faces as frowning or smiling and who are presented with an ambiguous drawing. Though the socially accepted criteria for the recognition of facial expressions cannot help us to predict their responses, it would not be surprising to discover that, all things being equal, people who have eaten breakfast that morning will categorize the drawing as smiling, while those who went hungry will categorize it as frowning. Lerner concludes that it 'is precisely in such moments of perplexity that "meaningless" behavioural factors such as the physiology of mood states, the mechanics of perception, and blind conditioned habit come to the fore. The effect of such 'meaningless' factors on the uniquely human vocation of following rules might be the subject of a specifically human yet explanatory science' (ibid., p. 50). And though Winch seems to allow for the physiological explanation of human behaviour, for him such an explanation is so impoverished compared with detailed interpretation of meanings that it is hardly worth the effort.

This prompts us also to take into account that the form of life, which is at the background of everything we do and which forms the bedrock, can hardly be thought as something of which the subject has a discursive mastery, i.e. in terms of concepts and rules. I am certainly not arguing that Winch holds such a position, but there is a problem about the proper place of the 'form of life' in his idea of a social science if it is taken together with his reliance on reasons and actor-centeredness. Finally, it seems that because Winch focuses so much on what we do freely, he radicalises the distinction between reasons and causes, thus neglecting the fact that natural laws too always are to be applied *ceteris paribus*, i.e. all things being equal. Of course, the falling of an apple is logically different from meaningful behaviour, but there are similarities as well. In cases of human actions new reasons or appreciations may be involved, in the same sense as in cases of natural events where other causes may have to be taken into account too. Where prediction in a strong sense may not be applicable in the social sciences, a robust conception of it can lead to analogous problems in natural sciences. In the latter though it has not led to the decision to abandon it, so one may question why it has to be abandoned completely in the social sciences. The consequence of all of this is that Winch seems to neglect instrumental behaviour. Though most human activities possess both communicative and instrumental aspects, he avoids mentioning instrumental behaviour and contrasts meaningful behaviour not with non-communicative behaviour but rather with thoughtless, animalistic habit and the behaviour of a lunatic. Some practical activities, while performed 'for a reason', are nevertheless not intended to express a symbolic meaning, so Lerner argues (ibid., p. 118).

It will be clear, however, that besides these problems Winch has reminded us of a fundamental insight for social science, one which we cannot do without, i.e. that the study of human action always involves taking into account the self-understandings of the people whom we study. A fresh start from this idea may just do the work that the idea of social and for that matter of educational research badly needs.

BEYOND THE DICHOTOMY: CAUSES AND ACTOR-CENTEREDNESS IN CONTEXT

Understanding the reality we live in demands an understanding of nature itself but also of the kind of beings we are. And if one accepts that human beings are of a different kind than physical objects, it follows that they have to be studied at least partly in a different manner. A major problem with Winch's position, however, seems to me that for him explanation is conceived either in causal terms or in terms of giving reasons for our actions,[6] the former paradigmatic for the natural, the latter for the social sciences. In as much as human action is also a function of physiological states, the explanatory power of these is downgraded. Evidently, Winch does not deny that human beings *are* also bodies (in Merleau-Ponty's sense), but in so far as they are *human*, this aspect does not seem to count for much. He attacks the Humean view of causality as no more than 'constant conjunction', a view that leads to a neo-positivist sociology. Things would be otherwise, however, if we took a realist stance and posited some intervening, actually existing and potentially observable mechanism that links A and B together which it is the task of the (social) scientist to discover.[7] In both cases the embeddedness of what we do in a horizon of inherited meaning, for instance how we understand ourselves, vanishes. But for both cases as well we are stuck with a logically exclusive disjunction of either causal or reason-giving explanation. It is this picture, to use Wittgenstein's words, that has held us captive. If there are reasons to accept that human behaviour may at least partly be explained in terms of the regularities one observes and grants for these other techniques and methods, not only the problem mentioned of our bodily nature but others as well could be 'solved'. It is possible that a confusion lies at the basis of the dichotomy which prevents us from seeing the true nature of what is involved.

It was argued above that in the background of what we do there are always normative or value-laden elements operative, besides distinctions between the meaning of concepts, which constitute the frame of reference of our activities, i.e. how we understand human reality. It has been the aspiration of science to bracket or eliminate these, and thus to be able to deal with 'reality as it really is'. The pitfalls of this positivist stance have for long become clear. Our move should therefore be in the opposite direction; that is, in accepting that concepts, theories, reasons etc. always presuppose a background in order to make sense. It is similar but broader than the position which argues that all sciences are theory-laden. If this is correct there is no longer a need to rule out causes or observed regularities when explaining human action. Do they too not presuppose a meaningful context? To give a causal explanation of human behaviour then only refers to the fact that it is described in certain terms, in the same sense as an explanation in terms of reasons presupposes a background of shared understanding. Some human actions may thus be characterized in terms of causes and effects, but it may also be possible to give descriptions in terms of regularities (how antecedent variables go together with subsequent conditions) or to refer to reasons. Some activities may almost exclusively be understood by using one type of explanation, while in other cases several will be possible. Thus whether something is *really* explained, or whether 'reality' here is merely a matter of not being fictitious, should not necessarily invoke a correspondence theory of truth where sense data are the exclusive building blocks. Instead, as Winch rightly argued, it is always about 'what is real for us'. It goes without saying that answering a research question in terms of causes and effects will not generate an answer in terms of the understanding of those involved. But this kind of circularity is not to be regretted, as it is characteristic of all explanation.[8] Science, as for that matter any kind of explanation, will always take the data which are to be interpreted at a next higher step of abstraction, thus invoking a particular theoretical construction which makes sense. This is a circular process in which each level is taken to account for, to derive from, or to elaborate on the other. Thus instances are explained by patterns and patterns by instances. For Winch too, as argued above, there is not just the practitioner's understanding, not just the concepts of those involved (i.e.

raw data as interpreted phenomena), but those of the 'student of society' as well. Clearly, here it is not prediction that may exclusively provide us with a point of reference, nor is the method of the natural sciences the only way to come to valid conclusions. But even if the possibility of prediction is what one is interested in, a meaningful background still cannot be absent. How could it possibly be doubted that we always start from making distinctions in terms of what makes sense for us?

Even if sense data and observations will play an important role, this still does not jeopardize the claim that concepts are involved. Possible exceptions occur only at a very basic level, for example that light of a particular intensity is painful. In such cases one may argue that particular phenomena have 'meaning in themselves', that is without presupposing a shared meaningful background. Obviously, what is 'shared' here is the human body and its particular physiology. These cases are rare, however and once we start speaking about them, a language in which we can determine 'what makes sense for us' is implied. Again this has to be distinguished from a context in which reasons can be given. One may recall Wittgenstein's position on language: 'You must bear in mind that the language-game is so to say something unpredictable. I mean: it is not based on grounds. It is not reasonable (or unreasonable). It is there—like our life' (Wittgenstein, 1969, # 559). Analogously, physical objects may affect us in particular ways. It is therefore not correct to argue that phenomena which have a 'meaning in themselves' play no role whatsoever in our understanding of human behaviour, but it would also not be correct to ignore that more is involved if they have a place in our lives. In that case they also presuppose some kind of shared meaning which will include elements above the physical, chemical, physiological or biochemical level. For example and at a slightly higher stage of abstraction, there seems at first sight to be a so-called objective point of reference in medicine (being healthy, living longer etc.). But it is not only the case that surgery or medication can have side-effects which may prompt one to give up on a particular treatment, there is also the debate about quality of life which plays a role in this decision process. And, as is clear for instance from the area of environmental ethics, there are in many cases conflicting interests which have to be dealt with. We have to decide for example whether to safeguard a particular wildlife area or to build in that location a new airport, thus relieving thousands of people of aircraft noise.

Though there are only very few elements which have in these terms a definite meaning in themselves they have to be given a place too if one wants to understand human behaviour. It is also the case that in many of our more purposeful activities they continue to play a role, as do the observed regularities and causal explanations of which the actors make use. An adequate methodology of the social sciences should therefore combine causal explanation with intentional understanding. Following Bohman (1997) I too accept that hermeneutic philosophers of social science—he mentions Taylor and MacIntyre, but the same goes for Winch—are in danger of ignoring this due to their one-sided arguments, which rule out every kind of causal explanation in this context, and also due to their claim that all explanations are superfluous in comparison with actors' own interpretation of their actions. Instead, Bohman argues that 'macrosociological and functionalist explanations supervene upon actor's intentions' (Bohman, 1997, p. 445), a thesis which I believe is very plausible. A pertinent example of this might be a university climate in which constraints of a macro-institutional nature may be observed on scientific production.

Thus a place has been found for instrumental behaviour which was difficult to accommodate in Winch's position. Moreover, it has become clear how different methods or ways of explanation can be used. It goes without saying that in the end the explanation that is offered will have to be subjected to the community of researchers and scholars but also to that of practitioners, to be judged on the basis of whether the position argued for 'makes sense to say', given 'what is real for them'. Clearly it is in principle always possible to offer another explanation referring to reasons, causes or regularities and to apply theoretical insights from philosophy, history, aesthetics etc., i.e. to describe what Winch identifies as 'modes of life'. Incidentally, it is interesting from this perspective to have a closer look at our use of the concept of 'rationalisation', roughly meaning the attempt to explain or justify one's own or another's behaviour, our attitude towards logical, plausible reasons, even if these are not true or appropriate. Clearly it will depend on the circumstances and also on our knowledge of the person concerned whether we will call a particular reason a rationalisation or not.

The fact remains that the acceptability of it will rely heavily on whether others can agree with this particular interpretation. Many justifications could be called rationalisations, but to make a Winchean or even Wittgensteinian point, not all of them can be convincingly argued for. This example should provide enough antidote against objectivistic science, just as it does against objectivistic forms of common sense. Evidently, structures of meaning have to be applied in particular cases, which always need to be contextualized. This is a matter which is generally accepted for social sciences, but it is no less true for natural sciences which require taking into account all the relevant and the possibly intervening factors. As it is always possible in the social sciences that practitioners appreciate a particular situation differently, it is similarly possible in the context of natural sciences that new elements, which one was previously not aware of, or new mechanisms occur. There is furthermore, parallel to the creativity of the practitioner who 'applies' insights, the demand for the scholar to raise creative questions and to offer inventive answers. Thus it is not only possible to give a place to what is newly discovered, but also to take up in our reflections new developments of what Wittgenstein calls our 'form of life'. (The demand for performativity which so strongly characterises present-day society supplies an example of this.) This is reminiscent of Winch's argument that it is a particular task of philosophical reflection to remind us of the kind of 'bedrock' that underlies what we do, though it may not be something of which we are fully aware in our conscious dealings.[9] If one accepts these amendments to the Winchean position, what more can be said of educational research and of an educational science?

EDUCATIONAL RESEARCH AND 'WHAT MAKES SENSE FOR US'

Educational research should come to terms with Winch's suggestion that it must be philosophical in character. Here philosophy is not just concerned with eliminating linguistic confusions, although there is a proper place for conceptual analysis, but is concerned foremost with 'what makes sense for us'. That implies that the starting point is the self-understanding of those involved: educators and parents, students and children. It does not make sense therefore to break down teaching into atomic skills and sub-skills; nor to conceive education almost entirely in terms of examination results; nor to regard moral psychology as a series of points on the scale of self-esteem; nor to talk of parenting in terms of developing particular skills and quality time to empower children. In empirical educational research nowadays there is typically a starting point (topic, research question etc.), then a procedure (the gathering of data, etc.) and then an analysis and discussion. A lot of attention is paid to the middle stage, concealing the fact that the really big questions concern the values at the heart of, or taken for granted, in, the identification of the topic and the question, and of course in the ensuing discussion. Winch's position implies that the discussion has to start from a particular social intercourse or 'practice'. If follows that the empirical observational methods (and statistical techniques) cannot possibly be the only yardstick. Instead, the human situatedness of the phenomena being researched requires that all our observations, arguments, and considerations must be based in our practices. Normative and value-laden elements have to play a crucial role throughout educational research and not just in the first or final stages.

In trying to be objective, and in identifying 'objective' with 'free of bias' the fact is concealed that we always and inevitably bring our pre-understandings with us into any situation. In this sense understanding, as the German philosopher Hans-Georg Gadamer insists, requires 'prejudices' in the sense in which he uses that term, as equivalent to 'pre-understandings'. This is no more than to make the familiar distinction between *verstehen* and *erklärung*. *Verstehende* social science concerns itself with interpretation and meaning: it asks for instance what drug-taking among young people means—is it to be seen as a rite of passage, a means of social bonding, a way of marking out a dissident identity? The kind of social science that fits the *erklärung* model seeks explanation (the meaning of the German term): it asks for example what causes young people to drop out of university, just as the physical scientist investigates the causes of chemical changes. Neglect of the distinction between *verstehen* and *erklärung* creates a world of confusion and often leads us to forget that social science does not always work like physical science. An example may help here. The researcher seeking to understand why teenage pregnancy rates are much higher in one part of the country than another may come to the tentative conclusion that for low-achieving youngsters in marginalized communities giving birth to and looking after a baby gives them status among their peers, and confers a sense of purpose on their lives. Perhaps it is the most meaningful thing they will ever do. Statistics have an important place here in marking out coherent categories of 'low-achieving youngsters' and 'marginalized communities'. At the same time the researcher could not formulate her hypothesis unless she understood what it is like to find life meaningful or meaningless. Thus her pre-understandings are a precondition of her work. By contrast there is a standing temptation to embrace the notion of objectivity that consists in imagining that the explanations of phenomena are waiting 'out there' for us to discover with our instruments and techniques. When we declare, for instance, that '42% of the sample had experienced significant periods of separation from one parent or from both' we may forget that such separation cannot be unproblematically identified. This is not to embrace the claims of a crude constructivism to the effect that all meaning is created *ex nihilo*, but only to argue that whenever we conceptualize a particular part of reality, this necessarily occurs within the boundaries of what already makes sense for us. Ideas about what is worthwhile, about the nature of a human being, necessarily enter into the picture. That is why we cannot without further qualification make statements such as that 'European explorers brought civilization to primitive people'. Unlike earlier generations we are aware that what is civilized and what is primitive can be contested. Similarly, the common claim that a particular approach to a problem 'works', or that research should endeavour to discover 'what works', must not be allowed to conceal how much is dependent on just how 'what works' is defined. Unacknowledged metaphysical and ethical assumptions are usually lurking here: for instance to the effect that this or that is an acceptable way of achieving results.

We are no longer aware of things in terms of their multifarious meanings and interconnections, but isolate them in order to study their 'reality' and then worry about how they are linked and connected to each other. We do this because we are unwilling to live with complexity. To replace scientism and doctrinaire empiricism with a more modest view of science is perhaps the first step towards wisdom. Of course this does not mean that scientific method has no role at all to play within social science, but that it must make out the case for its relevance in each particular instance against other approaches that also offer insight and understanding, whether in conjunction with measurement and statistics or apart from them.[10]

THE STUDY OF EDUCATION: IMPROVING UPON OUR PRACTICAL KNOWLEDGE

I will conclude with a number of characteristics that in my opinion mark the nature of educational research. I suggest that it may be better to speak of *educational research or the study of education* (1), than of an educational science, given the connotations the concept 'science' has in the English language. Furthermore, what has been argued for concerning human behaviour should also characterize the study of educational phenomena. That means that *various modes of explanation* (2) may find their place in trying to understand what is involved in teaching pupils and students, in child-rearing, in continuing education and in educational policy and evaluation and so on. There is indeed no need for a single method nor to prioritize one, but as Wittgenstein argues concerning philosophy: 'There is not *a* philosophical method, though there are indeed methods, like different therapies' (Wittgenstein, 1953, # 133). Much will depend on the problem that is studied, but also on *the kind of theoretical interest* (3) one is pursuing.

That not only reasons of an ethical or religious nature may be involved, but that there is also an appropriate interest in a more instrumental kind of reasoning may be illustrated by the recent debate on the French law banning in state schools Islamic headscarves and other religious symbols such as the Jewish skull-cap and large Christian crosses. The bill follows an official report on state secularism which was backed by President Jacques Chirac who argued that France needed to act to head off the danger to the nation's secular foundations. Former minister Bernard Stasi, who chaired the commission, consulted a wide cross-section of public opinion, including teachers, religious leaders, sociologists and politicians before handing in the report to the president. Critics condemned the law as an attack on religious freedom and said it would stigmatize the estimated five million Muslims in France. So far France is the only country in Western Europe that has banned head scarves in public schools. But the French government, which has a strong tradition of secularism, promotes restrictions on religious symbols as a means of promoting integration in a diverse society.[11] It is interesting to see that the report by Stasi explicitly states that the secular state cannot remain indifferent to issues of public order, to racist and discriminatory practices and the activities of pressure groups which undermine the principles of schooling. The state sets itself therefore the task to educate its citizens in a particular way, and so to avoid a double danger: on the one hand the fragmentation of society, on the other the denial of all diversity or plurality which the republican pact would render illusory. The report explicitly sees the school as the environment in which students should learn to live together. Thus it argues:

> *Dans un milieu partiellement clos, les élèves, pris en charge sur une longue durée, doivent apprendre et vivre ensemble, dans une situation où ils sont encore fragiles, sujets aux influences et pressions extérieures. Le fonctionnement de l'école doit leur permettre d'acquérir les outils intellectuels destins à assurer à terme leur indépendance critique. Réserver une place à l'expression des convictions spirituelles et religieuses ne va donc pas de soi* (Stasi, 2003, p. 28).[12]

By the particular measures it suggests, the report explicitly aims to deal with problems of de-schooling which may be the result of religious motives, and with the fact that many young women see themselves as victims of sexism through various forms of oppression, of verbal, psychological or physical violence. It remarks that young people too force some girls to wear covering and asexual cloths and observes that a refusal to conform to this results in their stigmatisation as 'whores'. The new law has to be seen as reacting against oppression and to assure anew the glue of society, surely too against particular forms of fundamentalism. The means to achieve this are partly sought within the educational system.

As an illustration of the complexity of an educational problem—and who could deny that the rejection of schooling and the fragmentation of society are such problems—this example is interesting for a variety of reasons. First, it exemplifies that particular societal developments are highly relevant for education. Surely, now that it is the law, schools will obey, but clearly the law-givers also expect particular results in instrumental terms such as a higher degree of integration and the countering of oppression. Second, since various modes of life are involved (the religious, the educational, the social, etc.) and various principles (for example rights and freedoms) must be taken into account, it shows that the issue has to be dealt with from a variety of theoretical stances. Finally, and this is clearly not an exhaustive list, I want to draw attention to the frequent references that are made by the report itself to certain aims which are envisaged. Whether or not the proposed measures *work* is another matter, but clearly if an educational researcher studied this issue for instance in the context of policy research, she would have to take such empirical outcomes into consideration. This moreover points to something outlined at various places in this chapter, that social research does not give us fixed and universal knowledge of the social world as such, but that it rather *contributes to the task of improving upon our practical knowledge of ongoing social life* (4). That this presupposes *dialogue between all those involved* (5), goes without saying. But when we realize that there are many and often highly contested versions of participants' self-interpretation, we will also see that though the latter are the only plausible starting place, more is needed for good dialogical and social scientific practice.

Here science is no longer seen as disinterested and value-free: instead there do not seem to be strict boundaries between science and society. In her contribution the researcher, the interpretive pluralist, will among other things explore the operation of many different practical norms, thus through her interpretation making implicit norms explicit. She will also and in my opinion necessarily *invoke a normative stance* (6). Here facts are no longer seen as exclusively made to refer to objective things in the world or things in themselves, neither are values seen as subjective states of the mind. In avoiding these and other conceptual confusions science reveals itself instead as a performative intervention. As Winch argued, what matters is 'what is real for us'. Though the researcher's work is in this sense also of a political nature, it does not coincide with that of the practitioner or the politician. As Pels writes in *Unhastening Science. Autonomy and Reflexivity in the Social Theory of Knowledge* (2003), 'In a nanoculture that glorifies the speedway and the "fast-forward mode", the university may still provide a resort of stillness and slow motion where "untimely" thoughts may be cultivated in relative liberty and leisure' (Pels, 2003, p. 24). Thus the writing of research may be seen as a case of *positive slowness* (7) that prevents us from being absorbed in the chaos of unmediated complexity. It allows us time to think and is performed at some distance in the interest of perspective and justice (Pels, 2003, p. 131).

Such a kind of educational research or study of education gives up a number of old distinctions such as values/facts, objective/engaged, researcher/practitioner, concept/fact, reasons/causes, qualitative/quantitative/interpretive. Not that these distinctions do not matter, they can indeed be quite helpful for particular purposes, but they do suggest too much the existence of dichotomies or oppositions which tend to lead a life of their own. Educational research employs various modes of explanation and pursues different kinds of theoretical interests. It participates through dialogue in improving our practical knowledge of ongoing social life but at the same time necessarily invokes a normative stance. In some sense one may say that it too is an educational practice, perhaps only of a slightly different kind. The reflection that is offered is philosophically engaged and will necessarily go beyond the empirical. It will go beyond means-end, instrumental reasoning and is thus unsettling in contrast to the kind of empirical research which draws on and reinforces the pull of precisely that kind of reasoning. This kind of reflective research does not sacrifice itself on the altar of prediction. And though it may want to start from the wisdom to be found in common sense, it will go beyond that in realizing a person's own values, in coming across new possibilities for education. What is at stake is correctly called by Peter Winch 'what is real for us'. This refers not only to the present and the past, but is equally relevant for the future.

NOTES

1. An exception to this is Wilfred Carr's study (see Carr, 1989).
2. See for instance the recent issue (2005, 55.3) of *Educational Theory*.
3. In the sense in which Plato famously reports Socrates as saying that the unexamined, i.e. unreflective, life is no life for humankind.
4. A more technical introduction to the basic Wittgensteinian concepts is given in Smeyers and Marshall, 1995, pp. 3–35.
5. Whether an explanation in terms of observed regularities presupposes in the end a causal framework has been the subject of many discussions. It invokes among other elements the issue of determinism or indeterminism as its frame of reference. This cannot be developed here, but a position on this matter does not seem to me decisive concerning what is argued for in this chapter.
6. As is well known Davidson argues that reasons can be causes, and thus his position may solve the problems Winch is confronted with. Following him Siegel equates 'the cause of an action or thought' with 'just whatever it is that brings that action or thought about' (Siegel, 1999, p. 212, footnote 18). I cannot go into the arguments Davidson develops nor into the critical discussion it has generated, but this clearly confronts us with the question whether causality as found in physics (and expressed by physical laws concerning material objects) is really of the same nature as the causality that explains our actions (for which we use concepts such as reasons, motives, intentions).
7. The nature of causality, whether it has to be conceived in realist terms or not, the latter a position which Hume holds, is a matter of a prolonged debate this chapter cannot go into. It has however as far as I can see no immediate bearing on my argument.

8. Dick Pels argues in a similar way: 'the epistemological break between science and (scientific) common sense, or between observer and observed, does not turn upon the conventional distinction between "merely partial" views and views that claim the ability to totalize, but upon the somewhat unconventional distinction between views that are self-consciously circular and views (both everyday and sociological-scientific) that deny this circularity in order to claim a "straight" transcendent foundation' (Pels, 2003, p. 176).

9. An example of this is the recent work by Mary Midgley (2004), *The Myths We Live By*. She considers several very potent ideas that have moved from ordinary thought to affect the course of science and have then returned to outside usage reshaped by scientific use. Thus she argues that 'We are accustomed to think of myths as the opposite of science. But in fact they are a central part of it: the part that decides its significance in our lives' (Midgley, 2004, p. 1). She discusses for instance the social-contract myth, the progress myth and the myth of omnicompetent science.

10. The examples given in the preceding paragraphs were developed in a previous study (see Smeyers and Smith, 2003).

11. Interestingly, the implementation of the law has resulted by way of compromise in some places in the acceptance of bandannas (which leave the forehead and the ears uncovered), while other heads of schools have prohibited these too, even if worn for fashion reasons.

12. 'In a relatively closed environment pupils are taken into care for a long period where they have to study and live together in a situation when they are still fragile and subjected to exterior influences and pressures. The functioning of the school has to permit them to acquire in the long run the intellectual tools intended to assure their critical independence. To reserve in this a place for the expression of spiritual and religious convictions is thus not straightforward' (my translation).

REFERENCES

Bohman, J. (1997) Pluralism, Indeterminacy and the Social Sciences: Reply to Ingram and Meehan, *Human Studies: A Journal for Philosophy and the Social Sciences*, 97, pp. 441–458.

Carr, W. (1989) The Idea of an Educational Science, *Journal of Philosophy of Education*, 23, pp. 29–37.

Eisenhart, M. (2005) Hammers and Saw for the Improvement of Educational Research, *Educational Theory*, 55, 245–261.

Howe, K. R. (2005) The Education Science Question: A Symposium, *Educational Theory*, 55, pp. 235–243.

Howe, K. R. (2005a) The Question of Education Science: *Experimentism* versus *Experimentalism*, *Educational Theory*, 55, pp. 307–321.

Lerner, B. D. (2002) *Rules, Magic, and Instrumental Reason. A Critical Interpretation of Peter Winch's Philosophy of the Social Sciences* (London, Routledge).

Midgley, M. (2004) *The Myths We Live By* (London, Routledge).

Moss, P. A. (2005) Understanding the Other/Understanding Ourselves: Toward a Constructive Dialogue about 'Principles' in Educational Research, *Educational Theory*, 55, pp. 263–283.

National Research Council. (2002) *Scientific Research in Education*, R. J. Shavelson and L. Towne (eds) (Washington, DC, National Academies Press).

Pels, D. (2003) *Unhastening Science. Autonomy and Reflexivity in the Social Theory of Knowledge* (Liverpool, Liverpool University Press).

Schwandt, T. (2005) A Diagnostic Reading of Scientifically Based Research for Education, *Educational Theory*, 55, pp. 285–305.

Siegel, H. (1999) What (Good) are Thinking Dispositions?, *Educational Theory*, 49, pp. 201–221.

Smeyers, P. and Marshall, J. (eds). (1995) *Philosophy and Education: Accepting Wittgenstein's Challenge* (Dordrecht, Kluwer).

Smeyers, P. and Smith, R. (2003) Two Dogmas of Measurement, *Measurement: Interdisciplinary Research and Perspectives*, 1, pp. 279–285.

Stasi, B. (2003) *Commission de réflexion sur l'application du principe de laïcité dans la république* (Rapport au président de la république. Remis le 11 décembre 2003). Retrieved August 31, 2005 from http://lesrapports.ladocumentationfrancaise.fr/BRP/034000725/0000.pdf

Winch, P. (1958) *The Idea of a Social Science and its Relation to Philosophy* (London, Routledge).

Winch, P. (1964) Understanding a Primitive Society, *American Philosophical Quarterly*, 1, pp. 307–324.

Wittgenstein, L. (1953) *Philosophical Investigations/Philosophische Untersuchungen*, G. E. M. Anscombe, (trans.) (Oxford, Blackwell).

Wittgenstein, L. (1969) *On Certainty/Über Gewissheit*, G. E. M. Anscombe and G. H. von Wright (eds) D. Paul and G. E. M. Anscombe (trans.) (Oxford, Blackwell).

17
Philosophy's Contribution to Social Science Research on Education

MARTYN HAMMERSLEY

What I will be presenting is, loosely speaking, a Weberian perspective on the contribution that philosophy can make to social science research on educational institutions and processes.[1] Max Weber's attitude towards philosophy was an ambivalent one. On the one hand, he drew heavily on neo-Kantianism, and also on Nietzsche. At the same time, he insisted on social science as a separate and largely autonomous activity, treating any engagement with philosophical issues by social scientists as, generally speaking, a distraction from their real work.[2]

In this chapter I want to focus on two areas where philosophy can make an important contribution to social science. The first, and perhaps the most obvious one, is methodology, where the task is to clarify both the goals and means of research. The second concerns the values that frame social science inquiries so as to make them relevant to human concerns.[3] I will contrast the implications of a Weberian position in each of these areas with other views that treat philosophy as having either a lesser or a greater role.

METHODOLOGY

If we look at the methodological literature of social science generally we can draw a crude distinction between methodology-as-technique and methodology-as-philosophy.[4] These orientations differ not just in their principal foci—one concentrating on specific research methods, the other on general methodological issues—but also in terms of their assumptions about how to produce good quality research: for instance, they differ over whether this is a matter of technique and skill or of having a reflexive grasp on the philosophical assumptions being relied upon. Furthermore, as we shall see, methodology-as-philosophy often raises fundamental questions about the very pursuit of social and educational research, challenging the goal of knowledge, the ideal of truth and the possibility of objectivity.[5]

Methodology-as-technique portrays research as the deployment of particular methods or procedures, those that are taken to be scientific. These are viewed as distinguishing science from humanistic disciplines, with the former being capable of demonstrating empirical conclusions and building knowledge, by contrast with the endless disputes and lack of cumulation characteristic of non-scientific fields. By definition, from this point of view, any science must break away from philosophy and no longer be dependent upon it.

What is wrong with methodology-as-technique is that it either forgets that doing research necessarily involves assumptions that sometimes require philosophical attention, or it assumes that the relevant philosophical problems have all been satisfactorily resolved; in other words, some philosophical view from the past is simply taken for granted, without recognising subsequent challenges to it and their methodological implications.

Let me try to illustrate this tendency with an example from a recent book on quantitative research in education. Under the heading 'We need an ideal', Stephen Gorard writes: '[. . .] the ideal experiment, by isolating cause and effect, can provide us with a universal template for the perfect piece of research which leads to safe knowledge. We can then judge our more limited studies against that ideal, and so understand and explain the ways in which our own findings are less than secure (for sadly such is the fate of all real-world research)' (Gorard, 2001, p. 2). Here, while recognising the imperfect and practical character of actual research, Gorard is putting forward a particular technique, the experiment, as a universal ideal; as a procedure that can produce 'safe' or 'secure' knowledge, against which other techniques can be judged as better or worse according to how close an approximation they provide.

Gorard is not alone in setting up a hierarchy of research procedures, or in seeing one method as producing virtually certain knowledge. This is also built into some accounts of what is required of research if it is to serve evidence-based policymaking and practice. For example, Chalmers treats the randomised controlled trial as the ideal method for determining which policies and practices work (Chalmers, 2003; see also Hammersley, 2005). Similarly, like Gorard, many other quantitative researchers using non-experimental methods seek to justify their work on the grounds that it can approximate the *logic* of the experiment, and can thereby produce valid conclusions in a way that approaches not exercising physical or statistical control cannot.

From this point of view, the experiment is the essence of scientific method. Yet much work in the philosophy of science over the past fifty years has denied that there is anything so specific we can identify as scientific method. Even a philosopher like Karl Popper, whose position places great weight on the need to try to falsify hypotheses, recognises that experimental method has not been central in all areas of natural science where progress has been made. And he also emphasises the role of critical discussion in assessing philosophical arguments; indeed, in some places, one could interpret him as subordinating experimentation to critical discussion, treating it just one tool that serves such discussion (see Popper, 1987). Moreover, for Popper what science can give us is a great deal more limited than many quantitative social scientists, including Gorard, assume: at best, it can only tell us what is false, not what is true—it does not provide 'secure' positive findings. And, as soon as one takes into account the possibility of error in experimental evidence, it cannot even tell us what is false with absolute certainty. Much more recently, Susan Haack has also denied that there is any such thing as scientific method, insisting that science as a whole is committed only to privileging certain epistemic goals and virtues, and that the various sciences draw on a variety of devices that facilitate the improvement of human perception and judgment (Haack, 2003). From her point of view too, the value of the experiment would vary sharply across sciences.

My point here is not to argue that experiments, or quantitative methods generally, are inappropriate in educational research, but only to resist claims, such as Gorard's, that there are reasons to believe that they represent the perfect method or ideal.[6] Moreover, the argument against methodology-as-technique, against the idea that doing research can be reduced to following some particular procedure, can be made more general. Of particular significance here is the work of Michael Polanyi on the essential role of tacit knowledge, and thereby of judgment, even in natural science (Polanyi, 1959). Like Popper and Haack, Polanyi is not someone who rejects the validity or value of scientific knowledge, or the distinctiveness of science as an enterprise, but his arguments count against the idea that science is a matter of following some method, or even approximations to it.

In fact, the issue of the role of experiments in understanding human behaviour relates to a whole set of questions about the nature of causality in the social world, what count as explanations in this field, and how they can best be produced. Social scientists are unlikely to make much headway in dealing with these problems by simply ignoring them. Moreover, while it may be true that these problems cannot be resolved by philosophical work alone, it would be foolish to neglect the considerable philosophical literature available that deals with them.[7]

Tying quantitative method to a narrow kind of positivism, in the way that Gorard seems to do in the statement quoted above, is unfortunate on at least two counts. First, it may lead researchers astray, through encouraging implicit reliance on a philosophical idea about the nature of science that was undermined long ago. Secondly, it plays into the hands of those who want to deny that social and educational inquiry can be scientific, so that they can be free to pursue ethical ideals, political goals, or aesthetic projects in its name. For them, the patent failings of positivism amount to a denunciation of the scientific ideal *per se*, either in general or as it applies to studying the social world.[8]

By contrast with methodology-as-technique, methodology-as-philosophy highlights the role of philosophical assumptions in research. However, I want to suggest that this is often done in a way that is excessive, and that this stems, in part, from a failure to draw on the full range of relevant philosophical argument. Once again I will select just one of many possible examples.[9] In a recent introduction to structuralism and post-structuralism, Ian Stronach uses the old philosophical example of a table as a way of reflecting on notions of representation. He opens his discussion by asking the reader to 'Think of a table', and then outlines what might be involved in defining this concept, by identifying the features of tables in terms of their functional interrelations. However, he goes on to challenge this procedure as follows:

> (a) there *is* no table there, only the writing of 'table', and (b) [. . .] the no-table—let's call it a 'writing-desk' by way of a pun—is available to you only in imagination as a 'reading-desk', and on my say-so, though you may resist that say-so if you notice as such, and [. . .] (c) the time and circumstance of 'writing-desk' is always political, pedagogically strategic, culturally coloured, quietly privileging.

> So what's the problem? The table is not there. It is only someone writing 'table'. The table is performed rather than represented and it is a command performance ('Think of a table'!). Writing performs the table, and positions the self who will read. The failure of the table ever to be neutrally *there* is repressed, and the impossibility of 'going back' is denied. The active engagement of the reader in this masquerade is demanded. The acceptance of the heuristic is imposed rather than proposed. What at first can seem to be an innocent attempt to recruit the reader to a new possibility in thinking can simultaneously be exposed as shot through with power-play, inauthenticity, manipulation and mis-representation. This is what has often been called the 'linguistic turn'—an acceptance that these 'flaws' no longer seem open to correction. We have to live with the mess—there can be no recourse to a level of discourse where 'pure' structures/concepts/theories really tidy up the everyday nature of complexity and contradiction [. . .] (Stronach, 2005a, b, pp. 310 and 312).

There are some important and interesting philosophical ideas raised here. However, they are highly compressed, compacted, and distorted. And in the resulting 'mess' quite a lot is obscured. First of all, notice that while Stronach's argument is about the 'impossibility' of representation, as conventionally understood, the way he formulates the example undercuts any claim to representation anyway. Had he used the example in its most usual form, where the writer describes the table or desk on which he or she is writing, then the issue of representation would have been a live one: it would *not* have been what he refers to as a 'command performance', or not in the same way. At least at face value, it would have been reasonable to ask whether the writer was indeed describing a table in front of him, and whether his description was an accurate one. Of course, some of the points Stronach raises would still need to be addressed, but our thinking about them would not have been undermined by the very formulation of the example.

Next, I suggest that his move from 'there is no table' to the existence of a 'no-table', a 'writing table' or a 'reading desk' is a logical error. What *is* true is that if readers accede to Stronach's request to 'think of a table' then they will have some idea of a table in mind, though there is no strong sense in which this has been written into their imaginations by the author, nor will the table necessarily be functionally designated as for either writing or reading. Indeed, to suggest that it will only exist in the imagination of readers on the author's 'say so' is to ignore the arguments of those, like Stanley Fish, who in other respects might concur with much of Stronach's argument: Fish argues that texts are always constructed by readers (Fish, 1980). And the claim that the 'time and circumstance' of the author's injunction to 'think of a table' is 'always political, pedagogically strategic, culturally coloured, quietly privileging' requires some unpacking, to say the least. One would hope that it was pedagogically strategic, given that the text is part of an introduction to social science research methods for students. Whether or not it is political depends a great deal on which of the many possible meanings is being given to that term (see Hammersley, 1995, p. 6). And much the same is true of the concept of culture embodied in 'culturally coloured'. Whether the author's injunction to 'think of a table' is 'privileging' (quietly or loudly, or in any other adverbial manner) is uncertain because of a lack of clarity about these terms. Furthermore, while it is true that selecting the example of a table, rather than, say, a school or college, as an object for reflection necessarily closes down some important issues, it is unlikely that doing this privileges some group of people at the expense of others. The conceptual uncertainties and problems are played on by Stronach's 'gaming' style; but, in my view, as a result of that style his discussion does not help us much in thinking about the philosophical issues surrounding social and educational research. In effect, it encourages scepticism about the whole enterprise, as conventionally understood, but does so without providing any cogent justification.

It is striking that, even though he is writing an introduction, Stronach provides no references to the philosophical literature that critically interrogates poststructuralism. Moreover, in this respect he is fairly typical. Very little use seems to be made by social and educational researchers of the now substantial literature of this kind (for examples of this literature, see Dews, 1987; Habermas, 1990; and Ferry and Renaut, 1997). This amounts to a serious neglect of relevant philosophical work.

A central point that Stronach is raising concerns whether it is possible ever to have knowledge of phenomena, even of those 'medium-sized dry goods'—such as tables—that are so often the preoccupation of (analytic) philosophers. Indeed, as Edwards *et al.* (1995) have pointed out, appeals to the reality of furniture (along with death) have been a staple argument of realists for a long time. Furthermore, as in the case of Stronach, they have also been used as a standard 'hard case' by those who would deny the commonsense idea that we have knowledge of phenomena that exist independently of our ideas or discourses about them.[10] In this context, much can be learned from Susan Stebbing's blistering critique of those physicists in the early twentieth century who sought to reduce the reality of tables to that of the atoms making them up (Stebbing, 1944). Even more instructive, in my view, are Wittgenstein's meditations on Moore's defence of commonsense realism (Wittgenstein, 1969), since he shows that it is simply nonsensical to doubt some things about the world, and this certainly extends to the existence of tables. Even if one does not accept these counter-arguments, they must be engaged with if methodology-as-philosophy is to be anything more than gaming or discursive dissemination; and if it cannot be more than this, then it is hard to see the point.

The kind of scepticism Stronach is promoting might seem more plausible in relation to social rather than physical phenomena. When we ask about the existence of particular forms of social organisation, such as families, schools, ethnic groups, nation states, and so on, we have to recognise that these are only constructed through the actions of human beings. However, while there are difficult issues here, most of the discussions to be found in the philosophical literature do not point strongly to scepticism (see, for example, Searle, 1995). As Weldon (1953, p. 49) commented long ago: 'the legal non-existence of the Communist Party in Tsarist Russia did not prevent the Bolshevist Revolution of 1919'. State legislation is a much stronger injunction than an author's request to 'Think of a table', and there is a sense in which it does indeed determine what has legal existence; but it does not determine what has *factual* existence, any more than do the sceptical arguments of an author.

Let me reiterate that I am not suggesting that recourse to the philosophical literature can resolve all of the methodological problems that surround social scientific research on education. But, at the very least, we can use the resources provided to recognise where we are being led astray by arguments that have been shown to be misleading, or by the language we rely upon. That literature should also help us to understand the full range of positions that are available—instead of assuming, for example, that one must either be a naïve realist, believing that the world simply is as it appears, or an extreme constructionist, denying the very possibility of knowledge simply because our experience is constituted through socio-cultural capacities and practices.

VALUE RELEVANCE

For Max Weber, social research had to strive to be value-neutral but also to be value-relevant.[11] He took this idea from the neo-Kantians, notably Heinrich Rickert (see Rickert, 1914). However, whereas Rickert thought that the values by which social scientists should select particular phenomena for study could be objective—in other words, universal and perennial—by contrast Weber believed that the values that social scientists use to identify particular phenomena for study are historically variable and subjectively chosen.

Now, I take it to be obvious that educational research is always framed in terms of certain values. Yet researchers are often not explicit about what those values are, and their implications; they also frequently fail to recognise that other values could have framed their inquiries. And this is another area where philosophy can make a very important contribution. What is required is what Weber referred to as 'value clarification': identifying key values and what implications can reasonably be drawn from them as regards particular issues in particular contexts (Bruun, 1972). Equally important, it can help in differentiating values from factual matters.

Let me illustrate this with the example of equity.[12] Many social and educational researchers focus their work on inequalities in relation to social class, gender, ethnicity, and disability. And, almost always, they are concerned with inequalities that they regard as inequitable. Indeed, the term 'unequal' has come to be treated as if it were synonymous with 'inequitable', so that to many ears the phrase 'equitable inequalities' would sound like a contradiction in terms. Yet there is an important distinction here: not all factual inequalities would be judged inequitable by everyone, and some probably not by anyone. As a result of this conflation between inequality and inequity, educational researchers often treat the inequitable differences they are concerned with as if these were simply factual matters, failing to make clear that the identification of inequalities as relevant matters for investigation, and evaluation of them as inequities, depends upon value assumptions, and ones that may well not be universally shared.

Westen defines descriptive equality as referring to 'the relationship that obtains among two or more distinct things that have been jointly measured by a common standard of comparison and found to be indistinguishable by reference to that standard.' (Westen, 1990, p. 33). This specification is important because it points to the comparative and relational character of judgments of equality and inequality. It simply makes no sense to refer to some person or category of person as being in an unequal position unless it is made clear with whom they are being compared *and in terms of what standard.* Moreover, in descriptive terms there are innumerably many ways in which any set of objects can be described as equal or unequal to some other set.

Prescriptive equality, or equity, presupposes descriptive equality, and so is also comparative and relational. But here the standard employed consists of some notion of justice, and there is also a clear indication that the implied descriptive equality should prevail. Equity is concerned, then, with what *ought* to be treated the same; though it also (necessarily) prescribes what ought to be treated differently. As Aristotle pointed out, it is just as wrong to treat people who are dissimilar the same as it is to treat those who are similar differently.[13]

Furthermore, judgments of inequity can be based on several sorts of ground. In the context of educational inequalities the most important distinction is probably between equity relating to the distribution of goods, and that concerning the distribution of opportunities to obtain a good.

The first of these two kinds of claim about inequity involves the argument that something of value has been unequally distributed between two or more categories of person when it should have been distributed equally; or, alternatively, that it has been distributed equally when it should have been distributed in unequal portions. We can see notions of equity at play in this distributional sense in judgments about the allocation of educational resources, for example of teacher attention between girls and boys or of classroom support between children identified as having 'special needs' and those not so identified. Even in these cases, the scope for reasonable disagreement about what is and is not equitable should be clear. For example, if teacher attention is to be distributed equally by gender, should it also be distributed equally in terms of social class and ethnicity? It seems very unlikely that this could be achieved, so that some priority would have to be given to these dimensions of inequality. Furthermore, what about the argument that teacher attention should be distributed where it is likely to produce the most benefit, irrespective of these social categories?

A rather different, and more complex, concept of equity underpins a great deal of educational research. This is concerned with differences in the *opportunity* to acquire an education or to achieve high levels of educational achievement. Equity of opportunity relates to goods that it is not within anyone's power to distribute. Thus, the level of academic achievement which students reach is widely held to depend on their ability and the effort they expend in its pursuit, not just on the activity of teachers.

In these terms, equity of opportunity requires that individuals who are similar in their potential to achieve a given level of knowledge, skill, or qualification experience an equal chance of getting it. However, as Williams (1962) has pointed out, the notion of equality of opportunity assumes that some conditions are to be equalised in order to allow inequality of some other (justifiable) kind to be revealed and rewarded; and there is no logically determinable stopping place in arguments about what should be equalised (see also Mackinnon, 1986). As a result, there is great scope for disagreement about what does and does not constitute equity of opportunity; over and above the question of whether the sort of meritocratic regime that it implies is justifiable.[14]

So, we are faced with a range of different interpretations of what equity implies. Indeed, Ennis (1978) argues that equity is a formal concept whose content must be supplied by one or other substantive conception of what would be desirable, just, etc.[15] We can get some sense of the sort of disagreement involved if we look at the redefinition of the problem of educational inequality which took place in Britain and some other countries over the course of the twentieth century. The starting position was the argument that the pre-1944 education system was inequitable because many children of working class parents who had the same ability as middle class grammar school entrants did not get a secondary education, because their parents could not afford the fees and because there were insufficient scholarship places. However, following the 1944 Act, views about equity of opportunity were revised: it was now argued by many that working class children still did not have equal access to an academic secondary school education because they did not have the same opportunities at home to develop academic ability as middle class children. Where previously the distribution of ability had generally been taken as given, as lying outside the responsibility of the education system, now it was itself treated as something the opportunity to acquire which was subject to legitimate (indeed obligatory) state intervention. One result of this was a proposal for compensatory education; another was the move to comprehensive secondary schooling. More recently, some have gone a step further, arguing that equality of opportunity requires that the criteria in terms of which educational achievement is assessed must treat the background cultures of all pupils as equal; in other words, what is defined as knowledge and ability within the education system must be diversified.

Here, then, we have variation in judgment about what constitutes equality of educational opportunity. Furthermore, the meaning of 'opportunity', like that of 'equality', is relational. Rubinstein (1993) has argued that the opportunities available to people cannot be defined independently of the goals, capabilities, and desires which they have; and that the latter are not simply a product of their circumstances. Because they have different orientations, people may respond quite differently to 'the same' situation. This is surely true, though it seems to me that, since attitudes may be changed and capabilities developed, it is legitimate to identify opportunities as open to people even though they would not recognise these or be able immediately to take advantage of them, given their current attitudes and capabilities. In other words, opportunities may be ascribed not just on the basis of the goals, desires, and capabilities *actually* possessed by the actors concerned but also in relation to ones which they *could* reasonably acquire or adopt. Yet here, of course, we introduce still further scope for reasonable disagreement about what would amount to equality of opportunity.

Despite all these complexities, most research on educational inequalities does not make clear the particular interpretations of 'equity', 'opportunity', and other concepts on which the value relevance of its focus has been determined. Moreover, as I noted earlier, inequalities are frequently presented as if their status as inequities were obvious and/or as matters that empirical research can determine. Here, then, philosophy could play an important role in drawing the attention of educational researchers to the logical grammar of the various value-laden concepts that can set the framework for their research, and the relationship of these to matters of fact.

Once again, though, what I am proposing is a limited role, and there are those who would not accept the limits. At a general level, there has been much criticism of Weber's position in these terms, from quite different directions. Strauss, Voegelin, and Habermas, for example, have all charged Weber with fuelling a destructive relativism by refusing to give philosophy the role of providing the values that should govern social science inquiry, so that such inquiry would serve not just the truth but also the good (Strauss, 1953; Voegelin, 1952; Habermas, 1971).

A similar argument has sometimes been put forward specifically in relation to education, for example by Richard Pring in his recent book *Philosophy of Educational Research*. He writes that 'it is difficult [...] to think about education, let alone about research into it, without addressing questions about the qualities which constitute or lead to a worthwhile form of life' (Pring, 2000, pp. 14–15). And later he comments: 'The central educational function of schools is to enable young people to learn what is valuable and significant. That then must be the defining focus of educational research' (p. 21). His argument seems to be that educational research should operate within a single value framework provided by the philosophy of education.[16]

There are reasons to disagree with Pring's argument. First, there is no single agreed conception of 'what is valuable and significant', and therefore of education, nor is there any immediate prospect of reaching one. As with many other words, the meaning of 'education' varies according to context, as well as on the basis of the value perspective adopted. Furthermore, education is not the only value (or complex of values) in terms of which we can investigate what goes on within educational institutions. I have already mentioned equity here, and it seems to me that this is distinct from, and perhaps sometimes even at odds with, a commitment to education.[17]

Another problem with Pring's argument concerns whether philosophy can in itself justify practical judgments about what is or is not of value, what ought to be done, and so on. For me, it is necessarily a meta-discipline, concerned with clarifying the concepts that we use to think about what is good, what is right, what ought to be done, and so on. Such clarification is extremely important, not just in relation to research but also for our practical judgments in the world, including policy decisions about education. However, it does not do all of the work that is required in coming to conclusions about what should, and what should not, be done. For one thing, factual assumptions will always be involved, on which it cannot adjudicate. Equally important, we necessarily make practical judgments in a situated way, as people with particular commitments and obligations, rather than in the disengaged terms in which, it seems to me, philosophy must operate.

CONCLUSION

In this chapter I have outlined a Weberian conception of the role that philosophy can play as regards social science research on education, focusing on two key areas: that concerning how best to pursue inquiry in order to gain knowledge; and that relating to the value-relevance of particular studies. I have argued that philosophy can play a very important role in both these respects, and that at present it is not given sufficient, or sufficiently careful, attention by most educational researchers. At the same time, I suggested that there are important limits to philosophy's contribution. It cannot tell researchers how best to go about investigating particular topics, because it cannot legislate concerning scientific method. Similarly, it cannot provide some single value framework that ought to govern social science research on education.

It may seem that what is being proposed here is that philosophy should play the role of 'underlabourer' to social science, in much the manner that Locke formulated the relationship between his own philosophical investigations and the work of contemporary natural scientists.[18] However, this is misleading. The metaphor needs revision: there are no underlabourers, only workers ploughing different fields whose crops can be of mutual benefit. My concern has not been with how philosophers should do their work but rather with how social scientists ought to make use of it. And it is probably just as important to assess the contribution of social science to philosophical work; in which context the roles would be reversed. Indeed, it could be argued that philosophers do not make sufficient use of the theoretical ideas and empirical evidence generated by social scientists; but that is not my concern here. My focus has been on ways in which the philosophical literature is not currently being employed to best effect by many educational researchers.[19]

NOTES

1. For a detailed account of Weber's position, see Bruun, 1972. Some writers argue for a distinction between educational research, which they believe should be geared to educational goals, and social science research in educational settings. For my views on this, see: Hammersley, 2003 and 2004.

2. Indeed, he complains about a 'methodological pestilence' (quoted in Oakes, 1975, p. 13) in German social science in the first decade of the twentieth century, with researchers becoming preoccupied with epistemological issues.

3. There is at least one other area where philosophy can make a very useful contribution that I will not discuss here, to do with research ethics.

4. These are best thought of as tendencies currently operating within the field; they certainly do not form an exhaustive pair of categories.

5. I will illustrate my arguments in this section by referring to the work of two currently influential authors: Stephen Gorard and Ian Stronach. My criticisms here are not intended to challenge all of their arguments. Furthermore, they are by no means unique in adopting the positions they do. They were selected because they recently engaged in a dispute with one another, and provide a sharp contrast in orientation within current educational research: see Gorard, 2005 and Stronach, 2005a, b.

6. Even if one believes that systematic comparison of the kind exemplified by the experiment is essential for causal analysis, and that educational research cannot avoid such analysis, it is important to recognise that there are additional requirements for validity, including those relating to description or measurement and to ecological generalisability. And, given that dealing with one methodological problem usually involves a trade-off against one's efforts to tackle others, any idea of a perfect single method, or combination of methods, is a mirage.

7. For an example of an educational researcher who has recently drawn on some of this literature in a sustained attempt to clarify these problems, see Maxwell, 2004. While Gorard does not employ the philosophical literature to address these issues in the book I am discussing here, he has done so elsewhere, see Gorard, 2002.

8. This rejection of science seems to generate much of the discussion that is to be found, for instance, in the latest edition of the *Handbook of Qualitative Research*: Denzin and Lincoln, 2005.

9. These other examples would include the methodological writings of Patti Lather and John K. Smith: Lather, 1991 and 1993; Smith, 1989 and 1993; Smith and Hodkinson, 2005.

10. Recent constructionist, relativist, and post-structuralist arguments need to be viewed in historical context as part of the waxing and waning of scepticism: see Popkin, 1979.

11. What he meant by 'value-neutrality' was that the exclusive immediate goal of research should be the production of knowledge.
12. For a fuller version of the argument that follows, and illustrations, see Foster *et al.*, 1996. See also Foster *et al.*, 2000.
13. The clearest presentation is in the *Nicomachean Ethics*, 1131a27, see Aristotle, 1925, p. 112.
14. From this point of view, the frequently drawn contrast between equality of opportunity and equality of outcome is rather misleading. In general, those who argue for equality of outcome are simply proposing a particular interpretation of equity of opportunity and/or a means of measuring it. This is clear in Halsey's (1981, p. 111) argument that, 'unless there is proof to the contrary, inequality of outcome in the social distribution of knowledge is a measure of *de facto* inequality of access' (see also Coleman, 1968). Rarely do proponents of equality of outcome argue explicitly that education is a good which can and should be equally distributed, in the way that educational expenditure or teacher attention can be—at least in principle. For a useful recent discussion of the complexities surrounding equity of opportunity, see Cavanagh, 2002.
15. Mackie has made much the same point about 'good': Mackie, 1977, chap. 2.
16. Here he is distinguishing between educational research and social science research on educational processes and institutions.
17. It may be that underlying Pring's position is the idea that ultimately all values belong to a single, internally coherent whole. Weber rejected that claim, and I believe he was right to do so. More recently, there have been other powerful arguments against it: see, for instance, Berlin, 1990; Mackie, 1977; and Larmore, 1987.
18. This appears in the 'Epistle to the Reader' at the beginning of his *Essay Concerning Human Understanding* (Locke, 1690).
19. An earlier version of this chapter was presented at a Symposium on Philosophy and Methodology of Educational Research at the British Educational Research Association Annual Conference, University of Glamorgan, September 2005. I am grateful to the participants in that symposium for their contributions, and to Stephen Gonard for his comments (though he will still not agree with my account of his argument here).

REFERENCES

Aristotle (1925) *The Nicomachean Ethics*, D. Ross, trans. (Oxford, Oxford University Press).
Berlin, I. (1990) *The Crooked Timber of Humanity* (London, Murray).
Bruun, H.-H. (1972) *Science, Values and Politics in Max Weber's Methodology* (Copenhagen, Munksgaard).
Cavanagh, M. (2002) *Against Equality of Opportunity* (Oxford, Oxford University Press).
Chalmers, I. (2003) Trying to Do More Good Than Harm in Policy and Practice: The role of rigorous, transparent, up-to-date evaluations, *Annals of the American Academy of Political and Social Science*, 589 September.
Coleman, J. (1968) The Concept of Equality of Opportunity, *Harvard Educational Review*, 38.1, pp. 7–22.
Denzin, N. K. and Lincoln, Y. S. (eds) (2005) *Handbook of Qualitative Research*, 3rd edn. (Thousand Oaks, CA, Sage).
Dews, P. (1987) *Logics of Disintegration: Post-structuralist thought and the claims of critical theory* (London, Verso).
Edwards, D., Ashmore, M. and Potter, J. (1995) Death and Furniture: The rhetoric, politics and theology of bottom line arguments against relativism, *History of the Human Sciences*, 8, pp. 25–49.
Ennis, R. (1978) Equality of Educational Opportunity, in: K. A. Strike and K. Egan (eds) *Ethics and Educational Policy* (London, Routledge and Kegan Paul).
Ferry, L. and Renaut, A. (eds) (1997) *Why We Are Not Nietzscheans* (Chicago, IL, University of Chicago Press), (First published in French in 1991).
Feyerabend, P. F. (1978) *Science in a Free Society* (London, New Left Books).
Fish, S. (1980) *Is There a Text in this Class: The authority of interpretive communities* (Cambridge, MA, Harvard University Press).

Foster, P., Gomm, R. and Hammersley, M. (1996) *Constructing Educational Inequality* (London, Falmer).

Foster, P., Gomm, R. and Hammersley, M. (2000) Case Studies as Spurious Evaluations: The example of research on educational inequalities, *British Journal of Educational Studies*, 48.3, pp. 215–30.

Gorard, S. (2001) *Quantitative Methods in Educational Research: The role of numbers made easy* (London, Continuum).

Gorard, S. (2002) The Role of Causal Models in Evidence-informed Policymaking and Practice, *Evaluation and Research in Education*, 16.1, pp. 51–65.

Gorard, S. (2005) How to Confuse a New Generation of Education Researchers, *Research Intelligence*, 89 November, pp. 9–10.

Haack, S. (1993) *Evidence and Inquiry: Towards a reconstruction of epistemology* (Oxford, Blackwell).

Haack, S. (1998) *Manifesto of a Passionate Moderate: Unfashionable essays* (Chicago, IL, University of Chicago Press).

Haack, S. (2003) *Defending Science–Within Reason: Between scientism and cynicism* (Amherst, NY, Prometheus Books).

Habermas, J. [1971] (1988) *Theory and Practice*, J. Viertel, trans. (Cambridge, Polity Press).

Habermas, J. [1987] (1990) *The Philosophical Discourse of Modernity*, F. Lawrence, trans. (Cambridge, Polity Press).

Halsey, A. H. (1981) *Change in British Society*, 2nd edn. (Oxford, Oxford University Press).

Hammersley, M. (1995) *The Politics of Social Research* (London, Sage).

Hammersley, M. (2003) Can and Should Educational Research be Educative?, *Oxford Review of Education*, 29.1, pp. 3–25.

Hammersley, M. (2004) Action Research: A contradiction in terms?, *Oxford Review of Education*, 30.2, pp. 165–81.

Hammersley, M. (2005) Is the Evidence-based Practice Movement Doing More Good than Harm? Reflections on Iain Chalmers' case for research-based policymaking and practice, *Evidence and Policy*, 1.1, pp. 1–16.

Keat, R. (1981) *The Politics of Social Theory: Habermas, Freud and the critique of positivism* (Oxford, Blackwell).

Larmore, C. (1987) *Patterns of Moral Complexity* (Cambridge, Cambridge University Press).

Lather, P. (1991) *Getting Smart: Feminist research and pedagogy with/in the postmodern* (New York, Routledge).

Lather, P. (1993) Fertile Obsession: Validity after poststructuralism, *Sociological Quarterly*, 34.4, pp. 673–93.

Locke, J. [1690] (1975) *Essay Concerning Human Understanding*, P. H. Nidditch, ed. (Oxford, Oxford University Press).

Mackie, J. L. (1977) *Ethics: Inventing right and wrong* (Harmondsworth, Penguin).

Mackinnon, D. (1986) Equality of Opportunity as Fair and Open Competition, *Journal of Philosophy of Education*, 20.1, pp. 69–71.

Maxwell, J. A. (2004) Causal Explanation, Qualitative Research, and Scientific Inquiry in Education, *Educational Researcher*, 33.2, pp. 3–11.

Oakes, G. (1975) Introductory Essay, in: M. Weber, *Roscher and Knies: The logical problems of historical economics* (New York, Free Press).

Polanyi, M. (1959) *Personal Knowledge* (Manchester, Manchester University Press).

Popkin, R. H. (1979) *The History of Scepticism from Erasmus to Spinoza* (Berkeley, CA, University of California Press).

Popper, K. R. (1987) On Toleration and Intellectual Responsibility, in: S. Mendus and D. Edwards (eds) *On Toleration* (Oxford, Oxford University Press).

Pring, R. (2000) *Philosophy of Educational Research* (London, Continuum).

Rickert, H. [1914] (1962) *Science and History*, English trans. (Princeton, NJ, Van Nostrand).

Searle, J. (1995) *The Construction of Social Reality* (Harmondsworth, Penguin).

Smith, J. K. (1989) *The Nature of Social and Educational Inquiry* (Norwood, NJ, Ablex).

Smith, J. K. (1993) *After the Demise of Empiricism: The problem of judging social and educational inquiry* (Norwood, NJ, Ablex).

Smith, J. K. and Hodkinson, P. (2005) Relativism, Criteria and Politics, in: Denzin and Lincoln (eds).

Stebbing, L. S. (1944) *Philosophy and the Physicists* (Harmondsworth, Penguin).

Strauss, L. (1953) *Natural Right and History* (Chicago, IL, University of Chicago Press).

Stronach, I. (2005a) Key Concepts, part of Miller, L., Whalley, J. B. and Stronach, I. From Structuralism to Poststructuralism, in: B. Somekh and C. Lewin (eds) *Research Methods in the Social Sciences* (London, Sage).

Stronach, I. (2005b) Reply to Stephen Gorard, *Research Intelligence*, 89 November, pp. 11–12.

Voegelin, E. [1952] (1987) *The New Science of Politics: An introduction* (Chicago, IL, University of Chicago Press).

Weldon, T. D. (1953) *The Vocabulary of Politics* (Harmondsworth, Penguin).

Westen, P. (1990) *Speaking of Equality: An analysis of the rhetorical force of 'equality' in moral and legal discourse* (Princeton, NJ, Princeton University Press).

Williams, B. (1962) The Idea of Equality, in: P. Laslett and W. G. Runciman (eds) *Philosophy, Politics and Society, 2nd Series* (Oxford, Blackwell).

Wittgenstein, L. (1969) *On Certainty* (Oxford, Blackwell).

18
US Graduate Study in Educational Research: From Methodology to Potential Totalization

LYNDA STONE

> Everywhere we remain unfree and chained to technology, whether we passionately affirm or deny it (Martin Heidegger, *The Question Concerning Technology*, 1954/1993).

INTRODUCTION

In his classic essay, 'The Question Concerning Technology', the German 20th century phenomenologist Martin Heidegger explicates a concept of 'the way'. He writes,

> We shall be *questioning* concerning technology. Questioning builds a way. The way is one of thinking ... through language ... We shall be questioning concerning technology and in so doing we should like to prepare a free relationship to it (Heidegger, 1954/1993, p. 311, emphasis in original).

Employed here as general frame of reference, contributions from Heidegger and others are offered in the chapter to follow as a 'way' to consider the relationship of technology to science, to persons, and to education. Contributing to the present volume on the state of education research, the specific focus is graduate study today for *educational researcher*s in the United States of America. The working premise is this: what graduate students learn determines what kind of researchers they become. Students tend to learn and to undertake research as their teachers learned and research; they are mentored into particular practices founded on particular belief systems. In contemporary education research, at least in a US context, the thesis of the chapter is that they learn principally and often exclusively about methodology. This 'way'—to use Heidegger's term—of training both 'technologizes' and potentially 'totalizes' research.

As foreshadow to the meaning of these terms and their use, the idea is that a methodological emphasis in research training turns process into narrowly construed preoccupation with technology that in turn portends limited research results.

There are, of course, other 'ways', other approaches, to considering the state of education research than by investigating graduate study. Focusing on education, these include intellectual histories of the field, accumulated results from specific educational research efforts, 'wisdom of practice' that generates research questions, and critiques of broader societal contexts and their impacts on education. In a 2003 piece in the influential journal, *Educational Researcher*, mathematics education researchers Hugh Burkhardt and Alan Schoenfeld name three general ways into doing research: the humanities approach, the science approach, and the engineering approach. For them, the first and 'oldest tradition ... has not worked well in practice' (Burkhardt and Schoenfeld, 2003, p. 5). The second has limitations because its products are assertions that, through testing, lead to additional assertions that do not in themselves 'generate practical solutions'. Instead they argue for the third, the engineering approach, with its long and respected history in such fields as medicine and electronics. Overlapping with the scientific approach, however, it appears to emphasize methodology in a technological sense as it produces 'tools and/or processes that work well for their intended uses and users' (ibid.). For present purposes, their three traditions might well be two.

Moreover, while there has always been some pluralism in approaches to research in education, this is currently being contested because of recent national US focus on and federal funding for 'scientifically based research' arising in the context of the accountability movement and specifically from the 2001 'No Child Left Behind' legislation. Except for occasional narrative testimony, 'science' as the paradigmatic source of information has nearly assumed hegemony in the policy arena. Significantly, governmental funding is tied to specific methodologies, that is, random assignment experimental and quasi-experimental designs that allow for replication (see Eisenhart and Towne, 2003, pp. 35, 36). The debate these developments have stimulated is centred on what counts as 'scientifically based' and more so on what other methodologies might be appropriate and fundable. What seems acceptable is a narrow range.

Based in the context just set out, this chapter is organized into two principal parts. In the first, the state of education research 'training' in the US is characterized with a claim that concentration on methodology has contributed to a kind of standardizing technology, what will be named 'technologization'. Its topics overview the organization and character of graduate study, the founding role of science, and the emphasis in training, through textbook exemplars, on methodology. In the second, attention is turned to technology in general and to its potential danger. Contributions from Heidegger and Jacques Ellul provide a frame of reference, and critiques from Henry Adams, Aldous Huxley, and Donna Haraway are the specific focus. Their theoretical writings, illuminating aspects of the relationships between science, technology and persons, posit the problem of 'totalization'. The chapter concludes with a suggestion that is intended to undermine a current over-emphasis on method in US graduate study in education research.

PART I

GRADUATE STUDY

The doctorate in the US has two forms, one for researchers and the other for continuing practitioners, the PhD and EdD respectively (see Richardson, 2003).[1] Those possessing doctorates in education share a central interest in the institution of education; they believe that it counts for social and individual good and that the institution requires and has possibility for improvement. In PhD programs topical focus varies but all recognize the importance of learning, teaching and schooling. Some conduct research on these realms specifically; others inquire either more broadly or narrowly. Processes and products, actions and accomplishments are among research preoccupations. Many seek direct application of their research results to educational practice, often as a matter of discovering 'what works'.[1]

Doctoral study consists of coursework and research internship that culminates in a dissertation. Along the way, future researchers work with mentors, advisors, project directors and more experienced peers. Many participate in supervised research prior to the dissertation project. Taking several years to complete, doctoral students typically undertake a program of study that helps establish a set of 'claims'. These are subspecialties that identify them for fit with faculty and research positions. Claims often relate to work in other disciplines besides education, education sub-fields, topics of study, and—importantly—methodological specialties. For example, a quantitative researcher in training has a Masters degree in statistics, is studying and utilizing advanced 'modeling' methods for application to the study of elementary classroom interactions.

Virtually all PhD study in education in the US is initiated through taught courses. These include an introduction to the field and often are organized around nationally published textbooks.[2] Examples indicate a shared definition of research. First, Donna Mertens writes, 'Research is a process of systematic inquiry that is designed to collect, analyze, interpret and use *data* to understand, describe, predict or control an educational or psychological phenomenon' (Mertens, 1998, p. 2, emphasis in original). Implied is both the empirical nature of research and its distinction from other forms of human inquiry. Second, Jack Fraenkel and Norman Wallen identify, as principal and potentially authoritative 'ways of knowing', ones that are based in sensory experience, others' views, expert opinion, and logic (Fraenkel and Wallen, 2003, pp. 4–6). Third, William Trochim (2001) claims that the interaction of empirical observation and measurement produces concept-related data on the basis of which theories can be formulated. This is effected through particular methodologies (Trochim, 2001, p. 4). What emerges from these examples is a rough, composite definition that, with the notion of 'methodologies' in the central place, becomes the 'standard' for all further coursework and research endeavors.

Students take required methodology courses first and foremost in quantitative methods and also in qualitative methods.[3] A first practical decision made by students concerns whether one is 'quantoid' or 'qualoid'; indeed students dig in and take pride in their membership of one 'camp' or the other. Also many have done empirical projects as Masters degree study. Quantitative courses entail not only initiation in general research strategies or techniques but also work in statistics. Typically there are many more courses and of more advanced levels in quantitative research than in qualitative. Qualitative courses still focus on 'how to do' research. In the sense of this chapter, both are technological. Moreover, except perhaps for a course in the history of education research itself, broad courses in history or philosophy or other foundations of education are most often electives—single offerings in which methodologies are seldom emphasized. In well-regarded programmes students do learn to apply excellent methods and they learn to modify and critique studies based on methodological flaws. What they seldom learn, however, is to question the entire science-research-methodology enterprise or to criticize its implicitly technological character.

SCIENCE IN EDUCATION RESEARCH

In modern philosophy, knowledge is typically defined as justified true belief; across the 20th century, knowledge and science became equated. In that relationship truth justification is through empirical processes of a universal scientific method. Furthermore since knowledge is foundational to education, it has generally come to be believed that education itself ought to be a science even while the meaning of this claim has remained 'elusive' (see Lagemann, 2000).

In response to federal legislation and funding, and particularly the 'No Child Left Behind' legislation of 2001 referred to above, a recent refocusing of research efforts in education was undertaken by the prestigious National Research Council (NRC).[4] Its 2002 report, *Scientific Research in Education*, then became a target of controversy but one which took the primacy of science in education largely for granted. How could one argue with this general articulation:

> To be scientific, the design . . . [of educational research] must allow direct, empirical investigation of an important question, account for the context in which the study is carried out, align with a conceptual framework, reflect careful and thorough reasoning, and disclose results to encourage debate in the scientific community (NRC, 2002, p. 6).

The NRC proposal is no simple positivist stance, no non-thoughtful use of scientific method. At the beginning of the 21st century, it reflects in sophisticated ways what the late historian Thomas Kuhn named 'normal science' (Kuhn, 1962/1970).

Utilizing Kuhn's term broadly, it is possible to discern a contemporary general form of normal science extant in US education research today. First, technology goes hand-in-hand with science and both are good for society. Second, given resources and past history of research, American know-how is 'exceptional' and continues to lead the world (see Ross, 1991). Third, the natural sciences serve as the model for the social and educational sciences. Fourth, methodological pluralism is acknowledged, yet the preeminence of quantitative methods continues. Fifth, post-positivist science acknowledges that truth as absolute is gone, generalizations do decay and human knowledge is fallible. Nonetheless, strong beliefs in cumulative results around individual topics remain; that is, there is continuing belief in small truths if not in some transcendental notion of truth. Sixth, the value of communal inquiry is great and some attention is paid to the idea of social construction. Seventh, there is even a general critical and political stance about research context: the question becomes 'who is researching for whom with whose interests in mind?'

Something more should be said about post-positivism in education research. Post-positivism as a philosophical perspective is a well-recognized corrective within philosophy of science and social science to the positivism of the early and middle decades of the 20th century. As a moderate position on knowledge formation, it theoretically retains the ideal of a pursuit of truth and knowledge. This is through emphasizing warranted assertability and allowing methods that are not solely experimental. The result is that knowledge becomes corrigible and none of its many sources is authoritative (see Phillips and Burbules, 2000, p. 26). Post-positivism, however, is largely found in philosophy, not in actual research practice. As James Paul notes, there remains a dominant 'positivist legacy' in US educational research (Paul, 2005, p. 1).

Graduate students tend to give post-positivist philosophy little more than lip-service because philosophy and/or philosophy of science are not typically part of their coursework. In their reaction to post-positivism, they are confused about truth, especially as participants in a general social context that recognizes relative cultural values. Then, while acknowledging their own and others' cultural influences, they have trouble with 'theoryladenness' (Hanson, 1958), still possessing a naïve faith in 'what they see'. Seeing, after all, is central to observation, central to empirical method, central to studying 'reality'. Next, influenced by the prevailing research ideology, they have mixed views about their own subjectivity: on the one hand, researcher agency is significant (they are becoming researchers!), while on the other hand its 'bias' can be overcome through objective method. Moreover there is little talk about research falsification as empirical inquiry is clearly a process of winners. One determines results not errors, even with the language of the null hypothesis (compare Mackenzie in this issue). Overall research domains develop definition largely through accretion and refinement; methodological tinkering is emphasized. Relatedly, there is also attention to the rationality that underlies research, as students question the idea of a universal form of reasoning, believing in 'minority' viewpoints. However they make an exception in considering their own logic, take it for granted, and do not think of it as one kind of rationality among others. Finally, even when they do value methodological pluralism they see it as limited in scope. At the last, post-positivism cannot overcome an obvious disconnection in their training between what graduate students distinguish as 'theory and practice'. It does not seem to matter that this post-positivist 'orientation' to science and research (Phillips and Burbules, 2000, pp. 25–26) offers a comprehensive, moderate base by which their own preoccupation with methodology might helpfully be informed.

METHODOLOGY

To begin, the terms 'method' and 'methodology' are used in graduate study and in education research itself in several ways. That 'something has method ... [is an assertion] that there is an order, a regularity ... that underlies an apparent disorder, thus rendering it meaningful' (Shulman, 1988/1997, p. 7), while methodology is the collective term (see Trochim, 2001, p. 348). Research 'methods' are specific sub-units, such as designs, techniques, and skills and, as well, their larger systemic organization into traditions. In general, present-day usage of 'method' means process, a regularly planned, systematic set of procedural steps. Finally, the term also means the science of method, of systematic classification.[5]

As indicated, graduate students take initial coursework in which methodological 'traditions' are divided into the quantitative and qualitative. In the introductory textbooks methodology is presented in two parts, as general processes of research that underlie both the qualitative and quantitative traditions and as specific designs or approaches that differentiate the two. Thus students are not-so-subtly urged to focus on a particular tradition (even if they ultimately use mixed methods), to specialize in specific designs and develop expertise, and in more advanced work to refine their methods. Repeating the central claim of this chapter, what results overall in their training is valorization of methodology that becomes for many 'methodolotry'. It entails emphasis on standardization that turns methodology into an unnecessarily narrow conception of technology.

A perusal of introductory textbooks on education research reveals this overwhelming discursive and practical attention to methodology. In texts ranging in size from 360 to 650 pages, the two traditions of methodology roughly occupy between 54% and 91% of a book. Turning to general processes, methodological designs or approaches are most often organized as the two traditions along with 'others' including evaluation and action research, and sometimes, historical research. Of the two, quantitative designs occupy a ratio of two to one or greater in coverage, with the largest difference four to one. A typical example of design is 'experimental research' in a 2005 edition of Gall, Gall and Borg's book, *Applying Educational Research: A Practical Guide*. The text encourages the reader to: explain steps in conducting experiments, indicate differences in types of experiments, understand threats to internal validity and relevant aspects of external validity, and overview common design forms (Gall, Gall, and Borg, 1999/2005, see beginning p. 248). Across all design forms in this section and others there is a strongly technical vocabulary.

Standard texts further demonstrate that in effect the logic and vocabulary of quantitative method is often the basis for the formulation of qualitative method. Others have recognized the dominance of the quantitative even as they pose alternative methods. For example, in the 1988 edition of *Complementary Methods for Research in Education* published by the American Educational Research Association (AERA), authors Tom Barone and Elliot Eisner, famous for 'Arts-Based Research', address issues according to the conventional logic of reliability, validity, and generalization even as they note that these terms and their assumptions may be inappropriate for their own method (Barone and Eisner, 1988, p. 85). Incidentally, a third edition of this 'introductory text' with a relatively moderate stance toward multiple methodologies has just been published by AERA (see Green, Camilli and Elmore, 2006).

The second methodological element, a general process of how to conduct research, is organized textually in a relatively narrow range of ways. To emphasize, as textbooks are set out, students are to marry a broad understanding of process to the idea of designs forming a seamless conception of methodology. The process or logic is recognized as 'the scientific method'. Few assume today that there is a simplistic linear step-by-step model of the research process; one can tinker with each step if necessary to conduct inquiry. But, it must also be noticed that a nearly homogeneous general process is reflected in standard reporting formulations (for grants, in journals, at AERA etc.), and that there is a related form for dissertations that is required by education departments, schools, and colleges very widely in the US.

Two examples of the standard research process help make the point. The first, from the National Research Council mentioned above, lists particular 'norms' that constitute steps: asking significant empirical questions (often 'a' or 'the' question), linking research to relevant theory (undertaking a literature review), employing methods appropriate to the question (refining through the literature and selecting among possibilities), providing reasoning (linking observational data to theory through analysis of evidence), replicating and generalizing studies (integrating and synthesizing across time and place) (NRC, 2002, introduction, pp. 3–5).[6] Another formulation (see Trochim, 2001, beginning p. 14) prescribes a 'structure' of research that begins with broad questions, narrows down focus to operationalize (puts what is to be studied in concrete form), observes, collects and analyzes data, reaches conclusions and generalizes back to questions. Whether expressed in terms of norm or structure, it is clear that such prescriptions constitute 'the standard' for research for students and practising researchers. While it is interesting to see that 'methods' are not directly listed by that name in either of these norm or structure based approaches, the move to early determination of a question that they emphasize can also overly standardize—and thus unduly limit— research.

PART II

TECHNOLOGY

In Part I, the preoccupation with and indeed domination of methodology in education research graduate study in the US has been described. It has been argued that there is 'standardization' of methodology in researcher preparation, with 'method' as a virtually ubiquitous preoccupation, as 'means' or procedure, tools and steps of research. Thus method is connected to technology and to a standardizing process of 'technologiza- tion'. This awkward term is used to emphasize that there exists a nearly unitary model, a 'tool-box' for learning about and doing research.[7]

In Part II of this chapter, the turn is to the issue of technology itself. The topic is introduced with reference to two European theorists, Martin Heidegger and Jacques Ellul, who analyze technology's essential meaning and societal influence. Then three critical stances toward technology that bring out ways it is related to nature, science and persons are presented, from Henry Adams, Aldous Huxley, and Donna Haraway. Each and in combination is meant to point to a danger of the movement of technologizing toward totalization. 'Technologization' constitutes a system necessity that takes on a life of its own, is valued in and of itself. Totality or totalization, a potential if not a present actuality, is the result of technologization, the emergence of a conception of education itself that is limited, unduly bounded, and not inviting of alternatives and diversities. At the least, 'No Child Left Behind' legislation in the US in the present moment appears to have this impact.

To begin, something should be said about the recent context of technology and its development. Science dominated the 20th century bringing civilization, many believe, to a level of progress unimagined in previous eras. However, the thoughtful have come to recognize that science has limits: hunger and disease still prevail, natural disasters occur, war continues. Adulation of science has become more cautious at least since the dropping of the atomic bomb in 1945; in general science can provide no guarantee of perfection. The desire for prediction and power over human social life however is still strong, and this is particularly shown in the admiration for and the continuing 'advancement' of technology. Better instruments make better science; in the common mind, technology is science.

For present purposes a very useful introduction to 'technology' is that developed by Heidegger in an essay written at mid-century, mentioned at the outset of this chapter. He begins with the statement that 'technology is not equivalent to the essence of technology' (Heidegger, 1954/1993, p. 311): that is, technology has a fundamental being that is not apparent in the examples of technology around us. Its essence is related to common meanings, as means to end and as human activity, but is not equivalent to them. These common meanings of 'technology', however, point to the 'will to mastery' of human control that is blind to 'the true essence' of technology. It is the latter which, as commentator David Krell explains, 'is nothing technological' (Krell, 1977/1993, p. 309) in our ordinary sense of the word. Krell indicates the possibility of realizing a free relationship of persons to technology that Heidegger theorizes but recognizes is not easily achievable in our time.

Based in his previous work on the history and essence of mathematical science (Heidegger, 1936/1993). Heidegger describes the steps to understanding technology's essence as the following. First, technology as means has instrumental connection to cause and to a history in western thought that is fourfold. The four causes are material, form, end and effect. For Heidegger, these causes, belonging together, constitute 'ways ... of being responsible for something else' (Heidegger, 1954/1977, 1993, p. 314). Second, this responsibility has its own unity, its primal meaning, 'starting something on its way into arrival' (p. 316), into appearance through 'bringing-forth'. Third, bringing-forth is revealing, unconcealing, 'correctness of representation' or 'truth' (p. 318). Technology, even with instrumentality as its principal characteristic, then, is 'no mere means'. It is rather, fourth, the way of revealing. Heidegger summarizes his argument thus far that 'technology comes to presence in the realm where revealing and unconcealment take place, where ... truth happens' (p. 319). Thus essence is substantiated when the roots and meaning of *techne* are themselves explicated. Fifth, there is a particular character to modern technology, revealed as 'setting upon' or 'challenging forth' (p. 321) that leads to negative results for humankind.

In an important move, Heidegger then asserts that modern technology differs from past relationships to nature; now nature's energy must be 'extracted'. He writes, 'unlocking, transforming, storing, distributing, and switching about are ways of revealing. But the revealing never simply comes to an end. The revealing reveals to itself its own manifoldly interlocking paths, through regulating their course. This regulating itself is ... everywhere secured' (p. 322). The impact of regulating is that everything is ordered, to be on call for further ordering; it forms an all-inclusive 'standing reserve' (ibid.). Finally, man takes part in the revealing, in the ordering, but he has no control over unconcealment itself. Heidegger explains that 'when man, investigating, observing, pursues nature as an area of his own conceiving, he has already been claimed by a way of revealing that challenges him to approach nature as an object of research, until even the object disappears into the objectlessness of standing reserve' (p. 324). This claiming he names 'enframing'. Enframing, and what might be a response to modern technology, is returned to in the conclusion of this chapter. Meanwhile,

Heidegger's point is that technology today organizes being, structures consciousness. It is much more than the pervasiveness of actual technological 'methods', apparatuses and processes.

The French social philosopher and theologian Jacques Ellul also posits that technology, what he names 'technique', is everywhere. His opening definition is this: 'Technique is the totality of methods rationally arrived at and having absolute efficiency (for a given stage of development) in every field of human activity' (Ellul, 1954/1964, p. xxv). Ellul describes the 'characterology' and historical development of technique through the economy, relative to the state, and as regulating human social life in his classic text, *The Technological Society*.

Several of Ellul's points have particular relevance here. The first concerns the way in which the conventional relationship between technology and science is reversed and technique is understood historically to precede the appearance of science. In the early modern era, science fostered the growth of technique but again the relationship has changed. Ellul writes that 'in fact, scientific activity has been superseded by technical activity to such a degree that we can no longer conceive of science without its technical outcome' (pp. 9–10). In his view, the terms have become synonymous. A second takes up the application of technique to social life including the economy and bureaucracy in which the former is the 'organization' that is both standardized and rationalized. He quotes the French sociologist, Antoine Mas: '[standardization] means resolving *in advance* all the problems that might possibly impede the functioning of an organization' (p. 11, emphasis in original). Drawing on but disagreeing with the British historian Arnold Toynbee, Ellul further identifies the consequences of application: this is the development of technical organization in which new problems are based in the very methods that created them in the first place. Thus there is assimilation of everything to the machine, based in the ideal that 'technique strives ... for mechanization of everything it encounters' (p. 12). A third is that technique has become autonomous, constituting a form of social reality independent of persons that nonetheless encompasses them. Indeed Ellul confesses, 'I am keenly aware that I am myself involved in technological civilization, and that its history in my own' (See Ellul, 'Author's Forward to the Revised American Edition, 1964, p. xxvii). Fundamentally 'we' are conditioned by a technological civilization in which we are potentially destined to live trivial technical lives (see pp. xxviii–xxix, p. 14). A fourth point is a definitional distinction between technical operation and technical phenomenon. The former, idealized in efficiency, is for 'every operation ... [to be] carried out in accordance with a certain method in order to attain a particular end' (Ellul, 1954/1964, p. 19). The latter, as 'one best means', is 'the main preoccupation of our time ... [in which] in every field men seek to find the most efficient method' (p. 21), entailing rational judgment, consciousness, and specialization. According to Ellul, 'a science of means comes into being' extending so that no human activity escapes 'this technical imperative' (ibid.). In the same spirit as Heidegger, the purpose of Ellul's theorizing is to intervene against technologization.

THREE CRITIQUES OF TECHNOLOGY

The writings of Heidegger and Ellul focus critical attention on the role of technology in 20th century western society. Across the century many writers considered technology and the more general question of its relationship to science and to persons. Sociologists such as Max Weber, C. Wright Mills and Robert Merton (who wrote the introduction to Ellul's *Technological Society*) conducted analyses similar to Ellul's. Others come out of more humanistic traditions in history, literature and philosophy. In this section, three perspectives are overviewed, each taking up in a unique way the issues of standardization and potential 'totalization' through technology. Both Heidegger and Ellul recognize dangers from universally unifying means or 'methodologies'. Additional contributions to this general stance come from Adams at the century's beginning, Huxley from the middle decades, and Haraway near the century's end.

Writing about a half century prior to Heidegger and Ellul, and from within an American literary tradition, the nationalist historian Henry Adams takes up his own exploration of totality, of 'Unity', that incorporates science and technology relative to the social order. His significant text is *The Education of Henry Adams* (1918/1946), 'part autobiography, part novel, part philosophy, and part social commentary' (Young, 2001, p. 9), in which the chapter 'The Dynamo and the Virgin' is best known. The theme here is 'force', indeed the new force epitomized for Adams in his visit to the hall of dynamos, the giant engines, at the Great Exposition at Paris in 1900. As commentator John Young explains, the historian 'was mesmerized, attracted, repelled, and almost paralyzed by the technological developments he saw as the driving force in western history' (pp. 7–8). Adams writes of the dynamo as a symbol of infinity, itself named variously as force and unity. A chief theme line in *Education* is Adams's later life-project of seeking 'order' (see Kariel, 1956, p. 1075) for the new century and his explorations of various forms of force as possibilities. Among these are religion (in the symbol of the Virgin), womanhood and science.

In his quest, Adams names himself a failure, for not succeeding in identification of a unity. Overall he came to see that 'nothing was stable, not even the precedence of the Adams family' (Brogan, 1961, p. xi), his Boston Brahmin lineage.[8] He came to see that human control of the natural as well as the social worlds was impossible. He came to discern a break from the old world order in his day and, still more, perceived that he 'no longer fit'. Adams writes,

> The child of 1900 would . . . be born into a new world which would not be a unity . . . . [In it] order was an accidental relation obnoxious to nature; artificial compulsion imposed on motion; against which every free energy of universe revolted; and which, being occasional, resolved back into anarchy at last (Adams, 1918/1946, pp. 457–458).

In a very useful essay, the American political scientist Henry Kariel claims that Adams almost despaired of his search but stopped short of either mysticism or self-destruction. He explains,

Adams counseled either control of conflicting ... forces in terms of a determinate, absolute law or else suspension of all articulation .... [In spite of this position] he never ceased taking part in the perennial human debate and thus never completed his alienation from society, hanging on as its diffident participant while ever departing from it (Kariel, 1956, pp. 1089, 1086).

One last point concerning Adams's interest in science and its place in his theorizing is in order. In *Education*, he analyzes the accomplishments of modern scientists for insight into force and unity and for supporters of his dynamic theory of history: these range from Bacon to Darwin, to Karl Pearson, the father of modern statistics. For Adams, the physical sciences assume metaphoric centrality:

Man is a force; so is the sun; so is a mathematical point .... Man commonly ... [takes] for granted that he captures the forces. A dynamic theory, assigning attractive force to opposing bodies, takes for granted that the forces of nature capture man .... [The] feeble atom ... called man is attracted; ... he is the sum of forces that attract him; his body and his thought are alike their product ... since he can know nothing but the motions ... whose sum makes education (Adams, 1918/1946, p. 474).

Even with a law of acceleration that Adams attributes to scientific advance of his day, he realizes that science itself holds no unity. As he puts it, 'In 1900 ... [scientists] were plainly forced back on faith in a unity unproved and an order they had themselves disproved' (p. 495). What is needed, in applying this lack of unity to the world in general, is 'a new social mind', and a new 'education', a contribution surely that he could not make. Drawing on his dynamic theory of history, Adams concludes by suggesting a future political order. 'New forces', he contends, 'would educate' and might well be 'violently coercive' (pp. 497, 498); about such totalitarian possibilities one commentator names Adams a 'prophetic genius' (Brogan, 1961, p. xvii).

Written several decades later, the second text, Aldous Huxley's novel, *Brave New World*, manifests what becomes the emblematic fictional picture of totalitarian society as an outcome of advancements in science and technology. The standardized unity or totality in this new world is stability, expressed at one point by the regional leader, the Controller, in these terms: '[Stability.] The primal and the ultimate need .... No civilization without social stability. No social stability without individual stability' (Huxley, 1932/1946, pp. 43, 42).

The novel takes place in a London of the near future in which various lives are disrupted by the presence of persons who are different. There are several shades of difference, ranging from desires for sexual excitement to great unorthodoxy. The latter, this time according to another authority, the Director of the Hatchery and Conditioning Centre, 'strikes at Society itself' (p. 148). Unorthodoxy is especially central to the lives of chief characters, Bernard Marx and Helmholtz Watson, each of whom struggle with 'being individuals'. In the story, they interact in everyday affairs of the society but also with significant others. Bernard attempts but fails to become accepted both romantically and socially; Helmholtz ultimately rejects conventional social life. The former is devastated, the latter resigned. Both also meet and become friends with John, The Savage, who comes into their London world from another—a reservation. This place, peopled by Indians and half-breeds, has 'no communication whatever with the civilized world ... [and still preserves] ... repulsive habits and customs ... [such as marriage and childbirth]' (p. 103) ... [containing] families ... no conditioning ... monstrous superstitions ... infectious diseases ... priests' (ibid.). John, actually born in the 'Brave New World', has grown up away but ultimately travels back with his mother, Linda. Ugly, very unlike the conventionally standardized women of the story such as the 'romantic' heroine Lenina and her friend Fanny, Linda suffers a terrible death. This allows her son to see the horrors of this 'New World' that lead to his own suicide at the end.

The principal figures each respond to societal standardization resulting from the impact of science and technology in social planning. In the book's Forward, Huxley writes that it is about 'the advancement of science as it affects human individuals'. In this future moment, 'triumphs of physics, chemistry, and engineering are tacitly taken for granted ... [while attention is to results of research] in biology, physiology, and psychology' (Huxley, 1946, p. xi). Consider this process of reproduction and its outcome:

> On a very slowly moving band a rack-full of testtubes was entering a large metal box .... Machinery faintly purred. It took eight minutes for the tubes to go through ... Eight minutes of hard x-rays being about as much as an egg can stand. A few died ... most put out four buds; some eight; all were returned to the incubators where the buds began to develop .... [This was] Bokanovsky's Process .... Standard men and women; in uniform batches. The whole of a small factory staffed with products of a single ... egg .... Ninety-six identical twins working ninety-six identical machines!' (Huxley, 1932, 1946, pp. 6, 7).

Such a society, explains the Controller, 'has chosen machinery and medicine and happiness' (p. 234), even self-indulgence, over nobility or heroism or even common emotion. There are no wars and no great loves. He declares, '[You're] so conditioned that you can't help doing what you ought to do. And what you ought to do is on the whole so pleasant ... that there really aren't any temptations to resist' (p. 237). In the story there is no positive human response to this societal totality.

Across the century, a western tradition in 'science studies' develops in which various debates concern the relationship of 'science and society'. This latter idiom, focusing on two primary entities, appears inadequate in dealing with complex theoretical matters of unity, foundationalism, neutrality, objectivity, and constructionism in science (see Hacking, 1999). In the 19th century up to the time of Adams, nature and science were symbiotic but seen as separate from persons. In the era and genre of

Huxley, science and technology are seen as directly and completely controlling society. A third perspective is located in the writings of the American philosopher, Donna Haraway.

From within a particular viewpoint of feminist techno-science studies, Haraway offers the trope of the 'cyborg', what amounts through implicit critique to a new 'unity'. It is a non-unity-unity, the term borrowed from cybernetics researchers Manfred Clynes and Nathan Kline, who in 1960 posited the need for an 'enhanced man—a cyb(ernectic) org(anism)—who could survive in extraterrestial environments' in space (Haraway, 2000b/ 2004d, p. 204). '[In our] time, a mythic time' . . . Haraway explains, 'we are all chimeras, theorized hybrids of machine and organism; in short, we are cyborgs' (Haraway, 1991, p. 150). Taken principally from science fiction but realized actually in such arenas as medicine and the military, cyborgs are 'creatures' who are both animal/man and machine living in worlds of ambiguous social relations. For Haraway, '[the] cyborg is a condensed image of both imagination and material reality, the two joined centers structuring any possibility of historical transformation' (ibid.). They are both figurative and literal, with 'a physicality that is undeniable and deeply historically specific' (Haraway, 2000a/2004c, p. 323). Central to the concept of the cyborg is 'blurring'; Haraway names three kinds of blurring: between animal and human, animal-human and machine, and physical and non-physical, kinds that are already existing and not, visible and not. Pertinently, she asserts that 'late twentieth century machines . . . have made thoroughly ambiguous the difference between natural and artificial, mind and body, self-developing and externally designed . . . . [Continuing, ironically our] machines are disturbingly lively, and we ourselves frighteningly inert' (Haraway, 1991, p. 152). Significantly, to pose the trope of the cyborg makes science itself political—not just something which may have political impact.

Haraway's cyborg signifies a new relationship between science and technology and persons. It is emphatically not that man has conquered machines, or that machines have conquered him as in Huxley's vision, nor that humankind has formed a synthesis with nature as was Adams' desire. The cyborg is 'new' science. Haraway explains, 'Science is practice and culture . . . . There is no core, only layers . . . . Everything is supported, but there is no final foundation' (Haraway, 2000b/2004d, p. 201; see also Haraway, 1992/2004a). As practice, science is both materially 'solid' and discursively 'liquid', incorporating aspects of culture that are at once historical, technical and political. For her science is about physicality with material effects; it is about culturally constructed meaning; it is about a particular historical moment, specific technologies, and the doing of politics. What results is scientific practice that is always ambiguous and changing and 'might be otherwise' (Haraway, 2000a/2004c, p. 326), and, significantly, in a culture that also might be different.

Acknowledging the always-ambiguous 'nature' of science has two results. The first is an altered form of its own operation. In this regard, Haraway has something additional to offer, in a revised form of 'objectivity'. In a paper from the late 1980s, she posits 'situated knowledges', in which 'only partial perspective . . . [not a transcendent now archaic unity] promises objective vision' (Haraway, 1988/1999, p. 177). The joining together of many partial perspectives, in webs of connections and shared conversations, produces a new form of scientific objectivity, one of practice not abstract ideal. The second is an altered phenomenon that recognizes its own political character. The cyborg itself is 'an act of resistance' (Haraway, 2000a/2004c, p. 321), a tool (a technology!) and a symbol that intervention is always possible, but not, in today's complex world, something simple.

CONCLUSION

The thesis of this chapter has been that US graduate study in education research entails a standardized over-emphasis on methodology. Such way of training technologizes method as both scientific process and specific techniques. The overall danger is that what results is a narrow view of research that limits possibilities for educational change and reform.

The chapter closes with a continued use of insights from the theorists from Part II. Heidegger, Ellul, Adams, Huxley and Haraway all recognize the potential for totalization from science and technology, and their writings help dramatize and make vivid that potential, negatively and positively. They help us, concerned both with education research training and beyond, to see what we may otherwise fail to notice. Taken chronologically across the 20th century, their insights into the relationships between science, technology and persons are as follows. Adams hopes for a positive totalization, the unification of a changing culture, and is nearly paralyzed in his historical 'discovery' that one is not possible. Huxley describes the ultimate negative totalization and fictionally in humanistic terms 'sees no way out'. Significantly, in his 1946 Forward he suggests another way of life for Savage. It is one in which '[science] and technology would be used as though . . . they had been made for man', not (at present and still more so in the Brave New World) as though man were to be adapted and enslaved to them (Huxley, 1946, p. ix, parenthesis in original).

The contributions of Heidegger and Ellul, both from the 1950s, explore technology as a basic human and societal presence, a pervasive phenomenon that has advanced nearly to the point of totality. In Ellul's closing comment on the future, he points to possible negative 'solutions' from within technology itself. Ironically, he suggests the possibility by the year 2000 of 'a golden age' of control and standardization, that is 'a future Huxley never dreamed of' (Ellul, 1954/1964, p. 433), as if yet further totalizing were possible. Heidegger's conclusion about the essence of technology contrasts with that of Ellul; his hope for positive intervention in technological domination in some ways prefigures Haraway's positive politics. Both require some concluding attention. First, the 'enframing' of technology that Heidegger writes of—the box that we find it hard to think outside of, as we might put it in today's terms—does not wholly deprive us of the capacity for questioning. Through questioning and 'listening' is revealed a 'free space' in which there is potential for danger *and* for a saving power. Danger comes in misconstruing the unconcealed as essence, that is God, Nature or Man; this is another sign of the ordering of technology. A saving power comes from understanding that 'enframing' is also potentially 'the granting that lets man endure . . . [so] that he may be the one who . . . is used for the safekeeping of the essence of truth' (p. 338). For Heidegger this is done through 'thinking', reflection through art that points to 'the bringing forth of the true into the beautiful' (p. 339). Here results the 'free relationship' to technology that this chapter sketches as an ideal.

Haraway's 'freedom' is a form of politics. She recognizes the potential power of language for positive change. Borrowing from the Russian formalist of the early century, Mikhail Bakhtin, her own 'technology' is *topos*, a rhetorical site. She creates such a space with the technological trope of the cyborg, pointing to a general 'contingency, thickness, inequality, incommensurability, and a dynamism of cultural systems of reference through which people enroll each other in their realities' (Haraway, 1997/2004b, p. 241). The cyborg's own blurred 'identity' undermines established categories of 20th century meaning; it shifts the relationship of nature, science, technology, and persons. It speaks to a cultural politics of intervention, of 'altering' a potential technological totalization.

Such intervention provides a significant lesson for graduate study in education research in the US. No one is claiming that a brave new world exists at present but there is overwhelming emphasis on methodology and a standardization that pervades initial training if not conventional research practice. The issue is not the familiar one of quantitative versus qualitative methods. It is rather that what counts is method itself, method that has become technologized. The concluding suggestion of this chapter is that what is needed is a new politics of education research, a kind of radical stance in which methodology is questioned. Questioning its potential totalization well might open up different possibilities for practical research that can reform present day education. At the least the very narrow context of 'No Child Left Behind' research can be broadened. At the least the preoccupation with empirical methodology can be altered. And, at the last, a start might be made toward undermining the domination of from empirical research as the sole basis for educational and social change.[9]

NOTES

1. See the collection from editors, Paul Smeyers and Marc Depaepe, *Educational Research: Why 'What Works' Doesn't Work*.
2. Textbooks overviewed for this interpretation are the following (many have previous editions): Best and Kahn, 2003; Fraenkel and Wallen, 2003; Gall, Gall and Borg, 1999/2005; Gall, Gall and Borg, 1963/2003; Glaser and Strauss, 1967/1999; Mertens, 1998; Scheurich, 1997/2001; Trochim, 2001.

3. Anecdotal evidence for much of this discussion is garnered from teaching a doctoral core course for many years. I note here that those who do not desire to be empirical researchers, such as philosophers, have no identity within this methodological duality.
4. NRC is related to the American Academies of Science.
5. Here discussion is informed by the *Oxford English Dictionary*.
6. A last norm is to open research to peer criticism.
7. The aspiration to develop such a methodological 'tool-box' goes back at least as far as Francis Bacon: see Richard Smith, 'As if by Machinery: The Levelling of Educational Research', in the first Special Issue.
8. For those unfamiliar with American history, this is the family of Samuel, John and John Quincy Adams, respectively a revolutionary leader and two presidents. Henry Adams's father was US Ambassador to England.
9. Thanks for assistance with this chapter from Silvia Bettez, Kathie Engelbrecht, Jim Diana, Dan Huff, Judith Meece, George Noblit, Jim Marshall, Paul Smeyers, Lynn Vernon-Fagens, and editors, David Bridges and especially Richard Smith.

REFERENCES

Adams, H. [1918] (1946) *The Education of Henry Adams: An Autobiography* (Boston, MA, Houghton Mifflin).

Barone, T. and Eisner, E. [1988] (1997) Arts-Based Educational Research, in: R. Jaeger (ed.) *Complementary Methods for Research in Education*, 2nd edn. (Washington, DC, American Educational Research Association).

Best, J. and Kahn, J. [1959] (2003) *Research in Education*, 9th edn. (Boston, MA, Pearson).

Brogan, W. (1961) Introduction. *The Education of Henry Adams: An Autobiography* (Boston, Houghton Mifflin).

Burkhardt, H. and Schoenfeld, A. (2003) Improving Educational Research: Toward a More Useful, More Influential, and Better-Funded Enterprise, *Educational Researcher*, 32.9, pp. 3–14.

Eisenhart, M. and Towne, L. (2003) Contestation and Change in National Policy on 'Scientifically Based' Education Research, *Educational Researcher*, 32.7, pp. 31–38.

Ellul, J. [1954] (1964) *The Technological Society* (New York, Vintage), Originally published in French.

Ellul, J. (1964) Author's Forward to the Revised American Edition, in: *The Technological Society* (New York, Vintage).

Fraenkel, J. and Wallen, N. [1990] (2003) *How to Design and Evaluate Research in Education*, 5th edn. (New York, McGraw-Hill Higher Education).

Gall, J., Gall, M. and Borg, W. [1999] (2005) *Applying Educational Research: A Practical Guide*, 5th edn. (Boston, MA, Pearson).

Gall, M., Gall, J. and Borg, W. [1963] (2003) *Educational Research: An Introduction*, 7th edn. (Boston, MA, Pearson Education).

Glaser, B. and Strauss, A. [1967] (1999) *The Discovery of Grounded Theory: Strategies for Qualitative Research* (New York, Aldine de Gruyter).

Green, J., Camilli, G. and Elmore, P. (2006) Complementary Methods in Educational Research, 3rd edn. (Washington, DC, American Educational Research Association and Lawrence Erlbaum).

Hacking, I. (1999) *The Social Construction of What?* (Cambridge, MA, Harvard University Press).

Hanson, N. (1958) *Patterns of Discovery* (Cambridge, Cambridge University Press).

Haraway, D. (1991) A Cyborg Manifesto: Science, Technology, and the Socialist-Feminist in the Late Twentieth Century, in: *Simians, Cyborgs, and Women: The Reinvention of Nature* (New York, Routledge).

Haraway, D. [1992] (2004a) Otherworldly Conversations; Terrain Topics; Local Terms, in: *The Haraway Reader* (New York, Routledge).

Haraway, D. [1997] (2004b) Modest_Witness@Second _Millennium, in: *The Haraway Reader* (New York, Routledge).

Haraway, D. [1988] (1999) Situated Knowledges: The Science Question in Feminism and the Privilege of Partial Perspective, in: M. Biagoli (ed.) *The Science Studies Reader* (New York, Routledge).

Haraway, D. [2000a] (2004c) Cyborgs, Coyotes, and Dogs: A Kinship of Feminist Figurations. Part I, An Interview with Donna Haraway, by N. Lykke, R. Markhussen, and F. Olesen, in: *The Haraway Reader* (New York, Routledge).

Haraway, D. [2000b] (2004d) Morphing in the Order: Flexible Strategies, Feminist Science Studies, and Primate Visions, in: *The Haraway Reader* (New York, Routledge).

Heidegger, M. [1936] (1993) Modern Science, Metaphysics, and Mathematics, in: *Basic Writings*, trans. W. Lovitt and D. Krell (San Francisco, CA, Harper).

Heidegger, M. [1954] (1993) The Question Concerning Technology, in: *Basic Writings*, trans. W. Lovitt and D. Krell (San Francisco, Harper).

Huxley, A. [1932] (1946) *Brave New World* (New York, Perennial Classics).

Huxley, A. (1946) Forward. *Brave New World* (New York, Perennial Classics).

Kariel, H. (1956) The Limits of Social Science: Henry Adams' Quest for Order, *The American Political Science Review*, 50.4, pp. 1074–1092.

Krell, D. [1977] (1993) General Introduction: The Question of Being, in: *Martin Heidegger, Basic Writings* (San Francisco, CA, Harper).

Kuhn, T. [1962] (1970) *The Structure of Scientific Revolutions*, 2nd edn. (Chicago, IL, The University of Chicago Press).

Lagemann, E. (2000) *An Elusive Science: The Troubling History of Education Research* (Chicago, IL, The University of Chicago Press).

Mertens, D. (1998) *Research Methods in Education and Psychology: Integrating Diversity with Quantitative and Qualitative Approaches* (Thousand Oaks, CA, Sage).

National Research Council. (2002) *Scientific Research in Education* (Washington, DC, National Academy Press).

Paul, J. (2005) *Introduction to the Philosophies of Research and Criticism in Education and the Social Sciences* (Upper Saddle River, NJ, Pearson).

Phillips, D. and Burbules, N. (2000) *Post-Positivism and Educational Research* (Lanham, MD, Rowman & Littlefield).

Richardson, V. (2003) *Carnegie Essays on the Doctorate: Education* (Stanford, CA, The Carnegie Foundation for the Advancement of Teaching).

Ross, D. (1991) *The Origins of American Social Science* (Cambridge, Cambridge University Press).

Scheurich, J. [1997] (2001) *Research Method in the Postmodern* (London, RoutledgeFalmer).

Shulman, L. [1988] (1997) Disciplines of Inquiry in Education: A New Overview, in: R. Jaeger (ed.) *Complementary Methods for Research in Education*, 2nd edn. (Washington, DC, American Educational Research Association).

Smeyers, P. and Depaepe, M. (2006) *Educational Research: Why 'What Works' Doesn't Work* (Dordrecht, Springer).

Smith, R. (2006) As if by Machinery: The Levelling of Educational Research, *Journal of Philosophy of Education*, 40.2, pp. 157–168.

Trochim, W. (2001) *The Research Methods Knowledge Base*, 2nd edn. (Cincinnati, OH, Atomic Dog Publishing).

Young, J. (2001) *Henry Adams: The Historian as Political Theorist* (Lawrence, KS, University Press of Kansas).

19
Shovelling Smoke? The Experience of Being a Philosopher on an Educational Research Training Programme

JUDITH SUISSA

The programme serves a number of purposes:
To equip you with the understanding, skills and techniques to enable you to carry out your doctoral research project.
To give you a broad understanding of research approaches and methods which will enable you to read and understand a wide range of research papers and articles in order to enhance your research competence and enable you to pursue future research activities (Doctoral School MPhil/ PhD Research Training Programme Handbook, Institute of Education, University of London, 2005).

Like many of my contemporaries in philosophy of education, I am suffering from something of an identity crisis. I am not referring to the way in which we find ourselves flung between various positions in the debate, within our own academic community, over what philosophy of education is. This debate, the contours of which are reflected in recent work such as Wilfred Carr's editorial Introduction to the *RoutledgeFalmer Reader in Philosophy of Education* (Carr, 2005), and which have already provided ample material for stimulating symposia and conference papers, is, to my mind, a sign of the health of the discipline. I personally am heartened by the broad focus of recent rigorous work by philosophers of education who draw on such varied traditions. And I am not too troubled by questions as to what our 'duty' is in this regard, having long ago been convinced (and reassured) by Harvey Siegel's position that, *contra* Soltis, the aims and obligations of the professional philosopher of education should be simply to 'produce good philosophy of education' (Siegel, 1988, p. 18).

No, what troubles me is my role within the academic institution in which I work, and the way in which the structures of this institution and the broader academic culture seem to force me to redefine what I do.

Apparently, what I do, or what I am supposed to be doing, is 'research'. David Bridges notes that philosophers are rather uncomfortable with defining what they do as 'research', given that the dominant paradigm of research is a narrowly scientific one (Bridges, 2003, pp. 22–23). The choice we are faced with, as Bridges explains, is either to accept that what we are doing is not research—a move that, for political reasons, in the current climate in UK higher education institutions, would be generally regarded as suicidal—or to broaden the definition of 'research' so as to include the kind of work done by philosophers. Most philosophers of education seem to have opted for the latter option, adopting something like the following definition of research: 'systematic and sustained enquiry carried out by people well versed in some form of thinking in order to answer some specific type of question' (Peters and White, 1969, p. 2). However it would be naïve to think that we could just get on with what we've always done, and simply call it something different. For those of us—the majority, surely—involved in teaching, especially in the training of PhD students—new 'researchers'—the problem does not end here. In fact, it is around questions about the role of philosophy in research training courses for educational researchers that several intriguing and often frustrating philosophical issues come to light, and it is these on which I want to focus in the following discussion, drawing on my own recent experience.

I first became aware that this field was fraught with problems when, as a PhD student, I was required to attend a number of core courses on the Research Training Programme at the Institute of Education. These courses had names like 'Collecting and Analysing Data', 'Becoming an Educational Researcher' and 'The Theoretical Underpinnings of Research'. Flipcharts and brightly coloured markers featured largely in them. It soon became apparent that I and the couple of other philosophy students were a bit of an anomaly in these forums. We tried to join in. It was often fascinating to hear about the educational research that students from various different disciplines were working on. We really did our best with the flip-charts, but when discussion turned to 'field-work', 'the literature review' or 'the methodology chapter', there were a lot of blank stares, uncomfortable silences, and a growing sense of exasperation on our part as we tried to explain, over and over again, that 'we don't do empirical research'. On one memorable occasion, driven to despair by yet another cosy session in which all 23 of us in the class sat in a circle and took turns to answer the question 'what is your research methodology?', a fellow philosophy PhD student, when it was his turn, looked earnestly at the lecturer, and said: 'I read; I think; and I write'.

This statement, amusing (and accurate) though it was, clearly would not do when, a few years down the line, the ongoing battle on the part of philosophy students to get the Doctoral School to recognise that there was nothing in the research training programme that addressed their academic needs, was won and the philosophy department was entrusted with the task of designing and teaching a new core module on the research training programme, aimed at philosophers. When I took over the planning and teaching of this course in the second year of its existence, it was emphasised to me by the programme coordinator that we should focus on what would best meet the research training needs of students whose degrees were wholly or partly philosophical; but the course *must not* be an introduction to philosophy of education. And it *must*—as the template for the description to go into the Students' Handbook made clear—focus on 'methodology'.

I had the summer to plan the module, which was initially called 'Philosophical Approaches to Educational Research'. My confused struggle to articulate what I wanted to do, and to find some framework in the relevant literature that would help me plan my approach, soon crystallised into a worry about the question of whether I should be thinking of philosophy *of* educational research or philosophy *as* educational research; this, in turn, led to some further questions about the nature of philosophy and its relationship with educational theory and research. These questions did not go away but rather accompanied me throughout my teaching, often being reframed by the experience of teaching, often intertwining with each other, and often themselves becoming the focus of discussion in class. What follows is a reflective account of this process.

I PHILOSOPHY *AS* EDUCATIONAL RESEARCH OR PHILOSOPHY *OF* EDUCATIONAL RESEARCH?

I decided pretty early on that I was going to focus, for both political and academic reasons, on the former of these. The academic reason was that several courses on the research training programme already had a component in them called 'epistemology'. Although these were not always taught by philosophers, the questions raised were without a doubt philosophical ones: what theory of truth underpins your research methodology? what concept of knowledge are you operating with? and so on. Ideally, I felt these topics should receive more in-depth philosophical treatment than the one or two sessions assigned to them in the research training programme. Had we been a large, well-staffed department, perhaps we could have done more in this direction, but given our current situation, this was not possible. And of course, there are many academics working in other disciplines who are capable of discussing such epistemological issues with the appropriate philosophical sophistication.

The political reason for my decision was that it seemed to me essential, in the current climate of puzzlement, if not downright derision regarding research that does not have immediately obvious practical 'applications', and the lack of understanding that I had so often encountered within my own institution concerning what it is that philosophers actually *do*, that I insist on taking the approach that what we do *is* a kind of research. I wanted to illustrate and support the point that simply doing philosophy, not as an analysis of the epistemological or ethical underpinnings of existing research projects, but as an enquiry into educationally relevant issues, constitutes a coherent and valuable research project in its own right.

Had my course been composed entirely of philosophy students, this point would have been self-evident. I would not have had to demonstrate to a bemused audience 'what it is that philosophers do'. However, we could not have predicted the popularity of the module. Over 20 people registered, out of whom only four or five were doing PhDs in philosophy. Thus, although my commitment was to teaching philosophy *as* educational research, and not philosophy *of* educational research, I soon discovered that this was not just a matter of avoiding 'the epistemology of . . .' and 'the ethics of . . .'. The meta-questions that had troubled me at the outset began to seem rather more complex. I had constructed a course-pack around a series of readings that I thought represented good examples of rigorous work by philosophers on issues that were broadly relevant to education. This included general work on the aims of education, analyses of particular educational concepts, discussions of the educational implications of certain positions in political theory, and philosophical approaches to particular aspects of the educational process, such as teachers' training or pedagogy. Yet I was very keen, early on, to get the students to talk about their own research, and to try and engage them in philosophical discussion around the substantive issues that they were working on. However, in doing this, I soon discovered that, in trying to promote a philosophical discussion around the kinds of issues that arose out of the students' research topics (as opposed to the methodology of their research), the philosophy *of*/philosophy *as* question seemed to mutate into a related, but slightly different question, which I later came to think of as:

II PLUMBING OR INTERIOR DESIGN?

The philosopher Mary Midgley once famously compared philosophy to plumbing. Her point was that 'Plumbing and philosophy are both activities that arise because elaborate cultures like ours have beneath their surface, a fairly complex system which is usually unnoticed, but which sometimes goes wrong' (Midgley, 2005, p. 146). Yet whereas 'about plumbing, everybody accepts this need for trained specialists, about philosophy, many people—especially British people—not only doubt the need, they are often sceptical about whether the underlying system even exists at all. When the concepts we are living by work badly, they don't usually drip audibly through the ceiling or swamp the kitchen floor. They just quietly destroy and obstruct our thinking' (ibid.). The point about plumbing is, as Midgley says, that we usually know when there is a problem with our plumbing. We only know this when something goes wrong: there is a leaking pipe causing water to drip down from the kitchen ceiling; there is no hot water in the shower. We may not understand what the problem is, or what is causing it, but we know *something* is wrong, and we know enough to call in the plumber (rather than the electrician) who comes in, fixes it, and goes away. Everything goes back to exactly how it was before—except for the fact that there is no longer water dripping down from the kitchen ceiling, and you can carry on as before, now secure in the knowledge that the broken pipe has been replaced with something solid.

Interior designers, on the other hand, are often far less modest in their ambitions. In a particularly alarming reality TV show that used to be popular in Britain, members of a household get in some interior designers to re-design a part of their house, unbeknownst to one member of the household who is conveniently away for the weekend. In a frantic race against time, a team of interior designers with visionary ideas remodels the kitchen as a hunting lodge, erects a conservatory, knocks down the wall between the dining room and the living room, replacing it with perspex bricks, or some similar makeover. The unsuspecting householder comes back from their golfing weekend aghast to find that their house is no longer quite what it was. It is still their kitchen, but it is almost unrecognisable, and they don't feel quite at home with the exposed brickwork. Crucially, unlike the case of the plumber, they didn't even call the interior designer in. In fact, they were unaware that there was anything 'wrong' with their lilac-tiled bathroom.

In the course that I taught that first term, one of my students was troubled by what seemed to her an inconsistent and confusing use of the word 'autonomy' in the literature on citizenship education that she was reviewing. She was not a philosopher, but was in the field of curriculum studies and was doing a critical cross-cultural analysis of programmes on citizenship and human rights education. She had been unable to find a satisfactory account of the difference between autonomy and freedom, and the confusion between the two terms seemed to complicate her analysis. I offered some philosophical analysis and referred her to systematic work done by philosophers on the notion of autonomy and related concepts. She seemed to find this helpful. It was clear in her mind, now, where the problem had lain, what had been the cause of confusion, and how she could adopt a coherent conceptual analysis of some key notions that would enable her to pursue her own research project and to draw important distinctions in her discussion.

Another student, however, was conducting an ethnographic study into the effects of equal-access programmes in higher education in Zimbabwe. In a rash attempt to draw the group into a philosophical appreciation of the complexities of the term 'equality' and related notions such as 'fairness', to which he referred several times in the course of describing his research, I opened up a discussion on these ideas. The student was, literally, panicked. He had got his research plan all sorted out; he had read the literature; he had collected a great deal of data, and he knew what he was doing. But now he was being told that the very conceptual framework within which he was operating was questionable. What was 'fair'? what was 'just'? what political values underlay his project? Where would it all end? I felt vaguely guilty. After all, he hadn't called in the plumber. He hadn't even noticed any leaks. Is every plumber secretly a frustrated interior designer? Was I being a bit too arrogant in my attempts to convince my students of the overarching importance of philosophy, and to demonstrate that it was relevant everywhere, not only in the epistemological assumptions behind their research or the ethical issues of how they conducted it? This dilemma soon led me into a related, but slightly different question:

III GADFLIES OR UNDERLABOURERS?

I had tried to move away from philosophy *of* educational research to philosophy *as* educational research, but I was now back with the age-old question of the very nature of the discipline and its relationship with other disciplines. In between the landmines of my weekly classes, I read whatever I could get my hands on in the literature on such meta-issues in philosophy, as I attempted to gain some clarity on these nagging questions. I was familiar with Peter Winch's work and had long ago felt fairly confident about rejecting the 'underlabourer' concept. But how does this play out in actual teaching work with researchers from other fields? Laurie Shrage draws a distinction between 'underlabourers' and 'gadflies', arguing that:

> Philosophers who are more attracted to the underlabourer conception tend to work in fields such as philosophy of physics, philosophy of biology, philosophy of psychology, or philosophy of mathematics and logic. These philosophers often want philosophy to find its institutional niche among the sciences, and to be recognized as the discipline that employs a kind of critical and historical reflection on the sciences that helps the latter avoid conceptual error and describe the world accurately. Accordingly, some philosophy programs have reorganized along these lines as departments of the history and philosophy of science, or logic and philosophy of science.
>
> Alternatively, philosophers who are attracted to the gadfly conception tend to work in philosophical subfields such as epistemology, metaphysics, ethics, political philosophy, aesthetics, or the history of philosophy. Philosophers in these specialties believe that philosophy has its own set of problems to address (about definitions of knowledge, existence, truth, meaning, good, beauty, obligation, etc.), and that these are problems that can be meaningfully confronted by philosophical reflection and reasoning alone. Philosophical gadflies tend to view philosophy as the queen of the humanities, as the discipline whose theories and speculations guide our understanding of human experience and artifacts. Philosophical gadflies work alongside other humanists in traditional philosophy departments, and when these don't exist, they find homes in departments of literature, rhetoric, politics, religion, ethnic studies, women's studies, legal studies, or in professional programs as resident ethicists (Shrage, 2007).

I find it interesting to note that philosophy of education does not appear on either of these lists. And yet it is, of course, somehow on both of them: psychological issues are commonly a feature of research in education, as are epistemological issues, ethics, and historical work. Yet in my own teaching, I was both attempting to demonstrate how problems about truth and meaning, ideas about the good, obligation, etc., were meaningful philosophical problems in their own right and that, being supremely relevant to education, they could constitute 'educational research', while at the same time, I was trying to show non-philosophers that their own research was prone to incoherence if they were not aware of the possible conceptual confusions underlying it. Could one be both underlabourer and gadfly at the same time? Was my increasing schizophrenia here simply the result of having to teach a group that contained both philosophers and non-philosophers? Richard Pring, in a discussion of educational research that seems to defend something like the notion of an underlabouring gadfly, notes that 'what is often seen as a straightforward empirical matter is often fraught with problems that are philosophical in nature—unclear concepts, questionable assumptions about verification of conclusions, naïve ideas about social facts and reality, and above all, unexamined notions of an educational practice' (Pring, 2004, p. 162). This certainly seemed to be the case with some of my students. Some of them were definitely using unclear concepts ('understanding'; 'equality'; 'progress') that could benefit from a bit of careful underlabouring. Crucially, though, Pring (ibid.) notes the danger of philosophy becoming 'yet another bit of theory in a theoretical course—something to be learnt, made sense of and applied' and indeed, my sense was that some people may take bits of the gadflying in which I was engaging in in a rather ad-hoc manner and relegate them to the role of underlabourer in their overall schemes. However, there is another danger, which Pring and other writers on this subject do not seem to address, and that is the danger of philosophy becoming something that disrupts, that causes an unnecessary and often confusing reframing of issues in research. Attempting to be both a gadfly and an underlabourer convinced me that while this distinction could be a rich source of meta-philosophical debate about the nature of philosophical questions and traditions and their relationship with other traditions and disciplines, it was not actually very helpful in the context of teaching educational researchers who may or may not be doing some philosophy. In puzzling over this point, I soon came to feel that a more helpful distinction was the related, but slighly different one of:

IV PHILOSOPHY IS EVERYTHING OR PHILOSOPHY IS 'WHAT I DO'

Philosophy, as Henri-Neri Castaneda reminds us, is ubiquitous (in Cohen and Dascal, 1989, p. 41). After a few weeks of teaching a diverse group of students, I felt pretty confident that, whatever my lack of familiarity with the field of educational research, if you gave me the title of any piece of research on an educational issue, I could construe it as an interesting philosophical problem. Yet this in itself is highly troubling. We are all familiar with the lampooning of philosophers as endlessly obsessed with questions of meaning and the infinite process of defining one's terms. 'Yes, but what do you mean by X?' is a common caricature of what we do. And although philosophers—even those within the analytic tradition—are quick to defend their discipline in the face of such a restrictive view of what it is that they are concerned with, I think we can all recognise the tendency to see problems of meaning and value in everything. In the context of training new researchers within academic institutions, this could have worrying implications; we seem sometimes to be cursed by a strange combination of insecurity and arrogance. We feel there are very few people out there who value or even understand our work, and yet everything, it seems, is potentially philosophical.

I began to wonder whether colleagues from other disciplines were afflicted with the same disciplinary illusions of grandeur. Do sociologists think everything is sociological? Do psychologists think everything is psychological? Perhaps, but is it not part of 'learning to become a researcher' that we develop a healthy understanding of and respect for disciplinary boundaries? There is an important distinction to be made between research projects that are intentionally inter-disciplinary, and PhD research undertaken by students who are being initiated into a particular academic discipline. While there are many exciting areas of educational research that lend themselves to inter-disciplinary work, and many successful examples of collaboration between, for example, sociologists, historians, psychologists and philosophers on educational issues, it would certainly not have been appropriate, or welcome, for a sociologist to tell me, while I was doing my PhD research, that there was an important sociological aspect to my research that I was overlooking. What then gave me the right to do such philosophical meddling in the conceptual and evaluative affairs of clearly defined research projects from other disciplines? I may think that, ultimately, the most important questions about education are philosophical ones: What is education for? Are there such things as educational values? Should parents be responsible for their children's moral education?—questions that cannot be answered by empirical enquiry. Yet no philosopher would doubt the value of rigorous, systematic empirical work—not just so that we have something to do philosophy *about*, but because in order to reach a fuller undestanding of something as important as education, we need an appreciation of both philosophical, normative, and empirical issues. In fumbling towards an articulation of this point, I was greatly helped by reading David Bridges' thoughtful discussion of these issues in *Fiction Written Under Oath?* (Bridges, 2003).

I agree with Bridges that given the way these two strands of our thinking are intertwined, to view the distinction between the empirical and the non-empirical as a strict dichotomy can be highly misleading.. But it is one thing to believe this, and quite another to adopt it as a strategy in teaching research students. Before students can appreciate Bridges' argument about the way in which the empirical/*a priori* distinction can collapse, and the historical and cultural context that makes sense of this, they have to first grasp the logic and meaning of this important distinction. Philosophers undergoing a systematic course of training that includes courses in epistemology and logic, are usually taught this distinction at a fairly early stage in their training. They may then go on to study more complex issues in epistemology, and at some point will probably encounter Quine's 'Two Dogmas of Empiricism'. By this time, they will be well equipped to appreciate the problems with the empirical/*a priori* distinction and to discuss the philosophical questions around it. However, most of my students on the research training module were not philosophers. Not only had they not had any systematic training in epistemology, but some of them did not seem even to have quite grasped the basic distinction between the empirical and the normative. I was obviously not in a position to offer an introduction to philosophy, but I had to first ensure that they had grasped this distinction before I began to suggest that perhaps it was problematic. There is, as Bridges notes, a 'complex interrelationship between, for example, observation and theory, between the *a posteriori* and the *a priori*', (Bridges, 2003, p. 30), but, apart from (and to the horror of) the philosophers in the group, some of my students were not even entirely clear about what these terms meant.

'Educational researchers', Bridges insists (ibid.) 'should resist traditions which identify some people narrowly as "empirical researchers" and others narrowly as "philosophers" and embrace an intellectual world in which the two constantly inform and challenge each other'. One implication of this view is that new educational researchers need to be trained so as to be able to 'move freely across these areas as conventionally defined'. However, the only way, it seemed, that I could ensure that my students could do this would be to provide them with a solid basis in philosophy—something clearly impossible in an eight-week course. Perhaps, indeed, while I could appreciate the truth and value behind Bridges' suggestion, I too would find it difficult to adopt such a stance in my own 'research' because, analogously to my own non-philosophy students, I am steeped in philosophical paradigms, and am not familiar enough with or confident enough in the paradigms of other disciplines in order to really appreciate their interaction. So at what level, and how exactly, is such ideal inter-disciplinary research to take place? Certainly many researchers, as Bridges is constantly reminding us, although they are not philosophers, are doing quite sophisticated philosophical work within research projects that are not wholly philosophical; and the same goes for philosophers who engage with other disciplinary traditions. But it would surely be putting the cart before the horse to attempt to offer such a perspective on research training programmes where students are still supposed to be 'acquiring skills' and 'familiarizing themselves with methodologies'. If discipline is, as Bridges says, to be the *sine qua non* of research, perhaps research training cannot be interdisciplinary? I thus found myself pondering the connected, but slightly different point that:

V IN ORDER TO BE INTERDISCIPLINARY, YOU NEED A STRONG BASIS IN A DISCIPLINE

While my confidence in my teaching abilities and the justification of my existence as an 'educational researcher' and trainer of educational researchers was rapidly ebbing away, I did feel still relatively confident in my qualifications as a philosopher. Thus I resolved, for the following term, in which I was scheduled to repeat the module, to stop prodding my students—the ones who were not philosophers—to see the philosophy in their own work, and to focus instead on offering examples of what good philosophy of education was. This would serve to complement the presumably solid examples they were getting from their own fields of what constituted good sociology of education, good enthnographic studies, and so on. Perhaps I should put my strange illusions of grandeur to one side, stop confusing my students, and address the rather more modest task of offering them an overview of examples of various different approaches to *doing* philosophy of education. My focus would be not underlying epistemological positions; not normative, ethical assumptions behind different educational theories or policies; not meta-questions about the role of philosophy, but simply an answer to the question of 'what is philosophy as educational research?'—the very question with which I had begun. And of course, as the course coordinator reminded me yet again, the module was supposed to be largely methodological. If sociologists and historians had research methodologies and skills, we philosophers, surely, had something akin to this. And so I found myself back with the familiar, but slightly different question:

VI WHAT IS A PHILOSOPHICAL METHODOLOGY?

A helpful conversation with a colleague who had designed and taught an earlier incarnation of the module encouraged me to construe it as demonstrating different ways of 'doing philosophy' about educational issues. I thus compiled the reader on the basis of a selection of texts, each of which represented a significant approach to philosophy in the sense of something that could broadly be defined, to satisfy the handbook description, as a 'methodology'. We began with a text by Plato, whose philosophical methodology was to imagine Socrates wandering around Athens with an obliging interlocutor, depicting bizarre thought experiments and occasionally asking his interlocutor what he thought of them. The students loved it. We spent an entire hour engaged in a really deep discussion about the relationship between knowledge of the truth and freedom, the role of the liberatory educator, the idea of false consciousness, and whether anyone could truly be said to be free. We then ended up discussing 'Educating Rita' for the remaining half-hour. I thought it was an excellent discussion ... but was it 'methodology?' Luckily, I had previously identified 'the use of metaphor' and 'dialogue' as particular aspects of philosophical methodology, and produced some readings by Ray Elliot and Nicholas Burbules on these ideas for my students. In the intervening week, I spent a long time thinking about these issues. Once again, David Bridges was helpful in reminding me that 'Some philosophical writing describes or represents a particular methodology—Socratic questioning, Cartesian doubting or linguistic analysis, for example—but a great deal more leaves it implicit or even invisible' (Bridges, 2003, p. 23) and 'it is certainly not a standard requirement of philosophical writing (in contrast with social science) that the author explains or defends his or her methodology' (ibid.).

There was also, however, the further question of whether philosophical method and content could really be construed as two different things. Well, of course they cannot, as the writings of the later Wittgenstein, amongst other things, constantly remind us. And while I was ostensibly focusing on 'methodology', the fact that discussions of methodology kept slipping imperceptibly and uncontrollably into substantive discussions did not seem to be posing any problems for my students. On the contrary, it soon became quite clear that the students on the Research Training Programme (many of whom had already been through several terms of flip-charts and coloured markers) were only too happy to be given the opportunity to engage in substantive, open-ended and fairly loosely structured discussion about the actual educational questions and ideas that they were encountering in their research, and the values that motivated them, as well as the various ideas and normative positions that emerged from the texts we were reading. I thus determined to stop agonising over the various taxonomical questions and distinctions that had been haunting me (was reflective equilibrium really a methodology? What constituted an Aristotelian approach as opposed to an application of Aristotelian ideas? Was Dearden's chapter on 'Happiness and Education' really the best example I could find of conceptual analysis applied to educational ideas?), to regard the title 'methodology' as simply a bureaucratic requirement I was forced to comply with in order to get the course description into the handbook, and just to accept that I was doing a bit of everything: part gadfly, part underlabourer; part methodology, part substance.

By the third term, I thought I had this pretty much sorted out. I used the term 'methodology' as a hook for organising the reading list, selecting texts on the basis of their philosophical quality and their potential to stimulate an interesting discussion about substantive issues that seemed highly important to enquiries about the meaning, value and process of education. Thus I muddled through another term, with varying degrees of success. By the end of it, however, I was plagued, not by the sense that I had completely failed to resolve any of the above tensions, but by a related, yet slightly different problem:

VII CONVERSATION ABOUT WHAT?

It was all very well to try and balance a demonstration of the kinds of things philosophers generally did—'conceptual analysis'; 'reflective equilibrium', 'applied philosophy'—with some discussion of the content of their work, but this often gave rise to practical problems in a group where so many of the students had no background in philosophy. I genuinely never knew, from one session to the next, how much I could assume about the points of reference for the discussion I had planned.

Thus, for example, I had put Jane Roland Martin's article, 'Sophie and Emile: A Case Study of Sex Bias in the History of Educational Thought' (Roland Martin, 1981) on the reading list as part of a session on 'feminist methodologies'. My plan was to outline some concerns about methodology and epistemological frameworks (there was that word again) raised by feminist theorists, and to discuss Martin's work as an example of philosophical writing that used a broadly analytical methodology but addressed feminist concerns. However, the discussion faltered at a fairly early stage when it became apparent that about half the students in the group had never encountered the work of Rousseau, let alone read *Emile*, so could not really appreciate the point of Martin's analysis.

Similarly, I had devoted a couple of readings to the tradition of conceptual analysis, including some pieces by analytic philosophers of education, and a historical overview of the tradition. It seemed impossible to do this justice without mentioning the work of Wittgenstein and so, realising that very few people in the group had ever heard of him, I found myself offering an account of Wittgenstein's life and background, the significance of the *Tractatus*, the central ideas of Logical Positivism, the different emphases in *Philosophical Investigations* and its impact on contemporary philosophy, and the history of analytic philosophy of education—with a brevity that would have put even the authors of the 'Short Introduction to . . .' series to shame. The philosophy students were, I suspected, a bit bored, and possibly horrified. The others made frantic notes. I felt terribly guilty of both falling into the trap Richard Pring warns us of (see above), and doing an unforgivable injustice to Wittgenstein, not least because so much of his life and writing testify to his tortured efforts to develop a form of doing philosophy the whole point of which is to get the reader and the pupil to think for themselves. What is more, I had failed, once again, to heed the warning of the course administrator who had insisted that this module 'must not be an introduction to philosophy of education'.

By the end of the term, I felt the internal tensions of the module were getting to be too much for me, and, at the next meeting of the Research Training Programme teaching team, we discussed completely reframing it so as to try and avoid these tensions. The team came up with the following proposal: we would make it clear that the course was intended for students doing non-empirical research, thus supposedly restricting the number of non-philosophy students. To make it more manageable and to accommodate other students who did not fit into the mainstream Research Training Programme, I would co-teach it with a colleague from History of Education. Priority registration would be given to Philosophy and History students. My colleague was as puzzled as I was by the assumption that historical research is 'non-empirical'—but that is another story. We found we shared an interest in the meta-question of the role of the so-called foundation disciplines in educational theory and research, and agreed to keep this question in the background and address it throughout the module. We put together a list of readings around a few general themes— 'the idea of the common school'; 'women in history and philosophy of education'—on which we could identify interesting work from both a historical and a philosophical perspective, and which we felt raised general questions about the nature of philosophical and historical research into educational issues and the relationship between the two disciplines.

The new format generally seemed to work quite well. As always, the success of the course depended largely on the unknown factor of who was in the group, their interests, and the dynamics between them. Luckily the people in our group were quite willing to enter into philosophical conversations about the educational ideas that emerged from their own research and from the readings. Unlike before, I could usually rely upon them having a basic grasp of what a philosophical question, as opposed to an empirical question, was, and an awareness of some basic philosophical distinctions. However, very few of them had any systematic training in philosophy. Increasingly, the classes took the form of a three-way conversation; between myself, my historian colleague, and the students, from various disciplinary perspectives. In my most optimistic moments, it did genuinely seem to me that I was, in fostering this conversation, 'doing philosophy' with my students, in a way that demonstrated the vaguely Rortian idea of philosophy as conversation—even, perhaps, an edifying conversation. Yet, relieved though I was not to have to prepare punchy 20-minute presentations on 'the history of conceptual analysis' or 'the political and educational thought of Rousseau', part of me missed the evangelical glow that had come with the knowledge that I was providing non-philosophers with a little philosophical content. For even if one goes along with Rorty's anti-foundationalist position on the role and nature of philosophy, from a pedagogical point of view there is no doubt that, as Rorty himself testifies, one cannot arrive at this position without first going through some sort of substantive philosophical training (Rorty, 1999, pp. 15–20). This may not be epistemologically foundational, but it surely has an educationally foundational role? One point that emerges very clearly from Rorty's autobiographical account of his gradual disillusionment with Platonism and his abandonment of the search for 'a luminous, self-justifying, self-sufficient synoptic vision' (ibid.) is that he could not have become the challenging philosopher he is without this process. As he says, 'I am very glad I spent all those years reading philosophy books' (Rorty, 1999, p. 20). My students, however, had not read many philosophy books, and often seemed to be demonstrating signs of anti-foundationalism without knowing what it was.

Was there any way I could teach philosophy without providing an introduction to philosophy? Was there any way I could get my students to do philosophy without implying that philosophy was simply another 'research methodology'? I realised that the same questions that had haunted me from the beginning of the first module, continued to echo in the background. However, I stopped agonising over them, largely because the students in the class seemed to be really enjoying it, the discussions seemed rigorous and interesting, and I was teaching with a colleague from another discipline who, in implicitly assuming that I would have a philosophical perspective on whatever issue we addressed, made me realise the obvious truth that philosophy is just what philosophers do.

VIII SHOVELLING SMOKE?

The task of philosophers who seek to define their subject is akin to that of fools who attempt to shovel smoke. It is not exaclty that there's nothing there, but whatever it is, it isn't amenable to shovelling. Those who discover smoke are well advised to look for fire, not to fetch their shovel. Similarly, when philosophers are discovered trying once again to define the nature of philosophy, it is better to examine whatever has precipitated their effort, not to pay too careful attention to what they newly profess (Mandt, in Cohen and Dascal, 1989, p. 78).

Had all my previous reflections over the nature and role of philosophy as and of educational research been simply another misguided attempt at shovelling smoke? Were they really just another symptom of the strange position we philosophers of education often find ourselves in, due to the institutional structure in which we work? Perhaps. But there are some firm convictions that I have come to hold, partly as a result of the experience of trying to deal with this situation. One is that what PhD students in philosophy of education need more than anything else at the moment is more philosophy. Perhaps if there was more rigorous philosophical training at MA level, PhD students could focus, in their 'research training', on honing their academic writing skills. The session in the last term that the students found the most useful was that in which I asked them all to write an abstract of their research. The group discussed these, and several people said they had found it hugely helpful to receive comments on the coherence and clarity of their abstracts from people outside their field, and from more experienced researchers. My ability to lead this discussion had very little to do with my being a philosopher and much to do with my having had experience in writing abstracts. This, it seems to me, is one of the 'skills' that research training programmes could usefully help students to develop.

The research training programme, remember, is meant to '*equip students with the understanding, skills and techniques to enable them to carry out their doctoral research project*'. What about 'understanding'? Surely, no research training programme can fully provide this. Whatever particular research project students are involved in, the issues they particularly need to 'understand' are the substantive topics that they are researching. In the case of philosophy students, there will be an almost infinite range of such topics. But some central philosophical issues, traditions and approaches may be relevant to several of these. The Doctoral School at my own institution offers, as an optional part of its research training programme, a number of reading groups on different theorists, traditions or specific issues that provide an opportunity for in-depth discussion and critique, facilitated by someone familiar with the material in question. In previous years I have both attended and facilitated highly successful reading groups on the work of John Dewey, on Hermeneutics, on Alasdair MacIntyre, and on philosophical conceptions of human nature. It seems to me that, for philosophy students and non-philosophy students alike, offering more reading groups of this type would be a far better way to develop 'understanding' than trying to develop yet another generic research training module focused on 'methodology'.

Finally, what about the aim of giving students 'a broad understanding of research approaches and methods that will enable you to read and understand a wide range of research papers and articles in order to enhance your research competence and enable you to pursue future research activities'? As I discussed above, it is clearly unrealistic to expect to familiarise students within a particular discipline with the research paradigms and substantive work of researchers from across a whole range of other disciplines. Yet in the course of my own research training, and in some of my classes, there were several moments in which two or three students, discussing their own research projects with others, or bringing different perspectives to bear on a substantive issue in which they had a shared interest, seemed to come close to developing something like this broad understanding. This, though, happened more often around the coffee table at break, or in a seminar that was not part of the research training programme; and when it happened in class, it did so in spite of and not because of the 'aims and outcomes' articulated in the handbook.

Should we, then, abandon attempts at serious philosophical input into 'research training'? Should we limit such input to an introduction to epistemology for educational researchers? I am not defending either of these options. On the contrary, the more philosophers we can draw into the conversation about just what such 'research training' should consist of, the better. Even shovelling smoke can be quite good fun when you do it with someone else.[1]

NOTE

1. I would like to thank Steve Bramall, Dianne Gereluk, Jane Hurry, Paul Severn, Tom Woodin and the research students who have participated in my courses over the past few years. This chapter could not have been written without them.

REFERENCES

Bridges, D. (2003) *Fiction Written Under Oath? Essays in Philosophy and Educational Research* (Dordrecht, Kluwer).

Carr, W. (ed.) (2005) *The RoutledgeFalmer Reader in Philosophy of Education* (Abingdon, Routledge).

Cohen, A. and Dascal, M. (eds) (1989) *The Institution of Philosophy: A Discipline in Crisis* (La Salle, Open Court).

Midgley, M. (2005) *The Essential Mary Midgley* (Abingdon, Routledge).

Peters, R. S. and White, J. P. (1969) The Philosopher's Contribution to Educational Research, *Educational Philosophy and Theory*, 1, pp. 1–15.

Pring, R. (2004) *Philosophy of Educational Research* (London, Continuum).

Roland Martin, J. (1981) Sophie and Emile; A Case Study of Sex Bias in the History of Educational Thought, *Harvard Educational Review*, 51.3, pp. 357–372.

Rorty, R. (1999) *Philosophy and Social Hope* (London, Penguin).

Shrage, L. (2007, forthcoming) Will Philosophers Study Their History, Or Become History?, in: D. Taylor (ed.) *Climbing out of the Ditch? Critical Perspectives on McCarthyism and American Philosophy* (Chicago, IL, Northwestern University Press) (accessed online at: http://www.csupomona.edu/~ljshrage/philosophyfuture.htm).

Siegel, H. (1988) On the Obligations of the Professional Philosopher of Education, in: W. Hare and J. P. Portelli (eds) *Philosophy of Education; Introductory Readings* (Calgary, Detselig).

20
Induction into Educational Research Networks: The Striated and the Smooth

NAOMI HODGSON AND PAUL STANDISH

INTRODUCTION

The idea of networks is now commonplace in understandings of the social and professional practices of late modernity. Educational research as an academic field can be understood as a network or group of networks and therefore consists of interconnected nodes that structure the way the field operates and understands its purpose. This chapter deals with the nature of induction into the network of educational research that takes place through research methods courses, the textual domain and the professional and social practices involved in collaboration, conferences and publication. Lynda Stone's (2006) critique is drawn upon to provide an illustration of the nature of the normalized and orthodox practices, driven by the dominant notion of 'what works', which shape the field and enable new entrants to access its networks.

Castells' (1996) understanding of the network highlights the importance of the power of flows between nodes in the network. The use of the term 'flow' here depicts an ease or freedom of movement. The use of the analytic framework provided by Deleuze and Guattari's (1988) notion of smooth and striated space problematises this understanding of flows, offering an alternative understanding of how the nature of thought and practice governs the route between nodes in the network. For example, it is suggested that although the network is amenable to adaptation and flexibility, the way in which critique functions in educational research has become domesticated and therefore does not challenge it. The suggestion of the domestication of critique, however, could be said to provide merely another binary—domesticated and undomesticated—through which to analyse the field. Deleuze and Guattari's concepts of smooth and striated space resist this dualist simplification and offer an alternative way of understanding the nature of thought in relation to academic practice.

MANUEL CASTELLS AND THE NETWORK SOCIETY

The term 'networks' is now commonplace in discussion of the nature of information technology or of the ways in which professionals come together to exchange ideas, to make connections with those of similar interests and to facilitate more productive working practices. Castells (1996) suggests that, although the idea of the network is not in itself new, 'the new information technology paradigm provides the material basis for its pervasive expansion throughout the entire social structure' (Castells, 1996, p. 469). Castells (1996) defines a network as:

> ... a set of interconnected nodes. A node is the point at which a curve intersects itself. What a node is, concretely speaking, depends on the kind of concrete networks of which we speak .... The topology defined by networks determines that the distance (or intensity and frequency of interaction) between two points (or social positions) is shorter (or more frequent or more intense) if both points are nodes in a network than if they do not belong to the same network. On the other hand, within a given network, flows have no distance, or the same distance, between nodes.... The inclusion/exclusion in networks, and the architecture of relationships between networks, enacted by light-speed operating information technologies, configure dominant processes and functions in our societies (Castells, 1996, p. 470).

The image of the intersected curve here denotes the action of the network in capturing the flow and channelling it in the desired direction. Castells (1996) characterises the organisation of production in late modernity in terms of the network as a response to 'the conditions of unpredictability ushered in by rapid economic and technological change' (Castells, 1996, p. 164). He describes the shift as being from vertically organised, autonomous bureaucracies to horizontal corporations in response to the network flexibility offered by the technological advances of the internet and globalisation. Flexibility and adaptability are, then, 'the key competitive weapon' (Castells, 1996, p. 172). Castells suggests that access to the network is governed to an extent by the already existing major corporations or power holders or by cooperation between them since 'entry into the strategic networks requires either considerable resources (financial, technological, market share) or an alliance with a major player in the network' (Castells, 1996, p. 192). As previously suggested, it is the ability to adapt and diversify that characterises the benefits of the network and as such it is involvement within it that is important rather than its products: 'The logic of the network is more powerful than the powers in the network' (Castells, 1996, p. 193). Once one is part of the network one has access to resources and the potential for adaptability to the economic, social and political forces that determine its focus. However, it is the logic of the network rather than the specific interests expressed through them that are determinant.

> The power of flows takes precedence over the flows of power. Presence or absence in the network and the dynamics of each network vis-à-vis others

are critical courses of domination and change in our society: a society that, therefore, we may properly call the network society, characterised by the pre-eminence of social morphology over social action (Castells, 1996, p. 469).

The use of the term 'flow' here depicts an ease or freedom of movement. The use of the analytic framework provided by Deleuze and Guattari's (1988) notion of smooth and striated space will offer an alternative way of understanding flows as potentially restricted by the network structure. The chapter turns first though to its substantive focus, the way in which students are inducted in to the field of educational research through courses and textual domains and through the social and professional practices of conferences, collaboration and publication.

LYNDA STONE'S CRITIQUE OF INDUCTION INTO EDUCATIONAL RESEARCH

Lynda Stone (2006) provides a critique of the induction of graduate researchers in the United States, where the notion of 'what works' dominates in education and in shaping research. Drawing on the work of Thomas Kuhn, Stone's (2006) critique is based on the idea that 'new generations of researchers learn early on what is "normal"', which can become limiting if it does not involve learning to reconceptualise problems and all that this entails (Stone, 2006, p. 1). Stone summarises the normalized beliefs about research that she identifies as governing the way in which graduate students are inducted into the field. These include the ways in which: the natural sciences serve as the model for research; the quantitative tradition predominates; efficiency is paramount and held as part of what science is; ethics is considered and requires compulsory 'institutional review to "contain" harm' (Stone, 2006, p. 2).

Stone (2006) notes how very early in their training, and sometimes prior to admission, graduate education students in the United States are required to state their methodological orientation, placing themselves in either the quantitative or qualitative camp. Stone notes that 'this community membership is a first founding component of belonging to the education research community' (Stone, 2006, p. 8). As such, graduate research students are inducted into a set of instrumental values:

> One message is to 'get in and get out'. A second is the necessity of funding and to locate projects and methods in order to 'get grants'. Still a third is to move quickly to focus on a research question and to narrow one's topic as one learns one's method. A fourth value is to adopt and perfect standardized routines and formats. These range from designing and conducting studies to reporting their results. All of these values are woven through courses and research experiences, through course papers and projects, articles and finally dissertations. All are constitutive of induction into a broad education research culture (Stone, 2006, p. 9).

These values are, it seems, instrumental in the sense of students producing (perhaps publishable) results in the most efficient way possible and their departments maximising their research output. Stone suggests that the normalcy in induction to the field is also indicated in what is missing from such courses, namely: background study of education; study of the founding disciplines of education; attention to theory. Stone's analysis also offers a sense of the rigid, linear nature of the way in which research is understood through such courses, as a process of design that seeks to overcome the problematic. While we are broadly sympathetic to the criticisms levelled by Stone, we seek in the present chapter to take matters in a slightly different direction and to relate it more closely to questions concerning the nature of networks.

Castells asserts that 'within a given network, flows have no distance, or the same distance, between nodes' (Castells, 1996, p. 470). This might be found, for example, in the way that one's presence on an email circulation list is unaffected by one's physical distance from other members, and as a member of that list one is as fully present, as fully or equally connected as all other members. Castells elaborates this, in topological terms, defined by intensities and frequencies of interaction and by flows: 'The power of flows takes precedence over the flows of power' (Castells, 1996, p. 469). Our purpose in the section that follows is to expose these notions of intensity and flow to a distinction that potentially casts light on different kinds or different possibilities of network. We shall refer to a topology that arises in the work of Gilles Deleuze and Félix Guattari: between striated and smooth space.

THE STRIATED AND THE SMOOTH

The idea of smooth and striated spaces is elaborated in Chapter 14 of *A Thousand Plateaux: Capitalism and Schizophrenia* (Deleuze and Guattari, 1988), though the distinction has a relationship with other contrasts elaborated earlier in that book, for example, between the rhizome and the tree, between nomad space and sedentary space, and between the War Machine and State science. We propose to make our way towards the distinction in question by referring first to these perhaps more familiar ideas.

The distinction between the rhizome and the tree, elaborated in the introduction to *A Thousand Plateaux*, serves to represent different modes of organisation and different modes of thought. The tree's central trunk, spreading branches, and tributary roots form a model of organisation and distribution that is replicated in, say, the management structure of a business or school, and, of course, the family tree, as well as in the conceptualisation of a disciplinary field, with its canon, its 'central' problems, its branches. The rhizome has a quite different form of growth: potatoes multiply in a process of cloning or lateral spreading; couch-grass extends across the sand-dunes, which form and extend with no centre; so too there is the ant-colony that reforms and regroups with seemingly endless permutability. In contrast to the American military, with its headquarters, there is the Vietcong and Al Qaeda, organisations with a spreading flexible body, with no head and no necessary organic arrangement. There is nomad existence in contrast to the *polis*. These distinctions model a difference in thought. Arborescent thought moves constantly within stable structures—this, on the one hand, that, on the other; delineations and demarcations; upright and sturdy; secure in its foundations; heavy with gravity and propriety. This thought displays what thought itself should be like. In contrast, rhizomatic thought flows freely and with affirmation, with a logic of *and + and + and + and . . .*— affirmation without negation. It is the logic of the Möbius strip, a surface with no underside, recto without verso.

In Hindu mythology, the gods Varuna and Mitra form a dyad—Varuna the despot and binder, Mitra the legislator and organiser. They function as a pair, in alternation and with symmetry, at once antithetical to one another and complementary, as though they together constituted a sovereign unity. The State then quite rightly acquires an army as a means of the juridical integration of war into its organisational functioning. In contrast, to Varuna, however, the warrior-god Indra, who comes to displace Varuna, stands outside this dyad or any symmetry of relations, in opposition to Varuna no less than to Mitra. Outside all dualities of terms as well as correspondencies between relations, and refusing to implement any binary relations between 'states', he bears witness to a *becoming*.

So, in Deleuze and Guattari's provocative terminology, this is a War Machine quite other to the State apparatus, a force outside any possible terms of its juridical integration. And this becoming, it is important to note, cannot become a model, for this would be precisely to fix and arrest it. Hence, it is forever in danger of escaping a thought too anxious to draw its distinctions, to assert its regime, and to establish its disciplinary domain. It suggests a thought whose hydraulic movement is not one of straight lines but rather of:

> . . . a curvilinear declination to the formation of spirals and vortices . . . It is the difference between a *smooth* (vectoral, projective, or topological) space and a *striated* (metric) space: in the first case 'space is occupied without being counted' and in the second case 'space is counted in order to be occupied' (Deleuze and Guattari, 1988, pp. 361–2, remarks cited from Pierre Boulez).

The movement is not from problem-elements towards over-arching theory, but towards the accidents that condition and resolve the problem, with the problem not an obstacle but a 'pro-jection', a movement to surpass that obstacle (ibid.). A nomad science such as this would develop eccentrically, in a way that is banned or barred by the conditions of State science.

Is this the space of Castells' networks, where flows have no distance and where connections are activated as if by light-speed operating information technologies (Castells, 1996, p. 470)? We note the emphasis on flows, but smooth space, Deleuze and Guattari tell us, is 'a field without conduits or channels'; it can only be explored by legwork (Deleuze and Guattari, 1988, p. 371); and they warn us also that one of the fundamental tasks of the State is 'to utilize smooth spaces *as a means of communication* in the service of striated space' (Deleuze and Guattari, 1988, p. 385). This is perhaps suggestive of the warning of danger and uncertainty that further fixes the direction of communication and action in striated space. For smooth space is not the place of straight lines of connection but of 'a movement that deviates to the minimum extent and thereafter assumes a vortical motion, occupying a smooth space, actually drawing smooth space itself' (ibid.). It is not the legislative determination of a domain but an ambulant thinking of deterritorialisation that extends the territory itself. This is the surging, spiralling movement of a critique that enables us to think what we could not think before.

The smooth and the striated represent ways of thinking and modes of operation within the network and are determinant of access to it. The 'principal elements of a State apparatus that proceeds by a One-Two, distributes binary distinctions, and forms a milieu of interiority' (Deleuze and Guattari, 1988, p. 325). We shall next consider this interiority as a feature of the research *domain*. Although the striated, like the network, works on the basis of inclusion and exclusion, and the smooth may be likened to the undomesticated and the nomadic, it is essential not to lose sight of a danger that constantly attends and threatens to compromise the very thinking we are trying to reveal:

> No sooner do we note a simple opposition between the two kinds of space than we must indicate a much more complex difference by virtue of which the successive terms of the oppositions fail to coincide entirely. And no sooner have we done that than we must remind ourselves that the two spaces in fact exist only in mixture: smooth space is constantly being translated, transversed into striated space; striated space is constantly being reversed, returned to a smooth space (Deleuze and Guattari, 1988, p. 474).

And at the end of this chapter Deleuze and Guattari warn: 'Never believe that a smooth space will suffice to save us' (Deleuze and Guattari, 1988, p. 500).

THE RESEARCH DOMAIN

The process of induction in to the field of educational research is achieved in the following ways. *First*, through research methods courses and a textual domain that are characterised by the ways in which: research design is presented as a process of creating an unimpeded conduit from designing to 'doing' research; the demand for 'evidence-based' policy and practice maintains the problem-solving linear focus of research design and practice; the critical has become orthodox and, therefore, been neutralised or domesticated; ethics is treated as a checklist of problem avoidance (sometimes with associations of purging and confession, e.g.

acknowledging one's 'positionality'). *Second*, through social/professional practices such as attending and speaking at conferences, and social and professional talk at such events, often in relation to seeking collaboration and publication—where the access to the appropriate network is predicated on adopting the language, style and manners of those who exert greatest influence within it—that is, the discourse through which the field's orthodoxy is constructed. Critique may, therefore, be impeded and the insular and self-referential nature of the field maintained. (We take the piety that is attached to referencing or to the formal structure of research design, as well as the importance of the genuflective reference to established scholars, as indicative of this.)

The terms 'domain' and 'domestication', with their shared etymological root, *domus* meaning house or home, represent part of the binary way in which much discussion during the process of induction into educational research proceeds. In relation to the network it has been stated that it is inclusion in the network that is important, and induction into educational research operates to ensure that students can access and speak in terms of the dominant discourses of the field. As such, the term 'domestication of critique' has arisen to describe the way in which the terms in which critique is conducted are those that shape the field itself and, therefore, fail to challenge its dominant discourses (cf. Heid, 2004; Ruitenberg, 2004). As Jan Masschelein (2004) has argued, critique has now become an integral part of the system and, therefore, does not represent the distanced, emancipatory potential of the critical tradition. Criticism of the field in terms of the domestication of critique, however, simply provides another binary with which to discuss the field of educational research. The delineation of striated and smooth space, with which the undomesticated and the domesticated might be aligned, is not a strict polarisation as spaces change between the two. Within educational research, however, the nature of the space is illustrated by the textual and discursive domain into which students are inducted.

The use of Deleuze and Guattari's notion of smooth and striated space serves to question the way in which educational research—even that which claims to be critical—proceeds in a way that is delimited by its terms of reference and by the nature of practice within the network. The network itself, extend though it may, comes to acquire the 'milieu of an interiority'. As such critique becomes domesticated and safe, and educational research as an academic field continues to reflect a striated space.

For Castells:

> Networks are open structures, able to expand without limits, integrating new nodes as long as they are able to communicate within the network, namely as long as they share the same communication codes (for example, values of performance goals) (Castells, 1996, p. 470).

The network does not insulate from innovation but is susceptible to it since it responds to flexibility and adaptability (p. 471). It is argued that, in the case of the field of educational research, the network assimilates only that which speaks the same language, the dominant discourse through which the field is constructed, in a process of homogeneous accretion and without the vortical dynamic we seek.

The insularity that this suggests is reinforced by a lack of engagement with disciplinary theory and philosophy in both research methods courses and texts, reflective of the field more broadly. Stone cites Thomas Kuhn's criticism of science textbooks that 'are systematically substituted for the creative scientific literature that made ... [their examples] possible' (Kuhn, 1962, 1970, p. 165, cited by Stone, 2006, p. 5). The same can be said of those that dominate the induction of students into educational research. Darrell Rowbottom and Sarah Aiston (2006) critique the way in which educational research methods texts refer to philosophical ideas but do not engage sufficiently with, or often misinterpret, them, reinforcing 'dubious bifurcations' characteristic of the way in which theoretical or methodological preferences are discussed, e.g. positivism *vs.* interpretivism. Again reflecting Stone's criticism that the scientific method is used as the standard for assessing the rigour of social science, interpretivist methods in educational research methods texts are often justified in opposition to positivism. The rigidity of the striated space of such methodological discussion is further maintained. The linearity and orthodoxy represent a space 'counted in order to be occupied' (Pierre Boulez cited in Deleuze and Guattari, 1988, p. 362).

The insularity and striation is further maintained by the field not engaging with the networks of other fields and disciplines. Despite reference to poststructuralist ideas and concepts that have emerged from other disciplines, the predominant concern with informing practice delimits the way in which the questions of the field are posed and maintains a belief in the irrelevance of philosophical and theoretical thought. That informing policy and practice should guide educational research is reflected in an outline of the nature of the field by the Economic and Social Research Council, which accredits and funds postgraduate research degrees in the social sciences in the United Kingdom:

> Educational research may include any enquiry which promotes theoretical and/or empirical social science understanding of educational and/or learning processes and settings, or which informs judgements about educational policy and practice (ESRC, F5, 1.1).

While this includes both theoretical and empirical research, it is possible to see that the focus on processes and settings and on informing policy and practice may be narrowly interpreted. The description of 'The Nature of the Area' continues:

> Educational inquiry draws upon a broad range of theoretical and methodological resources including philosophy and social science

disciplines. It may involve specific methods and techniques appropriate to the distinctive nature of educational knowledge and theories and the generation of new methods may itself be a focus of educational research. (ESRC, F5, 1.2)

This appears to be a usefully open definition of the area that enables research in education to be conceived according to multidisciplinary theoretical and methodological approaches and with appreciation of what is distinctive about education. When considered in relation to the guidelines for Social Anthropology, however, the above outline seems cramped or curtailed.

Social Anthropology works with a creative tension between empirical particularity and attention to the broadest theoretical questions about what it means to be a human social agent. Its theory, method and analysis are mutually constitutive. The discipline is noted for its fine-grained empirical detail. Its researchers achieve high levels of linguistic and cultural competence through long periods of fieldwork, complemented by ancillary sources of documentary information. Social anthropologists locate their evidence in as broad a context as possible, and the data they collect usually extend beyond the original focus of interest and specific research topic (ESRC, F13, 1.3).

The contrast illustrates the limited nature of how educational research is seen. In the context of normalised research the outline of the nature of the area of Education is unlikely to be interpreted broadly. The description of Anthropology suggests an intensity of experience, of allowing oneself to pursue uncharted directions.

ORTHODOXY TODAY

We have expressed concern about a certain domestication of critique, its too tidy integration within the regulated space of the domain. Is what we offer as an alternative to the binary distinctions and corresponding relations of this striated space in fact a kind of irrationalism or mystification, or perhaps, more 'alternatively', the 'smoothness' of a frictionless, cannabis-induced haze? On the contrary, it is the domain that itself is characterised by 'priestliness and magic' (Deleuze and Guattari, 1988, p. 373), and its standardised routines and domestication of critique have their own narcotic function.

In medieval Europe, we understand, one in five people were employed by the Church. It is difficult now to think of some of the activities they undertook as having anything other than a self-perpetuating and hermetic function, strange to our familiar ideas of usefulness, or as illustrating, perhaps ironically, anything other than a triumph of 'social morphology over social action' (Castells, 1996, p. 469). So too we ponder the thought that one day the practices of educational research may come to seem like the activities of a religious order. The orthodoxy with which the network of educational research operates brings to mind such an order with its evangelical qualoid and perhaps Jesuitical quantoid sects, with the affirmation of one's Theoretical Framework its creed, with Deferential Citation its genuflection, with Reflection on Positionality its confession, with Citation Indices its devotional icons, with Cohen and Manion its bible and Denzin and Lincoln its liturgy, with the winning of Research Funds its crusade, and with AERA its pilgrimage. Research students are novices to this order. It is elements such as these that we take to be the nodes of the network, necessary points of connection in the process of induction and professional practice. This, we think, suggests something of the kind of initiation and behaviour that is expected of the novice. It suggests also the striation of its domain, that inside into which things can be admitted or not. The nomad has no domain.

NETWORKS: STRIATED AND SMOOTH

To understand this further, we need to look also at the way that, in globalised, neoliberal times — in, that is, a Third Way politics of inclusion — the very sense of the inside of the domain takes a new form. For, as Lyotard's *Postmodern Fables* (1997) eloquently shows, this is an interiority with no outside, where the very possibility of what is other, of Indra, cannot come into view. In this context, binary oppositions provide little insight into the way in which the network operates in educational research or elsewhere. Educational and academic practice alike are implicated in this interiority. Criticism of the lack of engagement with philosophy and theory in educational research meets the response that it is practice that is important and, therefore, empirical research that is needed. The neoliberal policy context and the demands of performativity are taken as the backdrop to this and, hence, as determining its terms of operation. The way in which educational research is implicated in this is not adequately questioned. Critique comes in the form, suggested by Masschelein (2004), that the functioning of the system relies on. This response and the continued narrow concern with practice reinforces the striated nature of the field and denies the possibility of occupying a smooth space, even momentarily, in search of a more dynamic academic life.

Networks are not closed to change. Their strength lies in their flexibility and openness to adaptation. They are synonymous with neither striated nor smooth space, though they tilt, we have tried to show, towards the former. The omnipresence and taken-for-grantedness of the contemporary culture of educational research methods and the nature of its interiority make it all the more susceptible to striation, particularly given the value placed on inclusion within it. The research student is tutored in how to link the nodes in the network of Research Design, with a view to efficient and productive 'research'. Nomadic, unknown, perhaps random directions of thought cannot be pursued.

THE OBSCURING OF RESEARCH DISCOURSE, OR WHAT DOES THIS SHOW?

Looking at educational research in terms of the operation of the network begins to raise questions about how the purpose of academia is understood by the field. The contemporary language of education, we claim, dominates educational research such that no alternative can be considered. This is not only evident in the nature of induction and the way in which questions are posed but also in the assumption that empirical—rather than philosophical—research is the most appropriate means of gaining the required understanding of how to improve policy and practice. The relevance of philosophy to educational research is often denied. The assumption remains that philosophers speak *de haut en bas* and that their work is not concerned with practice. To not write in a manner that is instantly accessible is deemed exclusive and elitist. The irony is that so dominant is the discourse of inclusion that research that seeks to offer critique in these terms but that is not engaged with philosophical thinking provides no potential for emancipation, or empowerment, as much research would claim. To not be able to access a text often indicates that, in the manner of Deleuze and Guattari perhaps, it is the result of proceeding in a smooth space.

The ideas of smooth and striated space have offered a way of looking critically at the taken-for-granted practices that govern educational research networks, practices that are often not considered as anything more than instrumental in achieving the main purpose of data gathering and research output. The purpose has not been to provide another binary means of contrasting ways of thinking and working. The suggestion is not to seek smoothness as an endgame but to allow orientation towards becoming and uncertainty and to resist the smooth becoming striated. In educational research this requires engagement with the philosophical questions inherent in education, and therefore educational research, and dialogue with the knowledge of the social sciences in order to challenge its sense of its purpose, of its history, and of its relationship to that which it seeks to study and improve.

REFERENCES

Castells, M. (1996) *The Rise of the Network Society* (London, Blackwell).
Deleuze, G. and Guattari, F. (1988) *A Thousand Plateaus: Capitalism and Schizophrenia,* trans. B. Massumi (London, Athlone Press).
ESRC (2005) *Postgraduate Training Guidelines,* 4th edn., Economic and Social Research Council. Available at: http://www.esrcsocietytoday.ac.uk/ESRCInfoCentre/Images/Postgraduate_ Training_Guidelines_2005_tcm6-9062.pdf.
Heid, H. (2004) The Domestication of Critique: Problems of Justifying the Critical in the Context of Educationally Relevant Thought and Action, *Journal of Philosophy of Education,* 38.3, pp. 323–340.
Kuhn, T. [1962] (1970) *The Structure of Scientific Revolutions,* 2nd edn. (Chicago, IL, University of Chicago Press).
Masschelein, J. (2004) How to Conceive of Critical Educational Theory Today?, *Journal of Philosophy of Education,* 38.3, pp. 351–367.

Rowbottom, D. P., and Aiston, S. J. (2006) The Myth of 'Scientific Method' in Contemporary Educational Research, *Journal of Philosophy of Education*, 40.2, pp. 137–156.

Ruitenberg, C. (2004) Don't Fence Me In: The Liberation of Undomesticated Critique, *Journal of Philosophy of Education*, 38.3, pp. 341–350.

Stone, L. (2006) Kuhnian Science and Education Research: Analytics of Practice and Training, in: P. Smeyers and M. Depaepe (eds) *Educational Research: Why What Works Doesn't Work* (Dordrecht, Springer).

21

The Contested Nature of Empirical Educational Research (and Why Philosophy of Education Offers Little Help)

D. C. PHILLIPS

More than any other time in history, mankind faces a crossroads. One path leads to despair and utter hopelessness. The other, to total extinction. Let us pray we have the wisdom to choose correctly.—Woody Allen, 'My speech to the graduates'

INTRODUCTION

The discussion that follows is intended to goad philosophers of education into paying more detailed attention to empirical educational research—not just to its purported findings, but also to the 'nitty-gritty' details of its inner workings. This stems from the belief that both communities— philosophical and empirical—stand to gain from this increased attention; and both may come to realise how inquiry into educational matters resembles, and differs from, inquiry in the natural and social sciences. I use the expression 'empirical educational research' rather than 'educational research' because I do not wish to commit the mistake of implying that philosophers of education (among others) do not engage in research—of course we do, but we do not regularly or even often engage in empirical research, although sometimes our work helps to clarify the normative and conceptual terrain in which empirical labours are carried out. (But part of my concern, of course, is to stress that the work of our empirical colleagues falls within the domain of our professional scrutiny in some other ways that—I shall argue—have been neglected heretofore.) I also use the expression 'empirical educational research' to refer to a broad domain of inquiry that covers not only the work of teachers, but also covers inquiries into the processes in learners as they learn (or mis-learn or fail to learn) specific subject matter material, teachers' decision-making, the study of gender and cultural differences and their impact on learning and access to opportunities to learn, programme evaluation that is intended to reveal both the positive and unintended harmful consequences of classroom interventions, the 'design experiments' that are becoming more common as researchers and teachers and curriculum developers cooperate (see the symposium in *Educational Researcher*, 2003), and the broader interests of those who monitor or plan, at a regional or national level, the operation and organisation and funding of the educational system from K-12 and beyond. This is in contrast to the narrower usage adopted by numerous philosophers of education who take the domain of empirical research to be co-extensive with the work of 'practitioners', a term almost always used as a synonym for classroom teachers (see, for example, W. Carr, 1995, chs. 1, 2).

THE OPENING DILEMMA

The essay draws initial inspiration (if 'inspiration' is the correct term) from several short passages by well-known authors. The first is the passage already quoted from Woody Allen; the second is from Arthur Conan Doyle. Let us start with the dilemma presented by Woody.

On both sides of the Atlantic, and probably on both sides of the Pacific as well, empirical educational research (using 'empirical' quite broadly) stands at the crossroads. One might say the same about social science inquiry in general (on my own campus, for example, if one is interested in pursuing anthropology one has to decide with which of two rival departments to affiliate), but this more general picture is not my present concern (see Phillips, 1987, 2000, and Phillips and Burbules, 2000, for my views on several of the philosophical issues that arise where educational research and the social sciences share permeable borders). Empirical educational research currently has its own treacherous terrain to negotiate. On the one hand, there are influential figures who countenance only rigorous scientific research; they use as their model of science the randomised controlled experiment or field trial, and they point to experimentation in medicine as the ideal model for educational research. The existence of this group of hardliners fills many other members of the research community with feelings of despair and utter hopelessness. On the other hand—at the other extreme pole of opinion—there are those who see the members of the first group as advocating 'their father's paradigm' (to borrow an expression from Patti Lather, 2004)—a paradigm that is hopelessly modernist, positivistic and imperialistic; those clustering at this second pole want to see an educational research that (again in Lather's words) moves 'toward a Nietzschean sort of "unnatural science" that leads to greater health by fostering ways of knowing that escape normativity' (Lather, 2004, p. 27). This second position is so murky and fraught with danger that it is regarded by the advocates of scientific rigour as leading to the total extinction of the empirical research enterprise (how, for example, could an epistemology that eschews normativity lead to anything but relativistic chaos?). Let us pray we have the wisdom to choose correctly! Or rather, let us have the wisdom to reject *both* poles—for neither point the way to the development of an empirical educational research that can illuminate educational phenomena and that can be useful to practitioners or policymakers as they hone their practice or shape their policies.

Clearly there are other possibilities; a large and amorphous group of views about the nature of empirical educational research[1] lies stretched-out between Woody's two horrendous poles. But what a dilemma this poses. How are those who are interested in a defensible educational research enterprise going to choose between the various alternatives?

Hopefully this is a false dilemma, for perhaps those professional lovers of wisdom—the philosophers of education—have already discovered the Holy Grail, have already clarified the relevant issues. Maybe they have already answered the anguished cries of our thousands of colleagues who do (or try to do) empirical educational research, and who are finding themselves at Woody's awful crossroads. It is here that Conan Doyle becomes relevant.

THE CURIOUS INCIDENT OF THE DOG IN THE NIGHT-TIME

Most of us are familiar with Sherlock Holmes's famous remark (in the story *Silver Blaze*) about the curious incident of the dog in the night-time. Although dirty deeds were afoot, the dog did nothing, and *that* was the curious incident. Empirical educational research is facing the crisis alluded to above, a crisis that centres around differences of opinion about 'nitty-gritty' theoretical or methodological matters, including how rigour ought to be assessed—matters that, dare I say it, are at bottom philosophical; and here there is a curious incident that involves the majority of philosophers of education. But—I hear you cry—most philosophers of education have almost no interest in the arcane, technical and semi-technical details of empirical educational research[2], and have nothing informed to say about it. *That* is the curious incident.

In the educational research journals on both sides of the Atlantic debates about the crisis have been taking place for a couple of decades and lately (spurred by political developments) the heat seems to have been intensifying, but the sad fact of the matter is that by far the majority of contributors to these debates are not by vocation professional philosophers of education. The two recent, and large, volumes published by Blackwell that aim to depict the current state of our field of philosophy of education—the *Guide* and the *Companion*—contain not a single essay devoted to philosophical issues in research.[3] (The introduction to one of the volumes contains a few words to alert the reader that despite the lack of coverage there are, indeed, philosophical issues in educational research, and the other volume contains an entry on testing. But evidently the editors did not dare to take space away from the numerous discussions of liberalism versus communitarianism.) There are a number of recent books and essays that are aimed at budding philosophers of education or at teachers and prospective teachers that (in passing) dismiss the field as essentially being vacuous; David Carr, for example, in the course of a brief discussion of the dangers in generalising from research findings, remarks that:

> ... the strongest version of this complaint (to which the present author is sympathetic) is that the forms of human association characteristic of educational engagement are not really apt for *scientific* or empirical study at all ... (D. Carr, 2003, pp. 54–55).

Overall, then, hardly what one would judge to be a stellar record of avid interest.

Some will say that I have been guilty of an exaggeration: There is an increasing number of books wholly devoted to what might be called 'philosophy of research', and every year a small number of papers on research appear in print (one of the strongest of these last year was Howe, 2004) or are presented at conferences (Gingell and Winch, for example, presented another strong paper at last year's INPE conference). This is true, but on closer examination these books and papers, again on the whole but not quite invariably, are *about* empirical educational research but discuss it in a way that is bereft of detail—they adopt the interesting strategy of tackling the topic without paying serious attention (if any attention at all) to what actually transpires in real cases of research. There is almost nothing in the recent publications that matches the depth of Robin Barrow's two-decades old, twenty-seven page, detailed, conceptual, theoretical and methodological examination of Kounin's research on classroom management (Barrow, 1984; for a few other cases see Phillips, 1987, 2000, and Phillips and Burbules, 2000); even the otherwise admirable books by Richard Pring, David Bridges, Wilfred Carr, Gert Biesta and Nick Burbules, and Michael Peters and Nick Burbules, are deficient on the dimension I am referring to here.

To cite some specifics: The volume by Biesta and Burbules, that bears the title *Pragmatism and Educational Research*, has no examples at all of actual research in it, and it settles in a couple of places for a contrived example of a teacher in her classroom that is never elaborated beyond a sentence or two; the book is really about Dewey's epistemology, of which it offers a fine discussion. But is the failure to discuss real examples an acknowledgement that pragmatism has nothing significant to offer our empirical colleagues? Much the same can be said about a companion volume by Michael Peters and Nick Burbules, *Poststructuralism and Educational Research*; this volume focuses on the theories (dare one say 'philosophies') of Henry Giroux, Patti Lather, Foucault, Lyotard, Heidegger and others, and again discusses no examples at all of mainstream educational research. It seems that Burbules and Peters had from the outset given up the attempt to be relevant to such research, and indeed had decided to use the term 'research' in the legitimate but very wide sense in which poststructuralists pursuing their theoretical interests are doing 'research', but, this being so, it would have been less confusing for them to have titled their book 'Poststructuralism and Educational

Theory'. *Caveat emptor*! On the lookout, as always, for passages in the book that would refute my interpretation of it, my heart raced when I came across two pages discussing 'new practices of reading', for naively I was expecting an analysis of the research on the phonics versus whole language controversy; instead, this is what I found:

> The development of new reading practices is historically grounded in the flourishing of formalist and futurist poetics, and structuralist methods especially in linguistics. Its first impulse can be seen in pre-revolutionary Russia with the setting up of linguistic circles in Moscow and St. Petersburg by the luminary Roman Jakobson ... [who] later brought his new structuralist methods to New York and Paris ... strongly influencing Claude Levi-Strauss who modeled his anthropology on structuralist methodology (Peters and Burbules, 2004, p. 81).

Caveat emptor indeed!

Wilfred Carr's book *For Education* does not suffer from this type of defect; it has three chapters discussing the nature of empirical educational research, chapters in which important claims are made, and in which a spirited explication is given of the view that educational research should be seen as a type of critical inquiry that can reconcile the interpretive and scientific traditions (see W. Carr, 1995, Part 11). However, the volume has the defect that again there are no examples of mainstream empirical research at all. This is a problem, for without examples it is hard to evaluate or even to fully comprehend some of his key points—his critique of empirical research goes ungrounded, as does his discussion of interpretive research (Shirley Brice Heath's great study *Way With Words*, for example, and Clifford Geertz's call for 'thick description', and the case studies that illustrated what he meant, are not referenced let alone discussed); and even the type of research Carr does countenance is only discussed in a very general way with a few short (but interesting) examples drawn from the reflections of teachers on their own practice which hardly exhaust the domain of empirical educational inquiry. We, as readers (and as a community of inquirers), are not well-served by this lack of examples, but just as importantly Carr's overall case also is less strong than perhaps it could have been.

David Bridges' book contains a number of helpful discussions of the current issues under debate about educational research (such as the quality of research, and educational research as disciplined inquiry), but again there is no detailed consideration of actual examples; Richard Pring fares slightly better, for in *Philosophy of Educational Research* he briefly mentions (that is, names) a number of examples, but only three are discussed in detail—if 'detail' is the correct term, for two (see pp. 34–36) are dealt with in one paragraph each, while the third runs only for five short paragraphs (pp. 122–4).

I am suggesting that giving short-shrift to examples—or no shrift at all—is a deficiency, one that is striking when the discussion of educational research is contrasted with the way in which scientific research is treated by philosophers; a charitable judgment is that 'philosophy of educational research' is roughly at the stage that much philosophy of science was at six decades or more ago when real examples of research, discussed with historical richness, were relatively rare. As a corpus, the recent volumes in education fare badly when compared with the depth to which Popper, Kuhn, Lakatos, Cartwright, Gallison, Laudan, Sober and other contemporary philosophers of science discuss real cases drawn from the natural sciences. (The works of Jon Elster, Ernest Gellner, Jerry Fodor, Daniel Dennett and the Churchlands, among others, and the pages of the journal *Philosophy of the Social Sciences*, illustrate the same trend in philosophy of the social sciences including psychology.) The marked change in doing philosophy of science came about when it was realised that there was much to gain by taking scientific research seriously, rather than discussing an artefact of the philosophers' imagination. As Peter Machamer put it in the opening chapter of the recent *The Blackwell Guide to the Philosophy of Science*:

> In the late 1950s, philosophers too began to pay more attention to actual episodes in science, and began to use actual historical and contemporary case studies as data for their philosophizing. Often, they used these cases to point to flaws in the idealized positivistic models. These models, they said, did not capture the real nature of science, in its ever-changing complexity ... . Philosophers of science could no longer get along without knowing science and/or its history in considerable depth. They, hereafter, would have to work within science as actually practiced, and be able to discourse with practicing scientists about what was going on. This was a major shift in the nature of philosophy (Machamer, 2002, pp. 6, 9).

The present essay is making a call for a parallel revolution in philosophical discussions of educational research, a revolution that entails taking examples of educational research seriously. As a field, our critiques of educational research will not be taken to heart by the research community if we have not grounded them in specific examples about which we have detailed knowledge; but we, as philosophers, also shall benefit by being forced to think deeply about real problems rather than about problems that emanate from our 'idealised' but uninformed models of what happens in research and about how research-design decisions are made. Who can tell what we might find? But we must not play games here, and we must display familiarity not only with cases that patently are appalling, but also with cases of research that widely are regarded as exemplary—for all fields have a soft underbelly of incompetent work, and any field (including our own field of philosophy of education as well as empirical educational research) can be made to look foolish if the only examples that are discussed come from the realms of the disreputable! (Note that this is not to claim that educational research or many parts of social science have had the epistemic success of the natural sciences; but to point the way to improvement, or to assess the reasons for epistemic failure, fine-grained examination of cases seems essential.)

To some it will seem obvious that I am begging the question. Empirical educational research is standing at Woody's crossroads because overwhelmingly it produces *poor research*; the historian of American education Carl Kaestle captured the situation in the title of his well-known essay in 1993, 'The awful reputation of educational research' (Kaestle, 1993). Thus it follows that there are few if any specimens of research that deserve to be regarded as exemplary, as being worthy of the kind of discussion that Newton or Galileo receive within philosophy of science. The case of Robin Barrow proves the point—he was only able to write twenty-seven pages on Kounin because he was showing how bad the research really was!

It can be conceded that there is plenty of shoddy research, or worse (as there is, indeed, in the natural sciences—think of the cold fusion fiasco recently—and as there is, too, in philosophy and history of education), but its existence does not establish that no good work exists. And I fight back even more strongly: How can philosophers confidently assert that educational research is bad *sui generis* when they take *little or none of it* seriously enough to examine in detail? And if the charge about the shoddy nature of research is to be sustained as a generalisation about the field as a whole, sampling bias must be avoided at all costs!

WHY NOW?

Before discussing in more detail some elements of the current crisis in the realm of empirical educational research, and the role—or lack of role—of philosophy of education in helping to resolve this crisis (or in making it worse), it is appropriate to raise the question 'why now?' Educational research has always been faced with critics and sceptics; its 'awful reputation' did not suddenly spring forth fully developed in 1993, like Athena springing forth from the head of Zeus, with Carl Kaestle acting as midwife. So why has a steady undercurrent of disdain recently turned into a torrent of contumely? The following brief account is based on experience in the USA, but there are grounds for believing that the situation in the UK (and perhaps elsewhere) is tending in the same direction.

To make a long story short, in official government quarters—and nudged by some vocal members of the research community—the view has become dominant that the focus of educational research ought to be the rigorous establishing of the causal efficacy of educational programmes or treatments (and, along with this, the accurate measurement of effect sizes), and there is renewed determination (supported by governmental funding) to weed out sloppy research. If these things come to pass, the expectation is that educational policy making could be based on what has been shown to work—as (supposedly) happens in the public health and medical spheres (Mosteller and Boruch, 2002). In the following discussion I shall refer to this as 'the position'.

The battle has been won partly by attrition and partly by the passage of legislation (see Eisenhart and Towne, 2003); currently more than 80% of US federal discretionary research funds in education goes to work that is judged to be rigorous according to the notorious and narrow 'gold standard'—namely, how closely the research design comes to the randomised controlled experiment or field trial (RFT). Quasi-experimental and regression-discontinuity designs that approximate the gold standard in rigor are grudgingly tolerated, but qualitative case studies, mixed-methods research and ethnographies are beyond the pale. It is the imposition of this position—embodying as it does many controversial elements—that has been responsible for much of the present crisis in the field of empirical educational research.

Putting aside for a moment the draconian nature of the position's methodological strictures, it is important to be clear about the underlying logic. Educational policies are, logically, causal recipes—'if it is desired to produce effect or result R, then introduce treatment or programme P'— but in order for an educational agency to be justified in imposing this policy, strong or reliable evidence must be available that P will reliably produce result R. This logic is what grounds the powerful movement in both North America and the UK that marches under the banner of 'evidence based policy and practice'.[4]

Karl Popper once remarked that there was more to be learned by offering a critique of a strong rather than of a weak position, and so he advocated strengthening any position that is about to face the spotlight before launching into an evaluation of it. In that spirit, here is something that can be said in support of 'the position' that I have been outlining. Educational programmes are introduced, or ought to be introduced, in order to produce beneficial results in the lives of students (and others), and there is no good reason to suppose that students would be better off if they were subjected to programmes for which there was no warranting causal evidence, or if the supporting evidence was flawed—this would be tantamount to subjecting the students to programmes that were likely to be ineffective. Good evidence is better than bad, or none; and it is better that a policy be supported by evidence that it is likely to induce positive changes than it be supported only on ideological or theoretical grounds or on the basis of a twinkle in its supporters' eyes. This may seem like unbridled positivism, but it is not—rather, it is to take seriously the fact that the eyes of different educational reformers twinkle at different things; reformers make conflicting claims and propose rival nostrums, and of course they believe that their own nostrums are the ones that are warranted. But the inescapable questions arise: Do these nostrums all work equally well to the benefit of the target group of children? Do some of these treatments or programmes unexpectedly cause harm? Michael Scriven put the matter in his characteristic blunt fashion: 'Who wants their children taught to read using a method that is only half as effective and no more fun than another program of equal cost?' (Scriven, 1991, p. 25) Elsewhere Scriven, like Popper and others before him, points out that all programmes or treatments have unintended consequences, some of which might well be deleterious. The need for evidence seems inescapable.

All those who are sceptical about the value of educational research need to grapple more seriously with the facts that social resources are finite, that our problems outstrip the resources that are available to deal with them adequately, and that we are inundated with candidate programmes for public support. Thus supporting with scarce funds a program that cannot produce evidence to show that it produces the effect that was hoped for, or that generates evidence suggesting that it causes harm, is a drain on resources and also is a wasted opportunity to do good.

This, then, is the position that has come to dominate in official quarters and that is also influencing—via research funding decisions—the shape of the educational research enterprise. Little wonder, then, that there is a crisis!

It is high time to assess the reactions to the position; I have formed four groupings of these in a way that is convenient for my rhetorical purposes but that need not be taken particularly seriously. I will not pursue some key issues here, for they are dealt with in several forthcoming essays; instead, I shall focus on three issues about which philosophers of education have spoken, but in my judgment not well, and one on which I hope more will join me in speaking.

REACTION ONE: THE RATIONAL MODEL OF DECISION-MAKING IS OUTMODED

The emphasis on evidence based policy and practice, which is close to the heart of the position, seems clearly to be a version of what is often called the rational model of decision-making: A problem exists, a morally and educationally sound policy is proposed to solve it, and if this policy is justified by empirical evidence then it is adopted. It seems relatively uncontroversial to say that, as a description of how policies actually come to be promulgated, this model is quite deficient. (I omit from this discussion the reactions of radical postmodernists and feminists, among others, not because these are not worthy of discussion but because the issues are deep and require much more lengthy treatment than can be given here.)

There are several lines of attack that can be developed, of which the following two are most relevant to our present concerns. First, it is often the case that more than one policy can be formulated that will lead to the alleviation of a particular problem, and furthermore it might be the case that all of these candidates might have some evidence in their support. The decision-makers have to weigh-up the pros and cons of each policy, and evaluate each in terms of their own particular goals and values. In short, evidence of effectiveness does not *determine* policy, and does not make the policy-decision an 'objective' one.

In his recent book David Carr formulates a version of this first sceptical position. In a paragraph that directly follows a passage in which he expresses his doubt that forms of 'educational engagement' can be studied by empirical educational research, he discusses a manufactured example of the effect of rote learning on mastery learning in mathematics, and he makes the point that without further premises no implications for educational policy follow (a point I agree with, since I made it myself—using a similar example—in a book published more than two decades before David Carr's; see Phillips, 1971.). But he seems to believe—as I do not—that this point in some way vitiates the use of empirical research, for he writes that this leads to an 'impasse ... about the relationship of educational theory to educational practice' (D. Carr, 2003, p. 55). But the fact that empirical findings do not, by themselves, determine what we ought to do by way of policy or practice should not come as a surprise to anyone (even to an opponent of the fact/value distinction), and certainly should not lead one into a troubling impasse.

But a second, more sceptical line can be taken: A policy often is decided-upon *first* (perhaps on self-serving political grounds such as that it likely will sustain the power of the 'in group', or will foster their economic flourishing), and *then* some research-evidence is sought in order to disguise the crassness and to make the policy-decision seem less arbitrary and make it more widely acceptable. In short, on this scenario evidence plays a political justificatory role. Patti Lather reports a nice example; she was aghast when she attended a meeting addressed by US government officials who spoke 'about the need for policy research that supported the present administration's initiatives'. She added that 'this sort of nakedness was either strategic or naïve, and these folks did not look naïve' (Lather, 2004, p. 17). Another interesting example, from the field of drug-testing, was reported in a recent essay in *Scientific American* (Michaels, 2005); many drug manufacturing firms now hire consultants whose speciality is the *undermining* of reports by government monitoring agencies that show their products are unsafe (in one case cited, a consultant reported that the government's findings were correct, so yet another consultant was hired to undermine the work of the first one!).

Sobering as they are, the points above are not news to those who are familiar with the field of programme evaluation, where the relation between evaluation evidence and decision-making has been under the microscope for at least three decades. But do these arguments (and others like them) constitute decisive objections to the model that insists that evidence of effectiveness be available for guidance in selecting what treatment to advocate as part of an educational policy? I think not. Assuming that all those involved in decision-making—in addition to their own individual motivations that might or might not be crass—are concerned to act so as to alleviate a particular educational problem, then what is crucial is that the policy that is chosen has some chance of meeting with success. Thus, if there are three rival programmes, and two of them are supported by reliable evidence about their causal efficacy, then some other basis apart from evidence will need to be used to make the choice between the pair; the one for which the evidence is negative would only be supported by rogues except under truly exceptional circumstances (Michael Scriven, 1995, pp. 56–57, discusses a relevant example of this, in the context of evaluation research). Cost-effectiveness of each of the two viable programmes I take to be part of the empirical evidence that is relevant, as is evidence about the likely burden each policy would place upon the practitioners charged with putting them into practice.

Logically, the fact that certain social groups will profit from the chosen policy in addition to the targeted group of students, is one of the side-effects or consequences of the policy—and *all* policies have side-effects. Some of us who wish to see dramatic social reform might become advocates for the rival (but also beneficial) programme, on the grounds that social justice requires that a different group should profit from the side-effects, but this does not challenge the validity of the requirement that there should be reliable evidence of the causal effectiveness of whatever programme is chosen; indeed, social revolutionaries ought to be as interested as social conservatives in data about the effectiveness of the programmes that are open for them to use, for after all they want their revolution to be effective. To cut to the quick, except under extraordinary circumstances the availability of positive evidence ought to be a necessary (but it is not a sufficient) condition for deciding to enact a policy. In the next section I will be addressing briefly those who do not even regard evidence as being necessary.

REACTION TWO: THE APPEAL TO EMPIRICAL EVIDENCE IS IRRELEVANT (OR IMPOSSIBLE)

It certainly takes a great deal of hubris to suggest that the work of thousands of our colleagues is pointless, but some philosophers of education rise to this daunting challenge! They attempt to deliver a *coup de grace* that would bring an instant and dramatic end to the whole empirical enterprise. Early in this essay I referred to David Carr's remark that the 'forms of human association characteristic of educational engagement' are not apt for 'scientific or empirical study' at all (D. Carr, 2003, pp. 54–5). There are others (although Carr appears to be among them) who have been inclined to dismiss all talk of 'rigorously obtained evidence of effectiveness' (or tempted in some cases to label it as the embodiment of unbridled modernism or positivism), and they assert that programmes should be chosen instead on *a priori* conceptual or normative grounds.

(a) To start with selection on normative grounds. This position gains whatever rhetorical strength that it has from the valid point that education is a normative endeavour—when we educate, we change individuals for the better—and the train of reasoning seems to be that a policy needs to be evaluated in terms of our normative educational (and moral) values, and such evaluation is not a matter for research using empirical social science methods (see for one example, D. Carr, 2003, p. 132). W. Carr (1997) puts it slightly differently; he deplores the transition of educational inquiry from being a form of Aristotelian 'practical philosophy' appropriate 'to those morally informed and ethically principled species of social practice' (p. 206) to being a form of inquiry:

which could solve the narrow technical problems which were preventing the newly emerging system of schooling from effectively serving the political and economic interests of the state ... educational inquiry was transformed from a species of practical philosophy into a form of natural science in which the idea of 'method' was given a central place (W. Carr, 1997, p. 207).

This general position seems to be a non-starter; the goodness of a programme or treatment does not make seeking empirical evidence about it otiose for the simple reason that *many alternative programmes might pass muster morally*, but not all of them might be effective in producing their goals and some might unexpectedly do some harm when put into practice (Gingell and Winch, 2004, touch on this point). The great educational reformer Pestalozzi was close to adopting the same position more than two centuries ago, when in his 'Letters to Greaves' he wrote that a mother must consider:

> ... not only what sort of knowledge, but in what manner that knowledge should be communicated to the infant mind. For her purpose, *the latter consideration is even more important than the former; for, however excellent the information may be which she wishes to impart, it will depend on the mode of her doing it whether it will at all gain access to the mind, or whether it will remain unprofitable*, neither suiting the faculties nor being apt too excite the interest of the child (Pestalozzi, 1977, p. 246, emphasis added).

In short, some modes of teaching or some broad educational programmes that appear to be outstanding on *a priori* moral or educational grounds might turn out to be quite ineffective, or even positively harmful, when put to the test of practice, and we would ourselves be morally derelict to introduce them in the face of any negative evidence that was available.

Thus I have little sympathy for the position advanced by David Carr in his recent interesting book, a position that *inter alia* gives a very limited account of the nature of empirical educational research; he argues:

> ... that it is mistaken to construe human conceptual learning, or knowledge-acquisition, as a quasi-naturalistic process ... apt for investigation via some kind of empirical science: on the contrary, any meaningful (human) educational learning (rather than animal training) is a matter of *normative* initiation into socially constructed and/or constituted rules, principles and values that no statistically conceived processes could even begin to explain (D. Carr, 2003, p. 132).

He is not alone. Some years earlier Kieran Egan had argued for what appears to be a similar position: Human behaviour may be shaped by our nature, which is in part biological and in part (a large part) cultural; but culture is shaped in part by educators. Thus, 'regularities discovered by psychologists are products of the kinds of forces that it is the educator's job to shape' (Egan, 1983, p. 135). Thus (!), 'all empirical research based on any psychological theory has no implications for education . . .' (p. 139).

At the very least, our researcher colleagues might ask what there is about a normative process of initiation that makes it unfit for empirical study; or why the educational shaping of cultural practices and how these then shape psychological processes, cannot be elucidated by empirical research the findings of which might well have implications for the more effective shaping of these processes (which, *contra* Egan, would be a valuable educational implication). Processes that humans engage in, in the real world, whether normative or cultural or psychological (or all three at once) *can* be studied—and probably ought to be studied—empirically, but they also need to be assessed in terms of the values (and if relevant the conception of education) that they embody. But David Carr, no less than Wilfred, seems to be ignoring the point made by Pestalozzi that often there are *rival programmes* of 'normative initiation', and therefore it might be a matter of some interest to decide which one has more by way of evidence to recommend it. For example, Catholic schools currently are undergoing a surge of scholarly interest in the USA, at least partly on the grounds that they might be more effective in initiating their students not only into 'normative frameworks' but also (and perhaps relatedly) into traditional academic fields such as mathematics than are secular state-run schools; is Carr suggesting that empirical research on this matter is a 'mistake'? Is it of no interest to discover whether or not this conception is correct? And if it *is* correct, it would seem to be important for educationists to discover what it is about Catholic schools that actually produces the results—a causal matter that is resolvable on empirical grounds, not on conceptual ones (after all, there is nothing in the *concept* of a Catholic school that indicates which of its practices bear fruit and which are bereft of results, or even do harm to students). What precisely is wrong, for example, with the research of Tony Bryk and his colleagues in Chicago area Catholic and non-Catholic schools? (See, for example, Bryk *et al.*, 1993.)

The gathering of evidence about the causal effectiveness of educational programmes stands, then, as both rationally and morally justified, and cannot be ruled out on *a priori* normative grounds as a mistaken focus for educational research—and also cannot be ruled out on the grounds that an inappropriate notion of causation derived from the physical sciences is being used, for this is not always the case. (See, for example, Phillips and Burbules, 2000, ch. 4; for a sophisticated discussion of the 'social mechanism' approach to the explanation of social phenomena—that could fruitfully be applied to educational phenomena, but which so far has escaped the attention of philosophers of education—see Hedstrom and Swedberg, 1998.)

(b) There are other versions of the argument that empirical research in education can be rejected summarily on philosophical grounds, at least to a large extent if not as an entire corpus. The attitude of the critics I have in mind seems to be, 'take care of the concepts and the problems that remain will either dissipate or turn out to be trivial', a view that may be traceable back to Wittgenstein's remark that in psychology there are 'experimental methods and conceptual confusion' (*Philosophical Investigations*, Part II, p. 232). Although philosophers have become a little more cautious about the differences between definitional and empirical claims following Quine's dissolving of the analytic/synthetic distinction, the charge of confusing the two has not completely faded from view in philosophy of education. Thus, in the index of Robin Barrow's book mentioned briefly earlier in this essay, there are eleven entries for 'necessary truths in empirical research', two for 'truths of definition', and seven for 'conceptual problems' (and about half of these entries refer to multi-page discussions in the body of the text).

The trouble is, what seems true by definition at one time is challengeable empirically at another (as David Bridges nicely points out), and even at the time the judgment about *a priori-ness* is made it can be a tricky matter to be sure about. I cannot resist citing an illustrative example from Barrow, in which not only does his judgment seem to be in error, but he also is uncharacteristically unsure of himself and so hedges his bets: 'praise to some extent lessens anxiety by definition' (p. 182). One wonders to *what extent* it does so, and one wonders as well what dictionary he was consulting when he wrote this.

A related ploy to show the uselessness of educational research is to point out that it constantly 'proves' what is obvious to common sense. (Robin Barrow would have been on safer—but not absolutely firm—grounds to claim that 'praise tends to lessen anxiety' is so obvious that it is almost a platitude.) From this perspective, countless dollars and pounds from the public coffers have been used to fund needless investigation of the obvious.[5] The counter to this sceptical attitude was well argued by Gingell and Winch:

> One can imagine, say, a racist saying that it is commonsense that black people have low intelligence and fail to profit from school, while a liberal will claim the contrary view is commonsense. Who is to decide between these two versions of commonsense? ... [And] commonsense is not something fixed. Until the nineteenth century it was commonsense to think that God created the world and living creatures in seven days. In the early twenty-first century it is commonsense in many parts of the world to believe that life evolved as a result of billions of years of causally regulated natural selection, in which God played no direct role (Gingell and Winch, 2004, p. 139).

But we do not have to appeal to the Almighty to make the point. Consider the classic question of whether it promotes learning better to distribute practice examples on a new mathematics skill over time, or mass the practice following the teaching of the skill. *After the research has been done*, it might seem intuitively obvious that massing the practice until mastery is achieved is the more effective, but would we have made this choice beforehand? (And be alert here, for I might be playing a prank! Maybe the research shows that massed practice is *less* effective!) The point is that intuitions are unreliable here, and certainly do not substitute for careful research!

REACTION THREE: THE CONTEXTUALISED NATURE OF HUMAN
ACTION

Numerous writers, including educational researchers, social scientists, and
some philosophers of education, have pointed out that individuals are
embedded in ('thrown' into) specific historical and socio-cultural contexts
that influence how they act in particular situations, and that they carry with
them their own personal sets of beliefs and values and prior experience.
Thus an Australian émigré to the USA who is in his sixties may well react
to a problem situation differently to an American more than a decade
younger who has adopted Texas as his home, who comes from a family
with high-placed political connections, and who might (or might not) have
had formative experiences in the Air National Guard. It is argued that this
contextualisation undermines the attempt on the part of empirical
researchers to reach generalisable conclusions,[6] although evidently they
persist in trying to generalise over 'matters that cannot be generalised'
(D. Carr, 2003, p. 54).

On these kinds of grounds, Robin Barrow reaches a sobering conclusion
about the prospects for educational research:

> It is also clear that the major shortcomings of such research are its
> conceptual inadequacy and the inappropriateness of systematic observa-
> tion techniques to the subtleties of human interaction . . . . What is true is
> that most of the crucial and interesting concepts in education, not only
> have not been, but could not conceivably be, adequately framed in
> isolatable and observable terms, and therefore cannot be satisfactorily
> empirically researched (Barrow, 1984, pp. 213–4).

In a move bold enough to warrant its own name—I suggest 'the Barrow
Gambit'—he attempts to insulate his position from criticism emanating
from our empirical colleagues:

> . . . it should be apparent that it would not make sense for anyone to
> suggest that there are pieces of research I have not referred to that might
> have been more successful. I am arguing that in the nature of things, as
> they are, that cannot be so (Barrow, 1984, p. 145).

It is, of course, undeniable that individual human voluntary action is
deeply influenced by contextual factors. But are the critics right in
suggesting that this rings the death knell on social science and educational
research (at least as we currently know it)? There are several considerations
that suggest the answer is 'no'! In the first place, there are many
anthropologists (including ethnographers) who study humans acting in
specific socio-cultural settings, and who claim to be doing rigorous
science—although, crucially, they recognise that this is not science in a
positivistic sense of the term. I shall return to this point in the last section
below. Second, while some social scientists agree that generalisation from
specific contextualised cases is not possible, there are others who disagree.
Lee J. Cronbach (1982), among others, points to the fact that generalising to

new settings is possible but that it always involves 'plausible inference', and this seems as true in medical research, ecology, vulcanology, meteorology, engineering and other fields as it is in education and the social sciences.

Third, the critics seem to accept the travesty that educational research only investigates phenomena at what can be called the individual level—the level, say, of a teacher working with some students—furthermore, sometimes with the Quixotic aim of discovering the laws that govern individual behaviour! Among other things, this is to overlook the fact that many phenomena of interest occur at the group or aggregate or systems level (a level overlooked by several of the philosophers of education discussed previously). Here it is appropriate to draw a parallel with physics: At the subatomic level, chance phenomena predominate that preclude the making of accurate predictions about the behaviour of individual quarks and so forth, but nevertheless at the aggregate or macro-level there are law-like regularities in the behaviour of matter. And the same appears to be true in human affairs—at the individual level accurate prediction of the actions of individuals *might not* be possible, but even if so it does not preclude the existence of regularities at the group or societal level (see Phillips, 2000, where this point is developed in depth and examples are given; see also Phillips and Burbules, 2000, ch. 4). Earlier I made the point that consideration of examples is rare amongst those philosophers of education who write about research, but consideration of research at the macro or systems level is close to vanishingly small.

Finally, the critics seem to assume that all empirical educational research embodies an antiquated, positivistic view of science (see earlier references to Barrow, D. Carr, W. Carr and Lather, who constitute the tip of a large iceberg), which of course they correctly attack. But the point is, there is no need to adopt this particular view of science, and many researchers are enlightened enough to reject it—the broad *postpositivistic* position, which cannot be dismissed so readily, is quite commonly adopted, even in official reports (see Phillips and Burbules, 2000; NRC, 2002). This serves as segue to the next and final section, and also returns us to Woody's dilemma.

THE ATTTEMPT TO CHARACTERISE SCIENTIFIC EDUCATIONAL RESEARCH IN TERMS OF THE 'GOLD STANDARD'

The attempt to foster educational research that is scientifically rigorous, and thus productive of trustworthy results about what programmes or educational treatments work, embodies as its central plank the mandating of the use of a narrow range of research designs of which the randomised controlled experiment or field trial (RFT) is the most favoured—so favoured that it is now commonly referred-to as 'the gold standard'! As described earlier, this attempt has been given muscle in the USA by the withholding of federal research funds to recalcitrant researchers. This attempt has, thankfully, faced stiff opposition from many in the empirical research community who use a broader spectrum of methods, and also from a few concerned philosophers of education and educational theorists.

A report was commissioned from the National Research Council (NRC), the investigative arm of the US National Academies of Science, and this strongly advocated that a much broader view of the nature of rigorous scientific inquiry be adopted (NRC, 2002)[7]; a follow-up report was released in 2005 (NRC, 2005). There have been feisty and philosophically interesting symposia in the journals *Qualitative Inquiry* (2004), *Educational Researcher* (2002), *Educational Theory* (2005) and *Teachers College Record* (2005). British journals have also contained some relevant pieces. While many good points have been raised—alongside some weak ones (see Phillips, 2005b)—one key issue has not received the attention it deserves. It is this: Giving an account of science in terms of the RFT seriously distorts the scientific enterprise and makes a mockery of its history, and *inter alia* co-opts the notion of evidence in an unacceptably narrow fashion.

As the natural sciences (including here medicine and biology) are often taken as exemplary models by social scientists and educational researchers who suffer from what has been called 'physics envy', it is appropriate to look carefully at what can be learned from them; what is found does not confirm the common set of expectations. Instead, one cannot help but be struck by the huge range of activities engaged in by researchers in the natural sciences, and the variety of types of evidence that have been appealed to: establishing what causal factors are operating in a given situation; distinguishing genuine from spurious effects; determining function; determining structure; careful description and delineation of phenomena; accurate measurement; development and testing of theories, hypotheses, and causal models; elucidation of the mechanisms that link cause with effect; testing of received wisdom; elucidating unexpected phenomena; production of practically important techniques and artefacts. Rene de Reaumur constructing wire gauze containers for food to be placed inside the gut of a hawk (to determine if the food can be digested when protected from mechanical interference by movements of the stomach and intestines), William Harvey blocking a vein in his arm with pressure from a finger, Darwin observing turtles in the Galapagos and breeding pigeons on his farm, Hawking doing calculations, Kinsey and his co-workers administering questionnaires, von Frisch constructing a glass-sided bee-hive, Galileo rolling a ball down an inclined plane, John Snow locating on the one map the locations of water-wells and also the cases of cholera across London, Crick and Watson tinkering with a crude metal molecular model in the attempt to unravel the structure of DNA—all these are as much a part of science as a modern educational psychologist consulting a table of random numbers to select members of the control and treatment groups for a randomised controlled experiment or field trial. (These examples are documented in Phillips, 2005a.) If variety of both investigative methods and types of evidence is sauce for the pristine natural science goose, why is it not also sauce for the educational research gander?

Even if it were held that some of the activities mentioned above are logically or conceptually 'more central' to science than the others—a view I am sceptical about—it would still have to be acknowledged that *without* careful observation, testing, measurement, construction of ingenious apparatus, designing questionnaires, making models, doing calculations, drawing implications and so forth, scientific inquiry (however char- acterised) would not be able to get off the ground. A so-called 'logic of inquiry' would be sterile unless there also were means for the acquisition of some substance (data, observations, hypotheses). This suggests that attempts to delineate 'the central method of science'—the attempt to give a simple 'gold standard' account of the 'nature of science'—must always be quite arbitrary; perhaps it was recognition of all this that led Percy Bridgman, a Nobel Laureate in Physics, to remark that 'the scientist has no other method than doing his damnedest' (cited in Kaplan, 1964, p. 27).

This leads to the following line of reasoning: The over-emphasis on using gold-standard methodology as the unitary criterion of scientific rigour detracts from the main question at hand when one is assessing an inquiry, which is this: *Has the overall case made by the investigator been established to a degree that warrants tentative acceptance of the theoretical or empirical claims that were made?* The methodology used in a particular study undoubtedly is an important consideration here, but it is not an 'authoritative umpire' (to use Arthur Kaplan's expression, 1964, p. 25) that should rule in or out of play the various diverse considerations that the scientist puts forward in developing his or her case. A weakness here might be compensated for by a strong argument or relevant piece of evidence there. What needs to be judged is the overall case that is made— the cohesion and convincingness and rigour of the often-complex argument that the particular scientist or investigator is making, how well the evidence that is appealed to is woven into the structure of the argument (and how rigorously this evidence was gathered), how well counter arguments and counter-claims are themselves countered or confronted with recalcitrant facts or data. To use Dewey's felicitous expression, has a *warrant justifying the assertion of the claim* under consideration been established? (And of course the strength of a warranting case may well be judged differently at different historical periods and in different disciplines.)[8]

The importance of constructing competent cases is quite obvious in the scientific/engineering investigation of the cause(s) of the tragic disin- tegration of the US space shuttle upon re-entry early in 2003, and in the evidentiary trail-blazing that led to the verdict that smoking was the guilty party in the cause of most cases of lung cancer (a verdict now even accepted by cigarette manufacturers). In both these examples, sceptical communities existed that resisted easy persuasion, but that nevertheless were open to being convinced by a competently produced web of argument embodying evidence that resulted from the deployment of many methods (rather than from the use of a single 'gold standard' method— indeed, it is noteworthy that, in both these examples of high-quality inquiry, randomised controlled studies played no role at all). It certainly did not hurt, in the two examples cited, that there was intense public interest and some political and legal pressure; but it is arguable that pressure alone, without the existence of a compelling case, would not have been efficacious.

This, then, is the route I suggest that we should take to escape from the dilemma at Woody's crossroads, and it points the way to a productive and positive relationship between empirical educational researchers and philosophers of education—for the latter are, or ought to be, expert in the assessment of cases. But to do such work, the cases presented by their empirical colleagues need to be taken seriously.[9]

NOTES

1. As stated at the outset, the focus throughout is 'empirical educational research', but for the sake of brevity the 'empirical' will sometimes be dropped in the following discussion.
2. Philosophers of education, as Paul Standish stressed to me, do display some interest in the results of empirical research, especially—and rightly—those that spur their normative concerns, for instance findings about inequalities in funding, or about the impact of 'high stakes testing' on individual students, or revelations about the incidence of physical or sexual abuse. But my point is about lack of interest in the arcana of research.
3. One commentator has suggested that this might be because other volumes in these series discuss research in the natural and social sciences, making further discussion redundant. However, other volumes certainly devote ample space to Rawls, liberalism and related matters, so why is so much (redundant?) space devoted to these topics?
4. The following represent the tip of a large iceberg: The writings of David Hargreaves in the UK; the book edited in the USA by Fred Mosteller and Bob Boruch, referred-to above, which bears the revealing title *Evidence Matters*; the establishment, using millions of dollars from the public coffers, of the What Works Clearinghouse website in the USA, under Boruch's supervision, which evaluates how well particular studies have established that a given program definitely has causal effects; the establishment at the beloved London Institute of Education of a Center for Evidence-Informed Policy and Practice; and the policy of the US Department of Education to direct most of its discretionary research funding to rigorous experimental educational research. For further discussion see Atkinson, 2000; Bridges, 2002; Hargreaves, 1997; Mosteller and Boruch, 2002; Eisenhart and Towne, 2003; W-W-C.org.
5. Some modest empirical evidence can be brought to bear here, which should serve to moderate our philosophical hubris in claiming to be the professional experts on what is trivial and obvious. A doctoral dissertation written at Stanford under the supervision of N. L. Gage (I served on the dissertation committee) found that two groups of relatively sophisticated subjects each rated contradictory statements as 'intuitively obvious' and a waste of time and resources to investigate empirically. (This study is described in Gage and Berliner, 1988, pp. 13–15, where other examples also are provided.)
6. The Danish social scientist Bent Flyvbjerg recently put part of the case quite well:

> The problem in the study of human activity is that every context-free definition of an action, that is, a definition based on abstract rules or laws, will not necessarily accord with the pragmatic way an action is defined by the actors in a concrete social situation. Social scientists do not have a theory (rules and laws) for how the people they study determine what counts as an action, because the determination derives from situationally defined (context-dependent) skills ... (Flyvbjerg, 2001, p. 42).

Wilfred Carr (1995), among others, also develops this general point well.
7. In the interest of full disclosure I should reveal that I was a member of the committee that produced the NRC report.
8. The position developed here is close to, but not identical with, the revival of 'rhetoric' as found in Nelson, Megill, and McCloskey (1987) and Toulmin (2003). Both sources see the mounting of convincing cases as being a rhetorical activity, and furthermore they suggest that the rhetorical structures of different disciplines might on occasion differ.
9. This essay was based upon a keynote address delivered at the annual meeting of the Philosophy of Education Society of Great Britain, Oxford, April 2005. I have profited from discussions at that

conference, and from helpful comments made by Eamonn Callan, Harvey Siegel, Paul Standish, and an anonymous referee.

REFERENCES

Allen, W. (1981) My speech to the graduates, in *Side Effects* (New York, Ballantine Books).
Atkinson, E. (2000) In defence of ideas, or why 'what works' is not enough, *British Journal of Sociology of Education*, 21.3, pp. 317–330.
Barrow, R. (1984) *Giving Teaching Back to Teachers* (Sussex, Wheatsheaf Books).
Biesta, G. and Burbules, N. (2003) *Pragmatism and Educational Research* (Lanham, MD, Rowman and Littlefield).
Bridges, D. (2003) *Fiction Written Under Oath?* (Dordrecht, Kluwer).
Bryk, A., Lee, V. and Holland, P. (1993) *Catholic Schools and the Common Good* (Cambridge, MA, Harvard University Press).
Carr, D. (2003) *Making Sense of Education* (London and New York, Routledge-Falmer).
Carr, W. (1995) *For Education* (Buckingham, Open University Press).
Carr, W. (1997) Philosophy and method in educational research, *Cambridge Journal of Education*, 27.2, pp. 203–209.
Cronbach, L. J. (1982) *Designing Evaluations of Educational and Social Programs* (San Francisco, Jossey-Bass).
Educational Researcher, (2002), 31 (8).
Educational Researcher, (2003), 32 (1).
Educational Theory, (2005), 55 (3).
Egan, K. (1983) *Education and Psychology* (New York, Teachers College Press).
Eisenhart, M. and Towne, L. (2003) Contestation and change in national policy on 'scientifically based' education research, *Educational Researcher*, 32.7, pp. 31–38.
Flyvbjerg, B. (2001) *Making Social Science Matter* (Cambridge, Cambridge University Press).
Gage, N. L. and Berliner, D. (1988) *Educational Psychology* (Boston, Houghton Mifflin, 4th ed).
Gingell, J. and Winch, C. (2004) Is educational research any use? Paper presented at the INPE Conference, Madrid.
Hargreaves, D. (1997) In defence of research for evidence-based teaching, *British Educational Research Journal*, 23.4, pp. 405–419.
Hedstrom, P. and Swedberg, R. (eds) (1998) *Social Mechanisms* (Cambridge, Cambridge University Press).
Howe, K. (2004) A critique of experimentalism, *Qualitative Inquiry*, 10.1, pp. 42–61.
Kaestle, C. (1993) The awful reputation of educational research, *Educational Researcher*, 22.1, pp. 23–31.
Kaplan, A. (1964) *The Conduct of Inquiry* (Scranton, PA, Chandler).
Lather, P. (2004) This IS your father's paradigm: Government intrusion and the case of qualitative research in education, *Qualitative Inquiry*, 10.1, pp. 15–34.
Machamer, P. (2002) brief introduction to the philosophy of science, in: P. Machamer and M. Silberstein (eds) *The Blackwell Guide to the Philosophy of Science* (Oxford, Blackwell).
Michaels, D. (2005) Doubt is their product, *Scientific American*, 292.6, pp. 96–101.
Mosteller, F. and Boruch, R. (eds) (2002) *Evidence Matters* (Washington, DC, Brookings Institution Press).
National Research Council. (2002) *Scientific Research in Education* (Washington, DC, National Academies Press).
National Research Council. (2005) *Advancing Scientific Research in Education* (Washington, DC, National Academies Press).
Nelson, J., Megill, A. and McCloskey, D. (eds) *The Rhetoric of the Human Sciences* (Madison, WI, University of Wisconsin Press).
Pestalozzi, J. (1977) How Gertrude teaches her children: Pestalozzi's educational writings, in: Daniel Robinson (ed.) *Significant Contributions to the History of Psychology, 1750–1920; Series B, Psychometrics and Educational Psychology, Vol. 2* (Washington, DC, University Publications of America).

Peters, M. and Burbules, N. (2004) *Poststructuralism and Educational Research* (Lanham, MD, Rowman and Littlefield).

Phillips, D. C. (1971) *Theories, Values and Education* (Melbourne, Melbourne University Press).

Phillips, D. C. (1987) *Philosophy, Science, and Social Inquiry* (Oxford, Pergamon Press).

Phillips, D. C. (2000) *The Expanded Social Scientist's Bestiary* (Lanham, MD, Rowman and Littlefield. Original edition, Oxford, Pergamon, 1992).

Phillips, D. C. (2005a) Muddying the Waters, The Many Purposes of Educational Inquiry, in: C. Conrad and R. Serlin (eds) *SAGE Handbook for Research in Education, Engaging Ideas and Enriching Inquiry* (Thousand Oaks, CA, SAGE).

Phillips, D. C. (2005b) A guide for the perplexed, Scientific educational research, methodolatry, and the gold versus the platinum standards (Keynote address, EARLI, Cyprus, August 2005).

Phillips, D. C. and Burbules, N. (2000) *Postpositivism and Educational Research* (Lanham, MD, Rowman and Littlefield).

Pring, R. (2000) *Philosophy of Educational Research* (London and New York, Continuum).

Qualitative Inquiry, (2004), 10 (1).

Scriven, M. (1991) Beyond Formative and Summative Evaluation, in: M. McLaughlin and D. C. Phillips (eds) *Evaluation and Education, At Quarter Century* (Ninetieth Yearbook of the NSSE. (Chicago, University of Chicago Press/NSSE).

Scriven, M. (1995) The logic of evaluation and evaluation practice, *New Directions for Evaluation*, 68, pp. 49–70.

Teachers College Record, (2005), 107 (1).

Toulmin, S. (2003) *The Uses of Argument* (Cambridge, Cambridge University Press).

Wittgenstein, L. (1963) *Philosophical Investigations* Tr. G.E.M. Anscombe (Oxford, Basil Blackwell).

22

On the Limits of Empirical Educational Research, Beyond the Fantasy: A Rejoinder to D.C. Phillips

PAUL SMEYERS

In his address to the annual meeting of the Philosophy of Education Society of Great Britain in Oxford in 2005, Denis Phillips argued that philosophers should pay more detailed attention to empirical educational research.[1] Both communities, he claimed—philosophical and empirical—stood to gain from such increased attention. This chapter takes up his advice and has a closer look, first, at a qualitative study of the professional development of primary school teachers and, second, at a quantitative research project, that is, class-size. Though it is not within the scope of a single chapter to detail all the aspects of the research that is looked into, I am confident that the elements that are highlighted will give the reader an adequate understanding of what is at issue. There are, of course, many other cases of high quality empirical educational research that could have been chosen, but these two will suffice to illustrate the points I wish to address. After a brief discussion of the two examples, the chapter then turns to Phillips' argument and discusses some of his claims in more depth. Thus, it focuses on some of the problems that his position might entail. One is his insistence on evidence and on analysis in terms of causation; another is the more general matter of the elusiveness of the account he provides. Finally, I argue that it is not so much whether we need to study empirical educational research that is the issue, but the nature of the research that is helpful in order to understand the field of education. Finally, the characteristics of the kind of research that I think we need are sketched.

EXAMPLE 1: A QUALITATIVE STUDY

The first example of empirical research that I wish to consider is a study of the professional development of primary school teachers (Mahieu and Vanderlinde, 2002). The subjects of the research were recently qualified teachers, who for the first time had responsibility for their own class. This is plainly an important year for them in terms of professional development, which is conceived as lifelong and in terms of complex processes of learning. The reasonable assumption was made that teachers at this stage in their career still had much to learn, particularly things that could not be taught during their college training. The principal research question addressed was: how does the personal frame of reference and micro-political learning of these teachers evolve and change during the first year of their career? The research method employed was qualitative, in this case specifically biographical. After a questionnaire designed to elicit some background information, there was an initial interview and then three more interviews with a total of eight primary school teachers. The interviews were recorded and a transcript made. In each case the resultant text was subdivided into fragments, which were then coded (to facilitate a content analysis), and a text synthesising the interview was presented to the teacher for final approval. Two researchers were involved throughout the process, and they checked each other's interpretations concerning codes and syntheses. Following this, a 'vertical' (or in-depth) analysis was made for each teacher, while a 'horizontal' analysis was constructed for different aspects across the group. Checks were again made between the researchers, who also kept a log of everything that they did or that happened within the context of the one and a half year period during which the data were gathered. The researchers made clear that they were conscious of the part they themselves played in conducting this research and the way in which this might influence their findings. They tried to be as honest as they could and worked as methodologically as possible.

The research was detailed and sophisticated, and it showed an awareness of what can go wrong, as well as attempting to anticipate future problems. It used the lived experience of the teachers as related in the interviews (their own words reflecting their experiences), and thus it necessarily had a high degree of validity. It goes without saying that the researchers were also conscientious about the reliability of their data, and they constantly monitored the quality of what they were doing.

Having explained the nature of the research and outlined the design and the method that were adopted, we shall now briefly consider the results. Clearly a selection has to be made here, and I propose to focus on the elements that were used in the comparative analysis of the syntheses. The study drew the following responses from the research subjects, presented here in summary form:

- the first year was a year of intense learning, particularly learning about relationships. As a result of being responsible for their own class, the teacher needed to develop relationships with other personnel in the school, which brought its own problems, and this was a big challenge and an important task. Teachers at this stage in their career knew too little about this from what they had been taught in college.

- the micro-politics of the school as evident in the power of the local school governors was experienced very strongly by new teachers, especially at the time when they were applying for teaching positions.
- all spoke of the importance of the teacher who teaches a parallel class (as someone they could and would rely on) and of the crucial importance of their dealings with parents.
- the relation with the headteacher too was felt to be very important, as was the experience of functioning in a team.
- on the material level all were concerned with having to secure a job the following year, and, furthermore, all experienced some concern about material resources in the context of the day-to-day functioning of the school.
- in sum: all teachers experienced themselves as insecure, badly prepared, inexperienced and not fully-qualified.

I have deliberately explained this research in some detail, and I have tried not to caricature it. Moreover, I want to acknowledge that in my opinion this research has been carried out according to the highest standards. Yet, one cannot but wonder whether the findings—that is, what we know now, after so much work and such deployment of expertise—is really something that we did not know beforehand. To put this more precisely, when we say 'we know now' there is a kind of circularity at stake that is reminiscent of the Meno's discussion of virtue in the Platonic dialogue that bears his name: what we now understand is recognizable because we had already accepted its importance. But even if there is something we might not have come up with in our arm-chair thinking, is this kind of knowledge useful—and, if so, for whom, in what circumstances and to what extent? Certainly, if you know nothing at all of teaching and teachers, this research may well be very informative about the primary school teacher's first-year experiences. But would not you and I, and of course experienced schoolteachers, be able to tell a very similar story? And insofar as details are concerned, naturally they will be different from case to case, so there is not very much point in trying to be too specific here. I do not deny that the insights developed here and the well-written research report in which they are presented may be interesting for headteachers, and even amongst those responsible for teacher education, but the question is whether this is really more than a collection of truisms, more, that is, than 'common sense' drawing on a particular context.

Similar points might be made about research into the relationship between speeding and accidents, drinking and driving, being depressive and being suicidal, and so on. And though there is value, as Phillips remarks, in seeking empirical evidence for so-called generally held beliefs, it does not go very far. Of course, sometimes people need to be reminded of these general facts of human nature, but is that proper research? It comes as no surprise that critics of such qualitative research turn to its quantitative counterpart to look for what they regard as insights of a more robust and valuable kind.

EXAMPLE 2: A QUANTITATIVE STUDY

Class size and, more particularly, the reduction of the teacher-student ratio, has been discussed widely. There is indeed a widespread belief among parents, teachers and others that pupils learn most effectively in small classes. This, according to Peter Mortimore and Peter Blatchford (1993), is reflected in the fact that one of the main reasons cited for choosing independent schools is class size. That many people expect a lot from smaller classes is understandable as the size of a class is one of the most important facets of the school environment, and it is reasonable to suppose that this will affect children's learning and behaviour. Yet some people are hesitant and argue that the costs of providing small classes cannot be justified in terms of the benefits they generate for student learning (Slavin, 1990; Tomlinson, 1990). Though there is a lot of debate concerning this issue, some critics argue that the evidence gained by well-designed studies to support size reduction is by no means conclusive. Most of the research is piecemeal and would not survive serious methodological scrutiny, they claim, at least not sufficiently to support any general conclusion concerning class size. With regard to the UK, Mortimore and Blatchford claim that only correlations or associations between class size and average pupil attainment have typically been reported, with little or no firm evidence on the impact of a particular class size on the achievements of its pupils. It is widely recognised, they claim, that results from these studies are difficult to interpret because they do not account of intake (for instance, lower attaining pupils can be concentrated in smaller classes). Furthermore, it should not go unnoticed that there have been meta-analyses regarding this issue. But even if one takes these into account, it is not clear what conclusions should be drawn. The situation is somewhat different for North America where more research has been conducted on this topic, though again interpretations differ. Some argue that there is a clear and strong relationship between class size and achievement (Glass, Smith and Finley, 1982). Others criticise the idea that an optimum class size can be specified in isolation from factors such as the age of pupils or the subject matter being taught (Robinson and Wittebols, 1986). In conclusion, though a bibliographical search (ERIC) generates 456 references (to reports, journal articles, etc.) for the period 1966–2005, it is not, as many scholars have argued, transparently obvious that there is hard empirical evidence regarding the impact of class size on student learning.

Before engaging in a discussion into this matter, one may be tempted to ask a radical question: do we need empirical research to prove that size matters? Is it not self-evident that reducing class size will bring about many beneficial effects? For instance, there are likely to be fewer problems with discipline, and the workload for teachers will be lower. There will probably be more time and opportunity to give attention to each pupil leading to more individual-orientated teaching. This would be combined with more detailed knowledge of each child's needs as a learner ... Who really doubts these things? And if we do accept them, the only thing that remains is to decide how much money we want to spend on education, an issue that is clearly political. One is prompted, therefore, to question whether this will not always be the conclusion: the political matter remains, regardless of the empirical research. So, some might ask, what is the point of it? Yet the fact that thousands of researchers are engaged in empirical research of this kind surely suggests that something else must be at stake. It may be the case that scholars have a different agenda (or are placed within a particular context that foregrounds a particular agenda). Maybe the issue is not straightforwardly about the relationship between class size and student learning but about something else. For instance, what is at stake is perhaps the demand for a particular kind of research within a particular set of societal expectations. I shall return to this later and to the relevance of the conclusions empirical educational researchers can offer, as I think much can be explained by this. But first let us have a look at a paradigmatic example.

There is one reference point in particular that is central for many authors researching class size, because of its all-encompassing approach: The Tennessee Studies of Class Size, project STAR (Student/Teacher Achievement Ratio). In these studies very clear conclusions are offered. The project is described by Mosteller, Light and Sachs (1996) in an article published in the *Harvard Educational Review*, in which they use it to show that large, long-term, randomised controlled field trials can be carried out successfully in education. Project STAR is seen as an experiment that starts from the idea that in smaller classes teachers have more time to give to individual children. Smaller classes are presumed to cope with a number of problems, as children face much confusion when they first come to school. For instance, they need to learn to cooperate with others and to organise themselves, and of course they come from a variety of homes and backgrounds where their experience will be diverse. In the experimental classes, in kindergarten, first, second and third grades (ages 5–8), the class size was reduced from around 23 to 15, by approximately one-third; the children moved into regular-size classes in the fourth grade. There were three kinds of groups: classes one-third smaller than regular-size classes, regular-size classes without a teacher aide and regular-size classes with a teacher aide. The experiment was carried out in 79 schools in the first year; both children and teachers were randomly assigned to the classes. In the second year it included 76 schools with 331 classes including 6,572 children in inner-city urban, suburban and rural schools. The experiment was continued for four years (1985–1989). After this period there was a second phase, the Lasting Benefits Study, which followed participating children into later grades and recorded their academic progress.

What were its major findings on class size? First, smaller classes did bring substantial improvement to early learning in cognitive subjects such as reading and arithmetic. Second, the effects persisted into grades 4, 5, 6 and 7, after pupils moved to regular-size classes. Students who had been originally enrolled in smaller classes continued to perform better than their peers who had started in larger classes. Incidentally, minority students gained twice as much as the rest during the first two years before settling to about the same gain as the rest. Third, the presence of teacher aides did not produce improvements nor did their presence seem to have as many lasting benefits. Some more detailed results further corroborate this conclusion. Performance was assessed through the use of two kinds of tests: the standardised Stanford Achievement Test and the curriculum-based Tennessee's Basic Skills First Test: 'The effect sizes are around 0.25 for small versus regular-size classes without an aide and around 0.10 for regular-size class with an aide compared to regular-size class without an aide. Thus the small class size advances the typical student an additional 10 percentile points, to the 60th percentile, while the aide advances the same student 4 percent, to the 54th percentile' (Mosteller, Light and Sachs, 1996, p. 819). The authors hurry to add that although 'not huge, these improvements are substantial; when applied to a large population, they represent a solid advance in student learning (p. 819). Furthermore, it is encouraging to find that students' early experience of smaller-size classes has lasting effects that can be observed when they move to regular-size classes: the measurable effect after the first year was 0.12, and in the fifth grade the effect was nearly 0.20.

Mosteller, Light and Sachs finally indicate that there are many issues involved when a well-designed and implemented study comes out with a definite finding. Serious consideration has to be given to all the available alternatives, and to the costs and social consequences of implementing the new policy suggested by the findings. In this case, policy-makers thought about the most effective place to introduce this intervention and decided to implement it in the seventeen districts with the lowest per-capita income. Thus the method was used in about 12 percent of the state's districts and reduced class size in only about 4 percent of all K-12 classes in the state. They further point out that, at the time of the study (1996), no further information became available from the seventeen low-income districts after their students moved to regular-sized classes. Therefore, they stress that these findings do not automatically mean that reducing class size is the best way to improve schooling; this has to be compared to other measures (for instance, one-to-one tutoring by qualified teachers, peer tutoring or cooperative group learning).

As argued above, the matter of class size has been the focus of interest in various places. In the 1995 report 'Class size and the quality of education', OFSTED used data from inspections to examine the possible relationship between class size and the quality of pupil's learning in UK primary and secondary schools. I shall not go into details concerning this study, but it is interesting to have a brief look at its conclusions. Some of the main findings are that:

- no simple link exists between the size of the class and the quality of teaching and learning within it;
- small class sizes are of benefit in the early years of primary education. Once pupils have achieved competency in basic learning, particularly in literacy, they are more able to learn effectively in larger classes;

- within the range of classes inspected, the selection and application of the teaching methods and forms of class organisation have a greater impact on learning than the size of the class (Ofsted, 1995).

There really is an abundant amount of research to select from. In some reports, attention is drawn to the fact that numerous aspects of the classroom are changed when the class size is reduced. Furthermore, teachers who have been assigned to smaller classes report that the classroom environment is better. There are fewer reports of distractions. The changes lead to the noise level being lower, and the room arrangements are more flexible because there are fewer desks. Sometimes researchers have observed that, in small classes, the majority of a pupil's time is spent in individual communication with the instructor, while most of a pupil's time in a large class is evenly split between individual and group instruction. Moreover, many forms of behaviour that are not tolerated in large classes because of the disruption they create, such as walking around the room, may be acceptable in small classes.

Though the results of the STAR-project have not generally been disputed, some critics have pointed out that the effects seem to decrease after a number of years. One may want to remark that this is probably to be expected in the sense that the experience of the initial class reduction was a one-off event that could not possibly produce the same effects the following years. Others have claimed that the reason for the limited benefits that derive from small classes may be found in the fact that teachers maintain their old methods of teaching and do not take advantage of the new opportunities small classes offer. Thus Mortimore and Blatchford argue:

> It is difficult to know whether it is the opportunity for more individual attention for pupils, more opportunities for pupils to become involved in practical learning tasks, or enhanced teacher motivation and satisfaction in small classes, which indirectly benefit pupils. It makes little sense, therefore, to consider class size in isolation from teaching practices, because the potential benefits of reducing class size will only occur if teachers alter their behaviour and classroom organisation (Mortimore and Blatchford, 1993, p. 4).

There may be other elements as well that have to be considered, such as the preparation time for teachers, which is supposed to be higher for larger classes, whether larger classes are given to more experienced (or possibly better) teachers and the views of pupils themselves (whether they feel happier, believe they are less likely to be bullied and are more confident about speaking up for themselves and participating in practical activities). Other more general issues have also to be taken into account: the relationship between class size, teaching methods and the age of the pupils. It is suggested, therefore, that the effects of class size may be different at various ages, a matter that will interact again with the kinds of teaching and instruction that are offered. For instance, it could be the case that class size reductions will be more effective in the first years of school when children are more dependent on adult help, whereas peer tutoring and computer-assisted learning are likely to be more effective once pupils have been in school for a few years. It may, therefore, also be the case that reduced class sizes can prevent problems but are not sufficient to remedy problems later on. The complications go on and on. Other issues that are suggested concern the relationships between pupils and teacher, attitudes and morale, and the relationships pupils have with each other.

SOME COMMENTS ON THE NEED FOR A PARTICULAR METHODOLOGY

Given the success of project STAR, some authors have drawn conclusions concerning the kind of research we need to conduct. Mortimore and Blatchford argue that a carefully controlled British Research study is long overdue (1993) and, furthermore, that what is needed is 'experimental research which compares the progress of pupils who have been randomly allocated to classes of different sizes' (Blatchford and Mortimore, 1994, p. 418) because this is the only research that can give us conclusive answers to the question of whether children in smaller classes do better. In the same vein, Mosteller, Light and Sachs (1996) argue that having access to strong research and policy studies will enable educators to make wise choices. It should not be forgotten that educators have to work with scarce resources and constrained budgets, and that they must make decisions about decide how to organise students in classrooms. And they continue:

> Hunches, anecdotes, and impressions may have been the only available options in the year 1900, but as we approach the year 2000, society has a broad set of analytic design techniques, widely accepted and effectively used in many fields, that can offer more reliable evidence than hunches and impressions ... Not all questions can be tackled using controlled experiments, but many can be. We need larger scale investigations because studies carried out in single schools always have the limitation of doubtful generalization (Mosteller, Light and Sachs, 1996, pp. 822–823).

They suggest a list of issues that may be tackled in a similar way (that is, well-designed, randomised controlled field trials preparing for educational innovations) such as the appropriate amount of homework in different classes for children of different ages, the distribution of time to tasks among different school subjects and even the question of whether or not students are losing too much of what has been learned in the school year during summer months and vacations. I find these examples quite strange, and it is not clear to me how they could be studied by randomised controlled field trials. Even more remarkable is the fact that Blactchford and Mortimore (1994) express some doubts about the results of (quasi-) experimental findings or randomised controlled trials, while on the other hand, they do not give ample space for other alternatives. Though, in my opinion, they correctly point out that class size reductions and methods of teaching need to be considered together and that benefits are only likely to take place if we consider what kinds of teaching, classroom organisation and tasks are relevant to a particular size of teaching group, they insist that these issues should be approached in an experimental way. How else, given their earlier statements, should one interpret their plea for *sound information*, which appears in the same article (p. 426)?

I said earlier that it is strange to find, on the one hand, pleas for well-designed (experimental) research while, on the other hand, these empirical researchers are aware of the multiple elements that have to be taken into account and the problems to be overcome. It is clear that they fully realise the limitations of the methods they want to follow. For instance, in a study of 1998, in which Goldstein and Blatchford discuss observational studies and randomised controlled trials, they argue for the assumption that the point of doing class size research is to make statements about causation: 'By causation we mean the inference that, from an observed "effect" of class size on achievement estimated by research, we can assume that moving children from one class size to another will have a similar effect on achievement' (Goldstein and Blatchford, 1998, p. 256). Yet in the same study they argue: 'Even with the most carefully controlled study causal interpretations will be difficult, not least because we need to take account of the context in which the research has been carried out; and whether the "effect" may vary across schools, educational systems and other contexts such as social background'[2] (p. 256). They draw attention to several problems that may arise because researchers have ignored the problematic aspects of measuring or defining certain concepts. The following list is long, though not exhaustive:

- the actual size of a class is not the same as the student–teacher ratio;
- the number of students formally on the register may differ from those being taught;
- the experienced size is to be differentiated from the actual size;
- the sample population may differ from the target population;
- reduction of class sizes within a large school may not be the same as an equivalent change in a small school;
- because of the inherently historical nature of all social research, by the time the results are available that context normally will have changed;
- the institutions or populations that are most accessible for study are often atypical;
- in the case of randomised controlled trials the expectations about the effects of class size may be partly responsible for observed effects;
- teachers and children in classes of different sizes within a school may interact over time and possibly 'contaminate' the effects of the size differences;
- a design where randomisation occurs only at the school level may not be representative of the real world, where different sizes typically do exist within schools;
- teachers may alter their style of teaching (they may tend to use more whole-class teaching methods and concentrate more on a narrower

range of basic topics) and consequently compensate in a number of ways with larger classes;

• there will be other 'mediating variables and processes' (such as quality of teaching, pupil attention, teacher control).

In a reanalysis of the data of the STAR-project, Goldstein and Blatchford (1998) identify other 'shortcomings'. For instance, they point out that 24 percent of the children were removed from the project after kindergarten, and these had a markedly lower score than those who remained in the study. They also note that problems regarding dropping out continued at grades 1, 2 and 3.

In conclusion, one finds that, on the one hand, pleas are made for well-designed (mainly experimental) research while, on the other hand, these empirical researchers are aware of the multiple elements that have to be taken into account and the problems to be 'overcome'. Clearly they fully realise the limitations of the method to which they want to adhere but, nevertheless, decide that it is still the best path to follow.

Of course, it is interesting to know that reductions in class size have no negative (and indeed have some positive) effects on student learning, but the question remains whether the level of those effects substantiates the claim for greater investment—resources are always scarce. This necessarily requires a different line of research and of argumentation. Many other issues are involved, which the STAR study does not go into, such as the workload of the teachers and the feelings of happiness of the students, and there are other considerations that can hardly be measured in the same 'objective' experimental manner. This is also a problem because the various elements that are involved relate to each other. It comes, therefore, as no surprise to find in many studies that it is not so much class size that is important but the way the teacher deals with it—that is, the way she varies her teaching to accommodate optimal student learning. What lessons are to be learned from this debate? Does it rule out experimental or even empirical research? An overall picture of the research that we need, which takes into account the nature of what is studied, will generate the contours of a possible answer. But before offering that, I shall provide some more meta-level comments. Incidentally, what was observed in the above studies, in my view, holds for *all* empirical quantitative educational research, in a paradigmatic way.

So what may be concluded on a meta-level as regards this kind of research? First of all, it seems that, in these studies, the benefits of reducing class size are calculated in terms of factors (independent and dependent) that can be measured and manipulated in their constituent parts. What does not fit into this experimental pattern is simply left out. Although the wellbeing of pupils and teacher workloads are mentioned, there is no attempt to incorporate these factors into the design. Obviously it would be very difficult to analyse some of these relevant variables in random settings. Nevertheless, case studies are ruled out because the conclusions they offer cannot be generalised. It is true that most of the researchers working in this area accept that the higher cost of smaller classes is a relevant consideration. However, they are much more concerned with establishing whether or not there is an effect, rather than considering the strength of the effect that would justify higher spending on education. The latter, much more political issue, is *irrelevant* for such researchers and is not dealt with. This generates a picture that suggests that once the facts have been determined, the conclusion (that is, to decrease class size or not) follows as a matter of course. Second, it is difficult to see how long term studies can accommodate for situational/ historical change. Not only is it impossible to foresee which new elements have to be taken into account, but also what is ignored are the different elements that, in their interaction with each other, create something new (which is not just the result of addition or subtraction of variables seen as factors). Problems of discipline, for instance, may disrupt the interactions to such an extent that regularly observed relations between variables no longer hold. Conversely, we are told that one of the advantages of smaller classes is that many forms of behaviour, which are not tolerated in larger classes because of the disruption they create, may be acceptable in smaller classes. Third, and less technically but perhaps even more importantly, the favoured design seems to ignore the fact that teachers deal with class situations (or learning situations) in a creative manner. It comes as no surprise to find in many studies that it is not so much class size that is important but the way the teacher deals with it—that is, varies his teaching to accommodate optimal student learning. Teachers will look for opportunities for students to learn and thus act more in the spirit of 'making the most of it', rather than carefully 'following' regularities or causal inferences. They realise that there are many roads to Rome, and also that it may not be the only place worth going to. All three of these conclusions could be seen as strengthening the case for a more holistic approach, where the relation of the elements that are involved is given a more prominent place. It seems that in educational contexts it is not so much factors or elements that have to be studied as such, but the complex relationships between them. Here the presence or absence of something may change the whole picture and, consequently, the conclusions that can be drawn from a particular setting. Yet from the position that is generally embraced, such studies are seen as irrelevant due to their lack of potential for generalisation.

Yet in some ways we arrive at a similar conclusion for the qualitative approach: the more elements that are taken into account, the more an excellent picture of what is under study is possible, but the less will it be possible to generalise to other situations (which necessarily differ in some respects). Incidentally, I take it that what was observed in the above studies will hold for the study of the educational field in general. It does not only hold for class-size research or the professional development of teachers but, so I would claim, for any kind of empirical educational research. Does this rule out experimental or even empirical research? For some that is the conclusion, and it was to those that Phillips quite rightly reacted. I will now turn to some of his arguments and to what I consider problematic in his position.

PHILLIPS' PLEA

Phillips is right to argue against the dismissal of the findings of empirical educational research. But does his argument consist really of something more than the one or two logical points that he makes? Phillips takes great pains to substantiate the claim that it is better that a policy be supported by evidence (Phillips, this volume, pp. 311–331). Of course, whether certain interventions work or do not work is for sure something that can only be decided on the ground floor where the result is relevant. And thus philosophy of education should never simply ignore what these, as Phillips calls them, thousands of colleagues conclude on the basis of their research. Thus it is perfectly reasonable for him to insist on the importance of discussing cases of empirical educational research, and on doing this in some detail, rather than discussing artefacts of the philosophers' imagination (p. 316). To have sound knowledge of what one is talking about is indeed necessarily the first step. And the fact that empirical findings do not by themselves determine what we ought to do by way of policy or practice should not be held against them. Neither should one advance an argument against research evidence solely because in some cases it is sought in order to make a policy decision seem less arbitrary or to make it more widely acceptable. Furthermore, who could disagree with Phillips' view that it would be morally derelict to introduce broad educational programmes that appear to be outstanding on *a priori* moral or educational grounds but that turn out to be quite ineffective, even positively harmful.

But I wonder whether this is the full story and whether it does not carry with it too much the message that in the end we should rely on this kind of empirical research to decide what to do. For example, with regard to rival programmes of 'normative initiation' Phillips comments that it might be a matter of some interest to decide which one has more by way of evidence to recommend it (p. 323). But what does he mean here by 'evidence'? The problem seems to be that, notwithstanding Phillips' rejection of 'the Gold Standard', his giving of due attention to empirical research subtly and perhaps unwittingly endorses a particular kind of research—that is, research of positivist or empiricist kinds. I welcome, of course, his rejection of methodology as an 'authoritative umpire', just as I go along with his argument that what needs to be judged is the overall case that is made:

> the cohesion and convincingness and rigor of the often-complex argument that the particular scientist or investigator is making, how well the evidence that is appealed to is woven into the structure of the argument (and how rigorously this evidence was gathered), how well counter arguments and counter-claims are themselves countered or confronted with recalcitrant facts or data' (p. 326).

But does he not stress too much the importance of (and, by implication, a reliance on) 'careful observation, testing, measurement, construction of ingenious apparatus, designing questionnaires, making models, doing calculations, drawing implications, and so forth' (p. 328), with the consequence that this may obscure the relevance of ethical, religious, moral, political considerations, and so forth?

What can be found in so-called quantitative empirical research is indeed often of very limited use in an educational context. It belongs to a paradigm of causality that cannot (or only at great pains and by changing the meaning of 'causality', that is, by incorporating *reasons*) give a place for the reasons human beings invoke for doing what they do. Or, it is so piecemeal that, given the range of other intervening factors, it is hardly relevant. Incidentally, so-called qualitative research does not do any better, as often the conclusions that are offered are so obvious that it is difficult to imagine disagreement. Yes, it is, of course, important to know the facts, though there is always a wealth of assumptions that shape the way the salient facts are identified. And how far these findings can go is quite another matter. How helpful is it to know that primary school teachers do not feel up to the task, or that changes in class size require changes in teaching skills and methods? Can it seriously be doubted that the number of students in a group will affect the teacher's workload or the wellbeing of the pupils *in some respects*?

So what is Phillips really arguing for? There is a kind of elusiveness in what he claims that is not very helpful. Instead of arguing that there are good and inspiring examples in physics or even anthropology, it would be more helpful if he would give us what he regards as outstanding examples of empirical educational research that philosophers need to look into when they deal with those particular matters. I have tried above to give two examples that surely are relevant for a discussion of the matters they purport to address. But even though I think these are certainly not cases of incompetent work, I am afraid that, for the practitioners, researchers or policy-makers in the field, they will not take us very far. What I think we need is an idea of research that gives up a number of the old distinctions such as values/facts, objective/engaged, researcher/practitioner, concept/fact, qualitative/quantitative/interpretive. It is not that these distinctions do not matter, but given developments in philosophy itself they seem to be decidedly dated. The disdain directed at some of the achievements of so-called postmodern philosophy is hardly the issue here, and it is beyond the scope of the present chapter to enter into this. I shall, instead, characterise educational research somewhat differently and avoid the so-called philosophical/empirical dichotomy. If we start afresh then, what is it that we should bear in mind when we gather data that is relevant and come up with insights that are valuable for theory and practice—where these are not to be seen as different domains but rather as different ways of dealing with the envisaged problems? Much of the aforementioned oppositions or dichotomies tend, unfortunately, to lead a life of their own. Instead of being helpful they obscure the full picture of what is at stake. It may be better to see these, in each case, as two sides of the same coin. The fantasy that it is possible to isolate (observable) factors and still deal with something that is relevant in future cases should once and for all be buried. The most a researcher can come up with is a new angle that may be helpful for particular problems. And it is not clear beforehand which problems may be generated through particular 'new' interventions. Moreover, this is no different for a philosopher than it is for a so-called empirical researcher. There is not only Quine but also Kant to be kept in mind.

By arguing in favour of empirical research in this way it is not only the case that Phillips is in effect drawing attention to what works but also that there is at the same time a kind of rhetorical commendation of whatever bears the label 'objective'. Clearly the methodology here will be taken to be its warrant. Phillips is not saying this, but what his argument appeals to may blind researchers to what else is at stake. It is indeed difficult to formulate a position from which one looks at the various elements involved yet at the same time uses the paradigm of causation. It is not so important to identify the fact that there are many factors at work. Rather we should consider which of these factors are relevant and the extent of that relevance. But what we do as researchers is constitutive of the reality we claim to observe, which we shape together and which is unavoidably value-laden. If empirical research does not rise above the level of description, there is a danger it will degenerate into a kind of empiricism. It often plays things too safe, merely engendering more of the same—the Matthew effect, the amassing of more details of what is in the end irrelevant. Instead, in order to make real progress empirical research should take risks and play a more imaginative, possibly dangerous game. There is much more that is at stake in 'what works'.

It seems as if the community of researchers has created for itself a kind of industry, which constitutes its own needs and answers its own questions. There is too much research that we do not need or, to phrase that differently, that practice does not need and that is theoretically uninteresting. There may be other factors that explain why 'what works' does not work. In other words, it may be that we do indeed need more research. That we need more research is the conclusion to be drawn from most empirical studies. But we do not need just more of the same kind of research. Maybe, if one cares for the wellbeing of those with whom one is entrusted, hunches and impressions are after all not such bad starting points. Evidently judgment goes far beyond this, involving experience and the development of wisdom through participation in a community of practice (of practitioners and scholars). Weighing the evidence and the foremost arguments—that is, judgment as Richard Smith uses that term (2006)—may seem more crucial than so-called empirically based expertise.

A PLACE FOR EMPIRICAL RESEARCH: ON THE KIND OF EDUCATIONAL RESEARCH WE NEED

There is no need to rule out causes or observed regularities when explaining human action as they too presuppose a meaningful context. To give a causal explanation of human behaviour then refers only to the fact that it is described in certain terms, in the same sense as an explanation that provides reasons presupposes a background of shared understanding. Some human actions may, therefore, be characterised in terms of causes and effects, but it may also be possible to give descriptions in terms of regularities (how antecedent variables go together with subsequent conditions) or to refer to reasons. Some activities may almost exclusively be understood by using one type of explanation, while in other cases several will be possible. Therefore, the questions of whether something is really explained or of whether what one argues for deals with reality need not drive us back to a correspondence theory of truth, with reliance on sense data its keystone. Instead, as Peter Winch rightly argues, it is always about 'what is real for us'.[3] It goes without saying that answering a research question in terms of causes and effects will not generate an answer in terms of the understanding of those involved. For Winch, there is not just the practitioner's understanding, not just the concepts of those involved (that is, raw data as interpreted phenomena), but those of the 'student of society' as well. Clearly, here it is not prediction that may exclusively provide us with our point of reference, nor is it the method of the natural sciences the only way to come to valid conclusions. But even if the possibility of prediction is what one is interested in, even then a meaningful background cannot be absent. How could it possibly be doubted that we always start from making distinctions in terms of what makes sense for us?

A place has been found for instrumental behaviour that was difficult to accommodate from an exclusively 'reason'-giving position. Moreover, it has become clear how different methods or ways of explanation can be used. In the end, the explanation that is offered will have to be subjected not only to the community of researchers and scholars but also to practitioners—to be judged on the basis of whether it makes sense to say what is argued for, given 'what is real for them'. And, evidently, it is at least in principle always possible to offer another explanation, referring to reasons, causes or regularities and applying theoretical insights (of differing qualities) from philosophy, history, aesthetics, etc. Structures of meaning have to be discovered in particular cases—something that is generally accepted within social science. Particular cases need to be understood in terms of their contexts. But this is no less true for the natural sciences, which require that all the relevant and possibly intervening factors be taken into account—a matter observed by Phillips as well. As it is always possible, in the case of social sciences, that practitioners will appreciate a particular situation differently, it is similarly possible in the context of natural sciences that new elements, which one was previously not aware of, or new mechanisms will present themselves. Furthermore, a parallel can be drawn between the creativity of the practitioner who 'applies' insights and the demand for the scholar to raise creative questions and to offer inventive answers. It is, therefore, possible not only to give a place to what is newly discovered but also to reflect on new developments in what Wittgenstein calls our 'form of life'. An example of this may be the recent demand for performativity, which so strongly characterises present-day society. This calls to mind Winch's argument that it is a particular task of philosophical reflection to remind us of the 'bedrock' that underlies what we do, even though this may not be something of which we are fully aware in our conscious dealings.[4] I think Phillips would agree with most of the content of the preceding paragraph. But I think his discussion lacks focus on the kind of research we need in educational contexts. If we grant him the logical point that he makes about the need for evidence that has been sought at the appropriate level and by the appropriate means, what more can be said concerning educational research?

What more *can* be said about educational research? First of all, educational research should necessarily be characterised in terms of a pluralism of method and content. Much will depend on the problem that is studied but also on the kind of theoretical interest that one is pursuing. Furthermore, it is clear that there is a proper place for concerns of an ethical or religious nature, just as there can be an appropriate interest in more instrumental kinds of reasoning. Educational research should take into account (particular) societal developments, as various modes of life are involved (the religious, the educational, the social, etc.) and various principles (for example, rights and freedoms). The issue that is at stake has to be dealt with from a variety of theoretical stances. Finally—this is surely not an exhaustive list—whether or not the proposed measures work is another matter, but clearly if an educational researcher studies an issue in the context of policy research, she will have to take empirical outcomes into consideration. Social research does not seem to give us fixed and universal knowledge of the social world as such, but it rather contributes to the task of improving upon our practical knowledge of ongoing social life. This presupposes dialogue between all those involved. When we realise that there are many and often highly contested versions of participants' self-interpretations, we will also see that though such interpretations are the only plausible starting point, more is needed for good dialogical and social scientific practice.

Here science (within which I include educational research) is no longer a disinterested and value-free endeavour. Instead there do not seem to be strict boundaries between science and society. In her contribution, the researcher, characterised as the interpretive pluralist, will among other things explore the operation of many different practical norms, thus making implicit norms explicit through her interpretation. But she will also, and in my opinion necessarily, invoke a normative stance. Here, facts are no longer seen exclusively as statements that can read off objective things in the world or things-in-themselves. Conversely, values are not seen as subjective states of the mind. In avoiding these and other conceptual confusions, science reveals itself instead as a performative intervention. As Winch argues, what matters is 'what is real for us'. Though the researcher's work is in this sense also of a political nature, it does not coincide with that of the practitioner or the politician. Writing may be seen as imposing a desirable slowness to the extent that it prevents us from being absorbed in the chaos of unmediated complexity. It allows time to think and is performed at some distance so as to be 'fair', and it encourages, as Dick Pels argues, a 'temporary suspension of belief that prepares for *another* decision and *another* division' (Pels, 2003, p. 131).[5]

NOTES

1. A version of this paper was published as Phillips, 2005. References to Phillips in the present chapter are to the version collected in this volume (pp. 311–331).
2. Causality here and elsewhere is conceptually identified as law-like generalizations, paradigmatically used, for instance, in physics.
3. In the context of the present chapter there is no room to go into the subtle position Winch is arguing for. I have dealt with some of the basic insights of his position in Smeyers, 2006, also collected in this volume.
4. An example of this is Mary Midgley's recent *The Myths We Live By* (2004). She considers several very potent ideas that have moved from ordinary thought to affect the course of science and have then returned to outside usage reshaped by scientific use. Thus she argues that 'We are accustomed to think of myths as the opposite of science. But in fact they are a central part of it: the part that decides its significance in our lives' (p. 1). She discusses, for instance, the social-contract myth, the progress myth and the myth of omnicompetent science.
5. Part of this chapter was first presented at the annual meeting of the Research Community entitled 'Philosophy and History of the Discipline of Education: Evaluation and Evolution of the Criteria of Educational Research' in Leuven, November 2005. It was also presented at seminars at the universities of Durham and Sheffield. During my sabbatical year (2005–2006) I benefited from the academic surroundings of St. Edmunds, Cambridge, and The College of Education at the University of Illinois at Urbana-Champaign. I am grateful to many colleagues for their suggestions and questions. I particularly want to thank Richard Smith and Paul Standish for the various suggestions that, I believe, have helped make my argument stronger.

REFERENCES

Blatchford, P. and Mortimore, P. (1994) The issue of class size for young children in schools: what can we learn from research, *Oxford Review of Education*, 20, 411–428.

Glass, G., Cahen, L., Smith, M. L. and Filby, N. (1982) *School class size* (Beverley Hills, CA, Sage).

Goldstein, H. and Blatchford, P. (1998) Class size and educational achievement: a review of methodology with particular reference to study design, *British Educational Research Journal*, 24, 255–268.

Mahieu, S. and Vanderlinde, R. (2002). *De professionele ontwikkeling van beginnende leerkrachten vanuit het micropolitiek perspectief* [The professional development of recently graduated teachers from the perspective of micro politics], Unpublished master's thesis, Katholieke Universiteit Leuven, Belgium.

Midgley, M. (2004) *The myths we live by* (London, Routledge).

Mortimore, P. and Blatchford, P. (1993, March) The issue of class size, *National Commission on Education*, NCE Briefing Number 12.

Mosteller, F., Light, R. J. and Sachs, J. A. (1996) Sustained inquiry in education: Lessons from skill grouping and class size, *Harvard Educational Review*, 66, 797–842.

Ofsted (Office For Standards in Education) (1995) *Class size and the quality of education* (London).

Pels, D. (2003) *Unhastening science: Autonomy and reflexivity in the social theory of knowledge* (Liverpool, Liverpool University Press).

Phillips, D. C. (2005) The contested nature of empirical educational research (and why philosophy of education offers little help), *Journal of Philosophy of Education*, 39.4, 577–597.

Robinson, G. E. and Wittebols, J. H. (1986) *Class size research: A related cluster analysis for decision making* (Arlington, VA, Educational Research Service).

Slavin, R. (1990) Class size and student achievement: is smaller better? *Contemporary Education*, 62.1, 6–12.

Smeyers, P. (2003) Causality and (in-)determinism in educational research, in: P. Smeyers and M. Depaepe (eds) *Beyond empiricism. On criteria for educational research* (Leuven, Leuven University Press), pp. 207–217.

Smeyers, P. (2006) 'What it makes sense to say': education, philosophy and Peter Winch on social science, *Journal of Philosophy of Education*, 40.4, pp. 463–485.

Smith, R. (2006) Technical difficulties: The workings of practical judgement, in: P. Smeyers and M. Depaepe (eds) *Educational research: Why 'What works' doesn't work* (Dordrecht, Springer) pp. 159–170.

Tomlinson, T. (1990) Class size and public policy: the plot thickens, *Contemporary Education*, 62.1, 17–23.

Winch, P. (1958) *The idea of a social science and its relation to philosophy* (London, Routledge).

Index

a priori enquiry 14, 134, 137, 177, 179, 204, 290, 291, 321, 322, 323, 344
academics 71, 152, 172, 176, 285
action-research 36–9, 133–46, 149–50, 167–81
  challenge to academic research 167
  change 136–7
  German 169–82
  German and English differences 171
  history 134–7
  and philosophical research 167–82
Action Research: a Methodology for Change and Development 133
Action Research and Postmodernism 38
Adams, Henry 275–6, 277
aesthetic judgment 78–81, 84, 86
agreement, Wittgensteinian 97–8, 99, 103
Alexander, R. 75, 80
Allen, Woody 311, 312–13, 316
anthropology 44, 46, 62, 75, 119, 312, 315, 345
Arendt, Hannah 179
Aristotle 31, 39, 40, 118, 122, 124, 137–9, 142, 143, 151, 152, 161, 216, 257
Arizona State University 63
art 46
  analogy with research 94
  anti-colonial 47
  feminist 47
  judgments about 78
artificial intelligence 54
aspect perception 79
assessment 44, 82, 83
audit 44
Austen, Jane 84–5
Austria 171–2, 174
average man 192–3

Babbage, Charles 53
Bacon, Francis 4, 20, 31–3, 39, 40–1, 122, 276
Bakhtin, Mikhail 280
Barnum, P.T. 53
baroque 45–6, 48–9, 50, 51, 55, 56
Barrow, Robin 314, 317, 324, 325

Bartley, W.W. 19–25
Baudelaire, Charles 48
Becker, H.S. 201
behaviourism 61
beliefs 66, 69, 72, 73, 76, 78, 89, 100, 112, 117, 126, 140, 141, 142, 151, 209, 325, 335
Benjamin, Walter 47–8, 53–4, 55
Berlin, Isaiah 84
Bhabha, H. 52
Blatchford, Peter 336, 339, 340, 341
Bohman, J. 170, 241–2
Bohr, Niels 18
Bridges, David 176, 284, 290–1, 292, 315, 324
Bridgman, Percy 12, 328
Brown, T. 38, 39
Burns, R.B. 107, 108, 109

Campbell, Donald 202, 210
Carr, David 91, 314, 319, 322, 323
Carr, Wilfred 1, 6, 151, 152 171, 175, 177, 283, 315
Cartwright, Edmund 53
case studies 199–212
Castells, Manuel 64, 299, 300–1, 302, 303, 305
Catherine the Great 53
Cavell, Stanley 91, 97, 98, 99, 103
certainty 20, 31, 46, 92, 93, 186, 187, 188, 189–90, 195
Chatterji, Madhabi 121–2
China 207–10
Chirac, President Jacques 245
class size 336–9
Clifford, J. 47, 55
clockwork automaton 45, 53
closure 44
cognitive facility 35
cognitivism 61
Cohen, Morris Raphael 16–17
colonisation 52
commonsense 151–6
communities of enquirers 66
Comte, Auguste 192, 193

Conan-Doyle, Arthur   312, 313
conceivability   26
consensual validation   75–6
Consequentialism   160, 168
consistency   75–7, 87
constructivism   61, 117, 123
   narrative   80
convergence   77, 78, 80, 171, 174, 178, 211
critique, domestication of   305, 307
Cronbach, Lee   189, 325
Crow, Michael   63
curriculum   44, 135, 200, 203, 228
curriculum reform   33–4
cyborgs   54, 278–9, 280

Dancy, Jonathan   83
Davidson, Donald   223
Dead Poets Society   100
deconstructionism   91, 93
deduction   20, 107, 204
dehiscent gap   49
déjouer   56
Deleuze, Gilles   9, 50, 299, 301, 302, 303, 305, 309
Derrida, Jacques   38, 53, 177
Descartes, René   33, 123, 124, 215, 216, 222
determinism   15
Dewey, John   124–5, 158–9, 175, 296
Diderot, Denis   33
difference   93, 161, 220
differentiation   61, 62, 109
disagreement   78, 79, 86
disappointment   46, 48
Discourse (Descartes)   33
discourse analysis   34, 36, 71
distraction   48
dogmatism   22, 27–8, 92
dual epistemology thesis   118, 119, 120–4
Dunne, Joseph   152
Durkheim, Emile   134
Dylan, Bob   55

East Germany   173
eccentricity   43
economic theory   62
educational research
   analogy with aesthetic judgment   81, 84

balkanised   86
'Big Science'   155
compared with arts   75–87
compared to research on education   149–64
democratising   158–9
different kinds compared   84
discourse-based   96
non-scientific approach   91
'Practitioner'   155
qualitative   75–6, 77, 107–8
quantitative   107–8
science based   89–90
Educational Research Undone: The Postmodern Embrace   39
Educational Theory   90, 228, 327
Egan, Kieran   322
Einstein, Albert   14, 112, 121, 153
Eisenhart, Margaret   228–9
Eisner, Elliott   62, 75–6, 153, 271
Elliott, John   170–2, 175–7
Ellul, Jacques   272, 274, 275, 279
Emma   84–5
empiricism   22, 22, 32, 121, 122, 123, 127–8, 217, 244, 346
enchantment   48, 55
Encyclopédie   33
Enlightenment   44, 45, 46, 47, 48, 53, 54
enquiry   61–73
   classroom   36
episteme   19, 20, 124, 152, 157, 160, 162
erotic, the   47, 54
ethics   127, 288, 301, 304
   applied   139
   environmental   241
   meta-   83
   substantive   127
ethnographers   47, 61, 325
ethnography   47, 62, 90, 117, 119
ethnomethodology   34, 36
Europe   4, 53, 61, 169, 228, 245, 307
evidence-based practice   89, 100, 102, 160
existential questions   97
experimentism   119, 230
exotic, the   47

faith   21, 22, 23, 113, 269, 276
falsification   109, 123, 269
familiar, demented form of the   43–55
fascination   48, 51, 54–5

Fascism 48
Feinberg, Walter 127
feminism 92, 93
feminist theory 62
Feyerabend, P.K. 24, 77
fideism 22
Fish, Stanley 255
Fisher, Sir Ronald 110–12
Flew, Antony 35
flows 299–303
Flyvbjerg, Bent 95
folk psychology 76–7
Foucault, Michel 51, 70, 71
foundation disciplines 61–5, 294
foundationalism 92, 277
France 4, 47, 245
Franklin, Benjamin 53
Frederick the Great 53
French Revolution 33
frivolity 52–4
frustration 48
funding, research 185, 190, 212, 266, 268, 301, 317, 319

Gadamer, Hans-Georg 41, 140–3, 236, 243
Galton, Francis 193, 194
Gay Science, The 93
gender 92, 194, 257, 258, 311
generalisabilty 3, 7, 117, 120, 128, 155, 185–95
Germany 169–82
Gilbert, William 41
'gold standard' 12, 63, 89, 119, 127, 190, 228–9, 318, 326, 328, 344
Glaser, B.G. 204, 205
global 50
globalisation 52, 300
Gorard, Stephen 252–3
Gothic, literary 45
Graunt, John 191
Guattari, Felix 299, 301, 302, 303, 305, 309

Haack, Susan 253
habits 90, 103, 204, 234
Hacking, I. 194, 195
Handlungsforschung 169, 170, 172, 174
Haraway, Donna 278, 279
Hargreaves, David 157
Hegel, G.W.F. 122

Heidegger, Martin 125, 217, 224, 265, 272–4, 275, 279–80
historical political sociology 62
holism 81–3
Horgan, John 153–5, 159
Howe, Kenneth 230
Human Affairs: A Postdisciplinary Journal for Humanities and Social Sciences 63
humanism 169
Hume, David 33, 37, 78, 122, 128, 186–7, 204
Husserl, Edmund 123–4, 128, 217, 218
Huxley, Aldous 272, 275, 277, 278, 279

ideological history 62
idols 32, 41
imperialism 48
incommensurability 84–6
incomparability 84–6
inconsistency 78–81
induction, critiques of 186–7
infallibilism 92
inspection programmes 44
inspiration 100
intellectual fusion 63
intelligence testing 127
interdisciplinarity 63, 64
interpretivism 11, 306
interviewing 34, 36, 108, 220
intuition 22, 26–7, 107, 153, 154, 222, 324
irrationalism 22, 307

Jacquet-Droz, Pierre 53
Jones, L. 38, 39
judgement 33–4, 40–1, 78, 90, 100, 112, 138, 156, 217

Kaestle, Carl 317
Kant, Immanuel 36, 78, 122, 124, 177, 178, 181, 218
Kariel, Henry 275
Kemmis, S. 171, 175, 177
Kerlinger, F. 107, 108
Kerr, Dale 94–5
Kohnstamm, Dolph 225
Koopman, J. 189
Krell, David 273
Kuhn, Thomas 120–1, 269, 301, 306

Lancaster University Institute for Advanced Studies   63
language
    human investment in   101
    of research writing   96
Las Meninas   51
Latour, B.   50–1
Law, J.   50
Lerner, Berel Dov   237, 238
learning disabilities   96
legal analogy   128
Lewin, Kurt   125, 134, 135, 136, 171
Light, R.J.   337, 338, 340
literary studies   61, 62
Locke, J.   17, 122, 261
looping effect   194
Lord of the Rings   84–5
Loux, M.J.   16
Lowe, E.J.   16

Machamer, Peter   316
MacIntyre, Alasdair   155, 181, 227, 236, 241, 296
MacLure, Maggie   39, 46, 96
magic   45, 51, 54
magic lantern   45, 48, 54, 55
Magritte, René   94
Marxism   47
    in Germany   173
    Gothic   48
Maximisation   160–1
McDowell, John   83
McNiff, Jean   38
Mead, George Herbert   175
melancholy   48
Merleau-Ponty, Maurice   216, 217, 218
Methodology of the Social Sciences, The   134
methodology wars   118–20
Metricity   160
Midgley, Mary   286
Mill, John Stuart   33, 186, 187, 192, 193
mimetic machines   45
modernity   7, 45, 47, 48, 142, 143, 144, 145, 146, 186, 190, 299, 300
monadology   50
monism   84
moral particularism   83
Mortimore, Peter   336, 339, 340
Moss, Pamela   229

Mosteller, F.   337, 338, 340
multidisciplinarity   63
music, philosophy of   80–1

Nancy, J.L.   43, 46, 49
Napoleon   53
narcissism   123
narrative constructivism   80
National Curriculum   81–2
natural sciences   4, 11, 24, 77, 95, 108, 133, 163, 235–6, 239, 241, 242, 269, 301, 316–17, 327, 347
naturalism   124–5, 227
neo Marxists   61
networks   299–309
neurophysiology   61
New Atlantis   40
New Paradigm/heuristic/dialogic methods   62
Neyman, Jerzy   110–11, 112
Neyman-Pearson theory   110–11
Nicomachean Ethics   40, 137
Nietzsche, F.   93, 103, 123, 251
nihilism   5, 123
'No Child Left Behind'   119, 126, 127–8, 266, 272, 280
nominalism   13, 15–16, 154
normativity   98, 167, 181, 312
novels   75, 80, 94
Novum Organum   30–1, 40
Null Hypothesis Significance Testing Procedure   109–13
    problematic   111
    personal judgment in   111
Nussbaum, Martha   155–6, 160

O'Dea, Jane   93–5, 99
OECD countries   162
ontological objectivity   75
otherness   45, 51, 53 55, 93
Ospina, Nadin   52

p-value   109–10, 111, 112
pace   80
paintings   45, 56, 80, 94
pancritical rationalism   22, 23, 25, 26
participant observation   34, 36
Pearson, Egon   110–11, 113
Pearson, Karl   276
peep show   45, 54–5
Pels, Dick   246, 349

perception 215–19
Pestalozzi, J. 322, 323
Petty, Sir William 191
phantasmagoria 47–8
phenomenology 7–8, 117, 123, 215–21
Phillips, Denis 9, 92, 93, 97, 100, 101, 333, 335, 343–6, 347, 348
Philosophical Investigations 79, 227, 294, 324
philosophical problems 34, 254, 288
philosophy
    and action research 167–82
    pre-modern practical 137–40
phronesis 40–1, 138–9, 143, 151–2, 162, 164
phronetic research 95
physics 18, 24, 41, 326
Plato 34, 35, 36, 122, 126, 218, 292
Poe, Edgar Allan 53
poetry 100–1
poiesis 137–8
Poinsot, Louis 192
Polanyi, Michael 253
Political Arithmetic 191
Pollard, Andrew 36
Popper, K.R. 11, 19–24, 26, 28, 122, 203, 204, 235, 252–3, 316, 318
positivism 11, 15, 44, 122, 135, 159–60, 169, 170, 172, 192, 227, 228, 253, 269 270, 306, 318, 321
postcolonial theory 52
postdisciplinarity 61–5
postmodernism 5, 38, 40, 43–56, 91, 92, 118
postmodernists 61, 91, 92, 319
post-positivism 123, 124, 127, 269–70
poststructuralism 38, 91, 93, 255
power-knowledge nexus 71–2
practical philosophy 137–46, 149–50
pragmatism 91, 167, 171, 175, 177, 314
    transcendental 118, 124–7
praxis 137, 138, 144–5
prejudices 41, 142, 143, 144, 219, 243
Pring, Richard 34, 259, 289, 294, 315
procedural objectivity 76, 87
profane illumination 47, 54
psychoanalysis 61
psychology 61, 193, 324
    folk 76, 77

qualitative research 44, 107–8, 127, 129, 157, 203, 219, 227–8, 236, 335, 345
quantitative-qualitative divide 107–13
quantitative research 107–8, 117–8, 135, 157, 219, 268
quantum mechanics 18, 153, 154
Quetelet, Adolphe 191, 192, 193, 194
Quine W.V. 290, 324, 346

Ragin, C. 201
randomised controlled experiment 185, 312, 318, 326, 327
randomised experiments 119–20, 127–8
rationalism 24
Reason in the Age of Science 142
Reflective Teaching in the Primary School 36
relativism 92, 118, 125, 259
replicas 45
representation 17, 46, 49, 51, 67, 69, 254
representational gimmicks 45
representational seeing 79
research
    contrast in methodology 107
    definition 65
Research Assessment Exercise 62, 84
Rickert, Heinrich 256
Ricoeur, Paul 224, 236
rigour 158–9
Rise of the Network Society, The 64
Robert-Houdin, J.E. 53
Robertson, J. 32
Rorty, Richard 158–9, 161, 164, 295
rough texture, educational practice 90
rules 33, 40, 41, 64, 66–70, 100–1, 112, 143, 144, 200, 205–6, 212, 232, 234, 235, 237, 238–9
Rules for the Direction of the Mind 33
Rules of Sociological Method 134
Russell, Bertrand 187
Ryle, Gilbert 222

Sachs, J.A. 337, 338, 340
Sartre, Jean-Paul 215
Sayer, Andrew 34
scepticism 92, 93, 154, 255, 256
Schön, Donald 36, 64
Schwandt, Thomas 90, 160, 229
scientific community 69, 100, 135
scientific research
    guiding principles 119

paradigms   120–1
scientifique   66
scientism   40, 49, 229, 244
Scriven, Michael   317
Scruton, R.   79
Searle, J.   200, 205
Second Viennese School   80
Sen, Amartya   161
'sense data'   16, 20
Shrage, Laurie   288
simplicity   25, 26, 212
Sinclair, Sir John   191
Singularity   160
situational understanding   152–3
Smith, Roger   37
social relativists   61
sociology   46, 61, 62, 140, 231, 239, 291
Socrates   128, 292
Somekh, Bridget   133–4
Stake, Robert   94–5, 201–2
standardised test scores   185
statistical modelling   188–90
statistics   109–10, 111, 188–93, 244
Stasi, Bernard   245
Stebbing, Susan   255
Stenhouse, L.   65, 171, 172
Stone, Lynda   299, 301–2, 306
Strauss, A.L.   204, 205
Stronach, Ian   39, 46, 254, 255, 256
subjective reactions   78–9, 86
subjectivism   125
subjectivity   40–1, 51, 89, 91, 94, 125,
    141, 215, 219, 224, 269
Supernanny   102–3
surrealism   45–7
syntactical structure   68

Tann, Sarah   36
taste   78
Taussig, M   44–5
Taylor, Charles   125, 227, 236
teachers
    education   61
    ignore theories   150
    pedagogical aims   151
    practical judgments   163
    as researchers   36–8, 135, 155, 156, 172
    self-understanding   176
*Teaching as Learning: An Action Research
    Approach*   38

techne   124, 137, 138, 143, 145, 151, 157,
    162–4, 273
technology   272–9
textbook method   101
theory and practice   152, 160, 167–9,
    170, 176
Tolkien, J.R.R.   84–5
tradition   141–2, 151, 155
transcendentalism   122
Treatise of Human Nature, A   37
*Thousand Plateaux: Capitalism and Schi-
    zophrenia, A*   302
trompe l'oeil   51–2
true real   45
truth   75, 89–104
    artistic literary   93–4, 99
    empirical quantitative   93
Turk, the   53–4

UK   44, 135, 149, 160, 163, 284, 317,
    318, 336, 338
unconscious, the   47
United States   134, 160, 185, 301
University of East Anglia   64
US National Research Council   89, 119,
    129, 268, 271, 327

Van Fraassen, B.C.   22, 27
Vaucanson, Jacques   53
Velásquez, Diego   51
verification   123, 170, 289
virtual technologies   54
voluntarism   15
Von Kempelen, Wolfgang   53

Waal, Mieke de   220
Weber, Max   134, 237, 251, 256–7
Western Art Music   80
What Works Clearinghouse   2, 185, 190,
    195
Williams, Robin   100
Winch, Peter   227–8, 230–9, 240–3, 246,
    247, 288, 348
Wittgenstein, Ludwig   79, 91, 97–101,
    222, 223, 227–8, 230, 231, 232, 236,
    240, 241, 245, 256, 292, 294, 324, 347
World Wide Web   54

Zermelo-Fraenkel set theory   108
Znaniecki, F.   204